Business Communication

Strategies and Skills

Third Canadian Edition

Richard Huseman

Dixie Stockmayer

James Lahiff

John Penrose

Harcourt Brace Jovanovich Canada Inc.

Toronto Montreal Orlando Fort Worth

San Diego Philadelphia London Sydney Tokyo

Canadian Cataloguing in Publication Data
Main entry under title: Business communication : strategies and skills

3rd Canadian ed.
Includes index.
ISBN 0-03-922855-X

1. Business communication. 2. Business writing.
I. Huseman, Richard.

HF5718.B87 1992 658.4'5 C91-095234-5

Editorial Director: Heather McWhinney
Acquisitions Editor: Michael Young
Developmental Editor: Judith Kalman
Editorial Assistant: Debra Jarrett-Chase
Director of Publishing Services: Steve Lau
Editorial Manager: Liz Radojkovic
Editorial Co-ordinator: Marcel Chiera
Production Manager: Sue-Ann Becker
Production Assistant: Denise Wake
Copy Editor: Erika Krolman
Cover and Interior Design: Q.E.D. Design Associates
Typesetting and Assembly: Bookman Typesetting Co.
Printing and Binding: John Deyell Company

∞ This book was printed in Canada on acid-free paper

1 2 3 4 5 96 95 94 93 92

Preface

The rapid rate at which technological innovations emerge and yesterday's innovations become obsolete characterizes the business environment of the 1990s. Nevertheless, the human element remains at the core of any successful organization. Therefore, the primary goal of this third Canadian edition of *Business Communication: Strategies and Skills* is to develop the reader's ability to communicate and, consequently, work effectively with others.

Features of the Text

Like its American counterpart, this book balances basic communication theory with practical examples and exercises so that students can develop practical communication skills and, at the same time, understand the underlying rationale.

Each chapter begins with a list of learning objectives to help students focus on important information in the chapter. A preview case serves as a bridge between the learning objectives and the chapter content. Each of these vignettes describes an incident that illustrates the relevance of the chapter. Additional examples appear in the body of the chapter to relate the content to the business world.

Throughout each chapter, marginal notes highlight significant points. Figures and tables illustrate the text and make it more meaningful. Boxed guides provide additional structure for students. A chapter summary reinforces the chapter's content.

Developing effective communication skills is not a passive activity. Unless students work with the ideas presented in each chapter, they are unlikely to develop any new communication skills. Therefore, at the end of each chapter, review questions, activities, and discussion cases provide several opportunities to apply the chapter's content.

Structure of the Text

The sequence of the chapters as well as the sequence of topics within chapters is designed to facilitate the development of effective communication skills.

Part One introduces students to basic communication theory. Individual chapters cover an overview of communication in business, the nature of communication in business, and nonverbal communication.

Part Two discusses written communication and communicating in the electronic office. Beginning with discussions of the writing process, the characteristics of effective written communication, and the development of logical arguments, Part Two then introduces students to the standard formats for letters and memos. A separate chapter on the electronic office highlights the ways in which technological change is revolutionizing written communication. The remaining chapters of Part Two are devoted to specific types of written communication: routine letters, persuasive messages, informal reports, and formal reports. Part Two concludes with a sample formal report to show students how the various elements fit together.

Part Three discusses oral communication techniques. Individual chapters on listening, public presentations, and communication and decision making in small groups ensure that students will have the broad range of oral communication skills necessary in today's business environment.

Part Four describes those strategies useful to students looking for a job, including developing a personal marketing strategy, as well as preparing résumés and letters of application. It also tells students what to expect from job interviews and what skills will help them in those interviews.

New to This Edition

Although the structure of this edition of *Business Communication* remains essentially the same, important changes have been made. International business communication is treated within the chapters as each chapter's topics warrant. Increasingly, people in business must be able to communicate with people from other countries and cultures. While a detailed consideration of specific cultures is beyond the scope of this text, it does highlight the key issues students need to consider to ensure successful communication. Complementing this treatment of intercultural communication is the book's new and contemporary design, which reflects the dynamism of business in the 1990s and allows for a more pedagogically sound use of colour.

Part Two (Written Strategies) contains the greatest number of changes. Most significant is the increased emphasis on the writing process, with the addition of three chapters devoted to its various aspects.

- Chapter 4 (The Writing Process) describes how to plan and draft a document.
- Chapter 6 (Clear Thinking and Argument) describes how to develop clear arguments supported by details readers will require to make their decisions.

- Chapter 8 (Communicating in the Electronic Office), formerly Appendix B, describes how to use modern office technology to facilitate these processes.

At the same time, specific letter formats receive less coverage. Only two chapters remain on the topic: routine letters and persuasive messages.

Chapter 11 (Informal Reports) now includes a section on trip reports. As well, the sample report in the Appendix to Chapter 12 has marginal notes to emphasize the key features of the report.

Part Three (Oral Strategies) contains a new chapter on communication and decision making in small groups. Since everyone, at some point in his or her career, will have to work on team projects or participate in meetings, this chapter is essential to the development of well-rounded communication skills. Other changes to Part Three include the addition of brief sections on using the telephone (Chapter 13), writing for the ear, and colour basics for visuals (Chapter 14). Finally, the section on team presentations has been expanded.

Part Four (Strategies in the Job Search) has been expanded to include three chapters: Marketing Yourself, Writing a Résumé, and Job Search Letters and Interviews. The first chapter helps students identify their strengths and develop a comprehensive strategy for marketing themselves to prospective employers. The chapter on résumés contains several new sample résumés and all of them have been redesigned to reflect the design capabilities of word processing and desktop publishing.

Instructional Package

Business Communication is accompanied by an Instructor's Manual/Test Bank that includes chapter synopses, answers to review questions, brief case notes, and sample course outlines for one- and two-semester business communication courses keyed to the text. It also includes several multiple-choice questions that can be used to test students' understanding of the content.

Acknowledgements

Many individuals have contributed to this edition, including my friend and colleague Gonophore Knuckles, who helped with the sections on news releases and writing for the ear, and Lee Anne Esopenko, who redesigned the résumés in Chapter 17.

However, this book would not have been possible without the constructive criticism and suggestions provided by the following reviewers: June Baker, Samantha Baskwill, Doug Beardsley, Carol Bhakar, Mary Dunn, Stena Jaworski, Dennis Johnson, Bev McGill, Liesje McKenna, Dave Parsons, Susan Reinhart, John Roberts, Roger Semmens, Pamela Sims, and Al Valleau. Most of the new features in this edition are a direct result of their input.

I also owe thanks to Heather McWhinney, for her patience and support throughout the project. Finally I owe special thanks to Judy Kalman, freelance editor, and Marcel Chiera. Their thorough editing and excellent suggestions contributed significantly to the text's quality.

Dixie Stockmayer
Vancouver, BC
September 1991

Publisher's Note to Students and Instructors

This textbook is a key component of your course. If you are the instructor of this course, you undoubtedly considered a number of texts carefully before choosing this as the one that would work best for your students and you. The authors and publishers spent considerable time and money to ensure its high quality, and we appreciate your recognition of this effort and accomplishment. Please note the copyright statement.

If you are a student, we are confident that this text will help you to meet the objectives of your course. It will also become a valuable addition to your personal library.

Since we want to hear what you think about this book, please be sure to send us the stamped reply card at the end of the text. Your input will help us to continue to publish high-quality books for your courses.

Brief Contents

Contents

Part One

Theoretical Considerations

Chapter 1

Communication in Business: An Overview

Learning Objectives

In this chapter, you'll learn the importance of effective communication in business organizations. More specifically, you will be able to:

1. explain the extent to which organizations depend on communication
2. identify some of communication's monetary and nonmonetary costs to the organization
3. discuss the reasons for the increasing importance of business communication
4. discuss the value of training for improvement in sending and receiving messages
5. discuss the environment in which the business organization functions and its effect on business communication

Preview Case

Jeannie Wong was excited about the prospect of attending college. She was living away from home for the first time, sharing an apartment with a friend from her home town. Her first scheduled class was Business Communication 100.

Wanting to get off to a good start, Jeannie purchased the textbook she needed for the class and took a few minutes to locate the room on the map she had been given at registration. She arrived for the class five minutes before it was due to start. She checked the room number and stood in the doorway for a couple of minutes to get her bearings. She noticed another student sitting by herself in the large lecture hall and decided to join her. "Is this seat taken?" she asked, smiling at the young woman.

"No, please sit down. I don't know a soul here." They chatted quietly for a couple of minutes as they got their texts and papers ready. "This isn't going to be so bad," thought Jeannie. "I've already met one person."

Jeannie looked around. About thirty of her new classmates were already in their seats. The instructor was busy setting up at the front and had written the course name in large letters on the blackboard. Several more students entered the room and quickly found seats, just as the class began.

The instructor began to speak. "Welcome. My name is Nattanya Frieburg. I'll be your instructor for this course. My goal this term is to show you just how much you already know about effective communication, and how you can use that knowledge to develop the additional skills you'll need at college and on the job. Before we get started, however, there are a few housekeeping items to attend to."

At this point, several late arrivals interrupted Ms. Frieburg's lecture. "Sorry we're late," one of them volunteered. "I couldn't find the room." "And I had to stop by the office to pay my fees," said another.

Jeannie used the interruption to consider Ms. Frieburg's first statement. Just how much did she know about effective communication? Just listing everything she had communicated in order to get to this class convinced her she knew quite a bit. After all, she had written to the college for the application form, filled it out, and returned it. She had applied for and obtained a student loan. She had managed to survive registration day despite all the procedures that were foreign to her. She had obtained a list of required texts and purchased most of them the day before classes started. She had located the room by consulting her map and asking directions when

continued

she was lost. And she'd met a fellow classmate, just by smiling and asking a simple question.

Ms. Frieburg began to speak again. "Hmm," thought Jeannie, "this isn't going to be as difficult as I anticipated."

Overview

"The growth of the service sector has ... changed the way individuals work, with fully 70 per cent of all employed people in this country [Canada] in services of some kind," says business writer Carolyn Leitch. She goes on to say that "interpersonal communication skills will be crucial ... the most important thing you're going to be able to do is speak to people."[1] Moreover, an official with the Canadian Manufacturers Association has said, "We have to have graduates who have flexibility, basic communications, technical and literacy skills, international outlook and the ability to learn or else we're just not going to be competitive."[2] By all accounts, the business of communicating is all important, regardless of the type of organization in which you work or will work in the future.

Communication is a transaction involving information

Communication is an exchange of information between two or more people. When it is effective, everyone involved shares a similar understanding of the message. Just as the corporation requires certain kinds of information to survive, an individual depends on information to maintain a balanced perspective and a sense of belonging.

Frank Rhodes owns and operates a small, wholesale janitorial supply company. It is not a huge organization: the workforce consists of five warehouse workers, one secretary, and three outside salespeople. Several years ago, when he encountered problems such as salespeople not completing their order forms, warehouse workers losing bills of lading, and the secretary misfiling important papers, Frank went to his employees for suggestions on how to solve these problems. While no one came up with any earth-shattering solutions, Frank found that the more he talked with his employees, the less frequently problems occurred. Today, Frank's operation runs smoothly. When problems do occur, they are generally minor and can be solved quickly. Frank's employees believe their work is valued and do their best to meet his expectations.

Human communication has a crucial function even if it often appears purposeless

Much of the information individuals exchange on the job has little to do with work but is nevertheless vital to them. Human beings communicate even when they have nothing urgent to express. Much apparently purposeless conversation actually has the crucial purpose of satisfying our need to interact with others. To understand the importance of such communication, consider solitary confinement. Generally regarded as the ultimate punishment for prison inmates, it deprives the prisoner of the opportunity and right to communicate with others.

Improving communication is big business

Because communication is recognized as crucial, many organizations seek to train employees to become better communicators. Training programs may be structured around one of many aspects of communication. A quick glance at the in-basket for one department produced advertisements for the following seminars and workshops:

How to Make Presentations with Confidence and Power
How to Build and Improve Customer Service
Designing with Desktop Publishing
Communication Skills in the Workplace
An Interview Survival Kit
Interviewing Techniques
Leadership and Supervisory Skills for Women
How to Solve Communication Problems
Designing Effective Manuals
Powerful Writing Skills

This list suggests the varied nature of communications courses as well as the many organizational activities in which communication is vital.

Monetary Costs

Research has shown that enormous amounts of time and money are devoted to communication. Workers can spend up to 60 percent of their work day on listening alone.[3] A study of participants enrolled in writing courses found that more than half spent 20 percent or more of their time writing.[4] The bulk of their time was spent listening. The tremendous cost of time spent on business communication partially accounts for the intense interest in it.

However, perhaps even more important is the cost of failing to communicate. The U.S. presidential commission that investigated the space shuttle *Challenger* disaster in 1986 concluded that failure to communicate was at least partially responsible.[5] While this example is extreme, it does highlight the need for effective communication.

Communication's monetary costs are high

Even routine communication is costly to organizations. Consider the cost of a single business letter to an organization. For example, a manager earning \$50 an hour spends fifteen minutes drafting the letter (\$12.50). Her secretary earning \$16 an hour spends fifteen minutes setting up, keying, and proofreading the letter (\$4.00). Then the manager reads and signs it (\$3.00). Next, the secretary sends the letter to the mailroom, and its handling there means additional labour costs ($0.50). Finally, stationery and mailing costs are added ($1.00). The total cost of the letter? $21.00.

Consider the cost of a department meeting. If six staff members earning an average of $25 an hour meet for an hour, that meeting costs $150.

Nonmonetary Costs

The monetary costs of communication are important to an organization, but its many other costs are also important, though more difficult to compute. The full cost of a communications failure, for instance, may never be known, but such failures often have long-felt repercussions.

When Basil Coates of Calgary travelled on business to South America, he generally took only one of his credit cards with him because of the risk of theft. On one such trip, he checked into his hotel in Toronto on a Saturday evening, using his credit card. No sooner had he reached his room than the front desk clerk phoned to say that his credit card had been rejected. Several phone calls later, Basil was still unable to use his credit card and had to use some of his limited cash reserves to cover the hotel bill.

Since Basil was flying to South America the next day, he asked his wife to phone the bank first thing Monday morning. The bank incorrectly maintained that Basil had asked to have the credit card cancelled the week before; however, given the situation, the card was reinstated. At no time did the bank admit any wrongdoing, nor did they apologize for the inconvenience Basil had experienced. As a result, Basil decided to move his account to a competitor. Even more significantly, he told the story to several of his friends and colleagues.

The ripple effect of communication failures may make it difficult to determine the exact financial costs involved. Unquestionably, however, ineffective communication results in errors, misunderstanding, poor performance, and negative feelings.

Many intangible costs are involved in communication

Internal and External Communication

Organizational communication may be internal or external, formal or informal. *Internal communication* refers to messages sent and received

Internal communication occurs within the organization

within one organization. Such communication is *formal* if the messages are sent through channels of communication developed by management. Much of the communication that goes on in any organization, however, is *informal*: information is exchanged by individuals who, although not formally connected within the organization, do interact by telephone conversation, during chance meetings, or on social occasions.

External communication is with outside groups or individuals

Much business communication is with individuals or groups outside the organization. This *external communication* may involve any of the many segments of the public with which the organization interacts.

Advertising is a highly structured form of external communication. Many organizations have their greatest number of public contacts through advertising. Whether the approach involves television commercials, printed ads, or mailed brochures, advertising is an important part of external communication.

Most external formal communication is not so highly polished or so heavily bankrolled as an advertising campaign, but it all has a clear purpose and a target audience external to the organization. The efforts of plant management to keep the neighbouring community aware of how the company contributes to the local economy is an example of this kind of external communication.

All employees provide informal external communication

Another kind of external communication is much less planned and purposeful. All employees are unofficial spokespersons for their employers. Even though you may seldom talk to outsiders about your work or your employer, you are still representing your employer and providing a kind of external communication. Satisfied employees are often the best advertisement for the company. Others in the community often form an impression of the company through the comments of employees.

Faina Franklin plays volleyball once a week with friends. They can always tell what kind of day she's had as soon as she enters the dressing room. Faina works as a desktop publishing specialist in the public relations department of a major forestry company.

According to one of her friends, "Some days she comes in all friendly and talkative. Other days she is a completely different person."

One day Faina arrived very grim-faced. "That's it. I'm ready to quit. Everyone's an expert. I spent two days coming up with a new design for the company newsletter and my boss decided to go with a design his secretary suggested. It's terrible. I don't want my name associated with it."

Faina talked for ten minutes about her problems with her boss. Her friends felt that she had been treated unfairly because her recommendations, based on training and experience in page layout, were ignored. Now when they think of Faina's employer, they can't help but remember that negative experience.

The Importance of Communication to Modern Business

Several factors explain the importance of communication to the modern business organization:

- the growth of business organizations
- the increased specialization of tasks
- a lack of skill among senders and receivers
- the relationships between communication and organizational effectiveness
- the computerization of the business organization

The Growth of Business Organizations

An organization's size affects the ease of internal communication

Most business organizations are much larger today than those of even a generation ago. In a small organization, managers can know a sizable share of the employees personally. For many organizations, growth has now made close contact difficult.

As an organization grows, so also do its communication problems. Organizational development through planned expansion or consolidation may result in the addition of one or more levels of management. The increased distances between the different levels of management, the result of a firm's growth, greatly complicate the transmission of information.

The International Environment: Implications for Communication

International communication is increasing

The growth of business organizations is not limited to the size and complexity of the organization. Growth also occurs geographically, from across the street to around the world. International growth makes communication all the more important and, at the same time, frequently more difficult.

When two people attempt to communicate, each may assume that the other person "shares the code" and that the message sent is very close to the message received. However, individuals from different cultural backgrounds frequently do not share the code and, therefore, must be careful not to miscommunicate. Many linguistic and cultural influences can disturb the process of effectively getting a message across to someone from a culture different from the sender's.

Even individuals who share the same language may have difficulty communicating. For example, in England the terms "bonnet" and "boot" refer to the hood and trunk of a car, respectively, not what you might wear on your head and feet. Even within Canada, words can have different meanings. If you live in a rural, agricultural area, you may eat "dinner" at noon and "supper" in the evening, whereas, in the city, the terms "dinner" and "supper" are generally used interchangeably.

Effective communication between people of different cultures can be difficult. Because of this difficulty in exchanging meaning, your skills in effective communication internationally are crucial to your organization. Therefore, you need to pay special attention to written and oral communication with people who do not share your culture or for whom English is a second language.

Avoid costly and embarrassing errors

You can avoid costly and embarrassing errors by:

Learning about other cultures. If your organization regularly deals with people from other cultures, spend some time reading about those cultures. A visit to the library will yield a variety of books, videotapes, and articles on other cultures — everything from travel handbooks designed for the casual tourist to detailed guidelines for conducting business in specific areas of the world.

Being patient. To many cultures, North American society is fast-paced, aggressive, and even rude. If you are communicating with someone from another culture, take your time, listen and observe more than you speak, and seek advice from others who have more experience. Find out if someone in your organization shares the culture of the person you are attempting to communicate with.

Being courteous. Politeness is never out of place; however, most cultures place greater emphasis on formal courtesy than is done in Canada and the United States. For example, the custom of giving and receiving business gifts is a highly developed art in Japan. Thank-you letters for any individual effort or service are a must in all situations.

If you've ever studied a foreign language, you'll know how frustrating it is to have someone speak to you quickly, seeming not to stop to take a breath. On the other hand, you may also have had the pleasure of speaking to someone who pronounces words clearly, pauses between main ideas, and uses gestures and pictures to get the message across. When speaking to someone whose first language is not English, speak a little more slowly than normal, use visual aids whenever possible, and check periodically for understanding. If you are speaking through an interpreter, remember to pause long enough to allow the interpreter to translate your complete meaning. In many instances, your success in the international marketplace is only as good as your contacts in that marketplace. Therefore, take time to establish ongoing relationships with people you meet abroad. You'll learn a lot about their culture and frequently make long-term friends in the process.

As for most business dealings within Canada, confirming the details of a conversation in writing is a good idea. This confirmation ensures that both parties agree on the outcome of the conversation, and has the additional benefit of allowing the receiver to study the message at leisure and to obtain a translation if necessary.

Confirm conversations in writing

The Specialization of Tasks

Over the past few years, management has sought ways of increasing efficiency. One common practice is to make the individual worker's duties more specific. Narrowing duties can help individual workers become competent and more productive faster since they require less training to master their highly specialized jobs. However, such specialization also has its downside: workers are less able to fill in when their colleagues are especially busy or absent and they may find their highly specialized tasks boring.

Business communication is affected significantly by the use of specialized terminology, a verbal shortcut that allows specialists to communicate with each other more easily. An accountant, for example, uses terms likely to be understood by other accountants. This terminology depends on the assumption that specialists in the same discipline share a similar level of knowledge; it can help them be briefer and more specific. Consequently, it saves time and achieves understanding readily — as long as both individuals are specialists of the same sort.

Specialized terminology facilitates communication between specialists

However, problems occur when a specialist uses specialized terminology to communicate with someone who does not share the same background. When one psychologist tells another of a client who "ventilated," both understand that the client spoke in anger. A person unfamiliar with the terminology might think that the client opened a window. An economist uses "negative savers" to describe people who spend more than they earn; this term conveys the intended meaning to other economists but not to the general public. Specialized terminology is often called *jargon.* Misunderstandings and frustrations inevitably follow when specialists use jargon to communicate with people outside their own field.

Terminology is functional only when the sender and the receiver possess similar knowledge

In recent years, many companies have diversified their products or services to make themselves less susceptible to the ups and downs of single segments of the economy. Such diversification often increases the number of different specialists (and their jargon) within the organization. As a result, although the organization may have established channels of communication, they may be completely ineffective if the various groups do not have a common information base from which to work.

Diversification often leads to communication problems

Managers now realize, however, that specialization is not the perfect remedy. When workers are specialists, they are very dependent on the efforts of other specialists. For specialization to be effective, the specialists must achieve good communication.

Without good communication, specialization is ineffective

Lack of Skill in Sending and Receiving

Without training, one cannot reach one's full potential as a communicator

Many people consider oral communication to be as natural as breathing, eating, and sleeping. They maintain that, with maturity, human beings naturally develop into proficient communicators. One need not be very perceptive, however, to recognize that this belief is not true.

The ability to communicate ranks high among the attributes that employers seek in a potential employee. Business leaders frequently bemoan the absence of this ability among many college and university graduates. Workers often cite an inability to communicate as a prime shortcoming of their superiors.

Communication problems may be the fault of the sender or of the receiver

Until the last few decades, people invariably held the communicator responsible for any communication problem. They thought that transmitting information properly always led to effective communication. Now people recognize that the receiver plays an important role too. Getting the desired response from the receiver depends partly on whether he or she receives the intended message.

Training can improve listening ability

Listening ability can be improved. For this reason, listening is the subject of many training courses conducted in business and governmental organizations. Several courses are also available on tape.

Since Brenda enjoys working with numbers, she was especially pleased to be hired to handle the travel expense accounts. The job has proved an eye-opening experience for her, however. She always thought that an expense account clerk spent most of the day working with numbers.

After six months on the job, Brenda says, "I like my work, but it's different from what I expected. At least half of my time is spent getting and giving information. Sometimes expense accounts are incomplete and I have to call for additional information. Many times, too, people come to me for help even before they submit their claims. Because they're not trained in accounting, they want really clear explanations of what's expected. Mathematical ability is important for this job, but the ability to communicate with others is just as important."

Improper reception of information can be costly

Companies and individuals daily pay the price of problems caused by a lack of skill in receiving information. The drill press operator who did not listen carefully to the supervisor explaining how to work with the new alloy destroyed $300 worth of drill bits and wasted $1000 worth of raw materials. The salesperson who couldn't make sense of the memo explaining the procedure for writing orders decided to ignore it; the orders were delayed for as much as two weeks. An inability to receive information accurately contributes greatly to communication problems.

The Relationships Between Communication and Organizational Effectiveness

Improved communication usually leads to better morale

Management considers worker morale an important indicator of a healthy organization. Better morale usually accompanies better communication. Managers who are concerned about low morale should create additional opportunities for workers to communicate.

Communication is related to job satisfaction

Job satisfaction, which is closely linked to morale, is another important consideration, and many managers strive to make jobs more satisfying for workers. When workers feel that they are a part of their work group, they are more satisfied and don't feel left out. Workers are also more likely to be satisfied if they are happy with the amount of information they receive.

MBWA: A Style of Managing

A manager has several roles

Communication is a vital part of the manager's job. This communication occurs in a variety of settings and under varying circumstances. The variability in the communication process dictates that a manager must adopt any one of several roles to remain effective. These roles include interpersonal roles, which focus on interpersonal relationships; informational roles, which recognize the manager's vital position in the receipt and dissemination of information; and decisional roles, which focus on the essential managerial activity of decision making.

If the manager is to perform effectively in these roles, effective communication is a must. Tom Peters and Nancy Austin, authors of the book *In Search of Excellence*, introduced a concept of communication and motivation through informal communication: management by walking around (MBWA). This managerial technique uses informality to keep communication flowing instead of relying on the organizational chart as the path for information flow. Using MBWA, managers can increase their contact with subordinates, suppliers, and customers. This informal communication becomes the stimulus for managerial decision making as well as the vehicle for feedback to those individuals who are crucial to organizational success.

The Computerization of the Business Organization

Modern technology has led to the information explosion

Not long ago, many authorities predicted that modern technology would eliminate jobs and reduce the volume of paperwork in business organizations. Advanced high-speed printing machines and modern photocopiers have instead increased the volume of communication. These devices have so simplified preparation that paperwork is now disseminated more widely than ever. Some authorities are calling the result an information explosion.

Computers capable of processing and storing tremendous amounts of information have truly detonated this explosion. Equipped with a high-speed printer, a computer can turn out reams of paper daily and, in the process, inundate management with information.

Computerization has neither eliminated jobs nor reduced paperwork. Moreover, workers appear to be adapting positively to the changes in their jobs. *The Globe and Mail* reported that a 1986 survey conducted for the Public Service Alliance of Canada found that 77.8 percent of the employees surveyed said their jobs were just as satisfying after the introduction of computers as they were beforehand. "Significantly, 82.7 per cent said computers made their work easier."[6]

Computerization is increasing the need for skilled communicators

Modern technology has contributed greatly to management's access to information. It has also increased management's ability to transmit information quickly and economically. Modern technology has not, however, replaced the human communicator. If anything, computerization has increased his or her importance, for it is the manager who must ultimately determine the information to be retrieved and those to whom it should be sent.

More information is available now than ever before, and growing numbers of organizations employ a director of communications, a job title virtually unheard of until recently. The director of communications is responsible for managing the flow of information within the organization and for solving communication problems. No matter how sophisticated technology becomes, individuals who are skilled in communication and aware of the vital components in the communication process will always be needed. Chapter 2 describes the communication process and its many nuances.

Summary

This chapter has provided a general introduction to business communication.

- Business communication
  - has always been an important organizational function, whatever the size of the business
  - is vital to the organization's goals and to the individuals in the organization
- Management
  - constantly seeks ways to improve internal and external communication

  - often provides communication training for employees
- The cost of poor communication is difficult to calculate, but it is generally acknowledged to
  - be very expensive
  - have tangible and intangible effects
  - affect individuals far removed from the original problem
- Communication is significant because
  - the tremendous growth of organizations makes management difficult and necessitates good communication
  - increasingly organizations are competing in an international marketplace
  - specialized workers depend more on others and must exchange information with them
- Most individuals are not naturally skilful in sending and receiving messages, but they can learn these abilities
- Effective communication
  - improves workers' attitudes
  - encourages behaviour business considers desirable
  - is a characteristic of the most successful companies

Review Questions

1. Using the scenario at the beginning of the chapter as a starting point, discuss the types of messages students communicate to their instructors.
2. Discuss the types of written communication you have received or produced in the past month.
3. What is meant by the pervasive nature of communication?
4. Can monetary or nonmonetary costs be more accurately computed? Why?
5. Define internal communication.
6. Define external communication.
7. Compare formal channels with informal channels.
8. Why are patience, an open mind, and courtesy so important when dealing with people from other cultures?
9. Explain how task specialization affects communication between individuals within an organization.
10. Define jargon.
11. In what ways does computerization facilitate business communication? How does computerization complicate business communication?

Activities

1. Collect data on one of the following and summarize your findings in a memo to your instructor:
   a. writing done by people who are doing the job you are training for and by their supervisors
   b. writing done by important people in your life
   c. writing done by high school and college students
   d. writing done by professionals whom you know
2. Interview at least three people you know who already work full-time to find out:
   a. what bugs them about fellow employees
   b. how they are affected by a lack of communication effectiveness
   c. what type of communication makes their job easier

   Summarize your findings in a memo to your classmates.

Discussion Cases

The Big Bite: A Costly Transaction[7]

For some time, Rachel Ruddy, a 40-year-old professional mid-manager at the Burnaby Mountain Credit Union, had been considering having some extensive dental work. Although she made a point of having yearly checkups and cavities filled as they appeared, she felt her appearance was affected by a badly discoloured incisor, misaligned teeth, and noticeable fillings. A growing awareness of the importance of self-image and its relationship to job mobility led her to decide to invest in having her teeth crowned.

She enlisted the services of her regular dentist, Dr. Luke, who happened to be a casual social acquaintance. Her first step was to ask Dr. Luke about possible improvements. He explained that he would carry out an initial examination, which would include taking an impression, and then discuss a total package of work. The cost of the first phase would be $100, a charge to be subtracted from the full fee if she chose to have the work done.

After completing the impression, Dr. Luke explained the total procedure to Rachel at a professional appointment. She was so shocked at the figure he gave ($4900 for work she had assumed could cost half that amount) that she asked few questions at that session. She was hesitant to pay so much just to improve her appearance.

Later, after reflecting upon the importance of her appearance in her job and her desire never to have to wear dentures, she returned for another appointment to clarify her understanding of the process and charges. Most of her questions dealt with the process itself.

continued

From this appointment, she understood that the charge included five years of maintenance. In fact, Dr. Luke mentioned that at one time he had offered ten years, but had changed his policy when he found that figure unrealistic. He stressed that the decision to have this work done was the patient's. But he did mention that saving teeth and avoiding later problems with the temporomandibular joint were investments.

Rachel had the work done. When the bill arrived, she found that the diagnostic fee had not been subtracted. The doctor's secretary maintained that Rachel had misunderstood the total figure, and that the doctor had already subtracted the fee. Rachel did not believe he had but decided that it was not worth making an issue of $100.

A year later, however, Rachel was billed for $50 after a regular appointment with Dr. Luke's dental hygienist. When she protested this charge, she was told again that she had misunderstood. The package applied only to maintenance of the crown work that had been performed. Certainly a reasonable person would not expect "free" dental care for five years. The five-year period was for replacement of crowns that had not adapted to the mouth.

Rachel has no intention of going to court or changing dentists. She is fairly satisfied with the work but not with the colouring of one tooth. Dr. Luke has told her not to worry as within a year the shading will conform through natural staining. He has been right with other predictions about the teeth, but she is worried that, if she waits too long, she may be charged for changes or new crowns.

Case Questions

1. Who is at fault — the dentist for not putting his diagnosis and fee structure in writing, or the patient for not fully understanding the services?
2. How could some of these misunderstandings have been avoided?
3. Which services and fees should be communicated orally and which in writing?

A Costly Misunderstanding[8]

Kenneth Newson is a middle-level manager in a large forest company. With over fifteen years of managerial experience, he has faced many difficult communication situations. His effective communica-

continued

tion skill is one reason for his steady record of increased responsibilities and promotions.

Kenneth recently decided to invest a rather large sum of money he had been saving. He thoroughly reviewed several alternatives such as stocks, bonds, treasury certificates, and real estate, but was especially interested in a small new apartment building, near his home.

Jacobs, the real estate agent, was very persuasive while explaining the tax advantages and potential income of a newly built apartment building. Kenneth had confidence in him and agreed to buy the building at the asking price, contingent upon three things: landscaping had to be completed, a fence built around the back patios, and mail boxes installed in the lobby. Based on his managerial experience, Kenneth insisted that these items be written into the contract.

About 45 days after Kenneth took possession of the building, the mail boxes had been installed, but neither the fence nor the landscaping had been completed. Kenneth called Jacobs to ask about the delay. Jacobs replied that the contractor told him the job had been completed. Kenneth then called the builder directly, and again was told the conditions of the contract had been met.

Kenneth was furious. He didn't feel that the two pine trees in the front yard were "landscaping"; furthermore, short fences between the patios but no back enclosure did not meet the terms of the agreement. He believed that nearly $1000 worth of services and goods had not been supplied. The contractors replied that they provided everything that was agreed on and additional work could not be expected because of the low price at which the building was purchased. No agreement could be reached, so Kenneth took his case to small claims court.

Case Questions

1. Kenneth, Jacobs, and the building contractor are all experienced, well-meaning businesspeople. What caused the misunderstanding in this situation?
2. How could the parties involved prevent the extra expense of small claims court?
3. How would you define "fence" and "landscape"? Are these difficult terms to define? Why or why not?

Chapter 2

The Nature of Communication in Business

Learning Objectives

In this chapter, you'll learn about the nature and purpose of communication in business. More specifically, you will be able to:

1. explain how reinforcing and aversive stimuli can affect the behaviour of others in the communication exchange
2. discuss the myths and realities of communication
3. discuss the variables in the communication process

Preview Case

Edwina Neira was trying hard to maintain an honours average in her second year at university. Her grades on all her mid-term exams were good; however, she was concerned about her grade in psychology. Professor Harding had not scheduled a mid-term for that course, nor had he returned either of the short papers Edwina had submitted in the first two months of term. Wanting some feedback on her progress, Edwina scheduled an appointment with Professor Harding.

"I wanted to talk about my work in your class, Professor Harding," began Edwina. "Since you haven't returned my papers yet, I just wanted to make sure that I'm doing all right in your course."

Professor Harding reassured Edwina by telling her she was a good student and was doing "just fine" in his course. Edwina left the conference feeling confident about her progress; however, a week later, she was surprised when she received a B- on both her psychology papers. When she mentioned her disappointment to Professor Harding, he explained that anyone getting above a C is a "good" student in his class.

Overview

Communication can be deceptive. A message may seem perfectly clear, yet we learn subsequently that the sender was communicating something entirely different from what we understood.

As pointed out earlier, the major purpose of this book is to help you understand the nature of communication and how to communicate effectively. While most of this book deals with the particular skills involved in effective communication, this chapter provides a theoretical framework for them. In it, we attempt to set forth the nature and purpose of communication, to examine myths and realities about it, to present variables in the communication process, and to discuss encoding and decoding skills.

The Nature and Purpose of Communication

A basic goal of organizations is survival

A basic goal of any organization is survival. If a campus organization fails to meet the needs of its members, it ceases to exist. In private business, a major goal is making a profit. When businesses fail to make profits, they must eventually cease to function.

The behaviour of people enables organizations to meet goals

What are the factors that enable organizations to meet their goals and continue to exist? The behaviour of people in an organization is the major element. Whether a business organization is successful depends largely on the behaviour of the people in that organization. The judgements, decisions, and efforts of its members determine to a large extent its profitability. Admittedly, some other factors, such as government intervention and regulation, competing businesses, and natural disasters, also influence profits, but the behaviour of people in organizations has great influence.

The fundamental question is thus one of motivation. How does one motivate others to behave in the desired manner? First, we must realize that our behaviour affects the behaviour of others just as much as theirs affects ours. For example, imagine driving down a highway at night, exceeding the speed limit by just a few kilometres per hour. Suddenly, in the rearview mirror, you notice a car approaching rapidly. You take your foot off the gas in an attempt to reduce the car's speed to the legal limit. A blue flashing light on the approaching car confirms your suspicion. Your heart beats a little faster. Then you breathe a sigh of relief as the police car speeds by and continues down the highway, obviously in pursuit of some other speeding driver. The behaviour of the police officer influenced your behaviour, and your slowing down would no doubt affect the behaviour of drivers near you.

Taking another example, have you ever found an item at a garage sale that really caught your interest? "That's a good deal for the price," you thought, "but it's more than I can spend." This scene may have occurred:

> "That item over there that's marked $10 — does it work?"
> "Sure it works; it's almost brand new."
> "If it works, I'd be interested in it for $5, but I don't think it's worth much more than that."
> "You kidding? Those sell for $20 new and that's if you can find one. I got a new one for my birthday. That's why I'm selling this one. I'd have to get at least $8 for it."
> "It's probably worth that, but I only have $7.25 with me. If you'll take that, I'll buy it."
> "Okay."
> "Wow!" you thought. "I'd have paid the whole $10 if I'd had to."
> "I'd have let that old thing go for $5," the seller thought.

Your behaviour influenced the seller's as the seller's behaviour influenced yours. Interpersonal behaviour elicits responses — communication is a two-way process.

Influencing the Behaviour of Others

To understand how we influence the behaviour of others, we need a brief examination of reinforcing and aversive stimuli.[1]

Reinforcing stimuli have a positive impact on behaviour; aversive stimuli have a negative impact

Reinforcing stimuli have a positive impact on our behaviour. We find these stimuli pleasant when we experience them, through our senses, in such forms as the taste of good food or drink, the sight of an attractive man or woman, or the smell of a perfume or fresh bread. In brief, a reinforcing stimulus is one we seek out and want to experience. This type of stimulus is positive and can have a motivating effect upon behaviour because we seek to experience it.

Aversive stimuli have the opposite effect upon our behaviour. They are also sensory experiences and can include the taste of rotten food, a nasty smell, and the sight of something or someone we find ugly. These stimuli influence our behaviour in a negative way in that we seek to avoid them.

The spoken word is a forceful stimuli

Perhaps some of the most forceful stimuli, both reinforcing and aversive, come to us as spoken words. For example, the statement "You are really doing good work" can be a reinforcing stimulus that encourages the listener to work hard and long. On the other hand, "You really muffed that one" can have an aversive effect that causes a person to reduce effort and perhaps skip a day of work. If aversive stimuli are frequently repeated, they may cause an employee to quit a job altogether.

By this point, it has probably occurred to you that what is reinforcing to one person may be aversive to another. For example, drinking blood is aversive to most people in this country, but in some parts of the world it is reinforcing. Similarly, some people find the drinking of alcoholic beverages aversive, while others find it reinforcing. Any stimulus can be reinforcing or aversive, depending on the person and the situation.

A "paired stimulus" may produce a reinforcing or an aversive reaction

How does a stimulus become reinforcing or aversive? A stimulus paired or linked with a reinforcer becomes a reinforcing stimulus, while one paired or linked with something aversive becomes an aversive stimulus. For examples of how this pairing works, notice advertisements: "Eating yogurt leads to a long life." Using a particular kind of aftershave lotion leads to a kiss from an attractive woman. Or think about the pairing in the slogan "All my men wear English Leather or they wear nothing at all." Aversive stimulus pairing is sometimes part of the learning process. For example, a young child who puts a finger on a hot stove learns to associate the pain in the finger (stimulus) with the stove, which is now avoided (aversion).

Many important pairings take place in conversation

Many important pairings take place in conversation. The statement "Karen thinks you are doing a bad job" will cause you to react unfavourably to Karen the next time you see her. Likewise, "John says you are one of our best sales reps" will be reinforcing in your behaviour with John.

The discussion above has made three important points:

1. The behaviour of people enables most organizations to meet their goals.

2. Behaviour is greatly influenced by reinforcing and aversive stimuli.
3. Some of the most powerful reinforcing and aversive stimuli come to us through the spoken word.

Communication is the major way we can influence the behaviour of our business colleagues. Indeed, *the verbal and nonverbal communications of managers influence profits more than any other factor.*

Communication is the major way of influencing others' behaviour

Since communication has such a major influence in organizations, it is appropriate to examine its nature in detail. Many people give little thought to communication because they have been talking for as long as they can remember. But what is communication, really? For many of us communication is speaking. For some of us, it is primarily writing. For a few of us, communication is primarily listening. What communication is depends on the assumptions we make about it.

Seven Myths and Realities about the Nature of Communication

To understand more about the nature of communication, we need to confront some of the common misunderstandings or myths about the nature of communication.

The Myth: We communicate only when we consciously and deliberately choose to communicate.

The basis for this myth is the idea that we control our communication. Sometimes people do deliberately and consciously control their communication. For example, several days after interviewing a prospective employee, a manager decides to send a letter offering him a job.

Myth: we communicate only when we intend to; reality: we frequently communicate messages we are not aware of

Often, however, we are not aware of many aspects of our communications so we are surprised when they bring results that differ from those we had anticipated. For instance, the writer of the job-offer letter is shocked to learn that the prospective employee has already accepted a job at a lower salary with a lesser firm. Why? In a follow-up telephone call, the writer learns that, since ten days had passed after the employment interview, the job candidate assumed he was not going to get the offer. The message he received, just as if it had been communicated to him face to face, was that the company was not interested in him.

The Reality: We often communicate when we are not aware that we are communicating.

To continue the example, ten days had passed before the job applicant received his offer because one of the secretaries was sick and the other was busy typing a lengthy report. So, the would-be employer communicated a message he was unaware of. Indeed, all of us frequently communicate messages that we do not intend to communicate.

The Myth: Words mean the same thing to our listeners as they do to us.

Myth: words have the same meaning for both listeners and speakers; reality: words have meanings only in terms of people's past experiences

The basis of this myth is the assumption that words have the same inherent meanings for everyone. For example, on Monday, a project leader tells her secretary that there's no rush on a progress report she wants typed. On Friday, the project leader asks why her report isn't ready. "When you said there was no rush, I thought I could do it next week," replies the secretary. To the secretary who works for five other people, "no rush" means that a task can wait at least a week; however, to the project leader who is anxious to submit her report, "no rush" means in the next couple of days.

To illustrate further, when the word "apple" is spoken, some will imagine a red apple, some a yellow one, and still others perhaps will think of an apple pie. Why does the same word mean different things to different people?

The Reality: Meanings of words reflect people's past experiences and perceptions.

In the example, the words "no rush" mean different amounts of time to the project leader and the secretary because their perceptions differ. Because of the myth that words mean the same thing to everyone who hears them, we assume that others will get exactly the same message we do from a set of words. The reality is that words mean different things to different people.

The Myth: We communicate primarily with words.

Myth: we communicate primarily with words; reality: most of the message is nonverbal

The basis for this myth is a belief that a communicated message is one that is either spoken or written. For example, you go to your professor's office to discuss a topic for your term paper and hand her an outline of your proposal. After quickly glancing over the outline, the professor responds, "This looks good. Go ahead with the paper." But you feel somewhat uneasy about going ahead with the paper. Why? After leaving the professor's office, you realize that your uneasiness stems from the fact that she looked over the outline very quickly and several times glanced at her watch, as if she were late for a meeting. You now realize that something far more important than your term paper was on her mind. Indeed, the professor did communicate with words, but she also communicated without words — nonverbally.

The Reality: The majority of the messages we communicate are based not on words but on nonverbal symbols.

We all have become increasingly aware of nonverbal communication. Our tone of voice, eye contact, body movement, and even the clothes we wear communicate as much as or more than the words we use.

Even more important is the fact that our nonverbal communication frequently undermines our verbal communication. For example, at a lecture the speaker begins by saying, "I am pleased to be here to talk about my favourite topic — human motivation." However, his nonverbal communication is the following: he wears a wrinkled suit, he looks at his notes instead of at the audience, and he speaks in a monotone. The message communicated to you is that it is going to be a long and boring afternoon. When what is communicated nonverbally contradicts what is communicated verbally, why do we usually choose to believe the nonverbal message? It is primarily because we consider it easier for people to manipulate the use of words. Most of us believe that nonverbal messages are the most accurate reflection of what a person really is thinking and that there is truth in the adage "actions speak louder than words."

The Myth: Nonverbal communication is the silent language.

The term "body language" is often misused in place of "nonverbal communication." Many think nonverbal communication is never heard — that it is only seen.

Myth: nonverbal communication is the silent language; reality: nonverbal communication is received through all five senses

The Reality: Nonverbal communication is received through all five senses.

Gestures, body position, and the way we walk are silent nonverbal messages — so are the tone of our voice, the clapping of our hands, and the manner of our handshake. Nonverbal messages can be felt, heard, smelled, and tasted, as well as seen.

The Myth: Communication is a one-way activity.

The basis for the myth that communication is the act of telling is the assumption that our message moves without interruption to the receiver and ends there. All of us at one time or another have had people communicate in this fashion, talking *at* us rather than *with* us. For example, a supervisor may speak in such a tone of voice that you are reluctant to ask any questions or provide any response other than a passive, affirmative nod. Many times, when a subordinate fails to carry out an assignment correctly, we hear his boss say, "I *told* him exactly how to do it." All of us have been guilty of *telling* people rather than *communicating* with them. That brings us to another reality.

Myth: communication is a one-way activity of telling people; reality: communication is a two-way activity in which feedback is crucial

The Reality: Communication is a two-way activity.

Have you ever played the parlour game in which people sit in a circle and one whispers a message to the person on the right, then the message is passed to the next player, and so on? The rules of the game are simple: each person repeats the message only once, and no one can ask any questions. When the message finally gets around the circle, the last person states it aloud. Usually there is little, if any, resemblance to the original message. This game is a classic example of one-way communication. The message is passed quickly but without accuracy.

The same group of people can play the game so that each member, after hearing the message, is allowed to ask questions about it. This version of the game has two dramatic differences from the other. First, it takes longer to play. Two-way communication always takes more time than one-way communication. Second, and more important, the message is passed along much more accurately. The major reason for the increased accuracy is feedback.

Feedback is simply the listener's reaction to the sender's verbal and nonverbal message. A major function of feedback is to allow the sender to see how well he or she is accomplishing the objectives of the original communication. In brief, what distinguishes effective from ineffective communication is the ability to interpret accurately the feedback provided by the other party.

The Myth: The message we send is identical to the message received by the listener.

Myth: the message sent is identical to the message received; reality: the message received is never identical to the message intended

We all tend to assume that a listener receives the messages we send exactly as we send them. For example, suppose you send a letter to a friend in another province, inviting that person to be your guest next month. When you receive no response to your letter, you become irritated. Why did your friend not respond? Perhaps the problem is not that your friend did not reply but that the post office lost your letter. Or perhaps you left out a page when you put the letter into the envelope and your friend never received the invitation. The message that you send may be perfectly clear to you but not to your listener because of some obstruction that neither you nor your listener can control.

The Reality: The message as it is finally received by the listener is never exactly the same as the message originally sent.

Part of the reason the message received is never the same as the message sent has already been mentioned: words do not convey specific meanings. Meanings are based on individuals' past experiences. Since no two people have had exactly the same set of experiences, the message received by one person can never be exactly the same as the message sent by another.

The Myth: You can never give someone too much information.

Sometimes people in organizations say, "Nobody ever tells me anything; I just work here." Indeed, sometimes people do not receive the information they need to perform their jobs properly. On the other hand, the ease with which modern office equipment generates multiple copies encourages the assumption that the more information provided to employees, the more productive they will be.

Myth: you can never give someone too much information; reality: people can suffer from information overload

The Reality: People can be given too much information and suffer from information overload as a result.

Information overload means having too much information to make intelligent use of it. The problem is more common than most of us realize. In the last 50 years, machine copying and other types of reproduction have vastly increased our ability to generate and transmit information. But the human capacity to handle and process information remains unchanged. People speak, listen, and understand at about the same rate and level as they did 50 years ago. It is not surprising, therefore, that information overload is a major problem for people in many organizations. We need to understand that we do not solve problems simply by providing more and more information. We need to be concerned not so much with the *quantity* of information as with its *quality*.

Variables in the Communication Process

A brief look at the myths and realities of the nature of communication confirms that communication can be a confusing activity. In order to understand how it breaks down, we need to examine the variables in the communication process.

Communication can be broadly defined as the transmission of a message between two or more people. While some writers and thinkers discuss intrapersonal communication — that which occurs within the individual — our concern here is to examine interpersonal communication, communication between people.

Communication is the transmission of a message between two or more people

Communication between people involves many factors. The major variables in the process include:

The communication process includes six variables

1. sender (encoder)
2. message
3. channel
4. receiver or receivers (decoder or decoders)
5. perception
6. feedback

The way in which these six variables interact is illustrated in Figure 2.1, a model of the communication process. Too many of us take the art of communication for granted because we are ignorant of the mechanics involved. This model is intended to increase your awareness of the variables responsible for successful communication.

The Sender (Encoder)

The sender's basic task is to use symbols and skills to bring understanding to the receiver

The sender in the communication process is responsible for formulating the message in a way that accurately conveys an idea to the receiver. Since communication is essentially a process of creating understanding, sender and receiver must make a concentrated effort to arrive at a similar meaning. The sender, however, must bear the major burden. He or she needs to visualize the communication from the receiver's viewpoint. The sender's basic task is to search for communication symbols and use skills that will bring about understanding in the mind of the receiver. Specifically, the sender should (1) use verbal and nonverbal symbols that are on the receiver's level, and (2) secure feedback from the receiver.

The Message

Many important messages are complex

The message part of the communication process consists of the verbal and nonverbal symbols that represent the information we want to transmit. Each message we send is an attempt to convey an idea to the receiver. Some of the messages are relatively simple. A stop sign is an example of a simple message. While we may not always obey the message, it is clear and straightforward. Other messages are more complex and thus more difficult to impart to the receiver. For example, suppose you wish to convey to a group of employees that you want to increase production and improve quality control simultaneously. Getting that message understood by the entire group of employees could be difficult because the two

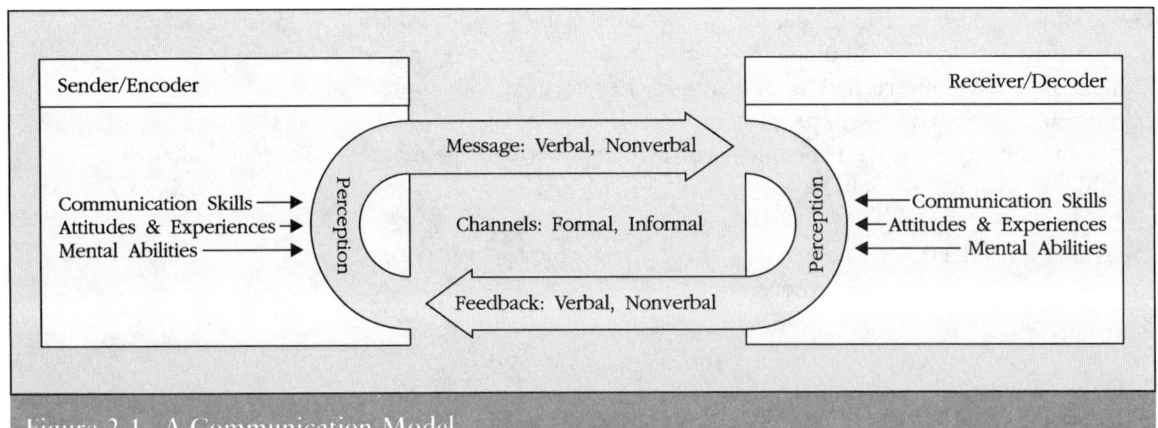

Figure 2.1 A Communication Model

components of the message, "improve quality control" and "increase production," seem on the surface to be incompatible.

The Channel

What is the appropriate channel for a given message? Should it be communicated face to face or on paper? The question of whether an oral or a written channel should be used can be partially answered by reviewing the following set of questions:

Consider whether oral or written communication is the appropriate channel for a given message

1. Is immediate feedback needed? Is it important to get the receiver's reaction to your message? If so, oral communication may provide the quickest feedback. Although written communication can generate feedback, it generally comes more slowly. Many messages require immediate feedback, and oral communication allows the sender to answer questions on the spot. However, the electronic office offers the possibility of immediate feedback in writing.

2. Is acceptance in question? The receiver may resist the message you are attempting to communicate. If acceptance is likely to be a problem, oral communication is better than written. When people receive a written communication, they feel they have had no chance for input. In face-to-face communication, you have the opportunity to do more to adapt your message to the receiver. Even though messages sent through electronic mail tend to be less formal, oral communication is still preferable.

3. Is a documented record of the communication needed? Many times messages in organizations may need to be verified or monitored at a later date. Frequently the receiver of a message is expected to be accountable for information contained in the message. If accountability is important, written communication is superior to oral communication. Ironically, because of the limited storage capability of many existing computers, electronic-mail messages are frequently printed and filed in traditional paper files.

4. Is detailed accuracy needed? If the message being communicated contains a lot of detail or precise information, or if it explains a complicated procedure, the written method is the superior means of communication.

In the final analysis, no method of communication is universally superior to another. In many cases, the message can best be communicated by a combination of both written and oral channels. Frequently, communicators follow an oral conversation with a written summary. In other

Combined written and oral communications are often needed

cases, they hand-carry written communications so they can provide a few words of explanation, thereby helping to ensure acceptance of the written statements.

All channels have costs and benefits

Whatever your choice of communication channel, be sure to weigh both its benefits and its costs. For example, most managers are short of time, a precious resource. The high cost of time can determine which channel of communication is the most appropriate. An announcement of an increase in employee health benefits should obviously not be communicated face to face to all 2000 employees. Rather, a written memo is the appropriate channel of communication, considering the number of people involved and the nature of the message. On the other hand, relaying a new business strategy against competitors to the director of marketing would definitely call for a face-to-face conference to ensure optimal understanding of the company's revised approach.

Communication channels can be formal or informal

Communication channels can also be characterized as either formal or informal. The formal channels include downward, upward, and horizontal communication. Generally, downward and upward channels of communication follow the organization's chain of command. As messages travel downward and upward in organizations, they tend to become distorted. In many cases, much of the message never gets through to the intended receiver. For this reason, many managers have adopted the MBWA (management by walking around) approach described in Chapter 1.

Some companies emphasize horizontal communication

In some progressive companies, hierarchical channels of communication are given less emphasis. For example, in some factories, managerial and office functions have been moved to the shop floor. Work teams assume much of the responsibility for solving production problems and managers adopt a "we're here to help you do your job" attitude. In these environments, horizontal communication assumes much greater importance. The tone of these channels of communication is much more likely to be consultative, persuasive, or suggestive than directive.

Informal channels help build positive relationships on the job

Informal channels of communication are also critical to the communication process. While informal channels can refer to the office grapevine or rumour mill, they also include social and non-job-oriented conversation. Such conversation helps employees to establish positive relationships with their co-workers and to develop a sense of belonging to the work group or organization. Many companies actively encourage informal channels of communication through social gatherings and after-hours sports teams.

The Receiver (Decoder)

The receiver can affect communication in a number of ways. How much does the receiver know about the topic? Is the receiver likely to be receptive to the message and the sender? What previous experience has the receiver had with the sender? These points and many others determine the impact of the message upon the receiver.

Specifically, the receiver is primarily concerned with two types of behaviour: listening and providing feedback to the sender.

The receiver must listen and provide feedback

Perception

Perception is one of the most important variables in communication. As shown in Figure 2.1, perception is an integral part of both the sender's and the receiver's involvement in the communication process. The receiver is a product of all his or her *past experiences. Attitudes* towards the surrounding environment also modify our perception of what's being communicated. Of course, *mental abilities*, or intelligence, greatly determine the capacity to discern the communication accurately. Finally, *communication skills*, in speaking or in listening, influence the way one sends a message and the way one receives feedback about it. In all likelihood, sender and receiver bring different attitudes, past experiences, mental abilities, and communication skills to the communication process. These differences in perception need not prevent understanding. Rather, an awareness of and sensitivity to them can facilitate open and productive communication.

Past experiences, attitudes, mental abilities, and communication skills influence perception

A person's position in an organization strongly influences his or her perception. One study cites the different perceptions of supervisors and subordinates as an example. It reports that 76 percent of the supervisors questioned said they "always or almost always" sought ideas from subordinates in looking for solutions to job problems. However, only 16 percent of the workers thought their supervisors sought their opinions.[2] As this example shows, perception greatly influences the way we send and receive messages.

Perception greatly affects the way we send and receive messages

Feedback

Feedback is the receiver's reaction to your message. The receiver may agree or disagree. The feedback may be verbal or nonverbal; it can be written or oral. Its importance is in providing guidance for the next message sent to the receiver. In brief, the sender can evaluate the effectiveness of the communication by the feedback he or she receives.

Feedback is the reaction the receiver has to your message

Encoding-Decoding Skills

We can understand the communication process better by considering encoding and decoding skills. *Encoding* is the process of translating an

Encoding means translating an idea into a message; decoding reverses the process

idea into a message. Imagine that you are writing a letter to a company about possible summer job openings. You have certain ideas you want to communicate in that letter. For example, you want to offer reasons why you chose to write to that particular company. Also, you need to provide some general information about your qualifications. As these ideas form in your mind and you put them on paper, the encoding process is occurring.

Decoding is the process of translating a message into an idea. Imagine the personnel manager of the company you have written to opening your letter of inquiry. As she reads it, she notes that you are asking about a summer job. At the same time she makes decisions about you and your qualifications. She decodes information about your work by noting how neat and attractive the layouts of your letter and résumé are. She decodes information about your previous work experience, courses you are taking, and interests you seem to have. All the decisions the personnel manager makes about your message are the result of the decoding process.

Encoding and decoding are complex processes essential to communication

Perhaps our descriptions of encoding and decoding have made them appear simple processes. They are not. As you learned from the discussion of the myths and realities of communication, people rarely assign the same meanings to our intended messages. Somewhere in the encoding-decoding processes, breakdowns in communication can occur. Bear in mind that the most important responsibility of the sender is to create understanding in the receiver's mind. In turn, receivers must make every effort to help the sender create understanding and make him or her aware of what has been understood.

To accomplish these goals as senders or receivers, we need the following skills:

1. We must have the ability to analyze the other person.

Receivers of messages are individuals. They are of different races and sexes, have varying family backgrounds, and come from all parts of the country or the world. And their personalities are different. For example, some individuals try harder when someone they respect criticizes them; others in the same situation simply give up and quit trying altogether.

Encoding-decoding skill 1: Analyzing the other person

As receivers, you must analyze the sender's frame of reference. If an instructor insists that you complete a major paper on time even though he or she knows you have another major assignment due at the same time, you may be angry. Yet consider what the instructor may be thinking: "This student thinks that other assignment is more important than mine." How would you feel in the same situation?

Whether sending or receiving messages, you must consider the other person in the communication exchange. He or she is unique. The extent of that uniqueness is the extent to which he or she will encode and decode messages in different ways from other people — including you.

2. We must have the ability to get and give feedback.

Encoding-decoding skill 2: Receiving and giving feedback

As a sender, you need to create a climate in which the receiver will be willing to provide feedback. Immediate feedback, of course, seldom occurs with written communication: that is one of its disadvantages. However, when you speak to a receiver, you must try to get immediate feedback to determine whether you have created the understanding you intended.

One way to get accurate and willing feedback is to ask a question and then pause. The pause lets your receiver know that you are really interested in the feedback. If you say, "Do you understand?" and immediately continue your message, you are not encouraging your receiver to ask for clarification.

Since a sender has difficulty getting useful feedback, giving feedback is an important responsibility of the receiver. Feedback tells senders about the understanding or misunderstanding they have created. (See the accompanying chart for some characteristics of effective feedback.)

Characteristics of Good Interpersonal Feedback

- **It is specific rather than general.**
  To be told, "You are dominating," is not as constructive as to be told, "You did not listen to what others said and thereby curtailed their suggestions."
- **It is descriptive rather than evaluative.**
  By avoiding evaluative language such as "You handled that badly," you reduce the need for the individual to react defensively.
- **It takes into account the needs of both the receiver and the giver of feedback.**
  Feedback can be destructive when it serves only your needs and fails to meet needs of the receiver.
- **It is directed towards behaviour the receiver can do something about.**
  Frustration is increased when people are reminded of some shortcoming over which they have no control.
- **It is well timed.**
  In general, feedback is most useful at the earliest opportunity after a given behaviour — depending, of course, on the other person's readiness to hear it. There are occasions when a cooling-off period should occur.

continued

- **It is two-way.**
  You get feedback about the feedback.
- **It is tailored to the individual.**
  A successful communicator recognizes the different needs and abilities of each person and interacts with each accordingly. You must guard against the desire to remake others in your own image. The changes in behaviour must be within the framework of each individual's personality and skills.

Encoding-decoding skill 3: Understanding perception

3. We must understand perception.

Perception, the process of assigning meaning to a message, is the major cause of communication breakdowns. When you perceive other people and their messages, you may misuse your perceptual skills in several ways.

First, people let past experiences influence their perceptions of messages. In an old riddle, a father and his son are driving to work. A terrible accident occurs. The father is killed instantly, and the son is badly injured. An ambulance rushes him to the hospital, where he is prepared for emergency surgery. The surgeon walks in, takes one look at him, and says, "I'm sorry. I can't operate on him. He's my son." How can this be?

Perhaps the boy is the "father's" stepson. Perhaps the "father" is a Catholic priest. Perhaps the boy was adopted. Other explanations abound. Actually, the surgeon is the boy's mother. Why can't many people think of this answer? It is because their past experiences have convinced them that surgeons are male.

Second, people often fill in missing information about messages received. In the earlier example, the project leader who said there was no rush to type a progress report expected to have it within a few days. The secretary assumed that the following week would be soon enough. Without feedback and without further information, the secretary simply assigned her own meaning to the project leader's message.

Third, people often perceive messages so that they are consistent with their own attitudes and beliefs. People tend to see the world through coloured glasses shaded the hue of their personal attitudes about themselves, others, and life in general. However, by recognizing this tendency in yourself, you can often learn to communicate more effectively.

Several barriers interfere with communication

Several barriers to communication affect the six major variables in the communication process discussed earlier in the chapter. One of the earliest and most complete lists of these barriers is presented by Thayer.[3]

1. **Meaning barriers:** problems with meaning, significance, and the sending and reception of the meaning of the message.

2. **Organizational barriers:** problems with physical distance between members; specialization of task functions; power, authority, and status relationships; and with the ownership of information.
3. **Interpersonal barriers:** problems with the climate of the relationship, the values and the negative attitudes held by the participants.
4. **Individual barriers:** problems with individual competencies to think and act, which would include physical ailments or handicaps; problems with individual skills in receiving and transmitting information, which would include poor listening and reading skills, and psychological considerations.
5. **Economic, geographic, and temporal barriers:** problems with time and dollar costs, different locations, and the effects of time on reception of the message.
6. **Channel and media barriers:** problems that confront the issue of how best to communicate a message; for example, it is sometimes best to transmit a message face to face rather than in writing.
7. **Technological barriers:** problems with too much information for the capacity of the recipient.

The encoding and decoding skills discussed earlier in this chapter can help to overcome these barriers.

Summary

In this chapter, we discussed the nature of communication.

- People's behaviour enables organizations to achieve their goals.
- Verbal and nonverbal communication influences the behaviour of others.
- Several myths and realities about the nature of communication exist:
    - *Myth 1:* We communicate only when we intend to. *Reality:* We frequently communicate messages we are not aware of communicating.
    - *Myth 2:* We communicate as if words mean the same thing to our listeners as they do to us. *Reality:* Meanings of words reflect people's past experiences and perceptions.
    - *Myth 3:* We communicate primarily with words. *Reality:* The majority of the messages we communicate are based on the nonverbal aspects of communication.
    - *Myth 4:* Nonverbal communication is a silent language. *Reality:* Nonverbal communication is received through all five senses.
    - *Myth 5:* Communication is a one-way activity. *Reality:* Communication is a two-way activity in which feedback from the other party is crucial.
    - *Myth 6:* The message we communicate is identical to the message

received. *Reality:* The message finally received by the listener is never identical to the message sent.
  - *Myth 7:* You can never give someone too much information. *Reality:* People can be given too much information. Information overload can be just as much of a problem as not having enough information.
- The chapter also included
  - a communication model
  - the encoding and decoding skills necessary for effective communication
  - a discussion of the importance of perception in the communication process
- The ability to perceive the other person's frame of reference accurately is a recurrent topic in this text.

Review Questions

1. In what ways can reinforcing or aversive stimuli affect behaviour?
2. Discuss the seven myths and realities about the nature of communication. Support your discussion with an example of each myth/reality.
3. What is the sender's major responsibility in the communication process?
4. "The more information we provide employees, the more productive they will be." Comment.
5. What important criteria determine whether an oral or a written channel of communication is more appropriate for sending a message?
6. Name the encoding and decoding skills that both sender and receiver should master to prevent communication breakdown. In the context of a business setting, give an example of each.
7. What are the characteristics of good feedback? Who bears the primary responsibility for good feedback? How can good feedback facilitate an accurate and willing information exchange?

Discussion Cases

Nick's Crisis[4]

Nick Young has worked as manager of the information services division of World Business Machines (WBM) for twelve years. His department's ratings have always been superior, and he is well liked by everyone with whom he works.

continued

Because of technological developments, WBM plans to reorganize the information services division. Any personnel changes resulting from this reorganization will be made on the basis of seniority.

Nick and his boss agree that the changes will benefit the organization, improve working conditions for current employees, and result in additional employment opportunities for members of the community, rather than layoffs of current staff. Nick's boss has asked Nick not to discuss any of the planned changes with anyone until all the details have been finalized.

Many of Nick's subordinates have noticed that, whenever they make suggestions about improving work procedures, Nick acts a little nervous and says, "Let's talk about this later." Additionally, Nick's administrative assistant inadvertently "leaked" to a subordinate that "some big changes are going to take place — technological changes."

Nick's subordinates begin to talk. Rumours spread about layoffs. Morale drops noticeably. Tardiness and absenteeism rise sharply. Work piles up, and work quality drops. Nick starts to spend most of his time disciplining his employees and writing reports for their personnel files.

Nick becomes very dissatisfied with his job; his boss picks up the signals and calls Nick into his office for some counselling.

Case Questions

1. What are some of the variables that have led to Nick's crisis? Use the Communication Model in Figure 2.1 to focus your discussion.
2. At what point might Nick have taken action and possibly avoided getting into the crisis?
3. What advice should Nick's boss give about (a) his own responsibility for the crisis, (b) Nick's responsibility, and (c) what to do next to try to restore peace to the department?

Whom Can You Trust?[5]

Joan Duncan is a registered nurse. One day, she took her son to the family physician because he was breathing with difficulty. After diagnosing a bronchial infection, Dr. Smithers prescribed an antibiotic. Duncan decided to have the prescription filled at the pharmacy

continued

in the neighbourhood mall.

Being a registered nurse, Duncan read the prescription before she brought it to the pharmacy. She told the pharmacist that her husband would pick up the medication later in the day.

When Mr. Duncan brought the medication home, Mrs. Duncan read the instructions on the label of the container. Immediately, she realized the pharmacist had indicated the wrong dosage and frequency of administration.

She phoned the pharmacy and, having made certain that she was speaking to the pharmacist, she asked him to check the prescription. The pharmacist's first response was that Conners Drug Mart doesn't make mistakes and that the instructions on the label were correct.

However, Mrs. Duncan insisted that the pharmacist check the prescription. Reluctantly, and somewhat indignantly, he agreed to do so. When he returned to the phone, he admitted that, in fact, the instructions were wrong. However, he passed off the error as a typographical mistake, refusing to admit that someone on his staff had made an error.

After discussing the situation with several friends who also deal with this pharmacy, Mrs. Duncan discovered that they had experienced similar problems. For example, just the week before, Mrs. Charboneau had been dispensed, and had used, the wrong eye drops. Fortunately, no serious complications had arisen.

Case Questions

1. Why might the pharmacist react as he did when Mrs. Duncan pointed out the error to him?
2. How would you feel if you were Mrs. Duncan? Why?
3. How might the situation have been handled?
4. What would be the appropriate steps to take to correct this problem?
5. Assuming the role of Mrs. Duncan, write a letter of concern to the physician, to the pharmacy, or to the Society of Professional Pharmacists.

Chapter 3

Nonverbal Communication: Messages Beyond Words

Learning Objectives

In this chapter, you'll learn about the pervasive nature of nonverbal communication. More specifically, you will be able to:

1. explain the importance of nonverbal behaviour in the communication process
2. improve your perception of body movement in nonverbal communication
3. explain how space is used to communicate in the business organization
4. recognize the impact of dress and appearance, colour, and time on those around you
5. recognize nonverbal indicators of relative power or status
6. explain how to change nonverbal behaviours that detract from the impact of an oral presentation

Preview Case

The eighteen members of staff working in the sales office were to be moved from one building to another. In the new location, because of lack of space, three people were seated across the aisle from the rest of their group.

Two of these three were juniors who had asked to be transferred to the factory floor. Their new jobs paid less and had less status, but they would be able to earn more because of increased opportunities for overtime. One reason for putting them across the aisle was to avoid the need to rearrange desks when they transferred to the factory at the end of the month. The third person to be put across the aisle was Jim, a middle-aged clerk who had been with the firm for twelve years.

The manager overseeing the move gave little thought to Jim's placement, although it did occur to him that Jim's responsible attitude would have a positive influence on the two juniors during their remaining weeks in that office.

Jim, on the other hand, worried that he might be forcibly transferred to the factory and he dreaded nothing more. He enjoyed his job and did not think that he would cope well with the added physical demands of a job on the factory floor.

Having speculated on the possibility of a move for some time, Jim recalled with alarm that his name had been omitted from the latest edition of the company telephone directory. With the exception of very junior workers and the factory workers, all other staff were usually listed.

The fact that his name had been omitted took on a new significance for Jim. It reinforced his fear that he was about to be transferred to the factory. He became so preoccupied over what might happen to him that he started applying for office jobs that paid less than his present one and involved less interesting work.

Overview

At the outset of this chapter, we need to underscore the fact that we use both verbal and nonverbal means simultaneously to convey our messages. The situation described above illustrates the power of nonverbal communication. More and more people who write about business communication stress the importance of nonverbal communication. For example, in your résumé you communicate not only with the words that describe your education and experience, but also with the quality and colour of paper you use, the neatness of the typing, and similar nonverbal qualities. So, while we will analyze separately several aspects of nonverbal communication, remember that in practice verbal and nonverbal aspects combine for the total message that is communicated.

Nonverbal communication can be defined as all those messages that are not encoded in words. The intended or implied meaning of many of these nonverbal messages varies dramatically from one culture to another. Therefore, when you encounter someone from a culture different from your own for the first time, you may have to learn more than the language to communicate effectively.

Nonverbal communication is a message not encoded in words

In the remainder of this chapter, we will discuss the pervasive nature of nonverbal communication and examine what we communicate by how we say something, how we communicate with our bodies, how we communicate with space, and how we communicate through dress and appearance, colour, and time. These nonverbal aspects of communication are what many authorities maintain is the key to most of our ordinary communication.

One authority on nonverbal communication, Albert Mehrabian, believes that our words convey a very small part of the message, arguing that only 7 percent of the total impact of any given message consists of words.[1] Nonverbal factors account for 93 percent of a message's impact. Of that 93 percent, 38 percent is attributed to tone of voice and inflection; the remainder to facial expression, body position, and gestures. If you carefully analyze the messages that others communicate, you may be surprised at how much emphasis is placed on the nonverbal aspects of communication and, therefore, confirm Mehrabian's findings for yourself.

More than 90 percent of the message may be communicated nonverbally

How You Say Something

Of all the components of nonverbal communication, how we say something is most like verbal communication. To realize how important this component is, perform a simple test. The next time a friend asks you to do something — go to a movie or to a particular restaurant for dinner — respond with the words "Sure, I would love to go," but let your tone of voice convey that you have little or no interest in going. Then watch your friend's reaction to *how* you communicated your response.

How you say something can reinforce or undermine the verbal message

At times we mean to communicate a particular message through the use of *emphasis*. The phrase "I would like to help you" can convey several meanings, depending on the word emphasized:

1. *I* would like to help you.
2. I *would* like to help you.
3. I would *like* to help you.
4. I would like to *help* you.

In each case, the emphasized word changes the meaning of the message.

Voice qualities include rate, volume, rhythm, pitch, and resonance

To better understand this component, we can look at *voice qualities*, including rate, volume, rhythm, pitch, and resonance. All of us at one time or another have been made aware of the quality known as rate — how fast or slow someone is speaking. Depending on what other messages are being communicated, an increase in rate can indicate anger, impatience, or anxiety on the part of the person sending the message. A decrease in rate can indicate thoughtfulness, a reflective attitude, or — on the other hand — boredom or lack of interest.

Volume is another voice quality that frequently conveys meaning, especially in conjunction with rate. When a supervisor says in a soft voice, "I would like to talk with you in my office," you feel somewhat at ease. But if your supervisor says the same words loudly, you feel disturbed. However, the implied meaning assigned to the volume of speech differs in other cultures. In some cultures, even quite personal conversations are held at a volume loud enough to cause a North American audience some discomfort. At the same time, the volume of North American conversations can seem excessively loud and impolite to people of other cultures.

The qualities of rhythm, pitch, and resonance are more difficult to understand than rate and volume. When you consider voice qualities, the major point is deviation from the speaker's normal voice. Noting differences in the sender's rhythm, pitch, and resonance can often increase your understanding of the message.

It is the voice qualities of rate, volume, pitch, and resonance in combination with *vocal qualifiers* that cause one's intended meaning to become most apparent. We already gave one example of the significance of emphasis as a vocal qualifier. Another example is evident in the phrase "I am going to the boss's house for dinner tonight." Placing emphasis on different key words can greatly vary the meaning of the sentence. For example, pausing on "I" and raising your voice slightly might indicate a sense of superiority, implying "I'm going and you're not." On the other hand, the sentence spoken quickly at an even volume and pitch might simply convey information.

Vocal cues express emotion

We frequently use vocal cues to convey emotions. For example, most children know instantly when their parents are angry by the volume and tone of voice. Unfortunately, it is easier to convey the emotions of impatience, fear, and anger than the emotions of satisfaction and admiration through vocal cues.

Communicating with Our Bodies

The face and eyes convey many emotional meanings

The face and eyes are the most expressive means of body communication. The ability to interpret facial meaning is an important part of communication, since facial expressions can facilitate or hamper feedback. Many instructors rely on their ability to "read" their students' facial expressions in pacing their classes.

Eye Contact

Eye contact is one of the strongest forms of nonverbal communication

Especially important in facial communication is the role played by the eyes. Eye contact is one of the most powerful forms of nonverbal communication. Authority relationships as well as intimate relationships are frequently initiated and maintained with eye contact. In North American society, looking directly at a listener is usually thought to convey openness and honesty. You usually feel it is easier to trust someone who looks right at you. On the other hand, you tend to distrust those who don't look directly at you and to attribute less confidence to those who avoid eye contact. But, in some cultures, making eye contact with a superior can indicate disrespect.

In addition, prolonged eye contact can signal admiration, while brief eye contact usually means anxiety. Although more eye contact is usually better than less, note that direct eye contact of more than ten seconds can create some discomfort and anxiety.

Gesture

Any part of the body can gesture

Another important element of nonverbal communication is the use of gestures. The language of gestures is usually thought of as movements of the hands and arms, but the entire body is capable of gesturing.

Gestures include signs that are the equivalent of words or phrases. For example, in Canada, the thumb and forefinger held in a circle say "O.K." The index and middle fingers held up in the form of a V indicate "victory." A shrug of the shoulders is the universal sign for "I don't know."

Other gestures are directly tied to verbal language and illustrate a speaker's words. When a speaker says, "My third and final point is ... " and holds up three fingers, his gesture helps to illustrate his point. When a baseball umpire calls someone out at home plate, he points his thumb up and jerks his hand upward to emphasize his words.

Still other gestures control oral communication by alerting the sender of the need to hurry up, slow down, or repeat something. For example, frequently looking at your watch or drumming your fingers on the table when someone is talking with you signals the need to finish the conversation quickly.

We have very little control over some of the messages our body communicates, particularly those that result from strong emotional states such as anger or embarrassment. Such displays of emotion are usually seen in facial expressions. Many people, for example, feel their faces turning red when they are angry or embarrassed but can do little to control this reaction. Sometimes we are not even conscious of such gestures as stifling a yawn or clasping the hands to the face in fear.

Posture

Posture can demonstrate status or interest

A person's general posture, even without specific gestures, communicates meaning. It frequently gives clues about a person's self-confidence or status. For example, an interviewer may conclude that an applicant is nervous if he or she sits with arms crossed and shoulders hunched. Posture is also a way of demonstrating interest in another person. Many people conclude that, when you lean towards the person with whom you are speaking, you demonstrate interest in that person. Sitting back, on the other hand, may communicate a lack of interest.

The Importance of Gesture and Posture

Understanding body movements can aid communication

The exact importance of gesture and posture as modes of communication is difficult to assess. However, they are assuming more importance in organizational life. Therefore, we need to have some understanding of what people are communicating with posture and gestures. M. Knapp, an authority on nonverbal communication, has provided a useful scheme for classifying the major types of body movements.[2] It is the basis for the following brief explanations, which are intended to aid your understanding of how we communicate with our bodies.

Our bodies frequently reflect our feelings about particular elements in our environment. The degree of someone's like or dislike of someone or something can be seen in terms of general body orientation, by noting if the communicator's legs and shoulders are turned towards or away from the other person, for example.

Our moods can also be interpreted to varying degrees by body movements. The head and face are thought to convey information about anger, joy, and happiness; other body movements are thought to convey the intensity of the particular emotional state. For instance, people who are seeking approval may nod their heads and smile more at the person whose approval they seek. In general, their bodies are more active. One can often observe this type of body movement when watching a subordinate present an idea to a superior.

Body movement can also provide cues as to whose side you are on. The positioning of the body, especially the way the legs are pointed, communicates, "I am on your side, not theirs." It can also indicate openness or closeness to the other person.

Certain body movements naturally accompany particular types of statements. Frequently, at the end of a statement a person gives a downward movement of the head, eyelids, and hands. These movements tend to be upward at the end of questioning statements. Other types of interaction markers include leaning back when one is listening and leaning forward when one is speaking.

While it is easy to oversimplify the above classifications, it is important to realize that body movement affects the communication process. Having some basic understanding of how we communicate with our bodies will make us more effective communicators.

Accommodating Different Cultures

People's movements and the different meanings they attach to these movements differ from culture to culture. For example, there are major differences across cultures in the amount of facial expression and eye contact that are permitted to show power, submissiveness, and respect. Because certain behaviours may differ from our own, we may sometimes be confused by them.

Communicating with Space

All of us communicate in our use of space

The third major type of nonverbal communication is how we communicate using space. How close or how far we stand in relation to another person, where we sit in a room, and how we arrange the office furniture has a real impact upon communication.

The manner in which buildings and other fairly permanent structures are laid out, and the way rooms and offices are placed have a considerable influence on communication. All things being equal, you will communicate more with those whose offices are closest to yours.

There is currently a great deal of emphasis on how business offices are arranged, particularly the placement and arrangement of objects such as desks and chairs. Increasingly, the person in charge will move from behind the desk and sit face to face with the person in the more junior position to make communication easier. Similarly, the communication patterns in meetings depend largely on how the room is arranged. Groups seated at round or square tables tend to be much more talkative because their members can easily see one another and no one has a position of authority. A formal seating arrangement such as rows of tables, on the other hand, tends to focus attention on the front of the room and discourages discussion.

Communication zones determine social interaction

The physical distance necessary for conversations varies with the type of interaction. Intimate conversations are generally held at distances ranging from a point of physical contact to 50 cm. In organizations, confidential information is often communicated within this range. The major form of intimate contact in business organizations is, of course, the handshake. Most people have positive feelings about people who give a firm handshake and negative feelings about those who give a limp handshake. Men traditionally responded positively to women who had a limp handshake; however, today, they are more likely to respond positively to a firm handshake. In general, a firm (but not crippling) handshake is probably the best bet in a business environment.

Casual and friendly conversations are generally held at distances ranging from 50 cm to 125 cm; however, most business communication occurs from about 125 cm to about 250 cm. Public-speaking distances can range from 350 cm to the upper limits of visibility and hearing. A good deal of communication within and outside an organization takes place at this range.

All of us are aware of some of the ways space is used to communicate in business organizations. In general, three basic principles apply:

The space occupied in the organization communicates much about status

1. *The higher people are in the organization, the more and better space they are allotted.* In many organizations, the president has the most attractive office, while the vice president, department heads, and lesser officers have successively smaller offices. The number of windows in the office and the way it is furnished are also commensurate with rank or position.
2. *The higher people are in the organization, the better protected their "territory" is.* The more status a person has in the organization, the harder it usually is to get to see that person. Outer offices and secretaries often protect the high-status person.
3. *People at or near the top of the organization, on the other hand, can easily invade the territory of lower-status personnel.* The supervisor can usually enter the subordinate's office at will and can also phone the subordinate at almost any time. However, the subordinate usually does not have the same type of access to the supervisor.

Accommodating Different Cultures

In Canada, we have common standards of how close people may come to us physically, but these are by no means world standards. We may feel ill at ease when people from other cultures, who in an effort to feel comfortable, approach us closely. We feel our space invaded and withdraw. This seeking of common and equally satisfying distances can make for an unusual dance. The opposite phenomenon may be encountered with other cultures, where even greater distances than our own are sought.

Touch differences also exist

Touch differences also exist. Some people, for example, are likely to exhibit extensive touching, using both their hands and their arms in greetings. They also confront each other directly. Others may well add a hug and some backslaps to their greeting.

Although touch between sexes in a business setting is kept purely professional in our culture, our standards probably allow much more touching between sexes than more male-dominated cultures, such as those of Japan or the Middle East. On the other hand, touching and remarks that Canadian women would regard as sexual harassment are commonplace in cultures where women do not enjoy equal status in the business world.

Other Modes of Nonverbal Communication

Now that we have discussed the three major categories of nonverbal communication, we can briefly examine some other areas of nonverbal communication that have received less attention, but nevertheless play an important role in communication.

Dress and Appearance

Clothing communicates much about us

All of us have heard the phrase "clothes make the person." However, most of us are not aware of the impact that our clothing has on those around us. John Molloy, a consultant on executive dress with major corporations, has conducted several experiments to see what various types of clothing communicate.[3] In one study, Molloy compared the impact of black and beige raincoats. He took a set of pictures of the same man in the same pose, dressed in the same suit, the same shirt, the same shoes, the same tie. The only difference was the raincoat — one was black, the other beige. Participants were told the pictures were of twin brothers and were asked to identify the "most prestigious" of the two. More than 87 percent of the 1362 people in the study chose the man wearing the beige raincoat.

For another set of experiments, Molloy found a group of 27 restaurants in New York where ties were not required. In each he asked the head waiter to divide the dining room into most preferred and least preferred seating areas. Those areas near the street door and the kitchen door were considered the least preferable. Invariably a disproportionate number of men without ties were in the less preferable areas; in fact, almost no men without ties were seated in the more preferable areas.

Top executives have an unwritten code for corporate dress

Molloy places the impact of dress in perspective early in his book, *Dress for Success*. The results of a study he conducted in preparation for writing the book showed that top executives have an unwritten code for corporate dress.

Using pictures of young men in various types of clothing, Molloy asked 100 top executives of medium- and mid-sized American companies to comment on the appropriateness of their attire.

When asked to identify whether or not outfits were appropriate for young executives, 92 percent said "expensive, well-tailored, but high fashion" outfits were not appropriate; 54 percent said "obvious lower-middle-class" outfits were not appropriate; and 100 percent said that "conservative, upper-middle-class" outfits were appropriate.

Molloy then asked these same executives "whether they thought the men in upper-middle-class garb would succeed better in corporate life than the men in the lower-middle-class uniform." Eighty-eight percent said yes. A further 92 percent said they would not choose "the men in the lower-middle-class dress as their assistant."[4]

Molloy's experiments on the impact of businesswomen's dress influenced how women dressed in the 1970s. In one, male executives listed skirted suits, a dress or skirt with a blazer, or a dress with a matching jacket as their top three choices for women's dress in the office.[5] Molloy, therefore, recommended that wearing a dark-coloured skirted suit with a contrasting blouse would give women the authority they needed in business.[6] In many conservative, large organizations, this recommendation still dictates the type of clothes women choose for the office.

However, Susan Bixler points out that this "corporate uniform may have been a necessary first step toward an accepted professional look, but it was a monotonous one ... the eighties have seen the softening of the business uniform, especially for women."[7] Instead of setting rigid guidelines, Bixler recommends dressing appropriately for your audience and the context in which you find yourself. She points out that regional differences and industry differences often dictate what is or is not appropriate for the office. Although written for an American audience, the principles she suggests also work well in the Canadian context. Before beginning a job search in a region or industry you are unfamiliar with, you would do well to seek out situations that will give you some cues about the appropriate dress for the specific environment.

Regional Differences

Dress standards tend to be more formal in large urban areas than they are in suburban or rural communities. The same is true for the major population centres in Ontario and Quebec as opposed to the West Coast or the Maritime provinces. This difference became painfully clear for a sales representative from a major Toronto company who travelled to an east-coast town on business for the first time. Wearing his blue suit, white shirt, and conservative tie, he wondered why he was being treated so coolly by the people he saw at the university. After a couple of days, however, he figured out that his attire represented "Central Corporate Canada" to this particular audience. Once he began dressing more casually in a sports jacket, he was treated more warmly and was able to accomplish what he had set out to do.

Industry Differences

Dress standards differ from one industry to another. Banks, insurance companies, and head offices for major multinational corporations tend to favour conservative, classic dress. In such organizations, even a minor blunder such as wearing a sweater vest under a suit jacket can influence a recruiter's impression negatively.

Supervisors and managers in a factory, on the other hand, may find that even a sports jacket is unnecessary for all but the most high-level meetings. In fact, more casual dress may improve their ability to communicate with workers on the floor. Some companies have even gone as far as eliminating ties in an effort to create a more co-operative, team-based workplace.

In post-secondary educational institutions, dress standards can vary from one department to another. In general, business faculty tend to dress in a more business-like fashion, whereas engineering and arts faculty dress much more casually.

In some industries, workers generally wear uniforms that clearly identify their function and/or their organization. For example, workers whose jobs take them into people's homes, such as appliance-repair technicians, hydro and telephone workers, and postal workers, are more likely to be required to wear a uniform so that they can be readily identified.

In summary, there can be little question that dress and appearance can communicate various messages in the business setting.

Colour

Colour is related to particular moods

The communication involved in the choice of colour is closely related to dress because colour in clothing affects communication. Most women in business today have at least one black or navy blue suit they refer to as their "power suit." These suits are the female version of the conservative suits favoured by executives in John Malloy's experiments. However, in general, the trend is to wear colours that complement complexion and hair colouring.

Colours that surround us affect us. In rooms with walls in warm or hot colours, such as reds or oranges, we are likely to be more creative, stimulated, and prone to quick decisions. Rooms with cooler colours, such as blues, will likely bring about slow, deep, and methodical thinking, and detachment.

Check the colours in a fast-food establishment, a church, and a classroom. There's a good chance that the colours enhance the desired image or mind set. If your classroom is devoid of colour, it is probably not an accident, but a carefully planned effort.

Time

Time factors reveal job interest and status

Being early, on time, or late communicates much in our society. The setting and meeting of deadlines is also important. The employee who is habitually late for work and misses deadlines communicates very little interest in the job.

High-status people usually have more flexibility in their working hours. We even hear talk about "banker's hours" as the working day for higher-status individuals. They are usually also able to get appointments sooner and their meetings with superiors are usually of longer duration.

Another way in which time communicates has to do with the amount of time it takes to provide or receive feedback. For example, if people respond "too quickly" to a written request, we may feel that they have not given it careful consideration. On the other hand, if a long time goes by without a response, we feel a lack of interest, even though formal communication has not taken place.

Not all cultures see time the same way. Depending on which attitude is taken by a culture, concerns about deadlines, emergencies, forecasting, meetings, and schedules can take on substantially different meanings.

Power

Nonverbal indicators of power are prevalent in the business world. How you perceive others' indicators, react to those indicators, and pick indicators for yourself may have substantial impact on your business career.

In addition to using clothing to express power, we also adorn ourselves with other power indicators, some of which may serve as clues to our wealth or our judgement as well. These three clues — power, wealth, and judgement — may stand alone but they often overlap and reinforce each other. For example, while we may be aware of a man's expensive cologne or a woman's expensive perfume, we may also be offended by them. Conversely, we are likely to be impressed by a person in well-co-ordinated attire with expensive, but not gaudy accessories.

Examples of power indicators can be found in all of the nonverbal categories, such as standing straight, using expansive gestures, speaking in a loud voice, taking large strides, and using a firm handshake. Physical examples of power with which we surround ourselves are recognition plaques, memberships in honorary or exclusive organizations, photos of powerful people, large and well-appointed offices, and private secretaries.

Often we are only slightly aware of a person's power symbols, but we are still cognizant of the presence of power and adjust our behaviour. Knowing when, where, and with whom to use power symbols and actions can positively affect how others see and react to us. At all levels of the business world, power is present; clearly, some use it and others abuse it. Understanding the intricacies of nonverbal power indicators can pay rich rewards.

Nonverbal Communication in Oral Presentations

Here are some nonverbal behaviours associated with effective oral presentations, and some suggestions on overcoming nonverbal problems:

- A relaxed speaker tends to gesture, but not too much. A nervous speaker either avoids gestures and movement, or tends to overdo it.
- The confident speaker doesn't show perspiration; the nervous speaker is not so controlled. Dress lightly so as not to start out too warm.
- Visual contact with the audience enhances a presentation. This visual contact also scares many speakers. One well-known approach is to avoid direct eye contact by looking just above the eyes of the audience. This technique often is not successful, however, because the audience recognizes the strategy. A more effective technique is to talk to one member of the audience at a time. Try not to think of the large group, but rather engage a person on one side of the room for a few seconds, then look at a person in the middle, and then one on the other side of the room. Most effective speakers use this technique not so much to overcome nervousness, but to convey a personal touch.
- Effective voice control greatly affects the impact of the speech. An over-rehearsed speech often comes out in a monotone no matter how enthusiastic the speaker. On the other hand, an ill-prepared speaker is likely to exhibit the cracking voice, gasping, or swallowing that we associate with nervousness. Try to pace yourself in the speed of the speech. A speaker who lacks confidence is likely to change delivery rate by either speeding up or slowing down. Aim for a normal delivery rate.
- Hands and fingers are not obtrusive for the confident speaker; they tend to shake for the nervous speaker. This shaking is amplified many times over if a pencil is pointed at a transparency during overhead projector use. Plant the pencil solidly on the film to prevent its shaking.
- Some effective speakers move around behind the podium, but usually not too much. Beware of the speaker's shuffle. This side-to-side balancing can often be overcome if one foot is put forward and one backward diagonally.

Summary

In this chapter, we discussed the importance of nonverbal communication.

- Up to 93 percent of the total impact of a message can come from its nonverbal elements.

- Nonverbal communication has several elements:
  - how we say something
  - how we communicate with our bodies
  - how we communicate with space
  - how we communicate with dress, appearance, colour, and time
- In decoding messages, you should
  - avoid putting too much emphasis on any single cue
  - analyze the entire context in which the communication interaction occurs
- When a discrepancy between the verbal and nonverbal message occurs, people favour nonverbal messages.
- Messages are more effective when the nonverbal cues reinforce the verbal message.
- As our world becomes smaller, we need to be especially aware of the potential dangers of misunderstanding nonverbal communication across cultures.

Review Questions

1. Why do nonverbal messages play such a critical role in communication?
2. Explain why the way we say something can reinforce or undermine the verbal message.
3. Cite examples of how facial expressions attach emotional meaning to our messages.
4. In what ways is gesture an important means of communication?
5. Discuss how posture can provide clues to the self-confidence or status of a person in a business organization.
6. Explain how space is used as a communication device.
7. In what ways might your dress and appearance and the way you handle time impress your business colleagues?
8. Discuss the types of nonverbal communication that are influenced by cultural differences.

Activities

1. Identify some nonverbal rules, such as the books and coat on a library chair that mark a person's territory. Then break the rule, in this case by moving the books and coat and sitting in the chair. Be prepared to discuss in the next class what happens.
2. Observe and record people's behaviour in elevators. List as many nonverbal behaviour patterns as you can. Compare these patterns to those of people using escalators. What are the differences? Why do you think these differences exist? Report your findings in a memo to your instructor.
3. Most of us feel comfortable in a classroom and think little about its

nonverbal aspects. Identify the nonverbal patterns of students and instructors on a given day. Report your findings in a memo to your instructor.

4. What is the appropriate dress and appearance in the type of business you want to work in after graduation? How much can you vary from this standard without being penalized? (You may have to consult friends and relatives to obtain data for this exercise.)
5. Does music create different moods in different people at different times? How? Give examples of how music is used in business. Report your findings in a memo to your instructor.

Discussion Cases

Body Language[8]

Ernesto Espinoza was seething. Every time it looked as if he had finally straightened out his production supervisor, Steve Kozlowski, Steve managed to blow another situation with one of the workers. This time the worker had walked out, and the line had to be slowed down while a replacement was found.

This was a critical time for Ernesto. The vice president in charge of production was coming from Montreal to inspect the plant, and Ernesto wanted everything to go right. His future with the corporation depended on it.

For the third time, Ernesto called Steve to talk with him. He had to make Steve understand that he was really in trouble. The worker who had walked off the job had twelve years' seniority and had always been a first-class worker. Under these circumstances, the union would want to see the matter resolved in favour of the worker. Ernesto had to be sure Steve was impressed with the seriousness of the situation.

When the secretary buzzed to tell Ernesto that Steve was in the waiting room, Ernesto said, "Let him cool his heels." Fifteen minutes later he asked Steve to come in the office. Ernesto did not raise his head and greet Steve, nor did he rise to shake hands as he would normally have done. Steve stood at the desk several moments before Ernesto looked up and said, "Sit down." The telephone rang, and Ernesto talked five minutes before putting down the receiver. He then turned to Steve, folded his arms, leaned back, and said, "Well, tell me about this one."

Steve was upset by the extremely negative attitude he felt from Ernesto. He dropped his eyes, lifted his hands in a hopeless gesture, and said, "Well, what can you do with some of these guys who think they know everything?"

Case Questions

1. Describe the negative nonverbal messages Ernesto sent to indicate his displeasure with Steve.
2. Describe the submissive nonverbal messages Steve sent to Ernesto.
3. Give a positive movement for each negative movement named.

The Disappointing Interview[9]

Dick Evans of CMG was out when Susan Kang arrived early for her job interview. In two weeks, Susan would complete her commerce degree. She had already been interviewed by two of CMG's competitors. Although these other jobs were promising, a job with CMG had been her primary objective in obtaining a degree.

Susan had an excellent academic record and experience that was more than adequate for the CMG position. Dick Evans's secretary ushered her into his office and said, "Dick had to check on something in the shop. He's been having some problems out there. I'm not sure how long he will be, so make yourself at home." The office was unusually large, with a desk and chairs on one side and a more comfortable area with a couch, table, and magazines on the other.

At first, Susan took a chair near the desk, but as time passed the magazines on the table across the office looked inviting, so she moved to the couch. When Dick arrived forty-five minutes later, she was so engrossed that he had to call her name before she realized he was in the room. Dick seemed a bit irritated and distracted throughout the interview. Although Susan responded well to his questions, Dick was not very receptive and at times was even abrupt. She left twenty minutes later thinking she had blown the interview. On the way home, she went over the day's events in her mind, concluding that she wouldn't want to work for such a grouch and that one of the other jobs would have to do.

When the phone rang the next morning and Dick invited her back for a second interview, Susan was surprised. The man on the telephone seemed a different person. Dick apologized for his bad mood and asked her to give him and CMG another chance. Susan agreed to the interview, but she continued to wonder how her first impression of Dick could have been so wrong.

Case Questions

1. What nonverbal miscues did Susan receive?
2. How might Dick have helped Susan?
3. Why was it difficult for Susan to be other than self-centred in this situation?

Part Two

Written Strategies

Chapter 4
The Writing Process

Chapter 5
Characteristics of Effective Written Communication

Chapter 6
Clear Thinking and Argument

Chapter 7
Introduction to Letters and Memos

Chapter 8
The Electronic Office

Chapter 9
Routine Letters

Chapter 10
Persuasive Messages

Chapter 11
Informal Reports

Chapter 12
Formal Reports

Appendix
A Sample Formal Report

Chapter 4

The Writing Process

Learning Objectives

In this chapter, you'll learn how to plan and draft documents quickly and efficiently. More specifically, you will be able to:

1. describe several ways to get started on your writing
2. choose the planning process that works best for you
3. write your first draft

Preview Case

Anita Gomez sighed as she thought about teaching her first business communication class of the year. She knew that she would again hear the same comments: "I'm not creative enough to be a good writer"; "I don't seem to be able to get started"; "I know what I want to say, but I can't get it down on paper."

"This year," she thought, "it's going to be different." Anita had attended a writing workshop over the summer that had forced her to think about her own approach to writing. For one thing, she found that she couldn't produce the nice, neat outline that she usually asked her students to produce. The writing process was much messier than that.

Anita discovered that she usually started off by asking herself three basic questions: What's my purpose? Who's going to read this? What do they need to know? As she would ask herself these questions, she'd jot down a few key words. From these key words, she'd write a few sentences. Then she'd get frustrated because her mind was working faster than she could write; so she'd get up from her desk and wander about. Sometimes she'd do two or three routine tasks. When she returned to her desk ten or fifteen minutes later, she'd find that she had a general outline in her head that she could get down on paper.

For a couple of the more difficult projects, Anita had actually given up late at night, frustrated because she had only a vague idea of what she wanted to say. However, in the morning she'd wake up ready to sit down and write the first draft. When the workshop leader asked the participants to describe their writing style, Anita called hers the "back-burner approach." She got started on her ideas and then put them on the "back burner" of her subconscious. Later, when she brought them back to her conscious mind, they had "simmered" into shape.

Anita had also discovered that writing was much easier for her if she talked it out — even if it was to herself. However, she found talking with others in the workshop most effective. It was as though she had to say the words before she could get them down on paper.

Anita had a few new ideas, now, about how to get her own students started on their writing.

Overview

For most people, even published authors, writing is not an easy task. It is a complex process that each person tackles in a slightly different way. However, the process has three main steps: plan, write, and revise. Anita Gomez discovered what works for her; however, each person approaches the task a little differently. In this chapter, we'll suggest several strategies for planning your documents and writing the first draft. In Chapter 5, we'll focus on the final step in the process: revision.

Getting Started

Start with three steps

Nothing is more intimidating to a writer than a blank sheet of paper. Therefore, you need to find ways to get something on that paper as quickly as possible. While strategies for generating ideas differ, your first three steps should always be the same: *determine your purpose, identify your readers, and describe the context for the finished document.* Once you have a clear picture of your purpose, your readers, and the context for the information, you'll find that ideas come more easily.

The process is a little like deciding what clothes to take with you on a trip. If you haven't clarified the purpose of your trip, you'll have considerable difficulty choosing which clothes to take. However, by determining the trip's purpose, you immediately narrow your choice of clothing. For example, for a business trip, your wardrobe would be quite different from that for a vacation.

Similarly, knowing your purpose, your readers, and the context within which you are writing helps you decide what information to include in a document. In this section, we'll look at these initial steps in some detail.

Determining Your Purpose

What results do you want?

In business, written communication helps to accomplish the goals of the organization: it gets things done. Therefore, knowing what you want to accomplish is critical to the success of your written communication.

In this chapter we will look at three examples to illustrate this process.

For Example 1, imagine you are the manager of the print materials production department of a major organization. It's April 5 and your boss has asked you for a departmental vacation schedule within the next couple of weeks so he can budget for summer replacement staff. In this case, your purpose is relatively straightforward: you want your employees to schedule their vacations for the coming year.

In Example 2, let's say you need to write a memo to employees about punctuality. They are late reporting to work in the morning, they take extended breaks, and their thirty-minute lunch periods often last forty-five minutes to an hour. Their behaviour clearly violates company policy and must change. To get started, you ask yourself: what do I want my readers to do when they read this memo? Obviously you want the employees to conform to company policy regarding coffee breaks and lunch periods. However, this answer omits a key element in the purpose: the element of persuasion. A more accurate statement of your purpose is: *I want to persuade employees to conform to company policy by taking fifteen- minute coffee breaks and a thirty-minute lunch period.* By writing out this statement, you accomplish two things: you clarify your purpose for yourself and you no longer have a blank piece of paper.

Jot down your thoughts

While most often you want a specific action to result from what you have written, sometimes your purpose is strictly informational and no action is expected. For Example 3, imagine that you've been to a conference in San Francisco on office automation at company expense. Policy states that anyone attending a conference at company expense must submit a trip report outlining what was learned at the conference. Your purpose, therefore, is to summarize the main ideas presented at the conference.

Identifying Your Readers

Who are your readers?

The individuals who receive your communication may not perceive the situation as you do; they may have limited or different information on the topic, or they may have different values and beliefs that colour their perception of the message. Therefore, you need to anticipate their reaction so you can shape your message to achieve the desired purpose. To help you decide what information to include, ask yourself four questions:

- Who are my readers (their names and positions)?
- What do they already know about the situation?
- How will they react to what I have to say? Why?
- What will motivate them to do as I ask?

Focus on specific individuals

Writing down the names and positions of the people to whom you are writing is a routine task that helps you put pen to paper. More importantly, writing them down helps you to focus on the individuals and their characteristics, particularly when more than one person will read and/or act on the information you provide.

In business, very few documents have a single reader. Most are circulated to two or more people. In Example 1 about the vacation schedule, the employees include fourteen writer-editors, two graphic artists, a page-layout technician, two clerks, and a secretary, all of whom are probably anxious to have their first choice of vacation times. These twenty people are probably the only ones who will read the memo.

In Example 2, concerning employees who are taking extended breaks, the task is more complex. You may be dealing with a relatively young group of employees who range in age from 19 to 25 and have limited work experience in other companies. But, they are essentially conscientious employees who don't recognize how much production output extended breaks can cost an organization. Also, they may not recognize the serious consequences of not conforming to company policy. Therefore, simply pointing out the costs and the consequences may be sufficient to motivate the workers to change their behaviour.

On the other hand, these workers may be members of a union. Since the memo you are writing affects working conditions, it's fair to assume that one or more union representatives may be shown the memo, particularly if the tone of your memo offends someone who reads it. Although the union representatives are not the primary readers, their access to this information and their biases need to be taken into account when you are drafting the memo.

Finally, in Example 3, the report on the conference in San Francisco presents a slightly different problem in audience analysis. Your primary reader is likely to be your immediate supervisor; however, because of the nature of the report, it's likely to be circulated to several people in the company. The purpose of the report, to summarize the main ideas presented at the conference, is somewhat vague. You know that your supervisor and her managers are busy people who are inundated with information every day. Therefore, your major goal in preparing your report is to focus on no more than half a dozen key concepts from the conference. In this instance, the most important information will probably come from the third step, analyzing the context within which the document is written.

Analyzing the Context

Business communications are not written in isolation. They must fit into the overall structure and culture of the organization. The structure and culture will determine the tone as well as the content of a particular situation. In some organizations, internal communications can be very informal. Even relatively major reports have a chatty, informal tone. In others, however, even the simplest memo is expected to follow strict company guidelines. In still others, the tone and content vary dramatically, depending on who will receive the communication. For example, in major corporations where there is a rigid hierarchical structure, communications, particularly those directed at people in supervisory roles, will tend to be more formal than those in small, owner-operated businesses. Similarly, communications directed at one's peers may be less formal, particularly if they are for internal use only.

What other circumstances are relevant?

Tone as well as content is important

In addition to these general conditions, the specific context within which a document is written will have a dramatic effect on its tone and content. Let's return to the three examples to see how the situation shapes the written communication.

Situation shapes written communication

In Example 1, let's assume your department has grown from a five-person operation just three years ago to its current complement of twenty people. Staff members work together as a team and socialize together after hours. You know that several of your more junior staff are anxious to get some time off during July or August, but that some senior people like a fall vacation.

In the past, the vacation schedule seemed to sort itself out and everyone got his or her first choice. You have no reason to think it will be any different this year, but you need to know well in advance so that you can advertise and hire replacement staff (usually senior students from the local university). Vacations are calculated on the fiscal year: April 1 to March 31.

Here, your task is relatively easy. You have a request that most people will be happy to comply with, and you can probably give everyone his or her first choice of vacation. Therefore, writing the memo is strictly a matter of giving people the impetus they need to make their decision.

Again, Example 2 is slightly more complex. The workers who are not conforming to the break policy are hourly rated, unionized workers and are paid overtime for work in excess of seven hours a day. They work alongside other workers who receive a fixed salary whether or not they work overtime. These salaried workers are expected to get their jobs done regardless of how much time it takes. Since they frequently work eight or more hours a day, they sometimes take longer coffee and lunch breaks. To make matters worse, you have had your supervisory position for only six months and your predecessor tolerated extended breaks.

This scenario illustrates the important role context plays in shaping the message. Not only must you persuade the workers to comply with company policy, but you must also do so in a situation where the same rules might not apply to all employees.

In Example 3, you need to analyze the context within which you are writing even more carefully than in the other two because you've been unable to focus your report clearly in the first two steps. Let's assume that the conference on office automation focused on local area networks for state-of-the-art personal computers, desktop publishing, voice-activated computers, integrated software packages, and electronic-mail systems. If you work for a company that has a mainframe computer and discourages the use of personal computers, you would obviously not focus on local area networks. However, if you knew that the company was planning to purchase an electronic-mail package for the mainframe, you could profitably focus on those sessions, giving less emphasis to topics unrelated to the interests of your organization.

Once you become accustomed to using this process for getting started, you'll find that you can quickly jot down key ideas related to purpose, audience, and context. Writer's block at this stage should be a thing of the past.

Brainstorming

Getting started on brainstorming

Once you have a clear idea of your purpose, your readers, and the context within which you are writing, you are ready to jot down points you need to include. At this point, writers differ dramatically in their approach. One way to get started on some ideas is to answer the following questions:

- What one thing do my readers need to know in order to do as I ask?
- What information will persuade my readers to do as I ask?
- What details do I need to include to give my readers a complete picture?

Here's how these questions apply to Example 1:

- What do my readers need to know to do as I ask?
  - I need their vacation schedule by February 15.

- What information will persuade them to do as I ask?
  - Make it easy: use vacation planner with completion instructions.
  - Give everyone an individual planner and then compile the results.
  - Try to accommodate everyone's first choice — if we know far enough in advance we can hire replacement staff.
  - Company policy says everyone gets at least two weeks in prime time (July or August) if he or she wants it.

- What details are needed for a complete picture? (Remember, there are several new employees in the department.)
  - Three or more vacation days taken together should appear on the planner.
  - Single vacation days need not appear.
  - Employees can request a change in their vacation schedule so long as it is requested far enough in advance that it does not interfere with production deadlines set on the basis of the original request.
  - Deadline for reply is important so that we can recruit on campus prior to exams in mid-April (company will be recruiting during the week of April 8).
  - Vacation entitlements are based on fiscal year of April 1 to March 31.
  - Everyone who has been with the company for at least one year is eligible for three weeks' vacation; employees with less than one

year's service receive one day for every month worked before April 1 of the new fiscal year.

Jot down as many ideas as you can think of as quickly as you can

At this point, speed and quantity of ideas are most important. You can review your list and weed out inappropriate information in the next step. Inexperienced writers often frustrate themselves by trying to prepare their final outlines before they have anything on paper. As a result, they increase the likelihood of writer's block at this stage of the task.

In Example 2, the analysis of the readers and the context provides a starting point for the following ideas:

- Unionized workers must conform to policy regarding coffee and lunch breaks.
- Employees who range in age from 19 to 25 and have limited work experience in other companies may not realize the consequences of their actions.
- Repeated tardiness has serious consequences (oral warning followed by written warning that goes in personnel file and so on through disciplinary procedures).
- Cost of lost output because of lost time (company statistics about output per hour and about amount of time lost in a year with 30 minutes lost per day).
- Benefits of conforming to time policies (increased profits for organization — bigger bonuses for workers).
- Review of policies (fifteen-minute break morning and afternoon; thirty-minute lunch break; oral warning, followed by written warning that goes in personnel record).
- Employees' role in the success of the organization.

Your list does not have a specific order. Instead, ideas are listed as they occur to you. However, they are now on paper, so you can focus all your attention on selecting and organizing the content.

Some people think in pictures or key words

Instead of writing out complete ideas, some writers prefer to work with key words and, sometimes, pictures. For these writers, mind mapping is a particularly effective technique. A mind map is a nonlinear representation of your thoughts, using key words, colour, and imagery. Proponents of mind mapping say it allows you to use both sides of the brain in a creative manner. It also allows you to put all your notes for even fairly complex topics on a single sheet of paper.[1] Figures 4.1 and 4.2 show how the information for Examples 1 and 2 might be organized into a mind map. If you want to try mind mapping for yourself, read the following guidelines adapted from a brochure entitled *The Mind Map*.[2]

Guidelines for Mind Mapping

1. Draw a picture of your topic in the centre of your paper. Although you could use a key word, a picture helps involve the right, or creative, side of your brain.
2. Use key words. They can be generated faster than sentences without sacrificing meaning.
3. Print your key words. Printing is easier to read and remember.
4. Print one key word on a line. You'll leave yourself plenty of room to expand on your ideas.
5. Write horizontally. Your mind map will be much easier to read if you don't have to rotate your page to read the various parts.
6. Use colours, pictures, and codes for emphasis. Colours and pictures encourage the involvement of your right brain. Codes, such as asterisks and numbers, help to show relationships between ideas.

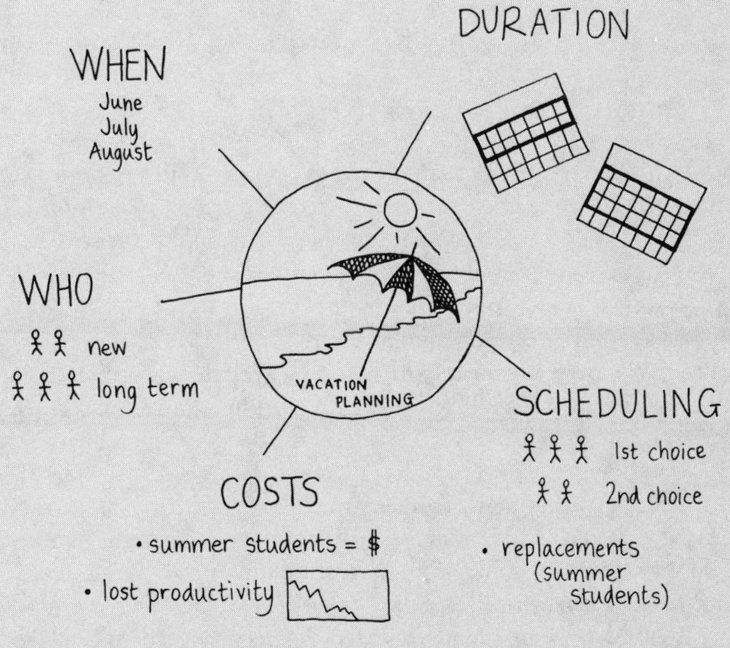

Figure 4.1 Vacation Memo Mind Map

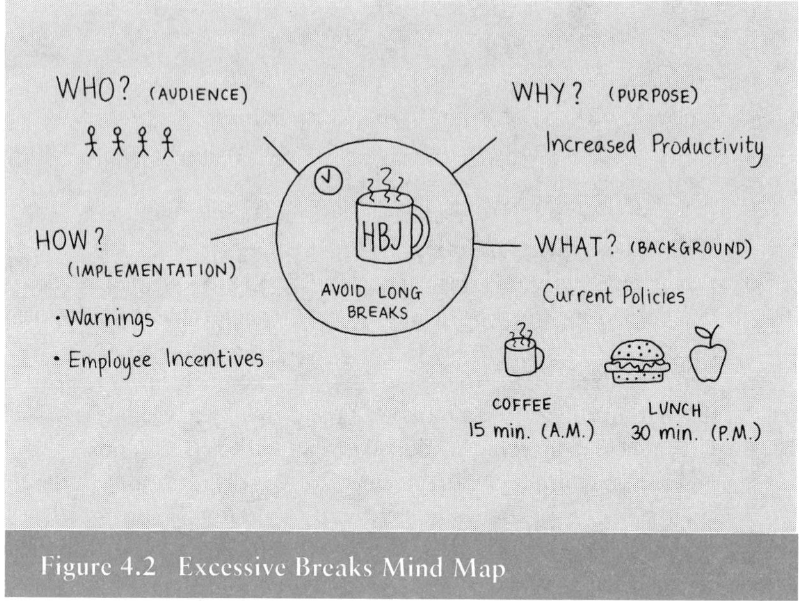

Figure 4.2 Excessive Breaks Mind Map

Selecting and Organizing Information

Selecting and organizing information is the final planning step

Once you've generated as many ideas as you can think of, you need to review your audience and context analysis to determine what information should be included and how that information should be organized. You can use your list of points or your mind map to accomplish this step. Begin by crossing out irrelevant information from your list of points, and use a series of symbols to group similar ideas. Alternatively, an outline is a convenient way to organize paragraphs or groups of paragraphs into a logical arrangement. Outlining means reworking your ideas before you begin to write your first draft; however, it does give you a neat, orderly plan to work from.

The outline is your plan

A technique that many students find effective is to imagine they are receiving the finished document. They consider what information they would like to have first, second, and so on, until they have a full understanding of the subject.

One student who found this step particularly difficult solved her problem by cutting out pictures from magazines of people she thought resembled her readers. When she had the pictures on the desk in front of her as she wrote, she had no difficulty deciding what information would be most useful.

North Americans in general expect you to get directly to the main idea of any message. They quickly become impatient with a lot of unnecessary information and skip through the message until they find the main idea. In Example 1, your employees are likely to be pleased to schedule their vacations, so that resistance or disagreement is unlikely. For that reason, you should present your main idea immediately. Getting to the point quickly results in a shorter message. Such an approach elicits the goodwill of the reader while saving time — both yours and the reader's.

But, just a minute. Who is your audience? If all of your employees were long-term employees, they would likely be familiar with the procedure, and a very short memo of two or three sentences would suffice. You would not need to spend much time organizing the information or preparing an outline. You might then prepare something like this:

Please complete the attached vacation planner and return it to me no later than Friday, April 12. This information will help me to plan for replacement staff over the summer months and to schedule your production deadlines so that they do not interfere with your vacation plans. If you need to check the number of days you are entitled to this year, please see me today.

Notice that the request or main idea comes first, followed by reasons for complying with the request. Giving the reasons acts as a friendly reminder of the need for prompt attention. The final sentence offers assistance for anyone who may need more information.

On the other hand, if you have several new employees, you may need to provide a lot more detail. Notice that we indicated the department has grown from five to twenty employees in just three years. Let's assume that ten have been hired within the last twelve months; those employees will not be eligible for a full three weeks of vacation. In addition, they may be totally unfamiliar with the policies and procedures on vacations. Review the Brainstorming section on page 65 that shows how you might decide to select and organize information for such a group. The original brainstorming sheet can be used to finish planning the message.

Write for the reader

Notice that what you want the employees to do comes first. The second section focuses on the benefits to the reader of complying with the request — writing for the reader rather than for the writer. Because so many of the employees have less than one year's service, it's prudent to give the highlights of the company's vacation policy before getting to the procedure for completing the vacation planner. The procedure itself is a matter of explaining the form and giving employees the correct code to indicate vacation days.

Planning a persuasive message

In Example 2 about breaks, persuasion will be an important component of the message. Therefore, you might decide to use the following sequence, recommended for persuasive messages in Chapter 10.

1. Attract the reader's attention
2. Create interest in the message
3. Show the benefits of performing the desired action
4. Tell the reader exactly what action you want

Notice how this outline is superimposed on the mind map for this topic (see Figure 4.3). Now you're ready to construct your outline.

I. Attention
A. Some statistics about output per hour
B. Some statistics about lost output because of lost time

II. Interest
A. Employees' role in company success
B. Reference to time policies
1. Tardiness
2. Break time
3. Lunch time

III. Desire
A. Consequences of conforming to time policies
B. Consequences of not conforming to time policies

IV. Action
A. Simple call for conformity
B. Expression of appreciation for conformity

Detailed planning saves time

Since you have outlined four basic ideas (Attention, Interest, Desire, and Action), your memo will need at least four paragraphs. It might be longer since you might easily have two paragraphs under "Interest" and perhaps two under "Desire." If the material is well organized, your chances of having it understood are increased.

By this time, many of you may be thinking that such detailed planning is time consuming and perhaps wasteful. However, experienced writers will tell you that it saves time in the long run. You're more likely to produce documents that are clearly focused and accomplish their purpose. And, with practice, you'll be able to go through these steps very quickly.

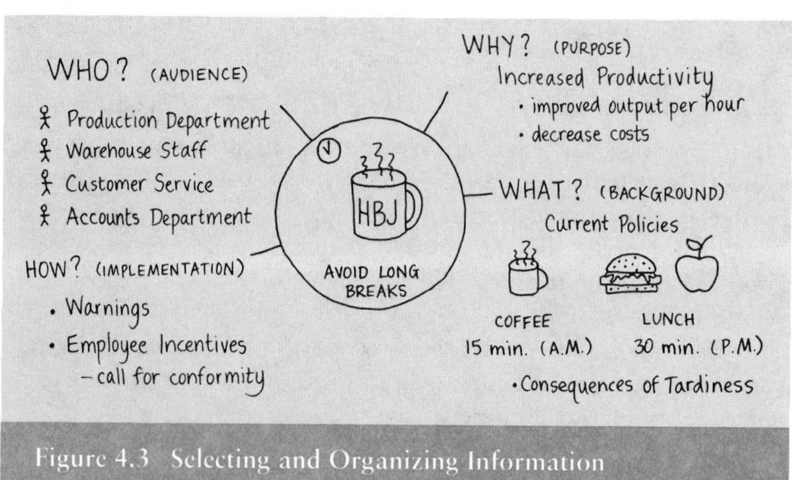

Figure 4.3 Selecting and Organizing Information

Drafting the Document

Don't try to revise and write at the same time

If your plan is sufficiently detailed, you should have no trouble drafting your document. At this point, speed is still your primary consideration. Avoid the temptation to revise as you write. Doing so will slow you down. Revision is much easier when you have the entire document in front of you.

Figure 4.4 shows the first draft for the memo for Example 1. Notice that the information is organized to answer five questions that readers might ask when reading the memo: (1) What do you want me to do? (2) Why? (3) How much vacation do I get? (4) How do I fill out this form? and (5) Where can I get help if I'm stuck? Senior staff may only skim the memo, just to make sure that the procedure is the same as it was in previous years. However, newer staff have all the details they need and a source of help should they require it. Before you proceed to Chapter 5, you and your classmates might want to discuss ways of improving the memo.

I need to have you complete the attached vacation planner by April 12, so that I will be in a position to accommodate all of your requests. We plan to recruit senior students from City University as summer replacement staff. Our recruiters will be visiting the campus early in April to interview prospective candidates.

Our company vacation policy provides that employees who have been with the company one full year as of March 1 are entitled to three weeks' vacation. Employees who have less than one year's service as of March 1 are entitled to one day for every complete month worked. For example, an employee who started on August 1 last year would be entitled to 7 vacation days this year.

Every employee with at least one year's service is entitled to at least two weeks' vacation during the summer months of June, July, and August. The attached vacation planner lists all the months of the year and days of the month. The final column on the right allows you to total the number of vacation days you plan to take each month. For your convenience, all the statutory holidays and weekends for the coming year have been shaded.

Please use code 03 to indicate which days you plan to take as vacation. Employees who are planning short absences of one or two days throughout the year do not need to show them on the planner. Don't hesitate to call me if you want more information. By the way, I will be out of the office for the rest of the week.

Figure 4.4 Draft Vacation Request Memo

Summary

The writing process has three main steps:

- planning
- drafting
- revising

Planning a document will be easier if you follow these steps:

1. To get started:
   a. determine your purpose
   b. identify your readers
   c. analyze the context
2. Brainstorm for the content by:
   a. listing ideas
   b. drawing a mind map
3. Select and organize the information

With a detailed plan, drafting the document should be a quick exercise.

Review Questions

1. Explain how planning can help you overcome writer's block.
2. Why is the context within which a document is written important?
3. Compare and contrast the two main methods of brainstorming.
4. What strategies can you use for selecting and organizing information?

Activities

1. For each of the following scenarios, write a statement of purpose and describe the information needs of your readers. Invent any details about the context that you think might be relevant and indicate how you might organize the document.
   a. You are a nurse on a surgical ward in a major hospital. Recently, a number of the housekeeping staff have accidentally punctured their skin on needles that have not been properly disposed of. Because of the risk of AIDS and the hospital's potential liability, the situation is serious. The head nurse has asked you to draft a memo to all staff reminding them of the correct procedure and the need to follow that procedure.
   b. This summer you are working as a counsellor at a camp for disabled adolescents. You recently purchased two packages of large, felt-tip markers at a total cost of $10. Each package contains ten different colours. You made a special trip into town to purchase the markers. When you used the markers for the first time, you found that four of the twenty were defective. While the markers were inexpensive, you are annoyed that 20 percent of

them are unusable. Write a complaint letter to the company that manufactures the markers.

c. You went skiing at Blackcomb last weekend. On the last run of the day, you fell and sprained your right ankle. Although you were in a great deal of pain, you were impressed with the speed and efficiency of the ski patrollers who came to your rescue. You decide to write a thank-you letter, even though you have no idea what their names are.

d. As a college recruiter for Stability Insurance Company, you interview many job applicants each month. When you interview Todd Robinson, you are impressed with his academic background as well as with his maturity. You feel that he may be well suited for an underwriting position you must fill, so you are fairly positive during the interview. Several days later, however, you interview another candidate who has completed a course in insurance underwriting and who is clearly the best candidate for the job. You have to write a letter to Todd Robinson to inform him that the company will not be offering him a job.

2. Using two or three samples of business letters (ideally mail you've received), analyze the content to determine the letter's purpose and the assumptions its writer made about the reader and the context within which the information is written.

Discussion Cases

Disciplinary Action Required

On October 31, 1990, six friends who were employees of Compuware Inc. were having a Hallowe'en party off the premises of the plant. After a few drinks, three of the employees returned to the plant to pick up a fellow employee who had been working the late shift. As they approached the security entrance, they donned Hallowe'en masks and ran past the security guard into a restricted area to find their friend.

Compuware Inc. had been awarded a major government contract and had undertaken to provide a high level of security for the government data. Only employees who had received special clearance were permitted to enter the offices where project work was taking place.

Elroy Ellsworth, the night security supervisor, was on duty that evening. He detained the four employees as they were leaving and had them arrested by city police. Although two of the four arrested did have security clearances for the restricted area, they were not

continued

wearing their clearance name tags at the time. The three employees who had worn the masks were detained at police headquarters and then released on bond.

The company decided not to press formal charges; however, internal disciplinary action was initiated against the three employees who were wearing the masks. Eileen Rosenberg, the assistant director of personnel, was responsible for drafting a letter of reprimand, which would be placed in their personnel files.

Case Questions

1. What made Ms. Rosenberg's task a difficult one?
2. Imagine you were one of the employees receiving the disciplinary letter.
   a. How would you feel about the situation?
   b. What questions would run through your mind as you read the letter?
3. From the company's point of view, what information needed to be conveyed?

The St. Claire Ski Race

Russ Martell is ski director at the St. Claire Mountain Ski Resort in the Eastern Townships. Each year his resort sponsors a women's professional downhill ski-cup race. This race falls in the middle of the pro-racing circuit season, a time when many of the top professional skiers take a short break from competition.

It is Martell's duty to attract some famous professional women skiers to this race. Because the race is well established, he has several drawing cards. This year there is $50,000 in prize money, an opportunity to gain points in the Women's Professional Downhill Ski Circuit rankings, as well as free meals and lodging at the resort. To the advantage of the skiers, a national television network plans to televise the race, providing an excellent opportunity for some extra publicity for the skiers.

Despite these drawing cards, the timing and location of the race have tended to work against it. Most skiers welcome their mid-season break, particularly when they are away from home for so many weeks. To make matters worse, the accommodations are rustic by resort standards and the temperature when the race is held can be

continued

−20°C. On top of everything else, airline and bus connections to the resort are poor.

Martell has been directed to write to all professional women skiers, informing them of the race.

Case Questions

1. What is Russ Martell's purpose in writing to all professional women skiers?
2. How might he convince at least some of the racers to include St. Claire in their itinerary?
3. How should he handle the disadvantages?

Chapter 5

Characteristics of Effective Written Communication

Learning Objectives

In this chapter, you'll learn to revise your own writing so that it demonstrates the ten characteristics of effective written communication. More specifically, you will be able to:

1. describe the ten characteristics that make writing effective
2. identify writing that does not contain the ten characteristics
3. explain how the ten characteristics work in combination to make writing effective
4. use specific techniques for incorporating the ten characteristics into your own writing

Preview Case

Michel Bissonette had been checking the mail anxiously all week. He'd been told by the Registrar's office that marks had been mailed out the previous Monday. Finally, they arrived. He tore open the envelope and scanned his marks with pleasure: 75 in Marketing; 83 in Accounting; 92 in Computer Systems ... But, what was this? 64 in Labour Relations. How could that be? His term average was at least 80 and term work accounted for 60 percent of the final mark. He'd been expecting a mark above 75.

Michel called the Administrative Management Department and spoke to Irene Divinsky, his instructor for the course. She listened politely while Michel protested that he must have made more than 64. Ms. Divinsky was polite but firm in maintaining that 64 was his final grade. Still not convinced, Michel decided to pursue the matter further and called the Dean of Student Affairs. The Dean advised Michel to consult his student handbook to find the procedure for handling the situation.

After a prolonged search, Michel found his handbook; however, he wasn't sure it was worth the effort when he read the following procedure for appealing marks:

In order to provide a mechanism by which students may air their problems concerning marks in academic courses, the College has established the following grievance procedure for all undergraduate students. First, the student should attempt to resolve his grievance with the course instructor. If not satisfied, then he may petition the head of the department in question, who will respond to the grievance in writing. If the student is not entirely satisfied, then his grievance may be submitted to the Undergraduate Petitions Committee, a three-man panel composed of two faculty members and one student who will render a final decision concerning the grievance.

Overview

Reread the handbook procedure. As you do, list the things that you find wrong with it. Since it was written for students, whatever you think is wrong with it probably is. After all, you're the audience.

This chapter will show you how you can make your written communication more effective, by making it

1. Readable
2. Tactful
3. Personal
4. Positive
5. Active
6. Unified

7. Coherent
8. Clear
9. Concise
10. Mechanically Sound

We'll analyze several pieces of written communication so that you can learn how to become more adept at analyzing and revising your own written communication. As we discuss each of the ten characteristics of effective written communication, we'll rewrite the material from the student handbook so that you can see the benefits of systematic revision.

Characteristic 1: Readable

Many writers try to impress their readers. They purposely choose long words and write lengthy, complicated sentences to show their command of the language and perhaps even their intelligence. Such writers prove that any idea, no matter how simple, can be communicated in a way that makes understanding difficult or even impossible for readers.

An overly complex writing style can prevent transmission of a message

The best business writing is readable because its style is clear and does not draw attention to itself. Readers are free to concentrate on the meaning of the message, rather than on the writing style.

Readable writing is clear writing

If you reread the material from the student handbook, you'll see that it's more complicated than it needs to be. Yet that style of writing is fairly typical of many business communications, including student handbooks.

Determining Readability

Analysts have developed several mathematical formulas to help judge the degree of complexity of written material — that is, the level of education the audience needs to understand a written passage. However, a less technical but more effective approach is to look at:

Readability formulas are not the answer; a less technical approach is more useful

- how the information appears on the page. Does your writing have paragraphs longer than 10 typewritten lines? If it does, you probably need to revise it so that you have smaller "chunks" of information separated by plenty of white space.
- how long sentences are. Do you have a variety of sentence lengths in your writing? While long, complex sentences may be confusing, reducing the length of every sentence might result in short, choppy sentences that could become monotonous and perhaps even offensive to your readers. A balance of short and long sentences is likely to be most effective.
- what words are used. Have you chosen your words because they are familiar and convey the precise meaning you intend? Choosing familiar, instead of obscure, words will ensure that you communicate with

your readers. This does not mean, however, that you should avoid longer, technical terms that will add precision to your writing. It does mean that you need to consider your audience carefully when choosing words.

Improving Readability

Write at or below your audience's level, but never "write down"

Your purpose in writing and the audience for whom the document is intended frequently determine your writing style and level of language. While you should avoid a style and language that is above your audience's level, your message should never sound as if you are "writing down." Your goal is quick and easy comprehension by your audience. One mark of an effective writer is the ability to write clearly at a relatively low level while maintaining an intelligent tone.

Clear writing increases readability

Your goal is always clearer writing. Here are nine suggestions for improving the readability of your writing:

1. Use headings, lists, and white space to make your writing more accessible to your reader.
2. Limit paragraph length to ten typewritten lines.
3. Aim for an average sentence length of twenty or fewer words.
4. Vary your sentence length and sentence construction. Variety sustains interest.
5. Use action verbs; avoid the passive voice.
6. Use familiar, concrete words your reader can picture; avoid abstract words.
7. Keep it short and simple (K.I.S.S.). Avoid unnecessary words and phrases; they "bury" your message.
8. Write as you talk. Your writing should have a conversational tone rather than a stilted or affected one.
9. Write to express ideas, not to impress the reader.

These suggestions will be demonstrated later in this chapter. For now, the student handbook material has been revised to show you that readability can be improved.

So **that students can air their problems about marks**, the College has **established the following** grievance procedure for all undergraduate students. First, the student should **try** to resolve **his** grievance with his instructor. If **this doesn't work**, then **his grievance may be filed with** the head of the department in question. **The department head** will respond to the student in writing. If the student is **still** not **entirely** satisfied, then his grievance may be submitted to the Undergraduate Petitions Committee. **This committee is** a three-man panel **made up** of two faculty members and one student. **Its decision will be final.**

Notice that complex and abstract words that create a stilted, formal tone have been replaced with simple, concrete ones. For example, in the first sentence, "mechanism" is dropped and "concerning" is replaced with "about." Since the last sentence was nearly twice as long as the recommended twenty words and not very clear, it's been rewritten so that each main idea in the original sentence is in a sentence of its own. Although the readability of the passage is now satisfactory, it has other problems. A look at the second characteristic of effective written communication will help identify some of them.

Characteristic 2: Tactful

Tactful writing avoids insulting or demeaning the reader

Regardless of who your audience is, material that is written tactfully does not offend the reader. Unfortunately, too many writers assume that what is inoffensive to them is inoffensive to everyone else. Off-colour, ethnic, or religious jokes are, however, inappropriate. As pointed out in Chapter 4, effective writers analyze their audiences to determine how they will react to the message. One outcome of such an analysis should be more tactful writing; writing that does not insult the reader.

Writing at too high or too low a level can be insulting

Tactful writing does not insult the reader's intelligence. To avoid insulting your reader, you need to write at a level that is neither too high nor too low for that reader. Tactlessness occurs when writers try to impress rather than express; the reader becomes confused and loses interest or, even worse, misinterprets the information and responds inappropriately.

One office manager alienated 25 co-workers when he sent out this message:

For the third time this year, I must remind you to turn off the light in the storeroom when you depart it. The light switch is a modern two-way switch. When the light switch is up, the light is on; when the switch is down, the light is off. I hope this is the last time I'll have to mention this.

Tactful writing does not categorize the reader. Consider the following:

People such as you are interested in the arts. That's why we're asking you to make a contribution to ...

Categorizing can be demeaning

As the sender of this message, you assume that everyone is interested in the arts. While many of your readers may well be interested in the arts, many will object to being categorized. "People such as you" puts the reader in the same category as everyone else. The extent to which you offend one, two, or several readers with such categories is the extent to which your potential contributions decline.

Take another example: imagine being a personnel manager who receives several hundred résumés from would-be employees each year. Many of these résumés are accompanied by cover letters that begin "Dear Personnel Manager." Many managers believe that you should take the time to find out their name if you are truly interested in working for the company.

Sexist language may offend many readers

Tactful writing is not sexist. Sexist language insults at least half your readers. Re-examine the student handbook material. Taken literally, it was written only for males. Notice also that the Undergraduate Petitions Committee is *three-man*. Whether or not you are offended by such language is irrelevant. Remember, someone in your audience could be.

One way of removing sexist language is to change *he* to *he or she* (or perhaps *s/he*) and *him* to *him or her*. But be careful: such phrasing can become cumbersome unless it is used sparingly. Pronouns are not the only — or even the most offensive — kind of sexist language. Here are some additional ways of avoiding sexist language:

1. Use the word *person*. For example:

Sexist	**When you schedule a meeting with a businessman, remember the importance of time.**
Nonsexist	**When you schedule a meeting with a businessperson, remember the importance of time.**

2. Use plurals. For example:

Sexist	**An employee is promoted on the basis of his ability and seniority.**
Nonsexist	**Employees are promoted on the basis of their ability and seniority.**
Sexist	**A good manager helps his subordinates develop.**
Nonsexist	**Good managers help their subordinates develop.**

3. Use the words *you* or *your*. For example:

Sexist	**An employee should punch his time card promptly each morning.**
Nonsexist	**Punch your time card promptly each morning.**

Many commonly used words in business communication are potentially sexist. Here are some examples of these words and their more contemporary replacements:[1]

Don't Say	Say
businessman	businessperson, business executive, manager

chairman	chairperson, moderator, chair
manmade	manufactured, handmade
salesman	salesperson, sales agent, sales representative
spokesman	spokesperson, representative
workman	worker
foreman	supervisor
stock boy	stock clerk

Tactful writing does not use humour in bad taste. Witness the collection message that began:

Maybe you've heard this one: Why are little birds so sad in the morning? Answer: Because their little bills are all "over-dew." It may remind you that we have a little bill that is overdue. If you feed it a cheque ... [2]

Tactful writing also avoids an accusatory tone. When your writing contains an accusation, whether implied or expressed, you risk offending your reader. Compare these two sentences:

Accusatory	**Perhaps you didn't read the instructions for your last assignment.**
Nonaccusatory	**Please reread the instructions for your last assignment.**

As you work to make your writing more tactful, remember that your own perception of tact is not what counts. What does is the meaning your receiver assigns to the message.

To make the student handbook material tactful, we need to remove the sexist language. However, don't think that you must always change *him* to *him or her*. One effective way to avoid sexist language involves our third characteristic of effective written communication — personal writing.

Characteristic 3: Personal

By personal, we mean that what you write should convey a "you" attitude. Such an attitude means that you must use the data from your audience analysis to help you focus on the readers' needs — answering their questions — rather than on yourself, the writer. You can also use language to create reader-oriented messages. By de-emphasizing the use of *we* and *I* and emphasizing *you* and *your*, you draw the reader into the document. Notice the subtle difference in reader involvement in the following examples:

The "you" attitude puts the reader first

We and I	You
We've mailed a cheque.	You'll receive your cheque in the mail.
Our savings accounts pay 6 percent interest.	You'll earn 6 percent interest from your savings account.
I want to express my appreciation ...	Thank you for your help with ...

Replacing *I*'s with *you*'s creates a you attitude

Using *you* and *your* makes the reader the centre of attention in the message. But writing with the "you" attitude can be done on two levels. The first is fairly mechanical and easy: Eliminate as many *I* references as possible. You won't be able to remove all references, but the tone improves with each removal. Insert some *you* references. Unless they are too numerous, they are valuable interest developers. Although some writers use the reader's name in a letter, you should use this technique sparingly. Many readers find it offensive.

Create a message to the reader rather than from the writer

The second level of applying the you attitude is more subtle. At this level, you are going beyond the mere substitution of *you*'s for *I*'s and are seeking a between-the-lines tone that the message is to the reader rather than from the writer. This is the level you should strive for.

Compare these two short messages:

The company wishes to encourage employees to take part in the suggestion system it has provided; the system has produced many money-saving ideas in the past.

Employees are the heart of XYZ Company, and each employee's ideas are enthusiastically sought and carefully evaluated. Many employee-volunteered ideas have produced time- and effort-saving changes.

Neither passage has an *I* or a *you*, but the second one has a tone that is directed *to* the employee rather than *from* the company.

At times, of course, you want to avoid the you attitude in order not to offend the reader. Tact is just as important as personal writing. Consider the following examples:

We and I	You
We didn't receive a cheque.	You didn't send your cheque.
Employees who are late three days without a valid reason will be dismissed.	If you are late three days without a valid reason, then you will be dismissed.

In the first example, "You didn't send your cheque" contains an accusatory tone. The *we and I* approach implies that the cheque did not arrive for reasons other than the reader's not having sent it. The second example is less explicit in its absence of tact. The *you* version communicates an expectation that every reader is considering being late. The more appropriate *we and I* version successfully communicates the company's policy but avoids the implication that all employees are irresponsible.

If the you approach might offend the reader, use we and I instead

Neither is it desirable to overuse the word *you*. When readers become aware of writing style, they cease to concentrate on the message. Generally, however, you want to put the reader first. After all, you are not writing to please yourself.

Here, then, is a new (but not perfect) version of the student handbook material. Compare it to what appeared earlier, since it also removes the sexist language.

The College has established the following grievance procedure so that you can air **your** problems about **your** marks, First, **you** should try to resolve **your** grievance with **your** instructor. If this doesn't work, then **your** grievance may be filed with the head of the department in question. The department head will respond to **you** in writing. If **you** are still not satisfied, **your** grievance may be submitted to the Undergraduate Petitions Committee. This committee is composed of three persons (two faculty members and one student). Its decision will be final.

Characteristic 4: Positive

Effective written communication is written in a positive tone. How people react to your writing depends in part upon the climate of communication you establish with them. Such a climate can be positive or negative. Compare the messages (shown in Figure 5.1) posted in two different doctors' waiting rooms.

A positive tone develops a positive relationship

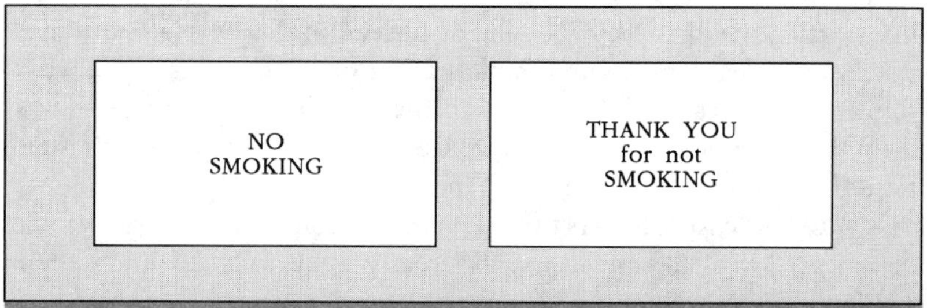

NO
SMOKING

THANK YOU
for not
SMOKING

Figure 5.1 The Climate of Communication: Positive or Negative?

Both messages have the same meaning. Yet they convey different ideas about the relationship the sender wants to establish.

When writing in business, we want to create as positive a climate as possible. Thus, we avoid using negative words such as *delay*, *can't*, *impossible*, *inconvenience*, and *trouble*. Here are some examples:

Negative	**You failed to enclose a cheque with your order; therefore, it is impossible to send you the merchandise.**
Positive	**As soon as your cheque arrives, we'll send your order via parcel post.**
Negative	**There can be no exceptions to this policy.**
Positive	**This policy must apply equally and fairly to everyone.**
Negative	**First-year students are never assigned single rooms in residence.**
Positive	**First-year students are assigned to double rooms in residence.**
Negative	**You should not ride your bicycle without wearing a helmet.**
Positive	**You should always wear a helmet while riding your bicycle.**

Correct use of reversal words and emphasis can help make writing positive

Two approaches besides careful word selection can help you gain maximum benefit from your message: *reversal words* and *emphasis*.

Reversal words change the direction or tone of a message from positive to negative or from negative to positive. *However*, *on the other hand*, *but*, and *unfortunately* are examples. When such a word or phrase occurs at a transition point, it identifies the upcoming change.

This identification can be valuable when you are moving from bad news to good news, for the reader now knows that the negative is finished. However, the change from a positive message to a negative message is unpleasant. For this reason, try not to add extra emphasis to the negative information by saying, in effect, "Brace yourself, here it comes."

In summary, you may wish to use reversal words between negative and positive thoughts, but you should always avoid them before negative thoughts. *Unfortunately* is especially to be avoided since it always signals a negative thought.

Emphasis also helps you focus most of the reader's attention on the positive aspects of your message. For *place emphasis*, you "place" your information at either the beginning or the end of the message since those are the locations of maximum emphasis. The opposite of this device works too. Putting negative information in the middle of a message — away from the beginning or ending emphasis locations — draws as little attention to it as possible.

Mass emphasis uses repetition for emphasis. A positive message might be repeated in both similar and different ways throughout the piece of writing.

To close our discussion of positive writing, let's take a look at the material from the student handbook. Obviously we are dealing with inherently negative material in a grievance procedure. However, we can use a more neutral term to describe the procedure: appeal.

So that you can air your problems about your marks, the College has established the following **appeal** procedure. **Please help us by following each step.** First, you should try to resolve **the problem** with your instructor. If this doesn't work, **your** appeal may be filed with the head of the department in question. The department head will respond to you in writing. If you are still not satisfied, **your** appeal may be submitted to the Undergraduate Petitions Committee. This committee is composed of three persons (two faculty members and one student). Its decision will be final.

Characteristic 5: Active

Which sentence seems more emphatic to you?

1. Effective business writers use the active voice.
2. The active voice is used by effective business writers.

Sentence 1 was written in the active voice, where the subject performs the action expressed by the verb. The active voice helps make your sentences come alive. Since people usually talk in the active voice, they are more accustomed to dealing with it. Therefore, you should use the active voice wherever possible in your writing.

Sentence 2 uses the passive voice. You can recognize the passive voice since it uses a form of the verb "to be" as an auxiliary verb and a main verb in the past tense. In addition, the passive voice implies the action was done "by" someone. Because people are less accustomed to dealing with the passive voice, you should use it sparingly in your writing.

In general, the active voice is strong because the subject is acting. The passive voice is weak because the subject is being acted upon. Consider the following:

Use the active voice to emphasize ideas

Passive	**A refund will be sent to you.**
Active	**You will receive a refund.**
Passive	**The report was written by Michel.**
Active	**Michel wrote the report.**
Passive	**The product's safety has been shown by laboratory tests.**
Active	**Laboratory tests have shown the product's safety.**

Using the active voice generally reduces the length of your sentences; however, you may choose to use the passive voice when you want to de-emphasize the doer, or when you don't know who is responsible for the action. But, the passive voice need not always be used to de-emphasize an idea. You can rewrite the following sentence in the active voice and still be tactful:

Passive **Your credit was checked.**

Active **To ensure that the use of credit is in the applicant's best interest, we do check all credit references.**

By making a general policy statement rather than simply saying, "We checked your credit," you do not risk implying that you were suspicious about this particular applicant.

Notice the use of the active voice in the following rewrite of the student handbook passage.

So that you can air your problems about your marks, the College has established the following appeal procedure. Please help us by following each step. First, **try** to resolve the problem with your instructor. If, **after talking to your instructor, you are still not satisfied, file** your appeal with the head of the department in question. The department head will respond to you in writing. If **you want further consideration, submit** your appeal to the Undergraduate Petitions Committee. This committee is composed of three persons (two faculty members and one student). Its decision will be final.

Characteristic 6: Unified

Too many short, simple sentences sound like a primary reader

Each sentence and paragraph in business communication should contain only one idea. When writing a sentence, your goal is to make sure that two unrelated ideas don't appear in it. Meeting this goal is easy if you write nothing but simple sentences. Limiting yourself to simple sentences, however, will result in a choppy writing style.

Experienced writers combine simple, compound, and complex sentences to bring variety to their style. In attempting such variety, remember to ensure that the different ideas within each sentence clearly relate to each other.

Poor	Better
Thank your for placing your order, and your new Beachcraft towels should reach you by July 15. (Compound sentence.)	**Thank you for placing your order. Your new Beachcraft towels should reach you by July 15. (Two simple sentences.)**

When you start the engine, adjust the motor speed immediately, and check your owner's manual if you have any further problems. (Compound-complex sentence.)

When you start the engine, adjust the motor speed immediately. If you have any further problems, please check your owner's manual. (Two complex sentences.)

Sentence variety is important, but remember not to sacrifice sentence unity for the sake of variety.

Paragraph unity: one central idea per paragraph

Unity applies in much the same way to writing paragraphs. In this case, our goal is to be sure that no paragraph contains more than one central idea. Often our thoughts get mixed together:

We need to talk about expansion plans tomorrow. The report is due next month, and I'm afraid we're running short on time. I can't figure out last month's profit statement. Need to go over it with you. We're over budget. Enclosed is a bill from the printer. Impossible! Did you authorize this?

You can see that this writer is dealing with three separate ideas — expansion plans, the profit statement, and the printer's bill. The passage can be improved by dividing it into three paragraphs:

We need to talk about expansion plans tomorrow. The report is due next month, and I'm afraid we're running short on time.

I can't figure out last month's profit statement. Therefore, I need to go over it with you. We're over budget.

Enclosed is a bill from the printer. Impossible! Did you authorize this?

Besides reading more smoothly, the material is now presented so the reader knows immediately that it has three important ideas, as opposed to only one.

Perhaps the best way to make sure that your paragraphs are unified is to begin all of them with a topic sentence. Then do not write any sentence not related to the topic sentence. Save unrelated ideas for future paragraphs.

Since our student handbook material was so brief, paragraph unity was not a problem. You'll find in practice, however, that many paragraphs are quite lengthy and require careful attention to unity.

Characteristic 7: Coherent

Coherent sentences and paragraphs are understandable because they "stick together"

Coherence is another quality important to both sentences and paragraphs. If sentences or paragraphs are coherent, the ideas in them are clearly tied together and easy to understand.

Sentences often lack coherence because we use pronouns such as *this*, *that*, and *it* ambiguously:

Unclear	**Your Grasscutter electric mower will operate quietly and quickly, and this will save you money.**
Clear	**Your Grasscutter electric mower will operate quietly and quickly. Its speed will save you money.**
Unclear	**They rented furniture for their apartment that cost $100 per month.**
Clear	**For their apartment, they rented furniture that cost $100 per month.**

Dangling constructions also make sentences incoherent:

Unclear	**Being a preferred customer, I'm sure you'll be interested in this offer.**
Clear	**Since you are a preferred customer, I'm sure you'll be interested in this offer.**
Unclear	**Having been run through the adding machine, the clerk rechecked his figures.**
Clear	**After running figures through the adding machine, the clerk rechecked them.**

Paragraphs can be coherent if you make a conscious attempt to use various devices to help the reader along. Unfortunately, if you assume the reader can read your mind along with your writing, you may produce paragraphs like the following:

You'll want to become a member of Highland Recreation Centre for several reasons. A one-year membership costs only $15 and entitles you to use all of the facilities, including the pool and weight room, at reduced rates. The Centre offers a variety of aerobics, handicraft, and special interest classes and workshops throughout the year.

Let's look at five devices that can improve paragraph coherence:

Use the same grammatical structure for items in a series

1. Use Parallel Structure

You'll want to become a member of Highland Recreation Centre for several reasons. A one-year membership costs only $15. It entitles you to use all of the facilities, including the pool and weight room, at reduced rates. It entitles you to attend a variety of aerobics, handicraft, and special interest classes and workshops throughout the year.

Parallel structure emphasizes all three of the reasons equally. Words, phrases, and complete sentences are said to be parallel when each item in a series uses the same grammatical structure. In the example above, each of the reasons is written in a complete sentence with "membership" as the subject. The reasons could also be written as phrases; however, the punctuation would change. For example:

You'll want to become a member of Highland Recreation Centre for several reasons. A one-year membership costs only $15, entitles you to use all of the facilities, including the pool and weight room, at reduced rates, and entitles you to attend a variety of aerobics, handicraft, and special interest classes and workshops throughout the year.

2. Use Linking Words

Linking words show relationships between ideas

You'll want to become a member of Highland Recreation Centre for several reasons. A one-year membership costs only $15. It also entitles you to use all of the facilities, including the pool and weight room, at reduced rates. In addition, it entitles you to attend a variety of aerobics, handicraft, and special interest classes and workshops throughout the year.

Linking words, as their name implies, show relationships or links between ideas. For example, items of equal value are often linked with "and," time relationships are shown with such words as "when" or "after," and cause-and-effect relationships are shown with the word "because." Other examples of linking words include *however*, *consequently*, *therefore*, and *if*.

3. Use Lists

Lists visually reinforce equal relationships

You'll want to become a member of Highland Recreation Centre for several reasons. A one-year membership:

- **costs only $15**
- **entitles you to use all of the facilities, including the pool and weight room, at reduced rates**
- **entitles you to attend a variety of aerobics, handicraft, and special interest classes and workshops throughout the year**

Notice that the lead-in to the list (the topic sentence of this paragraph) ends with a colon and none of the items, including the last one, is followed by a period.

Sometimes, stacked lists can show visually the same relationships that linking words show. In the example above, the reasons are "stacked" one on top of the other to show that they are items of equal value. However, lists will work only when you have a series of equal items. They cannot be used if your ideas have different relationships. For example, the following paragraph could not be written as a list:

A major snowstorm has delayed the start of our winter programs by one week. Therefore, we have extended the registration deadline from January 5 to January 12. Similarly, classes will start on January 15, not January 8 as originally planned.

Enumerating improves paragraph coherence

4. Give Each Idea a Specific Numeric or Chronological Label (Enumerate)

You'll want to become a member of Highland Recreation Centre for several reasons. First, a one-year membership costs only $15. Second, it entitles you to use all of the facilities, including the pool and weight room, at reduced rates. And third, it entitles you to attend a variety of aerobics, handicraft, and special interest classes and workshops throughout the year.

You can also use a numbered stacked list to make the paragraph even easier to read:

You'll want to become a member of Highland Recreation Centre for several reasons. A one-year membership:

1. costs only $15
2. entitles you to use all of the facilities, including the pool and weight room, at reduced rates
3. entitles you to attend a variety of aerobics, handicraft, and special interest classes and workshops throughout the year.

Headings improve paragraph coherence

5. Assign Brief Headings to Major Ideas (Signposts)

You'll want a membership to the Highland Recreation Centre for several reasons:
LOW COST – only $15 a year
GREAT FACILITIES – use of all facilities, including the pool and weight room, at reduced rates
GREAT PROGRAMS – a variety of aerobics, handicraft, and special interest classes and workshops throughout the year.

This is only one example of headings used as signposts. You'll find other examples throughout the text.

If you examine the final revision of the student handbook material below, you'll find that we've improved coherence by using enumeration.

So that you can air your problems about your marks, the College has established the following appeal procedure. Please help us by following each step.

1. Try to resolve the problem with your instructor.
2. If, after talking to your instructor, you are still not satisfied, file your appeal with the head of the department in question. The department head will respond to you in writing.
3. If you want further consideration, submit your appeal to the Undergraduate Petitions Committee. This committee is composed of three persons (two faculty members and one student). Its decision will be final.

Characteristic 8: Clear

Clarity in writing applies to the overall organization — paragraphing, sentence structure, and word choice — of whatever you write — letters, memos, or reports. Clarity is a general concept that means understandability. Naturally, readability is important to clarity. Unity and coherence are also important. Clarity involves several techniques, including planning what you write so that your content and organization meet the needs of your audience and accomplish your purpose. It also involves using topic sentences in paragraphs and choosing your words carefully.

Clarity includes readability, unity, and coherence

Clear Writing Through Topic Sentences

A unified paragraph, you may remember, has only one central idea. Usually, you'll express this idea in the topic sentence. This sentence clearly states the central idea of the paragraph.

The topic sentence presents the main idea of your paragraph

The topic sentence should be placed at either the beginning or the end of the paragraph. In business communication, it usually appears at the beginning. However, you might place your topic sentence at the end of the paragraph if (1) the main topic of your paragraph will be unclear unless the reader is first exposed to some details, or (2) you are attempting to persuade a reader whose reaction might be unfavourable. In the second case, presenting your details first helps you support the position you take in the topic sentence.

To see how topic sentences make writing clearer, examine the following paragraphs. Notice the relationship between each underlined topic sentence and all the other sentences in the paragraph.

Burns Brick Company has several employee relations problems. The turnover rate is 39 percent, up 10 percent from last year. Absenteeism has increased almost 25 percent this year, and the number of grievances has more than doubled during the past six months.

The turnover rate at Burns Brick Company is 39 percent, up 10 percent from last year. Absenteeism has increased almost 25 percent this year, and the number of grievances has more than doubled during the past six months. Obviously, the company is faced with several important employee relations problems.

By using topic sentences and by ensuring that every sentence in the paragraph is related to the topic sentence (unity), you help the reader better understand the written message.

Clear Writing Through Word Choice

Your readers will understand your message more easily if you avoid technical jargon and unfamiliar words.

Technical jargon can confuse your readers if they are not familiar with the terms

Avoid technical jargon. Every field of business has its own special language. A blow to the head can be a subdural hematoma to a doctor. If you spend more money than you earn, an economist calls you a negative saver. What the military calls a protective reaction strike is, nevertheless, dropping bombs. And if you do poorly in school, you'll probably be called an underachiever.

When writing in business, you should avoid using jargon unless you are sure that the reader will understand it. A nurse explaining a patient's problem to another nurse might refer to an embolism. In explaining the problem to the patient, he might simply say blood clot.

Avoid unfamiliar words. Jargon basically consists of perfectly appropriate technical words that are unfamiliar to most of us. Many often-used words, however, aren't really jargon, although they create just as much misunderstanding. Try this paragraph:

Fully cognizant of the inoperative nature of his vehicle, Anita's initial response was to institute repairs. Prior to modifying the timing, she found a defective wire in the anterior portion of the engine.

We have underlined the unfamiliar words. Now see if these changes make the paragraph more understandable:

Using familiar words can improve reader understanding

Knowing that his car was not working, Anita's first response was to begin repairs. Before changing the timing, she found a faulty wire in the front part of the engine.

Even the simplest ideas can be made almost unintelligible with unfamiliar words. Get out your dictionary and see if you can translate these old sayings into their familiar form:

- He who expresses merriment subsequent to everyone else expresses merriment of most superior quality.
- Precipitation entails negation of economy.
- Pulchritude is not evinced below the dermal surface.

To help make your writing clear, use words that are familiar to your reader. Here are some examples:

Don't Say	Say
Prior to	Before
Subsequent to	After
Accomplish	Do
Reimburse	Repay
Determine	Find out
Transmit	Send
Advantageous	Helpful
Locality	Place
Facilitate	Help
Encounter difficulty in	Find it hard to
Pursuant to your request	As you asked

Characteristic 9: Concise

Conciseness means few, precise words

Conciseness means saying what you want to say in the fewest possible words. The opposite of conciseness is wordiness. You can become a concise writer if you avoid (1) wordy expressions, (2) trite phrases, (3) useless repetition, and (4) abstract words.

Avoid Wordy Expressions

Wordy expressions are simply dead weight in a sentence. Many sentences beginning with *there are*, *it is*, or *there is* are wordy. Notice how you can say the same thing without phrases that make your sentences begin slowly:

Slow-starting sentences create wordiness

Don't Say	Say
There are three fine restaurants on Broad Street.	Broad Street has three fine restaurants.
It is important that all employees read the company handbook.	All employees should read the company handbook.
There is little time left for us to make a decision.	We have little time left to make a decision.

In just these three examples we have "saved" seven words at no expense to understanding.

"More matter, with less art," were Queen Gertrude's words to the rambling, wordy Polonius in Shakespeare's *Hamlet*. As she encouraged him to speak more concisely, we encourage you to write more concisely by avoiding such phrases as:

Wordy phrases are dead weight, no matter where they appear in your sentences

Wordy	Concise
A long period of time	A long time (or two weeks)
At the present time	Now (or the present date)
Consensus of opinion	Consensus
Due to the fact that	Because
During the month of November	During November
For the purpose of	For
For the reason that	Because
In many cases	Often
In some cases	Sometimes
In the near future	Soon
In the event that	If
In the province of Manitoba	In Manitoba
In view of the fact that	Because, since
With regard to	About
With reference to	About
The jar which is blue	The blue jar

Avoid Trite Phrases

Trite phrases can make you appear shallow

Trite phrases are worn-out, commonplace expressions. Because they are overused, they have lost their meaning, are dead weight in your sentences, and can reduce your credibility as a writer.

Although some trite phrases can simply be deleted from a sentence, others need fresher replacements. Here are some examples:

Don't Say	Say
Advise	Tell
Enclosed please find	Enclosed is
Numerous and sundry	Many
Permit me to say	*–nothing–*
It has come to my attention	I have learned
Under separate cover	Separately
Please be advised	*–nothing–*
Up to this writing	Until now
In accordance with your request	As you requested
Kindly	Please

Avoid Useless Repetition

Sometimes good writers repeat ideas for effect — to impress them on the reader's mind. Television advertisements, for example, contain many repetitions of the product's name so that viewers won't forget it. When you write, you may also have reasons for repeating ideas. But avoid the careless mistake of useless repetition of the same idea. The words in italics can be omitted from each of the following sentences with no loss of understanding.

Repeat ideas for effect, not because you forgot to proofread

- The two cars were *exactly* identical.
- His pay raise was small *in size.*
- We join *together* in wishing you well in your new job.
- If you can't use the new typewriter, return it *back* to me.
- What we need are some *new* changes.
- Please see me at 3:30 p.m. *in the afternoon.*

Avoid Abstract Words

Abstract words contribute to unclear writing because they are so general and vague that the reader is not sure what you are trying to say. Concrete words, the opposite of abstract words, have clear, specific meanings. They help readers create the image that you want created in their minds.

Here are some examples of abstract and concrete language:

Abstract words create unclear images in the reader's mind

Abstract	Concrete
Your savings account will earn the highest possible interest.	Your savings account will earn the maximum 6.5 percent interest each year.

The majority of our shareholders voted for the new plan.	**Sixty-four percent of our shareholders voted for the new plan.**
Your new, lightweight Solution Computer can be carried easily from room to room.	**Your new Solution Computer is feather light. Weighing only 2.4 kg, it can easily be carried from one office to another.**
You will receive your refund cheque soon.	**You will receive your full refund of $132.19 by July 15.**

To summarize, you can write concisely if you avoid using wordy expressions, trite phrases, useless repetitions, and abstract words. Writing concisely usually reduces the number of words used, thus saving the reader time and energy. Yet, conciseness may actually mean increasing the number of words to create a more vivid image.

Return to the student handbook material at the beginning of this chapter. Much of the wordiness was removed when we improved the material's readability. Otherwise, the material needed few changes to make it more concise.

Characteristic 10: Mechanically Sound

Grammar and format are important

Correct grammar improves understanding

Mechanically sound written material is free of two kinds of defects — errors in grammar and format problems. Perhaps you've wondered how an English teacher could be so cruel as to take three marks off for every comma splice in a term paper. Phrases such as "dangling construction," "faulty reference," and "subject-verb agreement" may nauseate you. Yet correct grammar is important. One reason for this importance is that correct grammar helps ensure reader understanding. Consider these examples:

A newspaper headline:
City Council Bans Gambling Behind Closed Doors

From a letter to an invited speaker:
Your speech will be followed by dinner, to begin promptly at 7:30 p.m.

From a newspaper article:
An audience of nearly 200 heard her lecture on "The Future of Endangered Species." A number of them have already perished.

A second reason for using correct grammar is that doing so will improve your credibility as a writer. No matter how good your ideas, if they are incorrectly expressed, many readers will discount them. Advertisers know that the package sells the product. Grammar is the package that helps sell your ideas. You'll find that many businesspeople are just as concerned about correct grammar as your English teacher was.

Correct grammar enhances credibility

Correct format is also important in written communication. As you read the following chapters about letters and reports, you will find that standard formats exist for each. Business letters, for example, typically have a heading, inside address, salutation, body, and complimentary closing. As a writer of business letters, you will be expected to adhere to this format. In addition, many organizations have specialized formats that they expect employees to use for all internal and external communications. Reviewing existing documents can also give you valuable clues about what's expected, even when no formal policies exist.

Effective International Communication

Writers who follow the ten characteristics outlined above are more likely to be read and understood by readers whose first language is English. When reader and writer have similar backgrounds, the probability of successful communication increases.

In international business, although English may still be the language of choice, cultural differences complicate communication. The writer whose cultural background does not include English as a first language will think and write differently.

For example, North Americans may need to adapt many of their linguistic patterns when conducting business in Japan. To many North Americans, the Japanese are so careful to respect one another's position they may appear evasive. For those Japanese who favour polite, formal language, Western speech appears too concise and abrupt. In addition, the concept of starting with the main idea is unfamiliar. Most Japanese prefer to explain first and follow the explanation with the main point.

Although Japanese business practices have changed somewhat with the times, such practices still reflect local customs and manners. Letters in Japan, whether business or personal, are characterized by extreme politeness, humility, and formality. The field of business has always provided challenges for the writer; intercultural differences now add another dimension to that challenge.[3]

As the volume of international business grows, so does the volume of international business communication. The business leaders of tomorrow will be those who are skilled in the basics of communication and who are flexible enough to adapt to the changing business environment.

Revising a Document

Use the ten characteristics as a checklist

To return to the memo drafted in Chapter 4 on vacation planners, Figure 5.2. illustrates how the ten characteristics can be used as a revision checklist. The handwritten items reflect the changes that would result when the ten characteristics are used as a checklist.

Booking Your 1991 Vacation

~~I need to have your~~ Please complete the attached vacation planner by April 12 so that I will be in a position to accommodate all of your requests. We plan to recruit senior students from City University as summer replacement staff. Our recruiters will be visiting the campus the week of April 8 to interview prospective candidates. ¶ Vacation Policy Our company vacation policy provides that employees 1. [who have been with the company one full year as of March 1 are entitled to three weeks' vacation.] ~~Employees~~ 2. [who have less than one year's service as of March 1 are entitled to one day for every complete month worked. For example, if ~~an employee who~~ you started on August 1 last year, you would be entitled to 7 vacation days this year.]

3. [who have ~~Every employee with~~ at least one year's service ~~is~~ are entitled to at least two weeks' vacation during the summer months of June, July, and August. ¶ How to Complete the Planner The attached vacation planner ~~lists~~ is a chart of all the months of the year and days of the month. The final column on the right allows you to total the number of vacation days you plan to take each month. For your convenience, all the statutory holidays and weekends for the coming year have been shaded.

Please use code 03 to indicate which days you plan to take as vacation. ~~Employees who~~ If you are planning short absences of one or two days throughout the year, you ~~do~~ need not ~~to~~ show them on the planner. ¶ For More Information If you have any questions, please see me today as ~~Don't hesitate to call me if you want more information. By the way,~~ I will be out of the office for the rest of the week.

Figure 5.2 Draft Vacation Request Memo

Has the memo been revised so that it conforms with the ten characteristics of effective writing?

Readable: The draft memo is fairly readable. Paragraphs are shorter than 10 typewritten lines; sentences vary in length from 10 to 26 words, with an average of 20 words per sentence. Only the word "your" needs to be changed to "you" in line one to make the memo readable.

Tactful: The draft memo is tactful. It is written at a level that will not offend and it does not contain any sexist language.

Personal: While most of the draft memo is written with the readers' interests in mind, the opening sentence focuses on the need of the writer. Notice how the direct request "Please complete ... " shifts the focus to the reader. Notice that, in some cases, "you" replaces "employees" to reinforce the personal tone.

Positive: Again, the draft memo is generally positive, but notice the next-to-last sentence. Phrases such as "don't hesitate" tend to have the opposite effect: the reader stops to think of reasons to hesitate. By combining the last two sentences, the writer conveys important information in a positive manner.

Active: The draft memo uses the active voice more frequently than the passive voice so that the overall tone of the memo is active.

Unified: Notice that each of the paragraphs in the draft memo contains unrelated ideas. Therefore, several revisions are required to ensure that each paragraph addresses a single topic. The first paragraph contains the request and the reason for it. The second summarizes the vacation policy. The third and fourth paragraphs instruct readers on how to complete the planner, and the final paragraph tells them how they can get more information.

Coherent: Although the paragraphs are readable, some of them lack coherence. Notice how paragraph two is improved by listing and numbering each part of the policy and by using parallel structure for each list item. Then, to improve the overall coherence of the document, a subject line and three internal headings are added to the memo. These headings tell the reader exactly what each section is about.

Clear: Although the memo is clear, notice that the third paragraph is improved by clarifying the topic sentence.

Mechanically Sound: A final check of the memo indicates that it contains no grammatical errors.

Once you've completed your revisions, you should review your audience analysis to ensure that you've provided your readers with the right amount and type of information. Figure 5.3 is one example of the final memo for the audience described in Chapter 4. Looking at this information from the reader's point of view, you can see that it answers five main questions: (1) what do you want me to do? (2) why? (3) how much vacation do I get? (4) how do I fill out this form? and (5) where can I get help if I'm stuck? These questions are often guides for the content of the subject line and the headings. The subject line and the headings in turn give readers access to the information they need quickly and efficiently. Senior staff may read only the first and fourth paragraphs, just to make sure that the procedure is the same as it was in previous years. However, newer staff have all the details they need and a source of help should they require it.

Notice that the overall organization of the final memo is much the same as that of the draft memo. This consistency is the result of careful initial planning.

You may decide to check the ten characteristics in a different order from the one presented here. For example, some writers prefer to consider clarity, coherence, and unity when they first begin to revise. Others decide on headings during the planning phase, so that their first draft often requires less revision for coherence. You will find that you modify the writing process suggested in Chapters 4 and 5 as you develop your skills as a business writer.

Summary

Evaluate the final rewrite of the student handbook material on page 93 against the ten characteristics of effective written communication.

Readable Short sentences and familiar words.

Tactful Sexist language removed. The material does not insult the reader's intelligence.

Personal Very reader oriented.

Positive As positive as possible for an appeal procedure, which must use some negative words.

Active Only one sentence in passive voice.

Unified Sentences have only one major idea.

Coherent All sentences and paragraphs clearly tied together. Enumerating used to enhance coherence.

Clear Much more understandable than the original at the beginning of this chapter.

Concise Dead weight removed.

Mechanically Sound Meets all the format specifications for a procedure. Grammar correct.

INTEROFFICE MEMO CANCO LIMITED

To: All Print Materials Production Staff

From: Lynn Goldmann, Director
Print Materials Production

Date: April 2,1991

Subject: Booking Your 1991 Vacation

Please complete the attached vacation planner by April 15 so that I will be in a position to accommodate all of your requests. We plan to recruit senior students from City University as summer replacement staff. Our recruiters will be visiting the campus in the week of April 8 to interview prospective candidates.

Vacation Policy

Canco's vacation policy provides that employees:

1. who have been with the company one full year as of March 1 are entitled to three weeks' vacation
2. who have less than one year's service as of March 1 are entitled to one day for every complete month worked. For example, if you started on August 1 last year, you are entitled to 7 vacation days this year
3. who have at least one year's service are entitled to at least two weeks vacation during the summer months of June, July, and August

How to Complete the Planner

The attached vacation planner is a chart of the months of the year and days of the month. The final column on the right allows you to total the number of vacation days you plan to take each month. For your convenience, all the statutory holidays and weekends for the coming year have been shaded.

Please use code 03 to indicate which days you plan to take as vacation. If you are planning short absences of one or two days throughout the year, you need not show them on the planner.

For More Information

If you have questions about the planner, please see me today as I will be out of the office for the rest of the week.

Figure 5.3 Final Draft of Vacation Request Memo

As you work your way through the remaining chapters in this section, look for ways to incorporate the ten characteristics into your writing.

Review Questions

1. What do we mean by "tactful" written communication?
2. Why should you adopt the "you" attitude when you write?
3. What is meant by "positive tone"?
4. When should you use the passive voice? The active voice?
5. How can you ensure paragraph unity?
6. What are some ways of improving paragraph coherence?
7. How can you enhance the clarity of your writing?
8. Suggest some ways of writing concisely.
9. Why is correct grammar important to mechanically sound written communication?
10. How do these ten characteristics of effective written communication apply to international business communication?

Activities

1. Get a copy of the student handbook for your college or university. As we have done in this chapter, evaluate part of it against the ten characteristics of effective written communication. Then rewrite the part you have evaluated and try to improve it.
2. Get a short article on a similar topic from each of three different sources: a professional journal, a textbook, and a popular magazine such as *Reader's Digest* or *Saturday Night*.
   a. Compare the paragraph and sentence length as well as the choice of language in each of the three sources.
   b. List reasons why you might expect to find differences in readability.
3. Examine the material below. (It was written for Teaneck employees only; customers will not see it.)
   a. Find at least five effective writing problems in the material.
   b. Rewrite the material so that all writing problems are removed.

Customer Refunds

Teaneck Department Store will refund a customer's money in the event that the customer is dissatisfied with his merchandise. If the merchandise is being returned by the customer, it should be accompanied by a sales slip. The merchandise should be examined by the salesman for potential abuse. Subsequent to merchandise inspection, the salesman should fill out a retail credit cheque form and acquire the appropriate approval (in the form of a signature) from his supervisor. The customer should be asked to sign the credit cheque and then refund the money. The credit cheque should be placed beneath the cash drawer.

4. Rewrite the following sentences so that they conform to the ten characteristics of effective written communication. Each sentence contains at least one error.

   a. Our regional director, a girl with substantial years of experience, will audit your accounts.
   b. If you don't pay promptly, a substantial discount won't be received by you.
   c. In view of the fact that you've had the merchandise for only six months, it goes without saying that your warranty covers the repair.
   d. If the employee has a grievance, the employee should take his grievance to the grievance committee.
   e. Smelling of liquor, the policeman arrested the driver.
   f. It is believed by the Board of Trustees that the new plan will work.
   g. Despite your delay in paying the bill, we will not cancel the account.
   h. I can say at this time that a lawyer could provide a solution to this problem, but that he would necessarily need to be a tax specialist.
   i. There can be no exceptions to this policy.
   j. A full report will be sent to you by the department chairman.
   k. Decentralization of the word processing centre was suggested by the report to improve work flow and reduce noise.
   l. You are not allowed to miss work if you don't have a good reason.
   m. At the present time the consensus of opinion is that employee turnover will increase during the month of May.
   n. Your performance was totally unsatisfactory.
   o. The purposes of the meeting was: (1) to communicate personnel policies; (2) encouragement of participation in in-service training programs; and (3) introducing several new employees.
   p. The report was intended for Fred and I, not for John and Susan.
   q. Each of the following pages have been proofread by the editorial staff.
   r. In accordance with your request, attached herewith is the surplus inventory report.
   s. Smoking is not permitted anywhere except in the lobby.
   t. We beg to inform you that unless you act soon, the contract will expire.

5. Examine the following letter, which was sent to a student inquiring about admission to a program and course credit for a business correspondence course.

a. List at least five problems with the letter.
b. Rewrite the letter so that these problems are corrected.

Dear Prospective Student

We are in receipt of your letter of March 15. Our Administrative Management program is very popular and we generally have an extensive waiting list. You are, therefore, well advised to inquire about admission well in advance of the registration deadline.

We're not certain that the correspondence course you referred to in your letter is equivalent to the one which is taught in the Administrative Management program. However, it appears that the course content is similar and that it will be given credit. Course credit applications are considered only after a student is admitted to the program.

The application process is quite complex. First an application form must be completed. Students must also prove they have the necessary prerequisites for the program. Basically though, students need a Grade 12 diploma with a C+ average.

A copy of our calendar is enclosed along with an application form. Applications must be submitted by May 31.

We appreciate your interest in our program.

Sincerely

Discussion Cases

An Expensive Lesson[4]

Jane Adams is a sales representative, College Division, for Bowan Publishing Limited. Her duties include visiting each college and university campus in her sales territory to meet new professors, to promote new textbooks and manuals, to supply information about upcoming publications, and to visit faculty members, both those who are currently using Bowan publications and those who are not, to persuade them to reorder or order texts that Bowan publishes. As well, her position requires her to promote a positive image of Bowan in the academic community.

continued

Ms. Adams decided not to visit Lakehead University in the spring even though she knew that professors order their texts for the fall term in April. Instead she sent the following letter:

Dear Secretary:

Please distribute these pamphlets and information sheets to the appropriate professors. If there is not enough, please put on circulation or copy. Should there be any books which the professors would like more information on, please contact me, as I would be happy to supply them.

Sincerely,

Professor Harry Gordon, a business communications instructor, had been using Bowan texts in his courses for three years. Generally, he had been satisfied with the texts and planned to use them at least one more year. However, after reading the letter, he decided not to reorder from Bowan; he also convinced three other instructors to do the same. Consequently, Bowan Publishing Limited lost a $10 000 order.

Case Questions

1. Were Professor Gordon and his colleagues justified in ordering texts from a new publishing firm?
2. What image of Ms. Adams and Bowan Publishing Limited does the letter project?
3. What principles of effective written communication are violated?
4. How would you interpret the statement "please put on circulation or copy"?

Creative Shirt Makers[5]

Creative Shirt Makers, your employer, is a Vancouver firm that specializes in making tailor-made dress shirts for men. The firm has been in business for five years. Business has tripled in volume since it started. Its shirts are sold through some specialty men's stores throughout the province, but a majority are made to order and sold

continued

directly to customers who appreciate high-quality tailoring.

This morning you received a letter from an influential customer, Yvonne Laroche of Prince George. Her November 15 order for ten tailor-made dress shirts that she planned to give her husband as a Christmas present totalled $550. Her letter reported that, when the courier delivered the shirts, the box was damaged and all of the shirts had blue ink stains on them. Naturally, she is very anxious to have the shirts replaced so that she will have them in time for Christmas.

In the five years you've been in business, this is the first time the courier has lost or damaged an order. After inspecting the shipping cartons, the courier reported they were not strong enough to withstand shipping. However, they agreed to pay you $250 — their maximum payment for uninsured items.

Your dilemma is that you cannot duplicate the entire shipment in the two weeks before Christmas. Several bolts of the cloth that Mrs. Laroche selected are on back order and you are two days behind schedule as it is. Nevertheless, because Mrs. Laroche is such a good customer, you will try to complete five of the shirts you have material for.

Case Questions

1. Considering the above information and the feelings of the customer, determine what you will say in the letter. Use the effective writing principles you have learned.
2. What is the purpose of the letter? What do you need to take into account about the receiver and the context? What will be your opening paragraph? What will be your explanation? What will be your closing paragraph?

Chapter 6

Clear Thinking and Argument

Learning Objectives

In this chapter, you'll learn how to judge whether an argument is logical and convincing or ineffective, and how to communicate the reasons for this judgement. More specifically, you will be able to:

1. recognize the importance of clear and logical thinking in business communication
2. distinguish between communication messages intended as arguments, and other forms of messages
3. distinguish between deductive and inductive argument
4. recognize the main fallacies that occur in arguments
5. describe some of the ethical problems involved in arguments

Preview Case

Erica Klausen, a recent graphic arts graduate, has been hired by Graphix Page Inc. to produce technical drawings for training manuals. Since most of her training focused on basic design principles and on the use of various graphics software, she has decided to purchase a computer so that she can develop her technical drawing skills at home. Besides, several of her friends have been able to make extra money doing contract work in the evenings and on weekends.

Because of her limited experience, Erica decides to ask some of her friends and colleagues to recommend two or three good computer retailers. She wants one who is knowledgeable about what products are available, but still offers competitive prices.

At coffee on Monday morning, Erica says to no one in particular, "I'm thinking of buying a computer system to use at home, but I don't know where to start. I've heard so much about firms that try to sell you their particular system even if it's not what you really need. Does anyone have any suggestions?"

Jarvis Peters is the first to reply. "I bought my system at a little place on Kingsway — Microworks — and I'm quite pleased with their service. They carry several systems and the sales clerk really took the time to find out what capabilities I needed. Besides, I think their prices are the best in town."

Denise Wong reacted strongly. "I wouldn't deal with Microworks if they were the last company in town. I bought my system there two years ago. My monitor literally blew up after only six months. When I went back to get warranty service, they told me that I had to go to the manufacturer. The manufacturer took three weeks to complete the repairs. I had to rent another monitor at my own expense, even though my monitor was still under warranty. I'm taking Microworks to small claims court next month to recover my expenses."

The conversation continued back and forth among the six or seven people at coffee. When Erica returned to her desk, she felt more confused than enlightened. For every satisfied customer, there was someone who had a horror story. What was she to do?

Overview

Erica's dilemma is typical of those we face every day at work or at college. We get conflicting arguments for and against a particular course of action. These arguments come in all shapes and sizes. Reading the newspaper over breakfast or listening to the morning news, we are influenced by people or organizations trying to convince us of the correctness of their views on everything from the best value in cereal to the candidate most deserving of our vote in the next election.

At college, we are expected to evaluate what we read in books and articles, and to produce reports and papers that are logical and well organized. At work, we may have reports to read (and write) in which it will be extremely important to judge whether the conclusions and recommendations reached are correct or not.

As we advance in our careers, the ability to think clearly becomes ever more important. Quick and accurate judgements have to be made about many people's arguments and submissions. So important is thinking clearly in relation to our own and others' ideas that even imagining a successful person who does not have this ability is difficult.

Differentiating between logical and illogical arguments is an important business skill

The purpose of this chapter is to introduce the main types of argument used in everyday life, with a view to recognizing a phoney argument when we see one, and to convincingly demonstrating — to ourselves and our "opponents" — the reasons for such a judgement. Most people have a rough, instinctive idea of the value of an argument, but lack the ability to put forward the exact reasons why the argument is good or bad.

Qualities of an Argument

Arguments occur in everyday life in the form of political speeches, newspaper editorials, letters to the editor, reports and submissions, sales brochures, and so on. However, not all communication falls into the category of a deliberately reasoned argument.

Understanding the qualities of an argument is important. Here is a preliminary definition that works in most instances: an *argument* is a piece of speech or writing that not only makes statements we are expected to believe but uses these statements as the reasons for other statements, which we are also expected to believe.[1] Obviously, not all, or even most, messages fall into this category.

Arguments differ from other kinds of speaking and writing. For example, narrative accounts of a sales meeting or the history of an industrial dispute simply present information; therefore, they are not arguments. Similarly, our descriptions of an organizational structure, the layout of a plant, or a brilliant manager are not arguments because we are not making statements to be used as convincing reasons for other statements.

Arguments differ from other kinds of speaking and writing

An argument has three essential elements:

1. at least one statement that is the point or conclusion of the argument
2. at least one statement that is alleged to support it
3. a signal or suggestion that an argument is happening, often indicated by expressions such as *therefore*, *points to the conclusion that*, *because*, and *in view of the fact that*

Examples

All employees must punch the time clock.
I am an employee.
Therefore, I must punch the clock.

Statements 1 and 2 are supporting statements. Statement 3 is the statement that is being reasoned for, the one that we are expected to believe on the basis of the first two. The word *therefore* signals that an argument is being advanced, that is, we are being asked to believe something on the basis of supporting statements.

As the next example shows, these elements can be presented in a different order:

My pet likes meat [conclusion] because [indicator that an argument is being constructed] all dogs like meat [first supporting statement] and my pet is a dog [second supporting statement].

In this argument, the conclusion depends on other statements that we are expected to believe. This mental process is quite different from simply describing one's pet eating meat, deploring the animal's carnivorous tendencies, or comparing people and their pets to determine how much they have in common.

We have reviewed the general qualities of arguments because the first step in clear thinking is knowing whether a message is an argument. This step precedes decisions about what type of argument is being considered or whether it is effective or not.

Inductive and Deductive Arguments

Although the philosophical aspects of clear thinking and sound argument can be exceedingly complex (logic forms a major part of courses in philosophy at universities), students of business communication can gain enough knowledge for practical use by grasping the main features of two very broad categories of argument: inductive and deductive. These two categories cover most of the arguments we are likely to analyze or construct in business situations.

Inductive Reasoning

Induction argues from the particular to the general

Inductive reasoning is a surprisingly simple process. It occurs whenever we reach general statements or conclusions on the basis of particular facts and cases. Because so many scientific conclusions are reached this way (that is, by observing hundreds and sometimes thousands of facts gained from experiments), inductive reasoning is often called the *scientific method*.

In many situations, we cannot hope to examine every single example of a phenomenon, particularly if some of these examples are going to occur in the future. We are forced to rely on inductive reasoning if we wish to reach conclusions about what does, might, or will happen.

For instance, when medical researchers conclude that smoking tobacco is unhealthy, they base this general conclusion (applying in the future as well as the past, if all other conditions are similar) on investigation of a certain number of particular cases. Even if this number is very large — say, several million people who smoke — it still does not cover every person who has ever smoked or who will ever smoke. The conclusion, therefore, that smoking is bad for you is inductive. In inductive reasoning, the size of the sample investigated is an important factor in judging the validity of an argument. Arguments based on a very small sample have a greater likelihood of error. In the case of smoking, only after the results of several hundred studies became available were tobacco companies required to place health warnings on cigarette packages.

Opinion polls and market research techniques are common examples of the inductive process at work. We examine a sample, and argue that what is characteristic of the sample will be characteristic of the whole group. By such methods, the results of elections can be predicted with a high degree of accuracy.

Most inductive arguments are one of three types: generalization, causal relationship, and analogy.[2]

Generalization

A generalization draws a conclusion about all cases that is based on the data from some cases. As such, generalization corresponds most closely to the explanation already given of inductive reasoning. It is the most obvious example of induction at work. We often make judgements without observing every possible situation or fact. Our views on the nature of polar bears, for example, are not based on the behaviour of every single polar bear that has ever lived. Nevertheless, by making generalizations, we can describe behaviours typical of polar bears: they are often found on ice floes and can tolerate very cold temperatures.

Generalization is a form of inductive reasoning

A generalization is formed by taking the "inductive leap." It can never be more than a statement of probability. The probability that a generalization is true varies considerably. For example, it is so probable that the sun will rise tomorrow that it is virtually certain; it is also highly probable, but less certain, that we will still be alive tomorrow; it is still probable, but somewhat less certain, that we will not be in a car accident tomorrow. But for thousands of Canadians each year, the improbable does happen and they are killed in automobiles, despite the strength of the generalization that it won't happen to them, based on their experience of many days without accident.

If generalizations are so simple, why do so many people reach generalizations that we think are stupid or dangerous? In business, managers who operate on the basis of faulty generalizations are likely to cause problems for their organizations. A view that all unions are run by extremists is likely to cause industrial relations problems, even though it may be true that some unions, some of the time, have members or leaders who hold radical views.

Care must be taken with generalizations

You need to be aware of two dangers when making generalizations:

Don't argue from a sample that is too small: "Don't buy a computer from Microworks. I bought one last year and the service was terrible."

The generalization here is that Microworks always or very often provides poor service. Because it is based on only one instance, this generalization is not very reliable, and we would be unwise to put much faith in it. On the other hand, if we know of hundreds of other dissatisfied Microworks customers, as well as of satisfied customers of other computer stores, we are in a much better position to make such a generalization with some confidence and authority. Faced with conflicting data, Erica Klausen, in our scenario at the beginning of the chapter, could have phoned the Better Business Bureau to get a more complete picture.

Make sure that your sample is reasonably representative of the whole.

Your sample should be reasonably representative of the whole

We cannot generalize about Canadians' attitudes to poverty if we talk only to millionaires; nor can we generalize about the benefits of nuclear power if we survey only employees of power companies. In each case, our sample must reflect as accurately as possible the whole group about which we are going to make the generalization.

When making or challenging generalizations, we must be careful of the small but very important terms *all*, *no*, *some*, *few*, *most*. If the generalization begins with *all* or *no*, even one exception destroys its reliability. We can allow for less certainty if we acknowledge we are talking only about *some* or *a few*. In this case, however, the generalization becomes less useful. For example, no one would want to fly with Air Canada if all we could say was that *some* flights arrive safely!

Causal Relationship

Cause-and-effect relationships are another kind of inductive reasoning

Establishing a cause-and-effect relationship between two things is also a form of inductive reasoning. In this type of reasoning, two events are taken into account to see if one caused the other. Causal relations can be considered in three kinds of problems.

The first is one in which two conditions exist that suggest one may in some way be responsible for the other. We must test to see if one really is the cause, or perhaps somehow connected to the cause, of the other:

- You turn on the television set and suddenly all the lights in the house go out.
- There is an $8542 error in the monthly cash flow in your video shop, and you have observed that one of the shop assistants, who earns $210 a week, has just bought an expensive new car.
- The cafeteria food smells "off" and the kitchen refrigerator is very old and sounds as if it's not working properly.

In these three examples, two conditions exist. The logical task is to determine what, if any, cause-and-effect relationship exists between them.

In the second kind of problem, a condition exists, and we must find out what caused it. The result, or effect, is known, so the logical task is to work back from the effect to the cause:

- The body of a dead man is found lying in a ditch alongside the road. Who or what killed him?
- You keep getting error messages on the screen of your computer. What is wrong?
- There is a bottleneck in the shipping department, with many complaints from customers not receiving their orders on time. Who or what is responsible?

Finally, consider the type of problem in which we know what condition exists, and we need to know what will probably result from it. In this case, we know the cause and are trying to find the result or effect. We are reasoning from cause to effect:

- The Prime Minister of India has been assassinated. What effect will this have on the people?
- I have turned the computer off while it is still working on one of the disks. What effect will this have on the files on the disk?
- There is a bottleneck in the shipping department. What effect will this have on my most important customers?

In real life, a simple relationship between one clearcut cause and one clearcut effect hardly ever exists. An effect of one cause becomes a cause of another effect and so on, until you have a long line of such causes and effects:

Jim Paterson dropped out of school as soon as he could. Therefore, he did not get a well-paying job. Therefore, when he had a family of his own, he had to struggle to make ends meet. Therefore, he took to drinking heavily to forget his problems. Therefore, he often had hangovers when he arrived at work and so made many mistakes. Therefore, there were many delays in the shipping department.

Obviously, this could go on almost forever. Thinking that any result has such a simple or single cause is naive. Many people who left school early are not alcoholics.

For these reasons, great care must be taken before assuming that one thing is the principal or only cause of another. To test this type of reasoning in practice, three questions can be asked:

- How probable is it that the cause you are considering could produce this effect unaided?
- Could the cause you are considering be only one of several that, operating at the same time, could produce this effect?
- Does some condition exist that could alter the relationship that you would normally expect between the causes and effects you are considering?

The difference between a necessary and a sufficient cause

A useful distinction to keep in mind when deciding what sort of relationship exists between a cause and an effect is the subtle difference between a necessary and a sufficient cause. A *necessary cause* is one that must be present for something to happen but is not in itself enough to bring about that particular result. For example, some capital is necessary to set up a successful business, but capital in itself is not enough without planning, hard work, and the right economic circumstances. Likewise, oxygen is needed for combustion to take place, but the mere presence of oxygen does not cause a fire.

A *sufficient cause* is one that is more than just necessary — it alone is sufficient for the result to occur. In this sense, a bullet through the heart could be called a sufficient cause of death.

Grasping this distinction between necessary and sufficient causes makes it much easier to be more certain of what relationships may exist between two events or circumstances.

Analogy

Analogy is a third type of inductive reasoning

An analogy is essentially a comparison between two things, the purpose of which is to determine whether, because a similarity exists between the two in some areas, they are similar in other ways as well.

To argue by means of comparison is very common. Politicians often make assertions about the national economy on the basis of what can or cannot happen in a household budget. In the case of cafeteria food that smells "off," each of the members of a committee set up to solve the problem might offer solutions based on his or her experience of similar situations (in other words, by means of analogies).

For example, one committee member might compare the food with what he used to eat at summer camp and conclude that the problem might be caused by a bad cook. Another might think of other examples of poor service caused when a licensee has a monopoly, and might recommend that a competing cafeteria service be set up. A third person might recall what happened at home when the fridge started to act up, and recommend an overhaul of the kitchen equipment. In each case, an argument is being made from analogy because each person is comparing this situation with another with which it has something in common and concluding that other important things also are similar.

Arguing by analogy is a useful method. But to test whether the analogy fits in each particular case, we must ask the question: are the two things similar in the characteristics that are important for this analogy?

In the above example, the first conclusion might be invalid because the personnel officer is sure that the cook is a well-qualified chef; the second might not hold because this catering firm also has an exclusive contract at another plant and there are no complaints there; and the third could be invalid because the problem is not constant, but happens only at certain times of the month.

When using or testing analogies, determine what is essential to the problem, and then see what similarities and differences exist between two cases.

Deductive Reasoning

Deductive reasoning moves from the general to the particular

Whereas inductive reasoning describes reaching general conclusions based on the observation of particular facts or instances, deductive reasoning proceeds from general or universal truths to conclusions that are particular applications of general ones.

For example, the company you work for might have a general rule that all employees must take their vacations within the calendar year they are due or forfeit them. From this, you deduce that you must take your vacation within the year. In this case, you have reached a conclusion by an obvious and simple logical process in which you have moved from the general to the particular. The name given to this process is deductive reasoning.

At work in deductive reasoning is a classification process: deciding in which category a given item belongs. In the above example, we have classified ourselves as employees in order to see that what applies to the general category of employees also applies to us. This classification might be more difficult if the company distinguishes between staff and employees, or hires part-time or seasonal workers.

Deduction is often a three-step process

Deductive reasoning can be summarized as a three-step process:

Universal statement:	**People who scuba dive like to take risks.**
Individual case:	**Joan is a scuba diver.**
Conclusion about this case:	**Joan likes to take risks.**

There are technical names for this process and complex rules governing the various forms it can take, but for our purposes in business communication seeing how the process works in practice is more important. Strictly speaking, the above example does not tell us whether our conclusion is true, only that it logically follows from the first two statements or premises.

Deduction is only as good as the quality of these premises. In the above example, it must be true that all scuba divers like taking risks and that Joan is really a scuba diver. Only if both these statements are 100-percent true (and in this example, this is surely not the case — we need to know of only one exception) can they be used to prove that Joan likes to take risks.

This argument cannot be used the other way around. Just because all scuba divers like taking risks, it does not follow that everyone who likes taking risks is a scuba diver. Similarly, it does not follow that, because Joan likes to take risks, she must also be a scuba diver. Using the classification system, we can place scuba divers within the larger category of all those who like to take risks. There is room in this category for people who participate in other risky sports.

No one would be likely to accept this argument about Joan's liking for risk-taking because it is overly dogmatic about a whole class of people. But groups of people *are* classified, mostly unfairly, every day of the week. For example, some people believe that everyone who collects welfare is lazy or that anyone who really wants to work can find a job.

Deductive reasoning is easily misused

People frequently build faulty arguments on this type of classification. In the letters to the editor sections of newspapers, we can read that unions are trying to ruin the country or that public servants do nothing but fritter away taxpayers' money. The wish to argue by classifying is a strong one. Human nature seems to want to stereotype people or lump them into categories to cope with them and avoid the difficult task of treating every case on its own merits. Deductive reasoning must be examined carefully for such flaws.

Deductive reasoning rarely seems to fit easily into the three-step form described above. Here is a piece of dialogue that relies on deductive reasoning for its argument:

"I'm afraid my father can't get around as easily as he used to."
"Well, he's getting on, isn't he?"

Putting this argument into deductive form, we get the following:

All old people are too feeble to get around on their own.
Your father is an old person.
Therefore, your father cannot get around on his own.

In this case, we can accept the conclusion only if we can accept the first and second statements. Deductive arguments stand or fall on the quality of these statements. Are they true? Are they true in every single case? It's only then that we can argue with the degree of certainty that is never possible in an inductive argument. The test with deduction is to make sure the assumptions are accurate and that each item under consideration is being correctly classified. In the above example, even if it were true that old people can't get around on their own, the father may not be correctly classified as an old person.

Common Fallacies in Argument

Flaws in arguments are called fallacies

As we have seen, each of the three main ways of using inductive reasoning as well as the process of deduction can be either used to good purpose or misused. We can misuse them either deliberately or unconsciously. To argue misleadingly on purpose is unethical. To argue illogically without realizing it will lead, at the very least, to embarrassment and possibly to serious consequences.

Usually, faulty arguments occur in a discourse (a body of spoken or written language) that is not a purely intellectual argument but a mixture of reasoning and other, more emotional and subjective elements. Aim for the ability to convincingly put forward a logical case in reports and submissions, and to be able to point out the weaknesses in the arguments of others.

A *fallacy* describes one or other of the many types of faulty reasoning that can occur. Fallacies, however, are not strictly the misuse of a logical process. They can also involve the masquerading of other uses of language as arguments when no argument is really present.

There are many common fallacies

Some common fallacies are outlined below. Try to recognize and explain the misuse of language and/or reasoning occurring in each. Included are fallacies that arise when subjective factors are put forth in place of argument, problems caused by the faulty use of evidence and other forms of material, and problems caused by a faulty logical process applied to that material.

Argument Against the Person

In this type of argument, a point of view is discredited by discrediting the person associated with it. The argument is attacked by trying to destroy the reputation. For example, a fast-food chain puts money into research on recycling yet continues to use nonrecyclable containers. Therefore, it makes no sense to support recycling research.

Misuse of Authority

The use of an authority can be convincing only when that person is an authority on the topic being discussed. Used otherwise, it is misleading and irrelevant. For example, the Prime Minister believes that there should be more French-Canadian scorers on the national hockey team. The coaches should therefore make the necessary changes as soon as possible.

Appeal to Common Sense

Using this approach, the speaker tries to win support for his or her case by implying that "everyone" already agrees with this position, and that to disagree is to be out of touch with reality. Such an argument might run: "You only have to read the newspapers to know that the crime rate is skyrocketing. Everybody knows it's time the government brought in higher fines and longer jail sentences."

Criticism Forestaller

A dishonest trick in an argument is the use of words and phrases designed to make fair criticism of the argument more difficult. For example, a woman whose letter to a newspaper condemning pornography is signed "Mother of eight" is making it harder to reasonably disagree with her point of view. One is almost attacking motherhood by doing so!

Emotionally Charged Language

No matter how rational we may think we are, we are affected by emotionally charged language, by the subjective feelings we associate with some words. Yet these associations are usually irrelevant to the logical strength or weakness of the argument. For example, as soon as we describe our opponents as "do-gooders" or "bleeding-heart liberals," we are colouring the argument unfairly. Everyone has deep-seated prejudices, and these are easily triggered by emotionally charged words. Depending on their point of view, the label "communist" or "capitalist" is enough to make rational debate impossible for many people.

Absolute Terms

Like emotionally charged language, the use of absolutes such as *always*, *never*, *hopeless*, *countless*, and *infinite* are likely to sway an argument unreasonably. Absolute terms are hardly ever accurate in a world that is mostly relative. It is simply not true that unions are always on strike, that companies never care about the welfare of their employees, that the cleaner is always late. The use of absolutes may be sometimes emotionally satisfying to the user, but such statements usually fly in the face of logic. Absolutes are often indicators of a desperate argument and should be avoided for this reason alone.

Faulty Generalization

Two types of faulty generalization were discussed in the section on inductive reasoning. Hasty generalizations base a conclusion on too little evidence. Unrepresentative generalizations base a conclusion on evidence atypical of the whole. For example, generalizations about Canadian society based on what only a few people think or only people in Toronto think are likely to be faulty.

"After This, Therefore Because of This"

This fallacy is an abuse of the causal relations component of inductive reasoning. Many people are strongly tempted to assume that because one thing happens before another, it is the cause of it. Such claims must always be treated sceptically, and other, more convincing evidence produced. For example:

> Before Martina Gorenko became company president, the firm had 100 employees and annual gross sales of $5 million. In four years, those figures more than doubled. Gorenko has certainly done great things for the business.

> Vitamin C can cure your ailments. I had a cold last week but it cleared up a few days after I started taking massive doses of Vitamin C.

False Analogy

False analogy, another misuse of inductive reasoning, is an argument resting on a comparison of two situations that are essentially different. For example, human society is often compared to a living organism. While useful up to a point, the analogy is misused if one implication is that a particular person should be the dictatorial head while all the others in society are just the limbs or working slaves.

False Classification

False classification is a misuse of deductive reasoning. It assumes that only two choices exist when several may be available. Another term for it is the "black-or-white fallacy." It does not allow for the full range of positions that can be taken on an issue.

Often the fallacy comes in the following form: John comes to work in jeans and a T-shirt. The only other people who come to work similarly dressed work in the warehouse. John must also work in the warehouse.

Misuse of Statistics

Statistics are an indispensable part of nearly every business discussion. Few business proposals carry much weight without convincing figures. However, it is worth remembering the adage "There are lies, damned lies, and statistics." Statistics can be easily misused, and should be treated with extreme caution.

A common misuse of statistics is the average weekly wage. When politicians try to convince us how high the standard of living in Canada is by pointing to average weekly earnings, they conveniently ignore the fact that more than half of Canadian wage-earners earn less than this figure. One needs only to listen to parliamentary reports to learn that politicians from different parties are likely to use different statistics for just about everything, including rates of inflation and unemployment.

Many other technical categories of fallacy exist, but these are some of the most commonly occurring ones. In most cases, little more than a critical scrutiny is needed to pick them out and show what is wrong with them.

Summary

The ability to distinguish logical and illogical arguments is an important business skill.

Arguments have three main qualities:

- the point or conclusion
- a supporting statement
- an argument signal

The two main types of arguments are inductive and deductive:

- inductive reasoning (or the scientific method) argues from particular examples to general statements and can include generalizations, causal relationships, or analogies

- deductive reasoning moves from the general to the particular and involves a three-step process: universal statement, individual case, conclusion about the case.

Arguments can include eleven types of flaws or fallacies:

- argument against the person
- misuse of authority
- appeal to common sense
- criticism forestaller
- emotionally charged language
- absolute terms
- faulty generalizations
- "after this, therefore because of this"
- false analogy
- false classification
- misuse of statistics

Review Questions

1. Why is clear and logical thinking important in all aspects of business communication?
2. How can you identify messages intended as arguments?
3. What is the main difference between inductive and deductive arguments?
4. What makes a generalization effective?
5. What makes a causal relationship effective?
6. What makes an analogy effective?
7. What are the limitations of deductive reasoning?
8. Generate your own examples to illustrate each of the eleven common fallacies in argument.

Activities

1. Are the following arguments? If so, what is the conclusion, and what is the signal or indicator? (If the indicator is presumed rather than stated, suggest an appropriate one.) *Note:* You are not asked to state whether these are good or bad arguments, but simply to determine if arguments are being made and, if so, how and why you know this.
   a. The company must be refusing to meet the union's terms, because the union has called a strike.
   b. I have a cup of coffee before I begin work in the mornings. After that, I go to my office.
   c. Each evening before dinner, I have a scotch and ice. It is a well-known fact that a little alcohol helps the digestive system tremendously.

   d. Every morning my boss arrives at the office in a bad mood. I am sure it will be the same thing tomorrow.
   e. I'm not travelling by bus any more. Every time I've been on one recently, it has been in an accident.
   f. If it is true that the managing director has been misusing company funds, then he should be dismissed.

2. Each of the following statements gives some evidence for a generalization. Rate each one according to the following scale: extremely reliable (error highly unlikely); well-supported (convincing for ordinary purposes); not reliable (not convincing enough to be accepted). Be prepared to justify whatever ratings you give.
   a. The poor level of care one can expect doctors to give under Medicare is shown by the surgeon who boasted of doing six operations in one day. This is what happens with socialized medicine.
   b. I didn't realize what the most popular soft drinks in this suburb were until my son started collecting cans in the park last Sunday. Behind the kiosk he collected 58 Fizzo cans, 39 Pinkpop cans, and 16 Bluecola cans. Fizzo and Pinkpop are definitely the most popular in our suburb.
   c. We carried out a poll in our suburb to see how many people supported the idea of an extra garbage collection each week. Of the first hundred people we saw in the street, 62 said yes, 20 said no, and 18 said they didn't care. It's obvious the majority wants more garbage service.
   d. I have been riding up and down in the elevator for the past fifteen years. Now they want to carry out a safety inspection. This is a waste of time and money because the elevator is obviously safe.
   e. While shopping in Paris, I never encountered a sales assistant who did not speak very good English. It is not necessary to speak French to shop in France.
3. Challenge each of the following generalizations by citing some conflicting evidence:
   a. Free enterprise produces the highest standard of living.
   b. The reason that there are wars is that it is in human nature to like to fight.
   c. The best movies are love stories.
   d. Natural resources should be used for the benefit of mankind.
4. Make up three generalizations about Canadian society that conform to the following requirements:
   a. One that you believe to be true, and are sure most people also believe.
   b. One that you believe to be true, but know most people reject.

c. One that you believe to be false, but know most people accept.

5. Assess the plausibility of the following arguments based on making causal relationships. If relevant, distinguish between necessary and sufficient causes in your explanations.
   a. Recent thefts of large amounts of beef and veal from the hotel kitchen have occurred since the new chef was hired. I suggest we fire him immediately.
   b. Last week, I was completely covered by a rash. I put on some aloe vera cream, and this week it has cleared up completely. Aloe vera cream is great for all kinds of skin problems.
   c. Since the new Prime Minister was elected, there has been a marked upturn in the Canadian economy. If only she had been elected earlier, we might not have had any recession.
   d. The most recent bushfires in Manitoba were caused by strong winds and unusually hot days.
   e. The company is run by an incompetent managing director who spends most of the day at a club. The local product is not as good as what we can import. These are the reasons why we have gone bankrupt.
   f. Every new customer who came into the store brought the handbill we delivered to letter boxes in this suburb. The reason for our increase in sales is this new form of advertising we have tried.

6. a. Consider the following statement: Four-wheel-drive station wagons have experienced tremendous sales since they were introduced in the United States. There is no reason they will not be equally successful in Canada and Africa.
      (1) What analogy is being made?
      (2) Make a list of the characteristics the United States, Canada, and Africa share that could justify this sales forecast.
      (3) Make a list of the differences that you think would affect the relative sales of four-wheel-drives.
      (4) What seem to be essential similarities and differences likely to affect this forecast?
   b. Identify the area of comparison for each of the following analogies, and determine what similarities and differences should be taken into account in evaluating them:
      (1) A dangerous person, like a wild beast, threatens the security of the people. Society gains when a dangerous beast is destroyed, and so it must gain when dangerous criminals are done away with.
      (2) The prudent housekeeper does not go into debt to buy the week's groceries. Likewise, we should never allow our government to run a budget deficit.

(3) New York has an efficient, 24-hour-a-day public transit system. Why can't Halifax have one too?
(4) In Switzerland, the government relies on the citizens to arrange to pay their income tax at the end of the year. Why can't a similar scheme operate in Canada?

7. A common form of criticism is to discredit an argument by attacking the reputation of the person who posed it. Offer an example of an argument from a newspaper, magazine, or any other relevant source in which you describe:
   a. the substance of the argument
   b. the identity of the arguer
   c. the nature of the misguided critic's attack against the arguer (be aware that if you agree with the critic, it is easy to overlook his or her fallacious reasoning)
8. What fallacies, if any, are present in the following statements? Discuss each fully.
   a. Art is unimportant because it is inaccessible to the poor.
   b. If Karl Marx had earned more money, maybe he would have known more about economics.
9. Advertisements often use the tricks of logic and rhetoric discussed in this chapter. Collect at least three advertisements from newspapers and magazines that blatantly argue a case without providing sufficient justification in their arguments.

Discussion Cases

Conflicting Views

Your local newspaper has been reporting in great detail the confrontations between environmentalists and loggers over the proposed logging of an old-growth forest stand. Several people, including Anthony Lowden, president of Treehigh Logging Inc., have written letters to the editor. The one sent by Mr. Lowden reads:

Dear Sir:

I am appalled and sickened by the latest round of protests of a bunch of bleeding-heart liberals who want to sacrifice well-paying jobs in the forest industry for low-paying jobs in the tourist industry.

Everyone knows that our high standard of living depends on our ability to harvest our natural resources and process them for the highly lucrative

continued

American and Japanese export markets. Unless we get on with the Forest Management Project (FMP) proposed by the local forestry consortium, the provincial economy will deteriorate even farther than it already has.

The FMP provides for the replanting of more trees than we've ever planted before. It also makes provision for public access to logged areas on the road system once active logging has been completed. This improved access alone should encourage more tourist trade.

If the environmentalists would spend less time blocking logging and more time getting their facts straight, we'd all be a lot better off.

Sincerely,

A. Lowden, President
Treehigh Logging Inc.

Case Questions

1. Is this letter likely to be published in the local newspaper? Why or why not?
2. Analyze the letter in detail, picking out all the devices of argument and word choice that the writer uses. Comment on the validity of their use in this case.
3. In a single paragraph, summarize how convincing the argument in this letter is to you.

Protect the Environment

As a market analyst at McMartin Inc., 16 South Boardwalk, Halifax, NS, H5J 3T9, your job is to conduct market studies on new products. New products are developed regularly by McMartin. Not all products are economically profitable; therefore, these studies are important. Your approval means substantial funds may be budgeted to produce the finished product.

A product for market testing has been assigned to you: two-in-one canvas shopping bags. The developer, Dr. Harry Peabody, claims the product will encourage people to stop using paper and plastic bags when they go shopping. "Everyone's concerned about the environment these days. Several supermarket chains are even offering discounts to people who reuse their plastic bags," says

continued

Peabody. "One bag is hardly enough for any serious shopping trip. By having bags fit into one or more exterior pockets on the main bag, people can have additional bags with them at all times."

Peabody sounds convincing, but McMartin's management knows that market demand, as opposed to an inventor's sales pitch, determines profits. You have surveyed 2500 volunteers at an area university to get their reaction to the reusable shopping bags. The responses to free samples of the bags are as follows:

1. Which styles do you prefer?

Male		**Female**	
two-bag model	20%	two-bag model	75%
three-bag model	80%	three-bag model	25%

2. Which colours do you prefer?

Male		**Female**	
White	30%	White	50%
Coloured	25%	Pastel	35%
Plaid	45%	Flowered	15%

3. What would you change about this product?

Colour	10%	Durability	30%
Fit	20%	Nothing	40%

4. Would you buy this product if it were available on the market today, priced at about $4.50 each?

Male		**Female**	
Yes	60%	Yes	75%
No	40%	No	25%

5. What form of media do you spend most hours with in an average week?

Television	60%	Newspaper	20%
Radio	10%	Magazines	10%
Number of Males	1552	Number of Females	948

Case Questions

1. What type of reasoning does this situation require? Why?
2. What conclusions can you draw from these data? For each conclusion, be sure to provide two supporting statements.
3. How valid are your conclusions likely to be? Why?

Chapter 7

Standard Formats for Letters and Memos

Learning Objectives

In this chapter, you'll learn how to use standard formats to prepare effective letters and memos. More specifically, you will be able to:

1. recognize the importance of the appearance of letters
2. use white space to make information accessible
3. identify the major parts of a letter
4. identify those additional letter parts that are used only occasionally
5. recognize punctuation styles commonly used in letters
6. explain why memos are important internal communications in an organization
7. recognize why memos are important
8. use an appropriate format for your memos

Preview Case

While a student, Bill Singh looked forward to three things: graduating, getting a job, and having his own secretary. He had expected the three events to occur more or less simultaneously, but that wasn't the way it worked out. At the time he graduated, Bill did not have a job; in fact, it took him six months to find one. Two years ago, he was hired as an assistant office manager, the position he presently holds. He does not yet have his own secretary, and he isn't likely to get one in the near future. When he needs a secretary, he uses one from the secretarial pool, if one is available. Otherwise he's on his own. Of these experiences, he says, "It's not exactly as I expected it would be — it's not enough to know how to compose a good letter; you've got to be able to put the whole thing together."

After several unpleasant episodes, Bill learned that the availability of a secretary does not necessarily ensure accuracy. When his boss found errors in two of his reports, Bill blamed them on secretaries. That was also when he learned that he was responsible for the content and appearance of his correspondence and reports, regardless of who had typed them. As his boss expressed it, "When you sign it, you're testifying to its accuracy." Bill learned the hard way that he must be knowledgeable about every aspect of business communication.

Overview

Much of the meaning of any message is nonverbal. If you close your eyes when talking with someone, you miss a large part of the message. The same principle applies to business writing. The reader sees many cues in addition to the verbal message. These cues, which together constitute appearance, create the first impression that the reader forms of the message and of its writer.

The appearance of a message should meet reader expectations without calling attention to itself

While the content of a message is certainly more important than its appearance, an appropriate appearance increases the likelihood of its being read. A written message must meet certain expectations if it is to be read and taken seriously. In this chapter, we focus on those expectations and what you should do to meet them. Since message content is of primary importance, the appearance should not call attention to itself. Instead, by meeting the reader's expectations, the appearance of a message should subtly aid communication.

The Appearance of a Letter

The overall appearance of an organization's correspondence will be influenced by:

1. The stationery
2. The letterhead
3. The use of white space

Stationery

One of the first things a reader notices about a letter or memo is the stationery. An important characteristic of stationery, of course, is that it is both seen and felt.

Good-quality stationery enhances the message

Since stationery should not detract from the message, it should be of the same quality as stationery used in most business organizations. Good-quality paper meets public expectations and sustains the image of your organization. Envelopes and second pages should be of the same quality as the company stationery.

The most common size of sheet is 21.6 cm by 27.9 cm (8 1/2 by 11 inches), but some executives use Monarch-size sheets of 18.4 cm by 26.7 cm (7 1/4 by 10 1/2 inches). Half sheets, 21.6 cm by 14.0 cm (8 1/2 by 5 1/2 inches), are often used for brief internal messages, such as memos or notes. Some provincial governments and international agencies use full sheets, 21 by 29.5 cm (about 8 1/4 by 11 3/4 inches) — a standard international size geared to metric measurement — and appropriate half sheets.

Paper should be of medium weight

The weight of business stationery ranges from 60 g/m^2 to 75 g/m^2 (16 to 20 pounds). Paper lighter than 60 g/m^2 is too fragile, and that heavier than 75 g/m^2 is too bulky and hard to fold, as well as expensive.

White continues to be the standard colour for business stationery, although increasing use is being made of pastels. Sales letters make greater use of colour than do other types of correspondence.

Letterhead

The printed heading on stationery is called a letterhead. A letterhead lends legitimacy to any business organization. Virtually all business organizations, whether one-person operations or much larger, use letterhead stationery.

Modern letterheads are subtle and nondistracting

At one time a letterhead took up a large part of a sheet of stationery. Such things as names of company officers and pictures of the company's plant were included along with the routine identifying information. A modern letterhead includes the company name and logo, address, and postal code. Many firms also include their telephone and fax numbers, including the area code. Companies engaging in international business may also include a code address for cablegrams in the letterhead.

White Space

Varying margin sizes with message length improves appearance

Planning is necessary to avoid sending out letters with an unattractive or disorganized appearance that is likely to detract from the message itself. The planned use of white space — areas of the page that are left blank — is an important determinant of appearance.

A letter that is balanced on the page is more attractive than one that is not. By surrounding your message with ample margins or white space, you can achieve a "picture frame" effect. Side margins of 4 cm are commonly used, as are top and bottom margins of approximately 5 cm. By varying the top and side margins on the basis of the length of the message, you can produce a letter with eye appeal.

Standard Parts of a Business Letter

Although letters may differ in appearance, their basic parts are similar

Compare correspondence from a variety of companies, and you will notice obvious differences immediately. Size and style of type, margins, and general appearance may, for example, vary considerably.

No matter how unusual a company's correspondence format is, its letters will contain the same basic parts. Regardless of the purpose of the letter, the reader has certain information needs that the following parts are intended to satisfy:

1. Return address of the sender
2. Date the letter was written
3. Inside address of the receiver
4. Salutation
5. Body of the letter
6. Close
7. Signature block

Return Address

The return address must be typed if letterhead is not used

The letters of most business organizations are written on stationery that has the company letterhead, including the address, at the top. When you write a letter on plain paper, this return address is the first information on the page. Thus it establishes the top margin. When using plain paper, the sender does not include his or her name in the return address.

Whether included in a printed letterhead or typed on plain paper, the return address must include street number and name (or post office box number), city, province, and postal code. For international correspondence (including communication with the United States), the return address also includes "Canada."

Date

All correspondence should include the date of writing

All letters and reports should be dated, since the date tells the reader something about the context in which the letter was written. The date also simplifies the filing of a letter; the arrangement of correspondence within a given file folder is usually chronological, according to the dates of the materials. The standard form for dates is November 19, 1991 (month/date/year); however, with the introduction of the metric system, 1991 11 19 (year/month/day) is being used more frequently.

When letterhead is used, the date should be typed two or more spaces below the sender's address. Shorter letters will have a greater number of spaces between the sender's address and the date to balance the message on the page.

When you use a plain sheet of paper, the date is generally placed two spaces below the sender's address. Figure 7.1 shows how the return address and date should be placed on a page.

Inside Address of Receiver

The inside address includes the name, title, and address of the person to whom the letter is being sent. Take care that all this information is correct.

Business letterhead and date

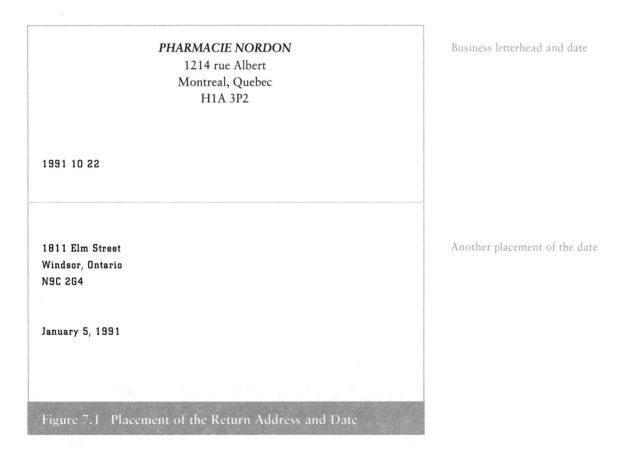

PHARMACIE NORDON
1214 rue Albert
Montreal, Quebec
H1A 3P2

1991 10 22

Another placement of the date

1811 Elm Street
Windsor, Ontario
N9C 2G4

January 5, 1991

Figure 7.1 Placement of the Return Address and Date

By misspelling the receiver's name or by stating an incorrect job title, you create unnecessary obstacles for the receiver. You also present yourself in a poor light by showing that you are inadequately informed about your correspondence.

The receiver's inside address is typed below the date line. The length of the letter determines the number of spaces between the date and the inside address; a separation of four to six line spaces is typical.

Information presented in the receiver's address is arranged from specific to general

The information presented in the receiver's address is arranged from the specific to the general. The most specific information, the receiver's name, if known, comes first. The receiver's name is most often preceded by *Dr.*, *Mr.*, *Mrs.*, *Ms.*, *Miss*, or other appropriate title. The person's initials or given name are included as well, followed by the receiver's surname. Next come his or her professional title, if any, the name of the organization, mailing address, city, province, and postal code. All provinces and territories are usually spelled out in full. However, if space is a concern, either the standard or the new two-letter abbreviations can be used (see Figure 7.2). When the city, province, and postal code appear on the same line, the postal code should be separated from the province by a double space. If possible, the postal code should appear as the last line in the address. A single space must separate the first three characters of the code from the last three.

Inside addresses are typically arranged as shown in Figure 7.3.

	New Form		Standard Form
Alberta	AB	or	Alta.
British Columbia	BC	or	B.C.
Labrador	LB	or	Lab.
Manitoba	MB	or	Man.
New Brunswick	NB	or	N.B.
Newfoundland	NF	or	Nfld.
Northwest Territories	NT	or	N.W.T.
Nova Scotia	NS	or	N.S.
Ontario	ON	or	Ont.
Prince Edward Island	PE	or	P.E.I.
Quebec	PQ	or	P.Q. or Que.
Saskatchewan	SK	or	Sask.
Yukon Territory	YT	or	Yuk.

Figure 7.2 Abbreviations for Provinces and Territories

1811 Elm Street
Windsor, Ontario
N9C 2G4

January 5, 1991

Dr. John Robinson
Registrar
University of British Columbia
Vancouver, British Columbia
V4K 2C3

Receiver's address arranged from general to specific

1811 Elm Street
Windsor, Ontario
N9C 2G4

January 5, 1991

Modern Office Supply
2226 Main Street
Winnipeg MB R2J 0V7

Figure 7.3 Format for Inside Addresses

The Salutation

Your relationship to your correspondent affects the style of the salutation and of the close

By asking yourself how well you know your correspondent, you should be able to select an appropriate salutation. The most frequently used salutations in business are *Dear Mr. . . .* , *Mrs. . . .* , Ms. . . . , and *Miss . . .* If you know your correspondent well, you may use his or her first name (e.g., "Dear Jack" or "Dear Marjorie").

In the past, salutations of *Gentlemen*, *Sirs*, and *Madam* were not only acceptable but widely used. These terms are seldom used today, even when a letter is addressed to a company. Today a writer who is unaware of an individual's name is more likely to omit the salutation, as shown in Figure 7.4.

If the recipient has a title, it should be used in the salutation (for example, "Dear Captain Pagonis"). Deciding how to address dignitaries in the church or high-level officials in government can be difficult. Most good dictionaries, however, include a reference section that lists such titles along with appropriate greetings for each.

Some writers use what we call a "salutopening" instead of a traditional salutation. Frequently used in sales letters, a salutopening presents the first few words of the opening paragraph and the reader's name in place of the salutation:

Yes, Ms. Jefferson

You are right to expect extended service ...

After the name in the salutopening, the sentence continues in the letter body a double space lower. Salutopenings eliminate the artificiality of greeting strangers as "Dear." Conventional salutations, however, continue to be used much more frequently than salutopenings.

The Body

The main message of a letter is contained in the body. The body begins a double space below the salutation or the subject line. Single-space within paragraphs and double-space between paragraphs.

The body of the letter should be no longer than necessary to cover the topic

The body of the letter should convey the necessary information without leaving significant questions unanswered. Many writers seem to feel obligated to fill an entire sheet even when a shorter message would accomplish the same purpose. The body should be no longer than necessary.

Short paragraphs make it easy for a reader to scan a letter and identify its important points. Longer paragraphs make the task more difficult.

PHARMACIE NORDON
1214 rue Albert
Montreal, Quebec
H1A 3P2

1991 10 22

Pharmacist
Gagnon Drugs
236 Government Road East
Kirkland Lake ON P0K 3H5

Subject: Volume Discounts

Many writers, unaware of a receiver's name, now omit the salutation

Salutation omitted replaced by a subject line

1811 Elm Street
Windsor, Ontario
N9C 2G4

January 5, 1991

Modern Office Supply
2226 Main Street
Winnipeg MB R2J 0V7

Please send me a copy ...

Salutation omitted, with no subject line

Figure 7.4 Letters without Salutations

Some authorities consider an average of four to six lines per paragraph reasonable. While these numbers are not sacred, they are a useful guide.

The Close

The close and the signature follow the body of the letter. Double-space between the last line of the body and the close of the letter. The wording of the close, like that of the salutation, depends on how well you know the other party. *Truly*, *sincerely*, *respectfully*, and *cordially* are the words most commonly used in closing letters. Each is ordinarily used with *yours* and sometimes also with *very* (e.g., "Very truly," "Yours truly").

Signature Block

Leave four lines of space below the close and type your name. If the letter is a business letter, type your job title directly beneath your name.

Some organizations have the name of the company appear in capital letters two spaces below the close and before the four spaces that precede the typed name. This format was originally used to clarify the company's legal responsibility for the letter. It is no longer considered necessary, and the prevalence of the practice is diminishing.

Additional Parts of a Business Letter

The standard parts described in the preceding pages are routinely found in business letters. You should also be familiar with some additional parts that you may sometimes use.

Attention Line

When you use an attention line, let it replace the salutation or place it between the inside address of the receiver and the salutation. The attention line indicates the specific person who should read the letter. The letter is not addressed to that person, however, nor is that person named in the salutation if one is included. The attention line is not widely used.

Allied Lenses, Ltd.
1418 Industrial Drive
Rexdale ON M5R 2T3

Attention: Mr. R. Jenkins

Subject Line

A subject line telling the reader exactly what the letter is about is frequently used in modern business correspondence. The subject line generally comes after the salutation. The subject line is a descriptive phrase that summarizes the letter's main idea. The following examples illustrate the type of subject line that might accompany each letter:

A subject line is a useful device that often appears in modern business letters

Main Idea	**Please send me information on your vacuum metallized flexible packaging.**
Poor Subject Line	**Request for Information on Vacuum Metallized Flexible Packaging [too long and detailed]**
Better Subject Line	**Request for Product Information**
Main Idea	**Please let me know by the end of the month when you plan to take your vacation this year, especially if you want time off in July and August.**
Poor Subject Line	**Vacation Entitlement [vague and misleading]**
Better Subject Line	**Booking Your 1991 Vacation**

Internal Headings

If your letter is more than two or three short paragraphs long, you may want to include headings for each of the main ideas. For example, if a client requests information on several products, you might introduce your description of each product with a heading.

Letters can contain headings

Reference Initials, Enclosures, and Copies

Reference initials appear at the left margin, two spaces below the last line of the signature block. When the sender's initials are used, they should be unspaced capitals. The sender's initials should precede the typist's initials, which are unspaced and lower-case. A colon, a dash, or a slash is used to separate the two sets of initials. The sender's initials need not be included if the sender also signs the letter.

If something in addition to the letter is included in the message, make an enclosure notation one or two spaces below the reference initials. *Enclosure* may be spelled out or abbreviated *Encl.* or *Enc.* If more than one enclosure is sent, the number should be indicated.

If someone other than the addressed receiver is to receive a copy of a letter, that person should be identified at the very end of the letter. List the names of those who are to receive copies after the single letter *c*, which refers to copies made by any means. This information is typed one or two spaces below the reference initials or enclosure notation:

JTD:nvp

Enclosures 3

c: Mr. Jenkins
Ms. Phillips

Blind copies are copies of which the addressee is unaware

A company may send copies of letters to someone without the addressee's knowledge. Such copies are called blind copies and noted with *bc*. This notation is typed on the letter copies but not on the original and usually appears directly below the usual copy notation.

Postscripts

A postscript conveys thoughts added to a letter after it has been completed in its usual form. A postscript may be used to present an afterthought or to emphasize a point. Postscripts do not often appear in business letters today; when used, they are usually for emphasis.

A postscript is often preceded by *P.S.*, but this indication is not necessary. A postscript should appear at the bottom of the letter, one or two spaces below the last line typed on the page.

Second-Page Headings

All subsequent pages need headings

When a letter continues beyond one page, each subsequent page should be headed by the receiver's name, the page number, and the date. While the first page may be typed on letterhead stationery, subsequent pages should be on plain paper (see Figure 7.5).

A second page should be typed 2.5 to 5 cm from the top of the page, and the body of the letter should resume four spaces below the heading. Two or more lines of the body must be included to warrant a second page. Never begin a second page for the signature block.

Letter Placement

Flexible spacing between letterhead, date, and receiver's address permits a balanced appearance

Figure 7.6 identifies the parts of a letter and appropriate spacing. In general, single-space within the parts and double-space between them. Remember that you have some flexibility in spacing between the date and the letterhead, and between the date and the receiver's address. Separate

-2-

A.J. Smith
1991 11 19

To confirm your acceptance of this agreement, please sign both copies of this letter in the space provided and return it to our office. If you have any questions, you can reach me at 432-7856.

Sincerely,

John T. Durrand
Director
Personnel Department

JTD:nvp

Enclosures: 3

c: Mr. Jenkins
Ms. Phillips

Approved and agreed to this ___ day of _________ 1992

_______________________ _______________________
Authorized Signature Social Insurance Number

Figure 7.5 Sample Second Page

these parts by enough line spaces to balance the letter on the sheet. The spacing between the other letter parts is constant regardless of the style of the letter placement used.

Letterhead	*WORLDWIDE ADVENTURE TRAVEL* *1835 Farnsworth Place* *Calgary AB M5H 7S2*
Date	1992 10 30
Receiver's Address	Mr. Don Ohajiah 3543 Oxbow Place Red Deer AB M5F 3N2
Salutation	Dear Mr. Ohajiah
Subject Line	Subject: Your Request for Information on Tours to China
Body	Worldwide Adventure Travel offers several adventure tours to China. Our 1991/92 brochure has detailed descriptions of each trip so I've enclosed a copy that you can read at your leisure. Our clients tell us they like knowing how much the trip will cost before they leave home. Therefore, our tour prices include airfare, ground transportation, hotels, and meals. Only the cost of alcoholic beverages and gratuities is not included. If you'd like to join us on one of the tours, send in your completed application form along with a cheque for $200 to reserve your place. If you have any further questions, please write, or phone me or my associate, Cynthia Klein, at (403) 253-6767.
Close	Sincerely
Signature Block	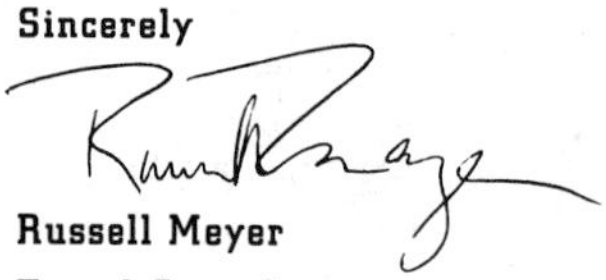 Russell Meyer Travel Consultant
Reference Initial	RM:ds
Enclosure	Enclosure: brochure
Copy	c: Cynthia Klein

Figure 7.6 Letter Format (Full-Block Style with Open Punctuation)

While the vertical spacing between the parts of the letter remains relatively constant, their horizontal placement varies. Some organizations provide employees with a manual or style sheet prescribing a certain style. There are two main styles from which to choose: full block and modified block.

Letter placement follows two main styles: full block and modified block

WORLDWIDE ADVENTURE TRAVEL
1835 Farnsworth Place
Calgary AB M5H 7S2

Letterhead

December 12, 1992

Date

Ms. Marcia Charboneau
City Travel
9400 Market Place
Regina SA
S4P 3N2

Receiver's Address

Dear Ms. Charboneau:

Salutation

Subject: Your Inquiry About Our Agent's Fees

Subject Line

Worldwide Adventure Travel is pleased to have travel agencies promote our tours. Because we are a small operation with a limited advertising budget, we depend on agents like you to let the travelling public know what we have to offer.

Body

We pay a 15% commission for all confirmed bookings. Also, as a bonus, we offer a complimentary tour to any agent who books more than 50 clients on our tours in a calendar year.

I'm enclosing 10 copies of our 1991/92 brochure for your clients, along with more detailed descriptions for your own reference. If you have any questions, please call me on our toll-free line, 1-800-403-5567.

Sincerely,

Close

Russell Meyer
Travel Consultant

Signature Block

RM:ds
Enclosure: brochure
c: Cynthia Klein

Reference Initial
Enclosure
Copy

Figure 7.7 Modified-Block Style with Mixed Punctuation

In the *full-block style*, every line (including the date, closing, and signature block) begins at the left margin. The full-block style is shown in Figure 7.6. Occasionally, a subject line replaces the salutation in full-block style, particularly if the name of the receiver is unknown.

In the *modified-block style*, the date begins at the centre of the page or is centred horizontally. The close and the signature are normally aligned with the date. This style is shown in Figure 7.7.

Punctuation Styles

In preparing letters, you can choose one of three punctuation styles: open, closed, and mixed. *Open-punctuation style*, as the name suggests, has no end punctuation in the introductory and closing parts of the letter. This style is preferred with the full-block style of letter placement. Figure 7.6 shows open punctuation.

Closed style uses punctuation at the end of each line in the introductory and closing parts of a letter. However, the closed style is seldom used today.

Mixed style combines elements of the open and closed styles. Only the salutation and the close have end punctuation: a colon follows the salutation and a comma the close. This punctuation style is commonly used with the modified-block letter placement style. Figure 7.7 shows the mixed-punctuation style.

The Memo

Memos are traditionally used for internal communication

A memorandum or memo is a message written for use within the organization. Traditionally, letters are used for external communication, while the memo is intended solely for communicating with others within the organization.

Memos are popular because large organizations have a great need for effective communication. As organizations grow, the problems of coordination become more difficult; memos can help to keep the various parts of the organization in touch with each other. Memos have many uses: to convey information from one department to another, to communicate between branches, and to provide records and reference. In fact, the memo is the most widely used form of written communication within an organization.

The Advantages of the Memo

Since memos are intended for internal communication, it might appear easier just to talk to the other person rather than write a memo. Sometimes it *is* easier, but memos have distinct advantages; for example, they

Memos have several advantages over oral communication

1. provide a written record
2. are suitable for transmitting complex information
3. can reach many persons simultaneously

Unlike a conversation, a memo can be filed for future reference. It is a written record for the writer, and the reader. By referring to a memo at a later date, you are reminded of its specifics, such as date, individual responsibilities, and deadlines. This documentation can be invaluable for reviewing completed projects and planning new ventures. Memos can also help to clarify the specific requirements of a task, thus ensuring it is completed correctly.

When a message contains highly specific or complex details, the listener experiences difficulty in remembering it. Complicated instructions are easily misunderstood under the best of circumstances, but when they are spoken, the chances for error increase. Consequently, a memo becomes an accurate memory-jogger.

If you must transmit information to a number of co-workers, contacting them individually is time-consuming. Schedule conflicts may make it difficult to assemble the group for a meeting. A memo, however, can reach many individuals easily.

Memos are generally economical, especially when they are handwritten or sent by electronic mail. However, when memos are dictated to and typed by a secretary, their cost is almost the same as that of letters.

The number of memos written in a given organization depends to a large degree on the climate within an organization. Some companies require employees to document every conversation and action with a memo; others regard memos as necessary only in very serious circumstances. When you join a firm, you'll be able to assess what your employer expects in the way of memos by talking to fellow workers or your supervisor.

The Significance of the Memo to You

In business organizations, people are judged in part by the memos they write

In larger organizations, the impression you make on your co-workers is determined partially by the memos you write. Your manner of communicating influences what others think of you. The farther removed the other person is from you, the stronger the effect of your memo.

When Linda Ikita sent a memo suggesting a change in price procedures, her superior, Marlene Hawn, did not have the authority to act on it. Hawn forwarded the memo to her superior, Max Whitcomb, who had never met Linda Ikita and knew little about her. In fact, his perception of her was created largely by the memo.

When you are working in a large organization, some people — often people who can affect your career — are linked to you solely through your memos. For example, Linda Ikita's managerial potential was recognized in part through her effective use of memos.

Occasionally you may find yourself writing a memo to protect your own interests within an organization. For example, you might want to document the decisions reached at a project meeting because some members of the team are noted for their ability to "conveniently forget" that they have agreed to perform a given task. Documentation is particularly important when their nonperformance affects your standing within the organization.

Preparation of Memos

The format of memos should encourage consistency in internal communication

The memo has evolved as part of an attempt to simplify communication within organizations. Some of the niceties of letter writing are sacrificed for the sake of conciseness. The format of the memo is also intended to simplify and speed up internal communication by ensuring consistency.

To guarantee consistency, some organizations provide employees with preprinted forms that have the basics of any memo printed at the top of the page. Figure 7.8 shows one format for positioning the names of the receiver and the sender, the date, and the subject. Notice that the amount of information given about the receiver and the sender is the same. If the receiver's title has been omitted, the sender's will be, too.

Modified Letterhead

INTEROFFICE MEMO WORLDWIDE ADVENTURE TRAVEL

Receiver's and Sender's Names

TO: **Marlene Hawn, Director Production Planning**
FROM: **Linda Ikita Production Planner**

Date

DATE: **February 17, 1992**

Subject Line

Alternate Scheduling Procedure

Figure 7.8 Sample Memo Form

By providing this format, a company can ensure that certain information always appears in the same place in all memos. Finding a particular memo in a file is easier if the subject of the memo always appears in the same place.

Uniformity in the arrangement of memos makes them easier to understand

Some organizations provide more structured forms, which further simplify the memo preparation process. One form consists of an original and two colour-coded copies, and includes space for the recipient's reply. In using such a form, the usual sequence of steps is as follows:

1. The initiator writes the message on the form and removes one of the copies to keep as a reminder.
2. The recipient replies in the space provided, removes the second copy, and returns the original to the initiator.
3. The initiator now has the message and its reply on one form and can take whatever action is necessary.

Memos are sometimes used for external communication

Although such forms are intended primarily for internal communication, they are sometimes used more broadly for routine correspondence with people outside the organization. For example, suppose that you order a lightweight tent from a sporting goods company. Although the company does not have the model you ordered in stock, a comparable model is available. The company might use such a form to notify you and await your response on the same form.

While creativity is desirable in many types of writing, it is not in memo writing. Since memos are intended to facilitate internal communication, consistency is an important consideration.

The subject line at the top of the memo serves two purposes: it focuses the writer on the topic, and it immediately signals the subject of the memo to the reader. In some organizations, the writer initials the typed name, which appears on the "from" line at the top of the memo. This abbreviated signature indicates approval of the completed typed message.

Memos vary greatly in length

Memos vary considerably in length. Some are brief, perhaps no more than a few sentences, while others are three or four pages long. Some companies provide half-sheet memo forms for short messages, thus reducing paper expenses. (Others feel that the savings are offset by the problems in filing and finding these smaller papers.) When a memo is longer than one page, each subsequent page should have a heading showing the addressee's name, the page number, and the date.

Since memos are less formal than letters, some writers mistakenly attach less importance to them

Although memos may vary in appearance, their purpose is always to facilitate internal communication. Because they are less formal than letters and are designated for internal use only, some writers do not apply themselves properly when preparing them. If a situation requires a memo, that memo merits care in both preparation and writing.

Summary

The appearance of letters and memos can improve or detract from the image of the organization or individual sending them.

- Stationery and letterhead are part of the appearance
- A business letter has seven standard parts:
  - return address
  - date
  - inside address of the receiver
  - salutation
  - body
  - close
  - signature
- A business letter may also contain
  - an attention line
  - a subject line
  - reference initials
  - notations of enclosures and copies
  - a postscript
  - subsequent page headings
- Spacing is important
  - body centred on the page
  - single spacing within blocks of information
  - double spacing between blocks of information
- Two main styles of letter placement are used
  - full block
  - modified block
- Open punctuation is preferred with the full-block style of letter placement, mixed punctuation with the modified-block style
- Memos are used in place of letters for messages sent within an organization

Review Questions

1. List the parts of a business letter.
2. How do the two main formats of business letters differ?
3. How are letters different from memos?
4. What are the advantages of the memo?

Activities

1. Imagine you are about to start your own business. Describe the kind of business it will be and create a letterhead for your stationery. In a memo to your instructor, write a brief description of the image you are trying to convey through your letterhead. Be sure to apply the ten characteristics of effective writing once you have completed your first draft.

2. Interview an office manager, the supervisor of a typing pool, or a typing teacher to find out what style of letter placement they prefer and why. In a memo to your instructor, summarize your findings. Be sure to apply the ten characteristics of effective writing once you have completed your first draft.
3. Imagine you are required to send letters to the following people. Prepare the return address, date, and inside address of the receiver for each case.
   a. the president of your college
   b. the mayor of your town or city
   c. the premier of your province
   d. your best friend's father
4. For each of the following main idea sentences, write an appropriate subject line:
   a. During my career as a business communication educator, I have become aware of certain recurring problems that students experience in their business writing.
   b. Please thank your second-year broadcast students for the professional manner in which they produced the peer coaching videotape.
   c. On February 15 and 16, 1992, I visited the British Columbia Institute of Technology to assist in the program review of the Operations Management Program. Here are the results of that review.
   d. Here is a summary of the evaluation questionnaire completed by the first-year financial management students.
   e. Because of the communication problems we've been having, I recommend that the company require a five-minute overlap of all production employees during shift changes.
5. Interview someone who has worked abroad for a multinational company. Identify the ways business communication in a foreign culture differs from business communication in Canada. In a memo to your instructor, summarize your findings. Be sure to apply the ten characteristics of effective writing once you have completed your first draft.

Discussion Cases

The Dilemma: Length Versus Format[1]

Mark Rothmark is a recent college graduate who was hired as a personnel consultant by a management consulting firm. The personnel director at Smith and Smith Manufacturing believed the com-

continued

pany employees seemed to be spending more time finding out the latest gossip about each other than working. The personnel director asked the consulting firm for a study of the employees' information needs, and Mark was assigned to the project.

Mark knew that the director, the son of the owner of the manufacturing company, liked one-page letters and memos. Mark is generally a pretty good writer. Although he had a lot of information to convey about the project, he tried to put everything in a one-page letter, even though in this instance he was not instructed to do so.

Fortunately, Mark showed the letter to his boss before sending it. His boss called it "terrible, very poorly written" and told Mark to redo it. Mark is trying to figure out what to do because he thinks the writing is pretty well organized and clear. He realizes, however, that the problem may be with the format.

Case Questions

1. What specifically could be done to make the letter (see Figure 7.9) more attractive and inviting to read? Make at least a half-dozen suggestions. Where and how could your suggestions be implemented?
2. Rewrite Mark's letter. Despite Mark's confidence in the letter's content, you should check that it meets the ten characteristics of effective writing outlined in Chapter 5.

Performance Communications
Suite 950, The Burrard Centre
55 Burrard Street
Vancouver BC V5H 3Y5

June 25, 1992

Mr. C. M. Moranis
Director of Personnel
Smith & Smith Manufacturing
3700 Beresford Avenue
Burnaby BC V5G 8H5

Dear Mr. Moranis:

This is in response to your April 30 request for a study to determine employee information needs. We find that your employees' high morale and efficiency have partially been lost as a result of recent personnel transfers. We therefore recommend that a company newsletter be established as soon as possible. As you know, many of your employees have been transferred to other plants or departments because the company has grown so much and so quickly over the past year. This growth was due in part to the high morale of the employees, who had formed tightly knit and efficient work units. The many transfers have caused those efficient work units to break up, in turn causes a number of problems for the company. Morale has declined somewhat as a result of the dissolution of the "family structure" that was created. Employees have been accusing the management of becoming "cold and impersonal" as a result of the breakups. Declining morale has led to declining production. The decline in production has been aggravated because employees frequently call or visit ex-members of the group on company time. The entire situation sets a poor example for newly hired workers, who see the workplace as a "goof-off" opportunity (which will further hurt production). Means must be found to re-establish employee morale, eliminate or reduce time away from the work place, improve current production, and set an appropriate example for new employees. Although nothing short of a full-scale employee

continued

Figure 7.9 Length Versus Format

relations program can be expected to meet your needs fully, I am proposing a company newspaper as part of that program, one which can be implemented very quickly.

I believe that the newspaper will help combat many of the problems indicated above. In order to help solve your current problems and meet the needs outlined above, the company newspaper should help re-establish the "family atmosphere" that led to your early success; re-establish respect for management by showing that management still cares about the employee; provide sufficient news about transferred employees so that remaining employees do not spend so much time inquiring about or making contact with those transferred; and through all of the above, convince new employees that they are to take their work seriously. If you can accomplish those four objectives, you should be on your way to increased productivity. The newspaper could be a 17-by-11-inch sheet folded to 8 1/2 by 11 inches, printed on both sides in one or two colours. Editorially, I recommend that the newspaper focus on news and events directly related to the employees' interests. Management notices and general news about the company should be included, but the paper must not be allowed to become a "puff sheet" for management. Instead, it must be "of, by, and for the employees" in order for it to accomplish its objectives.

The paper must be published frequently in order for it to become part of the work environment. I recommend that it be published once a week if possible, and no less than twice monthly. If it cannot be published at least twice monthly, I withdraw my recommendation, for the paper will contain "stale news" and not have the intended effect. A survey of employees indicates that they would like to see the following items: employee transfers, employee promotions, personnel and family news, community announcements, company news, and "getting ahead" articles. I will furnish addition information if you are interested in following up.

Sincerely

Mark R. Rothmark

Mark R. Rothmark, Consultant

P.S. I will call you next Thursday about this matter.

A Letter Worth Examining

Carmela Campolo is the sales manager for OfficeMATE, a company that manufactures custom-designed computer office furniture. Last week, she met with Maggie Rubin, the purchasing director at IDM Electronics. They discussed IDM's need to buy flexible modules. Carmela wrote the letter in Figure 7.10 as a follow-up to her meeting with Maggie. Read the letter and answer the questions below.

OfficeMATE Furniture, Ltd.
1423 Main Street
Vancouver BC V5F 3J2

February 17, 1992

IDM Electronics
P.O. Box 3435
Richmond BC V4T 2D3

Attention: Maggie Rubin, Purchasing Director

Madam:

Our meeting this past week was short, but much was accomplished. I always feel satisfied when I come away from such a meeting.

I understand our agreement as follows. We are designing custom computer desks and room dividers (Model 23-A-1.2a and b), which should work much better than the standard office furniture you currently have. When you buy ten or more units, we will send one of our technicians to assemble the furniture. If you purchase fewer than ten units, you will have to make your own arrangements for assembling the furniture.

continued

Figure 7.10 A Letter Worth Examining

You ought to be completely satisfied with our furniture. If not, we are working on a completely new series of designs, which should be ready within the next year or so. Perhaps these designs would be more appropriate for your situation.

We will be delivering your furniture as soon as we get the bugs out of our production line. Then we can set up the time for our technician to visit your site. Please have your assistant (I forget his name) so that we can work out the logistics.

Call if you have any problems or questions.

Respectfully,

Carmela Campolo
Sales Manager

Case Questions

1. If you were Maggie Rubin, how would you react to this letter? Why?
2. How would you improve the letter? Consider both content and format.
3. Write a revised letter that will achieve the desired goals.

Chapter 8

Communicating in the Electronic Office

Learning Objectives

In this chapter, you'll learn to recognize the impact of the electronic office on businesses today. More specifically, you will be able to:

1. explain the importance of the electronic office in today's business world
2. describe the components of the electronic office
3. discuss the advantages and disadvantages of various methods of electronic communication
4. explain how the electronic office functions
5. define selected terminology used in the electronic office
6. explain how the electronic office affects the writing process

Preview Case

Gunter Kaempffer was in a panic. His boss, Jennifer Jenson, had just informed him that the Kramer project report deadline had been moved up by two weeks. Jennifer wanted it on her desk by Friday morning — and here it was Wednesday noon. Less than a day and a half to pull together the data from a project that had taken more than three years to develop.

Gunter called his staff together and explained the situation. "No problem," said Lorraine Buchanan, one of his technical writers. "We'll make the deadline. That new word processing package we purchased makes it a snap. We can each write a section and then put it all together at the end."

"But it'll take a day and a half just to fit the sections together and to make sure that the format is consistent," replied Gunter.

"Not if we take some time right now to design a style sheet and put together a fairly detailed outline for the whole report. Besides, a lot of the data we need is already in project files on the computer. We all wrote a progress report every three months. We can probably transfer in whole chunks of the various progress reports without having to start from scratch."

"O.K., let's get started," said Gunter. "The sooner we get started, the better."

Overview

In the midst of the concern for increasing office productivity, technology has solved some of the problems. Project reports such as the one Gunter Kaempffer needs can be written much more efficiently than they could have been ten years ago because of word processing packages.

In the 1950s, approximately 1000 computers were operating in North America — all large, costly machines with very limited capabilities. Today, medium- and even small-sized companies are computerizing all or part of their operation. Computers are commonplace in the elementary and secondary school systems. In 1990, *The Globe and Mail* reported data from International Data Corp. (Canada) Ltd. that predicted portable computer manufacturers would ship 109.5 thousand units in 1992 alone.[1] Many of these portable computers will have as much or more processing power than minicomputers had just a decade ago.

This chapter describes the components of the electronic office and shows how they have changed the nature of communication in business and industry. It will show you how to take advantage of the features of computers so that you can write more efficiently and more effectively.

User-friendly Computers

Equipment is becoming less expensive and easier to operate

With every new development, the new tools in the electronic office are easier to operate. Instead of requiring special languages, "user friendly" computers respond to natural-language controls. Some computers even respond to voice commands. One of the newest developments is the pen-based personal computer, enthusiastically described by one writer in the following way:

> Pen-based computers are designed very much like notebooks, and are just about as simple to use ... Slip the untethered pen from its slot, and touch the tip to the page you want ... The document you pointed to will appear in a second or two ... the computer will open the application software automatically when it opens the file ... To insert text, you simply draw an upside down 'v' with the arrow pointing to the desired text ... and enter text by printing directly onto the screen.[2]

Business now must use electronic technology to stay competitive, and all employees must work to improve office productivity. For example, virtually all banks, credit unions, and trust companies have electronic banking machines so that customers can access their accounts 24 hours a day. Many also have teleservice banking, so that customers can do much of their banking by phoning a central location during the day or in the early-evening hours. A few are even experimenting with debit cards, which would replace cheques in most retail outlets. Customers using a debit card instead of a traditional credit card would have the amount debited from their account as soon as it was used to pay for something rather than receiving a monthly bill.

Manufacturers are using computers to automate their order processing, improve the efficiency of their assembly lines, and reduce the amount of inventory on hand at any given moment. Hospitals are using computers for keeping track of inventory, providing patient information to the health care team, as well as for personnel information, payroll, and other traditional tasks. In many retail outlets, goods purchased at the cash register are automatically deducted from inventory so that orders can be generated as soon as stock reaches a predetermined level.

The Traditional Office

Poor procedures and uneven workloads cause delays

In the traditional office, one secretary was assigned to one boss. The secretary performed a variety of duties, including answering the phone, greeting visitors, typing, running errands, filing, arranging meetings, and keeping records. Such offices had the usual four-drawer filing cabinets and electric typewriters. The supply cabinet held a large quantity of typewriter erasers, correction paper, white correction fluid, carbon paper, file folders, and labels, along with several types of office paper.

When managers had to produce an important report, the secretary worked at top speed — missing coffee breaks and lunches, and working overtime. At last, the report finished, the secretary sighed with relief. But, in the meantime, the manager had found information to add to the document. At this point, the working relationship became strained as the secretary contemplated retyping the document.

The Modern Office

In the mid-1960s, IBM developed an automatic typewriter called the MT/ST (magnetic tape selectric typewriter). By using the MT/ST, a typist could record keystrokes on magnetic tapes as well as on paper. The tapes simplified revision because only the changes had to be keyed again.

Form letters were produced more efficiently because the machine could type the same text repetitively at the rate of more than 180 words a minute. Also, errors could be corrected by merely striking over the previously typed character(s).

The revolutionary MT/ST launched the office into the electronic age, and the term *word processing* entered the language. Today written data — words as well as figures — are entered into, stored in, and manipulated by computer, then printed out many times faster than human fingers could manage.

New job titles have emerged

To take advantage of these new electronic tools, the role of the secretary has changed. Since the traditional secretary's day was filled with interruptions and task switching, one way to increase productivity was to divide the work differently. In many offices today, one group of secretaries prepares documents; another handles all other secretarial tasks. Secretaries who choose document preparation are called *word processing specialists* or *correspondence specialists.* Freed from the many daily interruptions, they can concentrate on streamlining the flow of documents. Those secretaries who choose the nontyping activities are called administrative specialists. They are assigned such duties as helping management with reports, composing letters, answering phones, filing, and planning meetings and itineraries.

Work group approach is an effective structure

As companies have gained experience with word processing, the work group structure has emerged. The work group is a small number of support personnel who function as a team. The group, composed of word processing specialists and administrative specialists, is assigned to a department or other entity.

This new office structure has many advantages. Managers are no longer dependent on just one person for support services. An entire team keeps the work flowing. Documents can be prepared more quickly and professionally. And, most importantly, many of the routine duties can be delegated to administrative specialists. Managers are free to address pressing problems. The secretaries benefit because their careers are no longer tied to the success of their bosses. A definite career ladder exists, and the specialists can be promoted on the basis of skills and abilities.

Input Components

Input is the beginning step in the creation of a business communication. The method the writer uses to get his or her words into a permanent form affects the efficiency of communication.

Longhand input is too slow

Because writing in longhand is slow, it is rarely used in the modern office. It is the slowest, least effective method of input. The average person writes ten to twenty words a minute, sometimes in handwriting that is hard to decipher.

Dictation to a secretary is expensive

Dictation to a shorthand writer is another method of initial input. With this method, the document creation process involves two people. This type of input is two to three times faster than longhand, but it uses the time of two people so that it does little to reduce office costs. Today, dictation is generally restricted to short documents and general instructions for the secretary.

Dictation to a machine is simple and cost-effective

A third method of input is machine dictation. Using a machine to record the dictation, the rate of input can be more than 100 words a minute. For writers who are not computer literate, dictation provides a relatively cost-effective input method that is easy to use and flexible. However, using dictation machines requires some basic skills.

Cassettes are the recording media

The usual recording media for dictation are cassettes. Standard cassettes hold 30 to 180 minutes of recording time, but mini- or microcassettes, which are becoming more popular, hold 30 to 60 minutes. Some central recording systems use *endless-loop tape*, housed in a tank in which it continually circulates. The tape need not be changed or handled in any way, and the dictator has no worry about its running out.

Dictation Procedures

The business communicator can make his or her most important contribution to efficient document production in the area of dictation. In fact, some companies set up their word processing procedures to give top priority to dictated documents. Here are some hints to help make you an efficient dictator:

Know Your Equipment. Become thoroughly familiar with your equipment. The vendor will provide help, but you should also read the instruction manual carefully. Your company may also conduct dictation training sessions.

Dictating skills are easily developed

Get rid of mike fright by simply reading a passage into the machine. Listen to your voice to evaluate the speed and clarity of your speech. Keep practising until you are sure your voice can be easily understood.

Before You Dictate. Set aside a certain time of the day to dictate. Prepare yourself in these ways:

- Gather information pertaining to the correspondence before you begin.
- Jot down an outline for the message. The guides given in this text can be helpful.
- Dictate the rush items first. Documents dictated in the morning can usually be transcribed and mailed the same day.

Set the Stage. Many companies have dictation procedures manuals that describe how documents should be dictated. Be sure to follow those procedures, if they exist. If they don't, the following guidelines may be helpful:

- Identify yourself, giving your name, your title, your department, and your phone number.
- Indicate the type of document — rough draft or final — letter, memo, report, and so on.
- Indicate when the document is required and how many copies are needed.
- Specify special stationery or paper if necessary.
- Estimate the length of the document: for example, short letter or a four-page report.

Dictate the Document. Hold the microphone about 5 cm from your mouth and speak distinctly at a natural speed, emphasizing past tenses and plurals. The following hints will improve your communication with the transcriber:

- Be sure to dictate unusual punctuation: capitals, quotes, underscoring, and dashes. If you have difficulty indicating punctuation by voice inflection, also dictate commas, periods, question marks, and paragraphing.
- Spell out difficult or confusing words or names. If necessary, tell the transcriber where to find reference material.

- Indicate document ends, errors, or insertions in dictation by using the cuing devices on the equipment. Consult the machine's manual to find out how to use your particular model's features. Marking the corrections saves time for the transcriber.
- Prepare the transcriber for charts or lists by indicating how many columns and column headings there will be. Dictate from left to right and from top to bottom. If possible, provide a written sample of the desired format.

Optical Character Readers

Another type of input is the optical character reader, or OCR. Optical character readers, when used in combination with word processing equipment, can be a rapid means of input. The OCR reads pages of previously typed documents, converts what it reads to electronic information, and places that information on a magnetic medium, usually a disk. The disk can then be placed in a word processing machine, and the document called onto the screen for editing.

The OCR can reduce keying time

For example, you are asked to update a report from another branch of your company; you write the changes directly onto a copy of the report. The report is scanned by the OCR. The word processing specialist views the document on the screen, incorporates the changes you have indicated on the copy, and prints a revised copy of the report. Making the changes on the original report is not recommended because the handwritten notes may reduce the accuracy of the data received from the OCR.

The OCR has several advantages: (1) previously typed documents do not have to be retyped; (2) the original document can be typed on any typewriter; (3) word processing equipment is used more efficiently for editing purposes; (4) optical character readers can read between 350 000 and 450 000 characters an hour (operators key 10 000 to 12 000 characters hourly).

These scanning devices are able to give input to small business computers, phototypesetters, computer mainframes, and communication devices, as well as word processing machines.

Prewritten Messages

The electronic office expedites the preparation of form documents. The word processing system can electronically store letters and paragraphs. After the word processing specialist has keyed the receiver's name and address, prewritten paragraphs can be recalled with just a few strokes, and a personalized document is ready to be sent. Total time necessary to produce the document is probably about three minutes or less.

Form letters speed up the communication process

Many software packages now come with form letters or paragraphs

A word of caution

for every occasion. While these letters or paragraphs can be very cost-efficient, business communicators would do well to examine the samples carefully before using them. Many are poorly written and do not meet the standards for clear, concise communication. Others can be quite helpful with a minimum of editing.

A form letter containing variable information can also be requested. The word processing specialist keys in the variable information, calls up the form letter, and the equipment automatically merges the document with the variables. Once again, producing the document requires very little time. And, once again, a word of caution is in order: sales letters that repeat the receiver's name several times within the text are not personalized; they are offensive.

Writer Keying

Increasingly, writers are drafting their own documents on their personal computers. They may then submit a diskette to a word processing specialist who completes the final formatting, editing, and production. To help the writer communicate what's required more effectively, a request slip such as the one shown in Figure 8.1 is attached to the rough draft copy.

For simple documents such as letters and memos, the word processing specialist may design a template that allows the writer to produce the final copy as well as the initial draft. Whatever input method is chosen, the author is ultimately responsible for ensuring that the documents are accurate, correct, and businesslike in their appearance.

Composing at a terminal is two to three times faster than composing in longhand. Writers can use the computer terminal to create the report and save time both for themselves and for the word processing specialists.

Writer keying also provides a more flexible work environment. With a portable computer, a writer can input text at home or on the road, and send either the computer disk by courier or the document via a modem to the word processing centre for output on a letter-quality printer. In fully networked office systems that have electronic-mail capability for notes, messages, and memos, writer keying is mandatory. Otherwise productivity gains are negligible.

Processing Components

The type of document-processing equipment available in your company depends on many factors, including the types of documents that are generated, the size of the company, the amount of money available for

WORD PROCESSING
REQUEST SLIP

Originator's Name: ______________________________
Department: ______________________________
Date In: ______________ Date Needed: ______________
Draft: ______________ Final: ______________

Check below: (paper to be used)

- ❑ Bond Paper
- ❑ Internal Communication
- ❑ Operations Bulletin
- ❑ Operations Manual
- ❑ OPC
- ❑ Employee Relations Manual
- ❑ Training Manual
- ❑ Directors Handbook
- ❑ Other
- ❑ Accounting Manual
- ❑ Legal
- ❑ Accounting Statements

Special Instructions: ______________________________
____
____
____

Operator's Initials: ______________________________
No. of Pages: ______________________________
Date Completed: ______________________________

000-000-001

Figure 8.1 Word Processing Request Slip

equipment, and the manner in which the company is organized. A company may have one or more of the alternatives discussed below.

Electronic Typewriter

The standard office typewriter is now electronic

The electronic typewriter has, for the most part, replaced the old-fashioned, electro-mechanical typewriter. The electronic typewriter has far fewer moving parts and possesses at least a few automatic features, such as a limited amount of memory, automatic lift-off of errors, automatic centring, automatic carrier return, automatic decimal alignment, and a choice of printing in 10-, 12-, 15-pitch, or proportional spacing.

Many electronic typewriters are designed for easy upgrading to more powerful capabilities (for instance, by adding a larger memory). Some can communicate with other pieces of equipment, such as computers.

The electronic typewriter is one of the first steps in automating the office. It is designed for original letters, memos, and short documents that will not have to be revised.

Dedicated Word Processors

Dedicated word processors are computers whose primary function is word processing. Some systems can also handle mathematics; however, they generally cannot handle spreadsheet packages or graphics. Because personal computers are less expensive and more powerful than they once were, dedicated word processors are becoming much less common. However, many organizations still use them.

Dedicated word processors fall into three main categories, which are described below.

1. Stand-alone Word Processor

Stand-alone word processors can handle many tasks

The stand-alone word processor is more sophisticated than the electronic typewriter. It consists of a central processing unit (CPU), a keyboard, a screen, and a printer. This equipment is capable of performing a large variety of text editing and repetitive processing tasks. The operator can be keying one document while others are being printed. This capability greatly improves productivity.

Since only one person at a time can use a stand-alone system, it is most useful in small businesses or departments of larger businesses.

2. Shared-logic System

Shared systems save money when several stations are needed

A shared-logic system (also called a cluster system) operates in much the same way as a stand-alone system, except that it has one CPU connected to two or more keyboards and printers. Some large systems can support as many as 132 pieces of equipment on one central processing unit.

Shared systems are appropriate for companies that employ more than one word processing operator. Because just one CPU controls the system, all work stations can share the same data base. When long documents must be processed in a hurry, the work can be divided among the operators. When all keying is completed, the document can be easily assembled and printed.

In a shared-logic system, all pieces of equipment depend on one CPU for computer logic and memory. If the CPU develops trouble, no part of the system can function until repairs have been made. Terminals in this system are called "dumb" terminals.

3. Distributed-logic System

A distributed-logic system resembles a shared-logic system, but there is an important difference. In a distributed-logic system, the individual pieces of equipment have their own "intelligence." If the central processing unit malfunctions, the other pieces of equipment may continue to operate.

Word Processing on Microcomputers

Microcomputers are even more versatile

Using word processing software on microcomputers is becoming standard in industry because it allows great flexibility. For example, many packages will now accept data from spreadsheet and graphic software, computer-aided design (CAD) software, and data base management systems. Moreover, managers can enter their own first drafts and then have their secretaries format and prepare the final draft. Or, they can prepare the final drafts themselves.

Desktop Publishing Software

Desktop publishing software allows integration of graphics

Desktop publishing software is the most recent development in word processing. These packages allow you to combine text from word processing packages and graphics from different software packages into a single report. Once you have all the information in a single file, you can then lay out your pages right on the screen so that what you see on the screen is what you'll get on paper. The versatility of desktop publishing software means that many small jobs, such as company newsletters and major reports that previously would have been sent for typesetting, can be handled on a single microcomputer.

Storage Components

Internal Storage

The type of storage needed will depend on the firm's needs and kind of equipment used

While documents are being processed, they must be stored in the computer. Today, more than a million bits (a *bit* is the smallest piece of electronic information) can be stored on a *computer chip* that is no larger than a fingertip. The chip, which is located inside the equipment, constitutes internal storage.

Hard disks are another type of internal storage medium. A single disk, which resembles a phonograph record, holds many millions of characters, so it can store information inexpensively.

External Storage

Floppy disks are the most popular form of external storage for small computers. Two sizes of floppy disks are available: 5 1/4-inch and 3 1/2-inch. The latter are becoming the industry standard because they are sturdier and can hold large quantities of data. Individual pieces of information stored on a floppy disk can be accessed instantaneously, making the editing process easy. It costs only a few cents per page to store information on a floppy disk.

File Management

In the traditional office, secretaries or clerks managed the office filing system. They established a standard system and set up reference indexes so that all office staff could find the files they needed. In the electronic office, many managers fail to recognize the need for similar attention to detail in the management of computer files.

Computer files are vulnerable to damage

Because files are stored electronically on the computer, they tend to be more fragile than paper files. For example, a power failure may result in the loss of any active files on the computer. Computer disks placed too close to a magnet can be erased. A speck of dust on the track of a computer disk may make the data unreadable. Therefore, computer files need to be copied or "backed up" regularly, preferably once a day, but at least once a week.

Labelling computer files saves time and frustration

No one would ever place a file in a file cabinet without a label that described exactly what the file contained; however, many first-time computer users pay little or no attention to the names of their documents on the computer. As a result, they are often unable to locate them without time-consuming searches.

A little planning can make every document instantly accessible. Computers allow you to store your files in *directories* and *subdirectories*. The directories are the equivalent of filing cabinets, and the first-level subdirectories are the equivalent of the drawers in the cabinet. With the computer, however, you can have several levels of subdirectories. Figure 8.2 shows a typical directory of files for a word processing package. Notice that each directory name has a maximum of eight characters. File names have the same limit; however, they are often followed by a period and three additional characters. The three characters following the period are generally referred to as an "extension" of the file name.

In Figure 8.2, the main directory is a document directory, labelled "document." Within that directory, there is a subdirectory for each major project the user is working on: "Bahamas," "Text," and "Guyana." Each subdirectory has its own series of subdirectories. For example, the "Guy-

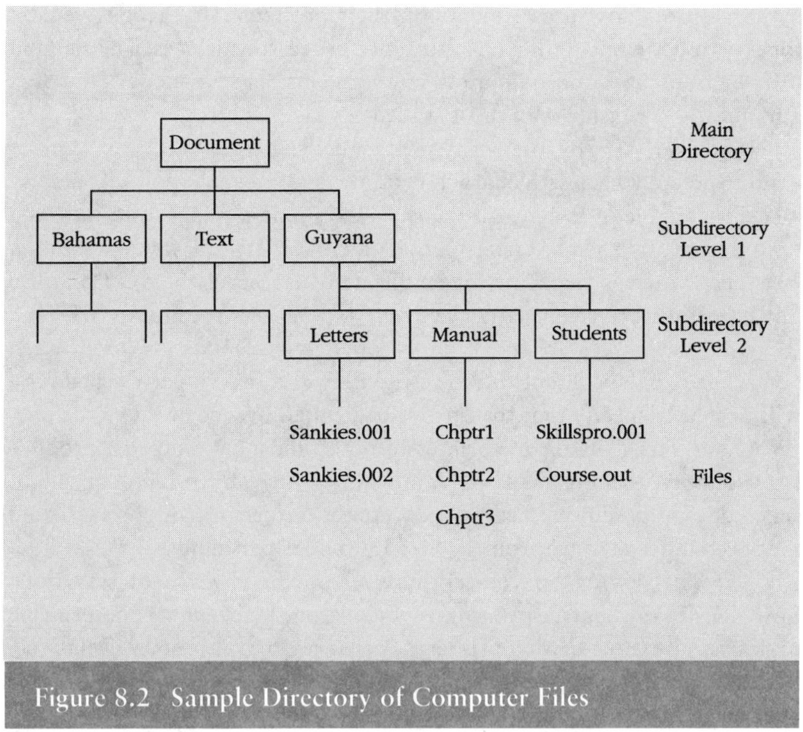

Figure 8.2 Sample Directory of Computer Files

ana" subdirectory is further divided into "Letters," "Manual," and "Students." Finally, each of these contains a series of files.

When you are establishing your directories and subdirectories, you may want to produce a diagram such as the one in Figure 8.2 to give you an overview of your filing system for quick reference.

Output Components

Although electronic storage is available in many forms, most documents are produced on paper at present. The output alternative you choose for a particular document depends on the use to be made of that document. In many cases you will have to specify the type of output you want.

Impact Printers

The kind of document and its use determine the type of output

Impact printers are familiar — a typewriter is an example. A device strikes the paper, producing an image. For many years, typewriters used typebars to print the letters. In the 1960s, IBM developed the "golf ball" or "selectric" element, more properly called a "single-element font." Other manufacturers now use elements on their products. The single-element font was a boon to printing on early word processing devices. The element printer could print approximately 15 characters per second, or 180 words a minute — far faster than most skilled typists.

In the early 1970s, the *daisy print wheel* was developed. It resembles a multispoked wheel with characters on the ends of each spoke. The daisy wheel is capable of faster printing than the single-element font; its speed ranges from 30 to 55 characters per second, or 350 to 650 words a minute. The daisy wheel is replacing the single-element font as the most popular impact printing device. Many electronic typewriters use a daisy wheel.

All these devices produce what is called *letter-quality printing*. When you want your document to look originally and individually typed, you will probably specify that the output be printed by one of these printers.

Other types of impact printers for the most part do not produce letter-quality documents. These *line printers* or *chain printers* are high-speed devices commonly used for computer output. Quality is sacrificed for speed. Speeds range from 100 to 3800 lines per minute.

Dot matrix printers have many advantages

The *dot matrix printer* produces characters by use of tiny dots. Low-density dot matrix printing is considered sufficient for the printing of drafts. The letter-quality printer is then used for final copies. Relatively high-density dot matrix printers that have near-letter-quality print are available. The advantage of a dot matrix printer is that, in addition to printing alphanumeric characters, it can also produce symbols and graphic representations. High-density dot matrix printers remain quite popular as an inexpensive yet versatile means of output.

Nonimpact Printers

The *electrostatic* (xerographic) *copier* is a familiar piece of equipment. The photocopier has largely replaced carbon paper as the method of reproducing one or more copies.

Intelligent copiers may soon be the high-speed printers used by many firms

Businesses that produce many documents may find that an *intelligent copier/printer* (IC/P) meets their needs. This device can be linked to a word processor and activated by the word processing specialist. The operator keys the document and, when the copy is ready, it is transmitted electronically to the IC/P, which can store the document for later printing or produce the output immediately. The IC/P can produce letter-quality documents with a wide variety of type styles, sizes, and line spacing as fast as 120 pages per minute.

This printer could replace more conventional forms of printing for many firms. In addition to printing words, the copier has a sophisticated graphics capability. And, the IC/P accepts data from computers and other IC/Ps as well as from word processors.

Phototypesetting saves time and paper

Another machine seen in the large modern office is the streamlined phototypesetting machine. Printing was once the exclusive domain of specialists working with large, expensive equipment whose operation required much expertise. Documents, such as annual reports, that needed a highly professional look had to be sent outside the firm. Today more than 50 percent of large businesses find it cost-effective to do their typesetting and even printing in-house. The savings are realized through streamlined procedures: the word processing specialist keys the document; the author edits it; the word processing specialist enters the corrections; and when the final copy is approved, the document is transmitted electronically to the phototypesetting machine. Special typesetting codes are entered on the document, and the phototypesetter produces a camera-ready copy. The copy is then run, often in multicolour, on a printing press in the firm or by an outside company.

This process has several advantages. It produces a professional-looking document that is keyed only once. Since the document never has to leave the premises, confidentiality can be maintained, deadlines can be met more satisfactorily, and the material is stored in-house for future use and revision.

Distribution of Information

Electronic mail speeds document delivery and lowers costs

At present, Canada Post carries the majority of mail generated in this country. However, hand-delivered mail may not always reach its destination in a timely fashion. In addition, hand-delivering the mail is the most time-consuming link in the document cycle.

For many years, businesses have been communicating by way of *Telex/TWX* machines. This system, operated by Bell Canada and CNCP, has made it possible for a firm with a Telex machine to communicate instantly with another firm that also has such a machine. Because an operator must key the Telex message into the machine, errors may occur.

With the introduction of the low-cost *facsimile machine* (FAX), many companies are finding that their Telex machines are becoming obsolete. The FAX takes an existing document, copies it, and sends it electronically to a receiving FAX machine, using regular telephone lines. It can transmit alphanumeric data as well as handwritten information, pictures, and graphs. Portable facsimile equipment is available for field assignments or trips.

To operate a FAX machine, the sender simply places the document face down on the document tray and then enters the FAX number of the receiver into the machine. The FAX dials the number, waits for an answer, "reads" the data electronically, and sends it to the receiving FAX. Since companies generally have dedicated lines for their FAX machines, the receiver's FAX machine answers the phone, accepts the incoming data electronically, and prints it onto specially coated paper. The sender's FAX prints out a status report indicating that the FAX message has either been received or failed to transmit. Because the operation can be handled automatically, materials can be sent to locations in time zones where offices are closed for the day. The message will be waiting for the receiver when she or he arrives at the office the next morning.

Computers can deliver electronic mail

Both Telex/TWX and FAX are examples of *electronic mail* or *telecommunications*. Though these technologies have been used for a number of years, these terms weren't used to describe them until recently. Other methods of electronic mail are now also available. Computers can be equipped with modems to communicate with other computers. For example, a branch office in Halifax develops a marketing plan that must be approved by the corporate office in Toronto. The plan is keyed on the computer in the Halifax office. The information is then transmitted electronically to a compatible computer in Toronto. No paper is used, no valuable time is lost waiting for the mail to be delivered. When the plan is received in Toronto, it can be printed or read from a screen. Suggestions can be made, approval given, and the plan transmitted back to Halifax within a short time. Companies can save thousands of dollars a month through the use of electronic mail.

Electronic junk mail can be a problem

As electronic mail becomes more common, it is increasingly used to transmit unnecessary, system-wide messages. Some organizations are attempting to limit these unnecessary messages by issuing policies limiting the types of messages that can be sent. Messages for all users of the system are then processed through a central location to ensure they are compatible with these policies.

Satellites are the carriers of the future

Today telephone cables are used as the work horses of electronic-mail transmissions, but satellites are the transmission devices with great potential. They already carry many of the telephone companies' signals. In addition, private companies provide services that allow firms to transmit voice, video, data, and graphic communications. Predictions are that satellite transmission will be available at a cost of 1.5 cents a page. It is therefore reasonable to believe electronic mail will become the future pipeline for business communications.

Multifunction Workstations

Multifunction workstations aid the executive

The multifunction workstation is an electronic device designed to improve managers' productivity. With it, the executive can view the day's appointment calendar electronically. Reminders placed in the tickler file will appear at the touch of a button. If a meeting with associates needs to be called, the associates' calendars will appear on the screen, a time for the meeting will be set, and the notices for the meeting will be distributed electronically. Incoming messages and mail will appear on the screen — no paper to shuffle, no message slips to lose. Electronic files, sometimes called "hot files," can be called to the screen at will. The need to rummage in the files or call the secretary to find a document is reduced.

Updating a report requires only these steps: the company's data base or a subscription data base such as Info Globe is accessed for the needed information; the previous report is called to the screen, revised, and new charts and graphs are generated; and the document is transmitted to the word processing centre for new formatting and/or printing if necessary.

Miniaturization enables workers to take the electronic office on the road

The executive who is used to having electronic technology as a tool in the office also wants to have access to it outside the office. The "office in a briefcase" fulfils this need. Computers, word processors, dictating equipment, and printers are now miniaturized to fit in a briefcase. With this equipment the executive can transmit orders, reports, letters, or memos from any telephone.

Until relatively recently, only executives had portable electronic offices; however, today many salespersons and delivery drivers also have them. They can track inventory and place orders easily while on the road.

Technology to Reduce Business Travel

Teleconferencing is emerging as an electronic tool designed to cut the need for business travel. Business travel is costly not only in terms of dollars spent but also in terms of time. Teleconferencing uses conventional closed-circuit television technology in which the participants are able to see each other on the screen.

At other times, a computer conference is useful. It uses terminals, printers, and telephone lines to access a computer for direct communication. Participants do not need to be at their communications instruments simultaneously; they can read others' input and give their own at their convenience.

Recent Developments

Artificial intelligence is another emerging electronic technology. An artificial intelligence system will react to memo-like requests, sort through knowledge stored in a computer, and carry out a line of reasoning. Experts predict that such a system will read our mail and tell us about the important parts. It will generate its own notices, monitor responses, and co-ordinate managers' schedules.[3]

Voice, graphics, data, text, and video information can already be integrated using laser disks with touch screen monitors to support business, education, and other presentation requirements. Inevitably, the processes will be refined, equipment production costs will decrease, and these sophisticated devices will be feasible for many businesses.

Writing in the Electronic Office

Computers have not changed the fundamental writing process; however, they have made parts of that process much less frustrating and more efficient. This section will show you how to take advantage of the features of word processing for writing business documents.

Basic Terminology

Both dedicated word processors and word processing software for microcomputers have several significant text-editing capabilities. Many changes that used to mean retyping an entire document can now be made with just a few keystrokes. Although most of these features are used during the revision phase of the writing process, a short description of the basic commands is included here to help you understand the descriptions that follow.

The functions available on individual equipment and software generally vary with the amount of money invested in the system. You'll need to refer to the word processing manual for specific instructions; however, the following features are most commonly available:

Delete/insert allows characters, words, sentences, paragraphs, and so on to be deleted or inserted anywhere in the text. Most systems can be set to "insert mode" where anything you type is added to the text or to "typeover mode" where new characters replace those already on the screen. If you are unfamiliar with word processing, you may want to use the "insert mode" so that you don't delete information unintentionally.

Copy/move allows any amount of information to be copied or moved anywhere within the document, or to any other document that is on the system. For instance, a paragraph that appears in one document but needs to be repeated in another document can easily be moved or copied without keying it again. This feature is sometimes called "cut and paste" to reflect the traditional step it replaces.

Block commands allow you to highlight large chunks of text so that you can move, copy, or delete them with only a few key strokes.

Format change allows the line length and tabs to be reset at any time. The system automatically adjusts all lines to the requested format. Vertical spacing can also be changed; single, double, triple, one and a half, and quarter spacing are among the options.

Hard returns allow you to separate paragraphs or chunks of information. Unlike typewriters, word processing packages automatically go to the next line (soft return) when the line is the length specified in the format. Therefore, you need to hit the "return" key only when you end a paragraph or have a line of a specific length (as for items in a list). Each hard return represents one line, so that you would hit the "return" key twice if you want a double space between paragraphs.

Tab and indent keys allow automatic spacing. Hitting the "tab" key indents the first line of a paragraph by the number of spaces specified in your format. If you want to indent an entire paragraph, you need to hit the "indent" key.

Pagination/repagination allows the selection of the number of lines to appear on each page. The operator keys in the desired number, and the system counts the lines and indicates the page breaks. When a document has been edited and text has been added or deleted, new page breaks can be automatically inserted and the revised document printed rapidly.

Justified right margin directs the system to produce a document with a straight right-hand margin. This feature is especially useful in newsletters and manuals; however, it should be used only on systems that have proportional spacing. Otherwise, "rivers" of white space tend to appear in the document because the amount of space between words is increased.

Merge allows the combining of previously keyed text, such as form letters and lists of names, to create repetitive letters that appear to be originals. The merge function can also produce form letters containing variables that change with each name.

Global search and replace locates a specified character string wherever it appears in the document. The characters can then be replaced with another set of characters.

Headers and footers allow specified information to appear at the top and/or bottom of each page in a document. For example, section titles can be placed automatically at the top of each page, and consecutive page numbers at the bottom of each page.

Dictionary allows spelling to be checked automatically. Incorrect words are highlighted and the operator can correct errors. This function should not replace careful proofreading of a document because the dictionary cannot recognize all errors. For example, the dictionary does not know that "their" was used when the correct word was "there." Neither can it check for word omissions or transpositions.

Thesaurus allows the writer to summon up alternative words. The writer identifies the word that he or she would like to change, and the computer supplies a number of choices. The writer makes a selection and the new word automatically replaces the previous one.

Subscripts and superscripts allow numbers to be placed slightly above or below lines for use in footnote references or formulas, for example, 2^{10} or CO_2.

Getting Started

Writing on the computer will be an exercise in futility unless you force yourself to learn how to type. If you time yourself writing out a few sentences, you'll probably find that you can write about 30 words a minute. Therefore, unless you can type at least as quickly, you won't save any time in getting your ideas down initially. Even a typing speed of 30 to 40 words a minute will allow you to increase your writing speed dramatically, because you won't have to rewrite your final draft. To learn how to type, you can borrow a "typing tutor" software package from most libraries.

In the pre-writing or planning stage of the writing process, you may find that a planning template such as the one shown in Figure 8.3 will force you to approach your task systematically. You just store the blank form as a separate document, and each time you begin a writing task, you open the file and enter your data. Because word processing packages allow you to insert any amount of data, you can write as little or as much under each question as you need to. When you have filled in the form, you simply save the completed form under a new name.

Figure 8.4 shows how the planning template could have been used for the memo in Example 1 in Chapter 4. Notice that we've eliminated "name" and "position" from the template because the memo is going to all members of the department and it's not necessary to list their names. This time, reader questions are used to organize the details of the memo. If you brainstorm the questions and put them in the order the reader is likely to ask them, you'll find that your first draft may be easier to write. In addition, key words from the questions can often be used as headings. For example, "What's the policy on vacations?" becomes "Vacation Policy" in the final memo.

What do I want my reader to do or know? (purpose)

To whom am I writing?

name:
position:

name:
position:

What do I need to remember about my readers? (audience characteristics)

What do I need to remember about the situation? (context)

If I could write only one sentence on this topic, what would I say? (main idea)

If my readers see this sentence, what questions would they ask? (include the details by answering the questions in point form)

Figure 8.3 Basic Planning Template

What do I want my reader to do or know? (purpose)

- That I need their vacation schedule by April 8.

To whom am I writing?

- All print materials production staff.

What do I need to remember about my readers? (audience characteristics)

- Some have worked for the department for several years; others have worked here less than a year.

What do I need to remember about the situation? (context)

- We have a policy that everyone must adhere to; short-term employees may not know that policy.

continued

Figure 8.4 Completed Planning Template

- My staff are busy so they won't appreciate something that's complicated.
- I can make the task easy by providing a vacation planner and instructions.

If I could write only one sentence on this topic, what would I say? (main idea)

- "I need to have your vacation schedule by April 8."

If my readers see this sentence, what questions would they ask? (include the details by answering the questions in point form)

- Why do you need the schedule this early?
    - So I can accommodate everyone's request.
- I'm fairly new; what chance do I have of getting the time I want?
    - We'll try to accommodate everyone's first choice — if we know far enough in advance we can hire replacement staff.
- What's the policy on vacations?
    - Entitlement is based on fiscal year of April 1 to March 31. Everyone who has been with the company for at least one year is eligible for three weeks of vacation.
    - Employees with less than one year's service receive one day for every month they have worked before April 1 of the new fiscal year.
    - After one year you get at least two weeks during July and August if you want them.
- How do I submit my schedule?
    - Matrix planner with boxes for every day of the year.
    - Weekends and holidays shaded.
    - Use code 03 for indicating which days you want.
    - Don't worry about taking one or two days here and there.
- Where do I go if I need help?
    - See me.
    - I'll be out of the office for rest of week.

Drafting the Document

Writing on the computer has a disadvantage. Paper notes can be spread out over a large surface so that you can see the entire document at a glance. On a computer screen, you can see only a portion of the document at any given time. Therefore, many writers prefer to print a copy of their planning document so they can see the entire plan at once. Some even prefer to do some preliminary drafting on paper — particularly if they are fleshing out the key points and putting them into sentences that can be transferred directly to the memo.

Preparing the Final Draft

The text-editing capabilities of word processors provide the greatest increases in writing efficiency. With a few keystrokes, you can completely reorganize your document, inserting, moving, and deleting ideas as necessary. Moreover, you get an absolutely clean copy every time you print the document so that you can more easily see the document from the reader's standpoint.

Advanced Word Processing Features

Once you have mastered the basics, you may want to experiment with some of the advanced features found on the more sophisticated word processing packages. Here are just a few that can help you write more efficiently:

The outline feature allows you to create a hierarchical document outline. Using this feature, you can specify the levels of your headings (moving from the general to the specific) and number them automatically. The outline feature is particularly useful for long research papers and reports.

Style sheets help you format documents automatically. Style sheets ensure that the same types of text (headings, lists, paragraphs, footers) in a document are formatted in the same way. For example, all headings might be in bold face to make them stand out. This feature is particularly useful when several people are responsible for producing a single report, because it ensures a consistent format throughout the document.

Macros allow you to save time by "programming" a series of keystrokes into the word processor and accessing your "program" with two or three keystrokes. For example, you may want to create a macro that types your company's name automatically. You can also create macros that will format your document automatically by setting margins, tabs, and page length.

Summary

The traditional office is giving way to the electronic office that uses a work group approach to get work done more efficiently. This team approach allows individuals to specialize and progress on the basis of skills and abilities. This chapter described the four components of the electronic office.

1. **Input** can take several forms:
   - traditional longhand (slow to produce and hard to decipher)
   - shorthand dictation (requires the time of two people)
   - machine dictation (simple and cost-effective)
   - optical character readers (reduces keyboarding time)
   - prewritten messages (form documents with variable information)
   - writer keying (preferred by many writers)

2. **Processing** uses up-to-date technology:
   - electronic typewriters with limited memory
   - dedicated word processors that fall into three categories:
     - stand-alone systems
     - shared-logic systems
     - distributed-logic systems
   - microcomputers with word processing software
   - desktop publishing software

3. **Storage** can be either internal or external:
   - file management is crucial
   - electronic storage media are vulnerable to damage
   - systematic labelling of files saves time and frustration

4. **Output** (hard copy) can be produced with
   - impact printers
   - nonimpact printers

Electronic files and electronic mail are making the "paperless office" a reality. With them, managers can:

- conduct research
- receive and answer mail and messages
- keep track of appointments
- search files
- access data bases
- construct charts and graphs

Information can be distributed in several ways:

- Telex/TWX
- FAX
- computers with modems
- satellites

The "office in a briefcase" is now a reality.
Teleconferencing saves time by reducing the need for travel.
The electronic office simplifies the writing process by providing:

- a wide variety of text-editing capabilities
- spelling checkers and electronic thesauruses
- the ability to design style sheets, macros, and templates.

Review Questions

1. What are the four components of the electronic office?
2. Give an example of each of the four components of the electronic office.
3. Describe three advantages of the electronic office.
4. Define a work group and discuss its advantages.
5. There are four primary methods of input for business documents. Which would you choose? Why?
6. Who should assume ultimate responsibility for the correctness of a business document? Why?
7. Why is it a good idea for the business communicator to understand the functions of word processing equipment?
8. How is the writing process affected by word processors?

Activities

1. You are employed by Datatech, Inc. Accounting Associates, 4721 Calgary Trail, Edmonton, Alta. T5H 2E7, has just placed a $7500 order for an accounting software package. This is Accounting Associates' first order with Datatech. You are asked to write an acknowledgement letter.
   a. Jot down a guide for the letter.
   b. Gain access to a dictating machine or tape recorder. Dictate the letter into the machine. Be sure to adhere to the procedures given in this chapter.
   c. Ask someone to transcribe your letter.
   d. Evaluate the transcribed letter to see if the transcriber was able to follow your directions.
   e. Indicate how you can improve your next dictated letter.
2. Survey six of your friends or your parents' friends who work in offices to find out what kind of technology their organizations use. Report the results of your survey in a memo to your instructor.

Discussion Cases

What's All the Fuss?

During 1991, Blackview Heights Technical College was expanding rapidly, particularly in response to demand from businesses in the area for courses in all aspects of computer literacy. The computer revolution meant a large demand from executives for courses that would help them get the most from the large amount of computer software now available for inexpensive personal and portable computers.

To cope with this growing aspect of their operations, the college decided to hire a technical services manager who would be responsible for the co-ordination of the college's computing facilities, which were to be used by the teaching staff, as well as for administrative purposes, including student record-keeping, documentation management, and general accounting.

The successful applicant for the job was Mary Rutgers, who had decided to transfer to the public sector from industry because the college was much closer to her home, and had better child-minding facilities.

After a week in the job, checking out what seemed to be going on, Mary decided to send the following memo to all staff (both faculty and support staff):

MEMO TO ALL STAFF (without exception!)

FROM: Mary Rutgers
Technical Services Manager

DATE: June 30, 1991

SUBJECT: Abuse of College Property

Since my arrival at the College, I have been appalled at the poor use to which the college computing facilities are being put. For about half the day, the mainframe is hardly touched. Then, it is overloaded between the late morning and early afternoon, with lengthy delays occurring before users are able to sign on.

This problem is easily solved. From now on, administrative staff will be barred from logging onto the computer after 1030 and before 1430. This will spread the load on the computer, and can be easily achieved if staff

continued

begin at 0800 or work until 1800. (Several staff have expressed an interest in working flexible hours anyway.)

It also appears that some academic staff are using the computing facilities to carry out their own work. In future, all instructors must discuss doing so with me first, and have permission in writing, before initiating any projects on the computer. If this law is infringed, severe disciplinary action may be taken.

From now on, students will not be able to access the computer from modems at home, because I have come across two students using the networking capability of the system to create a file of scandalous stories about their various instructors. This juvenile behaviour is not going to take place on my machines.

I have also decided to disband the Computing Resources Committee. Meetings are a waste of time. This Committee seems to me to be as slow as molasses in January in reaching decisions about what personal computers to buy, so I have decided I can do this job more efficiently myself.

These new rules are effective immediately.

Case Questions

1. How do you think that the staff who receive this memo are going to react? Why?
2. How would you deal with the three main problems that Mary has identified? Why?
3. Does using the computer for personal work present an ethical problem? Why or why not?

A Question of Security

Despite regular warnings, the staff at Evans Forest Products were often careless about computer security. The computer service manager, Dave Woo, decided that he would write to all users of the electronic-mail system to remind them of the need for security. Here's the memo he sent (on the electronic-mail system, of course):

continued

To: All E-Mail Users

From: Dave Woo
Computer Service Manager

Subject: Security and Electronic Mail

Usage of our electronic mail system continues to grow, replacing more and more the paper transfer of information. This allows messages to move much more rapidly between people, but we do require occasional reminders of the security issues involved.

Information stored on your IDs are protected from others viewing or altering that information providing:

1. You are the only one who knows your password
2. You sign off your terminal or PC when you are not physically present

Computer Services does not keep a log file of messages sent on the electronic mail system. Within Computer Services, a system administrator, a electronic mail administrator, and their backups have the only access to Password files.

We will be forcing you to change your password at the beginning of next month, but it should be changed three times a year. Here are the guidelines for selecting a password:

1. Make them something you can remember. We require a signed password release form before we can give you your password if you forget it.
2. Do not choose a password that is your spouse's, children's, pet's, or car's name. They are too simple to figure out.
3. Choose a mix of numbers and letters, or use a foreign word.

My personal method is to flip open a dictionary and point my finger. The word I point to becomes my new password.

You must sign off from your ID if you leave your desk. The computer system has no way of knowing who is pressing the keys. Besides, someone could sent a message using your ID and you would have no idea the message had been sent.

continued

Very confidential information regarding Personnel and Health matters SHOULD NOT be stored on the electronic mail system. You should keep it either on disk or paper, locked in a secure location. If you have any questions, give me a call at 7766.

P.S. From long experience with electronic mail, a good rule of thumb if you have to complain electronically is to wait for a few hours or until the next day before you send the memo. Without physical contact, it is very easy to give the wrong impressions by communicating electronically. Productive criticism via electronic mail is a difficult art to master. If you aren't sure, call or talk to the person.

Case Questions

1. Did Dave Woo proofread his memo before sending it? Why do you think he did or didn't?
2. How do you think that the staff who receive this memo are going to react? Why?
3. Other than having people send unauthorized messages, what other problems can result from leaving your terminal unattended?
4. What warnings might you add to Dave Woo's regarding security? Why?
5. Why is Dave Woo's advice about complaints particularly useful?
6. Compare the tone of this memo to the one in the previous discussion case. Which memo is more likely to be favourably received? Justify your opinion.

Chapter 9

Routine Letters

Learning Objectives

In this chapter, you'll learn how to write routine letters and memos that transmit information effectively. More specifically, you will be able to:

1. identify the characteristics of routine messages and the kinds of situations for which each is appropriate
2. recognize the strategic decisions that must be made in planning routine messages
3. make effective requests through letters and memos
4. develop appropriate written responses to the requests of others
5. use the indirect approach when a blunt refusal may offend or annoy the reader
6. identify the advantages and disadvantages of form letters and the kinds of situations for which form letters are appropriate

Preview Case

One of the things that Mario Gardini likes best about his job is the variety of his duties. As public information co-ordinator at a regional office of the provincial Ministry of the Environment, he deals with anyone from outside the ministry who seeks information from it. He meets with plant managers, property developers, newspaper reporters — anyone who, for whatever reason, wants information from the ministry.

He receives several dozens of letters each month from students who are writing research papers, and he is frustrated by many of them. Although he always wants to help these students, they often make it difficult for him. What frustrates him most is the poor quality of some of these requests for information. While some of the letters are clear and easily understood, others are not. In fact, some are so poorly written that he doesn't know exactly what to do with them.

Last week one writer requested, "Please send me information about what the ministry is doing to clear up water pollution related to the paper industry." Mario knew exactly what information to send that person.

Recently, however, one less understandable writer wrote, "I'm doing a term paper on the Ministry of the Environment. Please send information." Mario had no idea what that person actually wanted, so he could not help. Others are equally vague; some misspell words; others do not even include return addresses, thus making response impossible.

After two years on the job Mario has become very aware of the importance of letter writing. Having received thousands of letters, he says, "If people realized the impact that a well-written letter has, they would be a lot more careful in writing their letters."

Overview

Letters are crucial to organizations, despite the wide use of the telephone, other electronic media, and business forms

Despite the ever-growing use of the telephone and other electronic media for business communication, letters and memos continue to play a crucial role in business. While organizations have developed multitudes of forms that make it easier to convey certain kinds of information, letters and memos are still best for many situations. For instance, letters provide the most personal contact much of the public has with many businesses and government agencies; they are frequently the organization's sole contact with many individuals. The receiver forms an impression of an organization through such letters.

Writing letters and memos that work is not easy, but, as was pointed out in Chapter 4, the process can be simplified using a systematic approach. In addition, experienced business writers have developed guidelines for writing various routine letters. One purpose of this chapter is to show you how you can apply these guidelines in various situations.

In general, you can choose from two approaches: direct and indirect. The *direct approach*, where the main idea is stated first, is by far the most common. However, in certain limited situations, the *indirect approach*, which delays the main idea, is helpful.

Planning Direct Messages

Direct messages put the main idea at the beginning

As indicated in Chapter 4, stating your main idea near the beginning of your letters and memos helps busy readers determine quickly what they are being asked to do. Furthermore, when the main idea is at the beginning, readers can quickly decide whether they should act on the letter or whether it should be referred to someone else in the organization. Throughout the rest of this section, you'll notice that each of the examples uses the same basic organization pattern:

1. Start with the main idea(s).
2. Present the secondary details.
3. Close on a positive note.

While the requirements of a particular audience and situation may warrant a departure from this pattern, it provides a general framework within which to organize direct messages. The main idea may be a request for information, a routine response to a previous request, or simply a piece of information. The secondary details often consist of explanations. Providing the secondary details means anticipating the questions your reader may have and responding to them in the order they are likely to be asked.

Avoid clichés in your closing

The main function of the positive note is to provide a sense of closure or completeness to the message. Its omission will have no significant effect. Rather than ending with a cliché, such as "Do not hesitate to contact me if I can be of further help," you would be wiser to omit the close or, better yet, end with a brief and direct statement such as "Write me again when I can help."

Purposes of Direct Messages

The main-idea-first-followed-by-secondary-details principle of direct messages can be applied to several variations of the two main categories of such messages:

- requests for information or action, including placing an order, applying for credit, or making a claim
- responses to requests for action or information, including acknowledging an order, granting credit, or adjusting a claim

The guides in this section are intended to help you compose the various types of letters and memos, but are not meant to be used as outlines. The situations for which letters are written vary so much that most letter writing must be individualized. By viewing each situation as unique, you are more likely to write a letter or memo that will elicit the desired outcome.

Requests for Information or Action

Routine requests are common

Routine requests are often the subject of letters and memos written on the job. In requesting routine information, state the request (the main idea) in the first sentence so the reader knows exactly what information you want or what you want done. Next, provide whatever additional details may be necessary (secondary details). Last, point to the future by stating what you want the reader to do next (provides a friendly closing). Figure 9.1 is an example of a routine request that follows this pattern.

Problems occur when requests are not sufficiently specific

Business organizations send and receive numerous requests for routine information. The more specific a request is, the more likely it is to elicit the desired response. However, not all writers produce clear, specific requests. Consider the following request that the president of one company received after he had given the keynote address and had conducted one of the workshops at a local exposition. Both items were covered on the local television news.

On the six o'clock news last night, they showed a brief portion of the speech you gave yesterday. It sounded interesting, and I would like to learn what else you said in your speech.

Please send me a copy of the speech you gave.

Notice that the request comes in the final paragraph, not the first, and that the writer doesn't specify which speech he wants. Now, here's an effective rewrite of the request:

Please send me a copy of the speech you gave at Wood Expo on Tuesday, October 11, 1992. I believe the title was "My Customer, the Boss."

I saw a brief excerpt from the speech on the local CBC-news last night and thought you made several excellent points.

You can mail the copy to me at:

3535 Slocan Road
Coquitlam BC
V5C 3N9

#105-801 West 7th Avenue
Vancouver, B.C.
V5Z 1C5

1992 9 09

Vice President, Marketing
Canco Ltd.
31124 Old Orchard Road
Surrey, B.C.
V3B 1R2

Subject: Request for Product Information

Please send me information on your vacuum metallized flexible packaging. I understand that your company manufactures these products locally.

I am writing a term paper on innovative packaging materials and would like specific information on the uses of vacuum metallized flexible packaging and, if possible, the manufacturing process.

If you send me the information within the next two weeks, I will be able to meet the October 15 deadline for my paper.

Sincerely,

Frank Lofton

Frank Lofton

Figure 9.1 Routine Request for Information

Information Request Guide

- Main Idea
  - Make a specific request immediately.
- Secondary Details
  - Ask whatever specific questions are necessary to get the desired information.
  - Avoid wordiness by asking direct questions. "Will the machine ... " is preferable to "I am interested in ... "
- Friendly Closing
  - Make a positive and an appreciative reference to the action desired of the reader.

Placing Orders

Use the direct approach to place an order without an order form

When you order something from a supplier the process is simplified if you have an order form from the company. When you do not, the direct approach works best. Indicate in the letter exactly what you are ordering, the instructions for shipping, and the manner in which you intend to pay (see Figure 9.2).

Box 935
Cold Lake AB
TOA 1VO

April 23, 1992

Order Desk
Harris Hardware Supply
2435 Industrial Parkway
Edmonton AB
T5B 2C8

Subject: Order for X-365 Workbench

continued

Figure 9.2 Placing an Order

Please send me one X-365 Workbench before May 30. I've enclosed a cheque for $85.55: $69.95 plus tax and shipping charges.

I understand from your catalogue that you ship all goods through Able Couriers. They can deliver the workbench to my home address:

15 Marguerite Street
Cold Lake, Alberta
Phone: 654-1234

Since I intend to give the workbench as a birthday gift, delivery prior to May 30 is important to me. If, for any reason, the workbench is unavailable, please notify me immediately.

Irene Klar

Irene Klar

IK:ir

Whether using an order form or writing an order letter, you must include all of the necessary details. Delays often occur because the order letter omitted essentials.

Incomplete order letters are responsible for many delayed orders

Order Letter Guide

- Main Idea
  - Start with your main point. "Please send" or "Please ship" are appropriate openings and are likely to result in a fast response.
- Secondary Details
  - Provide all the details necessary for the seller to fill the order now. If details such as catalogue number, size, colour, and price are omitted, further correspondence will be necessary and a delay will result.
  - Indicate the payment plan you will follow.
  - Include shipping instructions if you have a preference.
- Friendly Closing
  - Close with your expectations of an appropriate delivery date.

Requesting Credit

An application for credit is a kind of order

Most requests for consumer credit are made by completing an application form furnished by the organization from which credit is sought. Even the person who writes a letter requesting credit will probably be asked to complete such a form. However, if applying for credit by letter, a standard order letter is required whether you are applying for individual credit (see Figure 9.3) or for credit for a company (see Figure 9.4). As in an order letter, you should get to the point immediately and then provide the necessary details. Headings are useful when you want your reader to find specific information quickly.

<u>Subject: Application for Credit</u>

Please open a charge account for me. I can demonstrate that I have used credit responsibly in the past.

<u>Name and Address and Phone Number</u>

Marcia O. Bonner
400 Tiffany Avenue, Apt. 908
Thunder Bay, Ontario
P7E 2R8
Phone: 555-3456 (home)
321-7654 (work)

In Toronto, I lived at 1011 Live Oak Lane, Building C, Toronto, Ontario, M6S 2G3, for three years.

<u>Credit History</u>

While living in Toronto, I had charge accounts with Eaton's, Sears, and the Bay. I paid these accounts on or before the due date each month.

In Thunder Bay, I bank at Royal Trust (Main Street Branch) where I have a combined chequing and savings account (#123456-7). In Toronto, I banked at the Yonge and Bloor branch of the Bank of Montreal.

<u>Employment History</u>

Since graduating from college five years ago, I have worked for B&J Electronics as a sales representative. I earn more than $40,000 a year.

If you require any additional information, please call me at work during the day.

Figure 9.3 Applying for Credit for an Individual

Subject: Request for a $1500 Line of Credit

Please open a $1500 line of credit for my company, Schief Clothes for Tots, Ltd., formerly known as Threads Unlimited.

On July 1, 1991, I purchased Threads Unlimited from the estate of Waldo Gillis. I plan to feature your Falcon line of sportswear as our highest-quality offering.

I have twelve years of experience in children's clothing, the last four of which were spent owning and operating Tiny Tots Togs in Saskatoon. The Saskatoon Credit Bureau has my complete credit history on file.

The grand opening of Schief Clothes for Tots will be held August 31 to September 2, Labour Day weekend. By that time, I hope to have a complete inventory of Falcon clothes for children.

Please send me confirmation of the $1500 line of credit and details about your payment plan. Also indicate the date by which I must place an order so that I will receive it by mid-August.

Figure 9.4 Applying for a Business Line of Credit

Making Routine Claims

Consumers understandably evaluate stores according to how the stores treat their customers. Similarly, the store's response to requests for adjustments is greatly influenced by the manner in which the customer asks for the adjustment. Consider this ill-conceived request:

In seeking an adjustment you should indicate immediately what is being sought

When I saw your humidifier advertised on television, I thought it was just what I needed. You said that it would solve the problems of dry air and static electricity, and both of these are real problems in my house. [This information is unnecessary since it does not advance the reader's understanding of the problem.]

One thing I didn't anticipate was the way its colour would clash with most of the furnishings in my house. I thought that grey would blend in with the surroundings, but it doesn't. [Overly wordy and beside the point.]

After using it for one week, I've decided that I can't get used to it. None of the colours in which it comes would be any better for my house. [Writer now states the problem, but reader still has no idea of the specifics of the humidifier — model, size, etc.]

I would like to return my humidifier to you. If I do so, would you please send me a full refund? I would certainly appreciate it. [Writer finally requests a specific action.]

This letter is wordy and rambling. It delays the main idea unnecessarily, moving from very general information (seen on television) to the specific request (a full refund).

When writing to seek a routine claim, you should use the direct sequence, from specific to general. Tell the reader the action you are seeking and the reasons for the request. Here's a more appropriate request for an adjustment:

Are you able to offer a full refund of $245 on the Airflow humidifier [model AC345-97] I purchased from your company on August 31? The grey exterior clashes with the furniture in my family room and this particular model does not come in any other colours.

I have enclosed a copy of the invoice that accompanied the humidifier. Please advise me on the procedure for returning the humidifier.

Routine Claim Guide

- Write promptly.
- Request a specific action in the first sentence.
- Explain why such action would be desirable.
- Express confidence in the reader's judgement and appreciation for the action you are seeking.
- Avoid sarcasm, name-calling, and threats.

Granting Routine Requests

When you can say yes to a request, you should do so enthusiastically. Since it is the answer that the reader is hoping for, you should say it immediately. When a grade six teacher wrote to ask for a tour of a soft drink bottling plant, the manager was happy to oblige:

Yes, I will be happy to give your grade six class a tour of our plant on the afternoon of May 5. Your students will probably be especially interested in the assembly line, but I will also show them one of our research labs if they care to see one.

The enclosed brochures will acquaint your students with our full line of products. If you have them read and discuss the brochures before your visit, the tour will be more interesting.

I look forward to meeting you and your class in the lobby of Building B at one o'clock next Wednesday afternoon. I have enclosed a map of our facility for your convenience.

When the manager of a textile plant was asked to donate the plant's scrap materials to a charity drive, he responded with enthusiasm and sincerity, as follows:

You can enhance the image of your firm by the manner in which you grant routine requests

Yes, we will gladly contribute the scrap materials from our mill for the next four weeks to First United's charity drive. Many of the poor and elderly of the community will benefit from the blanket-making project. It is certainly worthwhile, and we are pleased to be a part of it.

We will deliver the scraps to your temporary warehouse on each of the next four Fridays at 2:00 in the afternoon.

When granting routine requests from potential customers, your letter should display those characteristics likely to create a positive image of your firm.

To convey a positive image, you must avoid certain pitfalls. The writer of the following letter, unfortunately, did not avoid them in responding to an inquiry about when a specific course would next be offered:

Thank you for your letter of February 29 in which you requested information concerning Auto Repairs for the Layperson.	This statement is obvious and unnecessary since the letter is in response to a request.
This is one of our most popular courses, and you are one of many who have expressed an interest in it. The practical nature of the course and the present shortage of auto mechanics seem to explain the popularity of this course.	This information is irrelevant. Besides doing nothing to meet the needs of the reader, the paragraph is oriented more to the writer than to the reader.

You will be happy to learn that we will offer Auto Repairs for the Layperson in the fall quarter. Classes begin on September 8 and will meet Monday and Wednesday evenings from 7:00 to 10:00.

This is the information the reader asked for, and it should appear at the beginning of the letter.

I have enclosed the necessary registration form. Please complete the form and return it to me as soon as possible along with your tuition payment for the amount indicated on the registration form.

This information is necessary and helpful, but too vague. The writer should state a specific date rather than "as soon as possible."

We feel sure that you will benefit greatly from this course. Please continue to think of us when you want to enrol in additional courses.

This paragraph is inappropriate. Since the reader has not yet taken any course, it is not the time to sell future courses.

Use the direct arrangement when granting routine requests

The writer of the above letter could have made a better impression and conveyed the information more efficiently by using the direct arrangement:

Our course, Auto Repairs for the Layperson, will begin on September 8. The class will meet on Monday and Wednesday evenings from 7:00 to 10:00 during the fall quarter.

You may register by completing the attached form and returning it to me by September 6. By enclosing your tuition payment of $150 you will be able to avoid the delays often encountered when paying tuition on the first night of the quarter. Many have already expressed interest in Auto Repairs for the Layperson, so register early to avoid disappointment.

Please call me if you have any questions.

Similarly, you can create a positive image of yourself within the organization by the manner in which you grant routine requests to subordinates. What image of the writer would the following memo suggest?

It's good to see that you're taking an interest in your professional development. We like to encourage our employees to do so.

We've been dealing with restraint for the past three years, so there hasn't been much money to go to conferences. However, I did manage to get some money for your request.

And by the way, you won't have to use your holidays to get the time off to attend. The company can do without you for a couple of days.

While the writer may have been trying for a "folksy," friendly style, this memo is more likely to elicit the responses shown in brackets below:

It's good to see that you're taking an interest in your professional development. [But I've been taking courses for years and you've never commented on it before.] We like to encourage our employees to do so. [Oh, oh, here comes the bad news.]

We've been dealing with restraint for the past three years, so there hasn't been much money to go to conferences. [Just as I thought, I can't get any money to go.] However, I did manage to get some money for your request. [You're kidding.]

And by the way, you won't have to use your holidays to get the time off to attend. The company can do without you for a couple of days. [Now, what does that mean? Maybe I shouldn't go after all.]

Here's a rewrite that would create a positive image of the writer:

Pack your bags! Your request to attend the annual meeting of the National Society for Performance and Instruction has been approved. You will have the three days off with pay and $2500 to cover the course fee as well as travel and accommodation costs.

Please complete the attached Request for Authority to Travel form so that we can have your advance ready for you by Friday. Then, when you get back, submit your receipts to Mrs. Mott in the finance department.

Give me a call if you've got any questions.

Request Response Guide

- Main Idea
  - Say yes in the first sentence.
  - Do so wholeheartedly.
- Secondary Details
  - Express interest in the request.
  - Provide any necessary instructions or information.
- Friendly Closing
  - Point towards the future.

Acknowledging Orders

Acknowledging orders is good business

Many businesses live or die according to the volume of orders received. The link between orders received and business success is clear; the link between acknowledgements and success is less clear. For that reason, business people tend to play down the importance of letters of acknowledgement and to see them as nothing but a routine and time-consuming chore.

Some organizations send only preprinted postcards in acknowledement. Other sellers, reasoning that the promptly shipped order will soon be delivered to the buyer, consider acknowledgements unnecessary. While the postcard is preferable to no acknowledgement at all, a letter is more personal, and for this reason, best.

The manner in which present orders are handled often determines future orders

Correspondents should recognize that, while orders are routine for the seller, they may not be so routine for the buyer. Future business with the buyer often depends on the way the seller handles the present order.

Whether the message is in the form of a letter or a postcard, it should be changed at regular intervals. When a seller persists in sending the same message over a long period of time, customers begin to feel that they are being taken for granted. Customers most likely to feel this way are those who are most important to you — your best customers.

Francis Genet has worked as a purchasing agent for three companies for a total of eighteen years. During that time he has observed a variety of business practices on the part of suppliers. One of the most irritating practices, he feels, is the repeated use of the same letter acknowledging an order. "In some cases," Francis says, "a company will send out the same letter of acknowledgement for years. After a while you start thinking that your business means nothing to the supplier."

An order acknowledgement influences the receiver's perception of the sender

No matter how small the order being acknowledged is, its significance may be considerable. If served well, today's new customer may be tomorrow's major purchaser. Customers — whether old and valued or brand new — are receptive to a statement of appreciation and to an assurance that the order will be sent promptly. Consider the impression likely to be made by each of the following approaches:

- a letter of acknowledgement
- a preprinted fill-in postcard
- a completely preprinted postcard

The letter in Figure 9.5 gets down to business immediately by referring to the item ordered and to its shipment. It also seeks future orders and remains personal throughout.

Order Acknowledgment Guide

- Main Idea
  - Tell the buyer that the order was received and is being filled according to directions.
  - Identify the order clearly enough to prevent the reader from confusing it with another order.
- Secondary Details
  - Give the buyer the shipping details on how and when the buyer should receive it.
  - State the financial arrangement if it was not made clear prior to shipment.
- Friendly Closing
  - Express appreciation for the order.
  - Encourage more orders in the future.

Harris Hardware Supply
2435 Industrial Parkway
Edmonton, Alberta T5B 2C8

April 30, 1992

Ms. Irene Klar
Box 935
Cold Lake AB
T0A 1V0

Dear Ms. Klar:

Subject: Your Order for an X-365 Workbench

Your order for one X-365 workbench is being processed and will be shipped within 48 hours. Since you included a cheque for the full purchase price and shipping charges, we are pleased to give you a $10 credit on your next purchase.

continued

Figure 9.5 Acknowledging an Order

We hope that you will be pleased with the workbench. You will find that it truly resists all types of scratches, dents, and burns. This feature, plus the stability ensured by the four sturdy legs that support the table, means that you will be able to enjoy it for many years to come.

Remember that Harris Hardware Supply carries a full line of manual and power tools. These tools, like the workbench, are designed to provide good service and take hard use.

Use the enclosed order blank and postage-paid envelope for placing your next order. We look forward to serving you again.

Sincerely,

Julie Harris

Julie Harris
Sales Manager

JH:rm
Encl: 2

A Preprinted Fill-In Postcard

The preprinted fill-in postcard (Figure 9.6), though impersonal, is more specific than a completely preprinted one. Julie Harris can insert the name of the buyer in the space provided on the postcard. She can also insert the name and model number of the ordered item, the method of shipping, and the expected arrival date. This postcard thus provides some specific information, although it is not as informative as an individualized letter of acknowledgement.

Completely Preprinted Postcard

Even the most impersonal order acknowledgement is preferable to none, since it tells the buyer that the order is being filled

The completely preprinted postcard (Figure 9.7) informs the buyer that the order has been received. If the buyer happens to have placed several orders with Harris recently, however, this postcard will not clarify which order is being filled. Although such a postcard is completely impersonal, it does tell the buyer the order is being filled.

Dear ______________________

Thank you for ordering ______________________ from Harris Hardware Supply. Your order will be shipped within 48 hours by ______________________. You should receive it no later than ______________________.

Please let us serve you again soon.

Julie Harris
HARRIS HARDWARE SUPPLY

Figure 9.6 A Preprinted Fill-In Postcard

Dear Customer:

Thank you for your recent order. We at Harris Hardware Supply are pleased to count you as a customer.

We are filling your order now so that you will receive it promptly.

HARRIS HARDWARE SUPPLY

Figure 9.7 Completely Preprinted Postcard

The benefits of a personal letter of acknowledgement must be weighed against its cost. Such letters are expensive, but they can be justified if an opportunity for significant further business exists. In many cases a form letter will suffice, but it is unwise to rely solely on forms to acknowledge orders. An organization will be most effective in acknowledging orders through a rational use of a combination of completely preprinted forms, fill-in forms, and personal letters.

Choosing the best kind of acknowledgement requires weighing costs and benefits

Acknowledging Delayed Orders

Delayed orders must be acknowledged, at least by a preprinted form

Certain merchandise may be out of stock occasionally. In acknowledging the order, the seller should inform the buyer of this and advise him or her of when the merchandise will be available. Many organizations that receive a tremendous volume of orders do not acknowledge orders unless shipment will be delayed. Major retailers fill most orders almost immediately — the goods arrive as quickly as any acknowledgement would.

When a delay does occur, a form such as the one in Figure 9.8 acknowledges the delay. The customer's address is written on the front of the postcard, along with the information necessary for the customer to identify the order. Without this information those customers who have placed several orders will not know which order was delayed.

> Thank you ...
>
> ... for your order. We are temporarily out of stock of the goods you ordered and expect to make shipment on or before the date indicated on the front of the card.
>
> Should you write about this order, please return this card with your letter.
>
> Goodman's

Figure 9.8 Postcard Informing Customer of Shipping Delay

Extending Credit

Few business organizations insist on cash payment from customers. The extension of credit has become the rule rather than the exception. Consumers are applying for credit in ever-increasing numbers, and the degree to which it is extended grows proportionately.

When a person seeks credit and a business organization sees fit to extend it, the situation calls for a direct letter. What applicants want to know is that they are being given credit.

Although the main purpose of such a letter is to extend credit to the reader, this is not its sole purpose. In writing such a letter the writer should:

1. tell the person seeking credit that it will be granted

2. compliment the person for meriting the faith implicit in any credit approval
3. explain the terms of the credit plan
4. point towards future business with the customer and express appreciation for the credit request

A letter in which credit is granted is an example of a routine letter

Dear Ms. Saunders

Because of your excellent credit rating, we are pleased to send you a Rusk Brothers credit card.

Bills are mailed on the 20th of each month and are payable by the 15th of the next month. There is a finance charge of 1.5 percent on the unpaid balance each month.

The enclosed brochure describes many of the special services we offer our charge customers. As a charge customer, you may easily shop by telephone, and you will receive advance notification of sales.

Thank you for thinking of us when you decided to open a charge account. We appreciate the opportunity to serve you, and look forward to dealing with you again in the future.

Sincerely yours

In extending credit, the writer should express trust and acceptance

A letter offering to extend credit to an applicant should be phrased in a positive fashion. It should welcome the applicant to the preferred group of customers he or she is joining and express acceptance and trust of the new charge customer. Here is how a furniture factory informed a retailer that credit was being granted and the goods were being shipped:

The Deltina cane-back chairs you ordered on May 1 are being shipped to your store via Canadawide Shipping. They should arrive in Halifax by May 5. The amount of this merchandise has been debited to your new account.

Your excellent record with other creditors allows us to extend to you our regular terms of 2/10, n/30. As a new customer you may carry as much as $5000 of our products on account.

Included with your order are some suggested window and floor displays that other dealers have found helpful in attracting customers. Once customers pause to look at the chairs, they will recognize their stylishness and durability.

Use the enclosed order forms for placing your next orders. You can always count on prompt delivery and on our full co-operation.

Notice that this credit-extending letter was to a dealer. Dealers are generally interested in the sales potential of a product and of ways to display it; consumers are more interested in price and durability.

In writing to extend credit you should certainly adapt your message to the interests of the customer. Whether you are writing to a dealer or to a consumer, however, the same principles apply. In both cases, the structure of the message is the same.

Credit Extension Guide

- Indicate at the start that credit is being extended.
- If the goods are being shipped, give the details immediately.
- Specify the goods and the method of shipment.
- Mention how the reader earned the credit.
- Resell the reader on the wise choice.
- Point to future orders in the close.
- Avoid sarcasm, name-calling, and threats.

Approving Adjustments on Claims

Include a resale-attempt in a letter approving an adjustment

Being able to approve an adjustment calls for a prompt and direct response. This approval is positive throughout and it includes an attempt at resale:

You will receive a brand-new Deluxe Glide steam iron later this week. Thank you for returning the other iron to us. Our technicians are analyzing its performance in order to learn how to improve our inspection procedures. By calling the problem to our attention you are helping us to serve you better.

You should receive our summer sale catalogue of high-quality products next week. And remember, we promise satisfaction with your purchases.

When a customer seeks an adjustment and the error was the company's, most firms grant the adjustment immediately. Many cases are not clear-cut, however. Sometimes neither party appears to be at fault. A third party may be responsible, or it may be impossible to determine responsibility.

Many firms assume responsibility for an error, even when responsibility is unclear

Many firms, not wanting to lose a customer, automatically assume responsibility even though actual responsibility may be unclear. For example, a woman ordered a dozen plants through the mail. On opening the package, she found that only two appeared healthy; the remainder had died. Although she had never done business with it before, the company responded in this way to her request for replacement plants:

We are mailing a dozen healthy plants to you today. Under normal circumstances plants from Richard Brothers are extremely resistant to those conditions likely to harm lower-quality plants. In the five years we have been shipping plants in our patented stay-moist containers, more than 99 percent of the plants shipped have arrived in greenhouse condition.

To ensure that plants will arrive in good condition, it is important that they be removed from the carton and transplanted within 24 hours of receiving them. Doing this will result in healthy plants that will add much to your pleasure in gardening.

From now on you will receive our Green Thumb newsletter each month. It features unadvertised specials that are likely to enhance your garden at a fraction of the usual price.

Yours truly

Adjustment Approval Guide

- Indicate immediately that the adjustment is being granted.
- Grant the adjustment wholeheartedly.
- Play down the negative aspects by avoiding negative words.
- Briefly explain the reason for the problem or imply it when describing the adjustment measures being taken.
- If the reader must take some action, indicate clearly what it is.
- Look to the future in the close.

Refusing Routine Requests

From time to time, you'll have to write letters and memos in which you refuse routine requests from writers who are expecting a positive reply. Although some experts prefer the indirect approach discussed later in the chapter, many now favour the direct approach since the reader can guess almost immediately that the answer will be no. For example, a student inquiring about course credit believes she has taken an equivalent course, but it is not acceptable to the college she's planning to attend. Here's how the request might be refused:

The direct approach can be used to refuse routine requests

In your letter of November 10, you asked about course credit for Business Communication 117.

We are unable to grant you course credit for Business Communication 117 on the basis of your having taken English 100. Business communication and university-level composition courses cover very different content.

The business communication course has been specifically developed to teach you how to write effectively on the job. It shows you how to plan and write letters and memos that achieve a specific purpose and are directed to a specific audience.

If you want to complete Business Communication 117 before you enter your full-time business program, you can take it by correspondence over the summer.

I've enclosed a brochure describing our correspondence program. The course you're interested in is described on page 5. Please call me at 432-7878 if you have any questions about the course.

Sometimes, as a supervisor, you must refuse requests from your subordinates. These refusals may create hard feelings and poor working relationships if they're not handled well. However, with a little care, you can refuse a request and still maintain your subordinate's respect and goodwill:

Because your contract states that vacations must be taken no later than January 31 following the year in which the vacation was earned, you will need to schedule all of your 1991 vacation prior to January 31, 1991. Therefore, you will be unable to carry three weeks over until April 1992. However, should you wish to take six consecutive weeks, you have two options: take the last three weeks in January and the first three weeks in February, or take a three-week leave of absence without pay in April 1992 along with your three weeks' entitlement for 1992.

Please let me know when you'll be taking your vacation so I can arrange for temporary help.

Problem Orders

The success of any business organization often depends on the speed with which the organization can satisfy its customers. The term *turnaround time* often describes the length of time business firms take to provide customers with goods and services after receiving an order.

Even the most efficient organizations sometimes experience delays in handling orders. Regardless of who is responsible for the delay, you may have to write a letter to convey information likely to displease a customer. Nevertheless, because the customer is anxious to receive the merchandise, the direct approach is often most successful.

Out-of-Stock Items. When an item temporarily out of stock will be available soon, you should inform the customer. You want to inform the customer about the delay, but you also want to retain the customer's business. Here is a letter of refusal that uses the direct approach, but still manages to maintain a positive tone:

Out-of-stock items necessitate letters of refusal

Thank you for your order of April 7. We will be able to ship your Classic circulating fan by May 10. The growing volume of orders for the Classic has resulted in a backlog of orders. Our increased production levels have permitted us to limit the delay to one month. At the same time, we are maintaining the quality you associate with the Classic.

You will be enjoying the comfort and economy of a Classic circulating fan well before the onset of hot weather. The Classic will make the heat and humidity of summer disappear in a breeze for you.

Notice that, although the first paragraph conveys news of the delay, it focuses on the anticipated delivery date and emphasizes the popularity of the product. In the second paragraph, the reader is assured that the fan will be delivered before the hot weather arrives.

When informing a reader that an order will be delayed, you have two main purposes: (1) to convince the reader to wait for the order, and (2) to retain the reader's future business.

Discontinued Items. In the best of all possible business worlds, as soon as a company stopped handling a certain item, all orders for that item would cease. What actually happens is that orders continue to trickle in for the item, sometimes long after its discontinuation.

In response to an order for a discontinued item, you must inform the customer of the discontinuation while seeking to offer a substitute. Do not, however, offer any substitute that is not clearly appropriate. It is better to lose one sale and retain the goodwill of a customer than to provide a substitute with which the customer will ultimately be displeased.

Offer an appropriate substitute, if possible, for a discontinued item

When a retailer ordered a brand of videotapes from a wholesaler who had stopped carrying that brand, the wholesaler sought to offer an appropriate substitute:

Thank you for your March 17 order for 100 T-450 videotapes. We have replaced the T-450 with the superior T-900 line. This new product offers 30 percent higher picture quality and 50 percent longer life than does the T-450. By refining high energy tape particles, Superchron has created a tape that is mirror-smooth and provides perfect pictures for replay after replay. Although you

may be able to order some T-450 tapes directly from the Superchron Company, your customers will prefer the T-900 once they learn of it.

Once they know how much they will save because of the longer life of the T-900, your customers will agree that the T-900 is worth an additional $1.50 for a 60-minute cassette. Call me at (601) 592-1313 any weekday between 9:00 and 5:00. I'll fill your order that same day at a price of $15.25 per tape on orders of one dozen or more.

Too Small an Order. Many misunderstandings may occur when customers place orders for quantities too small to merit the discounts they expect. Although the direct approach is often the best one, you need to be careful to maintain a positive tone.

To stimulate sales, the Green-Gro Company offered a 5-percent discount on purchases of 100 or more 25-kg bags of lawn fertilizer. When a retailer requested the 5-percent discount on an order of 50 bags, the wholesaler responded in this way:

Thank you for your order for fifty 25-kg bags of Green-Gro lawn fertilizer. To qualify for the special 5-percent manufacturer's discount, you will need to increase your order to 100 bags.

This year marks the twelfth year you have purchased your supply of Green-Gro products from us. The growth of your orders over these years suggests that your customers enjoy dealing with you as much as we do. Your adherence to sound business practices in placing orders, making prompt payments, and customer follow-up have been appreciated.

By increasing your order to 100 bags, you will be ready for the upcoming seasonal rush. Regardless of the size of your order, you will still receive our regular terms of 2/10, n/30.

You will be receiving our new catalogue within three weeks. It features several new garden products that your customers will soon be seeking.

Using the Indirect Approach

Refusals are difficult to write because you are denying the reader's request. The reader is unlikely to respond favourably to such a message, so the directness of the routine good-news message can be inappropriate. Many authorities, therefore, suggest that bad news be presented in an indirect (inductive) manner.

As we indicated earlier in the chapter, some business writers maintain that *all* messages, positive or negative, should be direct in approach. "Get to the point!" is the advice they offer. Sometimes, however, a direct turndown early in a letter results in the reader's not reading any farther and thus remaining unaware of the logical reasons for the refusal. By refusing directly, the writer lessens the probability of a gracious acceptance of the refusal. The reader may then become frustrated and alienated.

Present bad news indirectly so the recipient must read the reasons for the refusal

When the writer uses the indirect approach, the reader may likely read the entire document and so understand the reasons for the refusal. In this way, the approval and the business of the reader may be retained. You might not have to sacrifice a continuing business relationship if you can get the reader to suspend judgement until the entire message is understood.

Imagine that you are the plant manager of an electrical parts manufacturing company. You received a letter from a grade six class requesting a plant tour for a 40-member group. According to company policy, tours are available only to persons aged sixteen and older, and to group sizes no greater than ten.

The company benefits from this policy by restricting the number of individuals likely to take a plant tour and, therefore, causing less disruption to plant operations. Members of the public excluded from such tours may be considered to benefit by not being exposed to the potential dangers of the machines, noise, and fumes of such a plant.

An effective writer tries to point out how the reader will benefit even though the request is denied. In some cases you may be able to make a helpful suggestion or offer an alternative plan. The plant manager, for example, may be aware of a film that would introduce the students to manufacturing processes and could be a substitute for a tour.

Point out how the reader may benefit from the refusal and suggest an alternative

Occasionally, pointing out a benefit is impossible. Generally, however, a writer who looks at the situation from the reader's point of view can suggest at least one alternative.

A key to using the indirect approach to accomplish the intended purpose is to know the facts of the situation. While situations requiring such letters or memos are sometimes similar, they are rarely identical. By knowing the relevant facts, you can develop a line of reasoning that the reader is likely to understand and accept.

The indirect approach generally has four steps:

1. Start with a neutral comment that indicates some form of agreement.
2. Present an explanation in a positive manner.
3. Clearly state the refusal.
4. End on a positive note.

1. Neutral Comment. Your opening comment should let the reader know the subject of the correspondence, but it should not imply either a

A neutral opening should indicate an area of agreement between writer and reader

yes or a no. After reading the first paragraph, the reader should be aware that you are responding to a request. Ideally you should indicate some form of agreement with the reader. However, in writing a neutral opening, avoid these pitfalls:

- Don't imply that the request will be granted. If the reader is led to expect acceptance, the letdown will further damage the relationship. "We at Baily Motors take pride in the service we provide our customers" would be inappropriate since the reader could understandably expect acceptance.
- Don't express too much pleasure in responding to the request. "We at Baily Motors are always pleased to hear from our customers" suggests that the writer is enjoying the difficulties the customer is experiencing.
- Don't begin too far afield from the subject. The opening should clearly identify the subject. "For the past 50 years, Baily Motors has been a leader in sales and service" leaves the reader uncertain as to the subject of the letter.
- Don't ignore the need for a smooth transition from a neutral statement to an explanation of the reasons. For that reason do not begin a sentence with such words as *however*, *although*, or *but*. These words signal to the reader that a rejection is coming.
- Don't use negative words in the opening statement. *Won't*, *can't*, and *unable* are the kind of words that suggest some form of disagreement.

An explanation of the reasons for the refusal should precede the actual refusal

2. Explanation. If you have succeeded in your neutral statement, the reader will be interested enough to continue reading your letter. At this time, you should give the reasons for your decision. Note that the reasons precede the actual denial of the request. By getting recipients to read the reasons, you increase the likelihood of their understanding them. While understanding does not guarantee acceptance of the reasons, acceptance seldom occurs without understanding.

In writing the explanations avoid these pitfalls:

- Don't be overly apologetic. "We at Baily Motors regret to tell you" reeks of insincerity. Assuming that the refusal is based on good reasons, an apology is unnecessary.
- Don't fall back on "company policy" as a reason for refusing a request. "For 50 years Baily Motors has had a policy that prohibits" is not an adequate explanation. Organizational policies are difficult to understand. If the writer does not blame policy but clearly explains the specific reasons in a plausible fashion, acceptance is more likely.
- Don't talk down to the reader. "Our experience in 50 years of serving the public has taught us" sounds like a parent addressing a child.

Readers do not respond favourably to this approach. In explaining, don't be so brief or so general that the relationship between your explanation and the problem is unclear.

Whenever possible, emphasize reasons that might benefit the reader. To inform a customer that a service contract would not pay for certain auto repairs, one correspondent wrote:

Your service contract pays for all necessary engine repairs, as long as the car is brought in for inspection every six months. In the absence of a six-month inspection, the contract ceased to provide coverage.

Regular inspections are intended to identify minor automotive problems before they become major, and costly, ones. Regular inspections also help us to balance our work load so that each work day is quite predictable.

In the second paragraph, the writer explained not only how customers benefit from service contracts but also how the auto dealer benefits. By describing how the dealer will benefit, the writer comes across as candid and honest. The whole message becomes more believable. Although the explanation is based on organizational policy, the writer never refers to policy. Policies are cold and impersonal, and people have difficulty relating to them. Reasons that are clearly stated and plausible are better received.

Clearly stated, believable reasons are likely to gain acceptance for the refusal

In some instances, of course, the only reasons for refusing a request are, plainly and simply, company reasons. In these instances you should not try to dream up imaginary benefits for the reader. Instead, just state the company's reason(s) and let it go at that.

3. Refusal. In the third part of the indirect message, you get to the heart of the matter, the actual refusal. If you have explained the reasons clearly, the reader can probably infer a refusal before actually reading it. Ideally, the refusal flows logically from the reasons.

Sometimes you don't have to state the refusal directly — the reader can infer it easily. When a personnel director writes to tell job applicants that they are unsuitable for the job in question, a statement such as "We need a person who has had actual supervisory experience" transmits the bad news. Saying "You do not meet our requirements" is unnecessary.

Many refusals need not be stated directly since they can easily be implied

In stating the actual refusal, avoid these pitfalls:

- Don't emphasize the refusal any more than is absolutely necessary. Devote enough space to the refusal to convey it, but do not belabour it.
- Don't structure the letter so that the refusal stands out. The refusal

should not call attention to itself; it should be embedded in the letter.

- Don't make a direct negative statement of refusal. Telling the reader, "Since you forgot to oil the motor, we are unable to give you a refund," conveys the message; however, its accusatory tone may be alienating. "We would refund the purchase price if the maintenance instructions had been followed" is preferable.
- Don't use the active voice in stating the rejection. "The admissions committee voted against your application for membership" is overly blunt and calls undue attention to the refusal. "Your application for membership was denied by the admissions committee" is more muted, but it still conveys the refusal.

If the message may be misunderstood, the refusal should be stated directly. The clearer the relationship between the reasons and a refusal, the less necessary it is to state the refusal explicitly.

4. Positive Ending. A letter or memo of refusal should end on an upbeat note, leaving the reader as favourably disposed towards you as possible. After conveying the refusal, you should try to regain some of the good feelings that may have been lost. Even though you have turned down a request, you may be able to suggest an alternative. One department store, for example, suggests its layaway service when it rejects an application for credit. When you are unable to offer an alternative, you may still be able to make a constructive suggestion.

To end on a positive note, avoid these pitfalls:

- Don't bring the refusal up again.
- Don't apologize for the refusal. You should leave the reader aware of your concern and good wishes rather than of the refusal. An apology will merely recall the refusal.
- Don't resort to tired phrases in the closing. "If I can be of help in the future, please contact me" is so shopworn as to be meaningless.

At the close, the reader should be aware of the writer's concern

The purpose of the ending is to show the reader that you remain interested. Even if no suitable alternative exists, you may be able to resell the reader on your organization.

Adjustment Refusals

Adjustment refusals are difficult since you are denying a request the customer considers reasonable

Customers who request adjustments generally consider themselves and their requests reasonable. Most companies take pride in their equitable adjustment policies. No matter how liberal a company's attitude towards claims is, however, certain requests are bound to be refused. Writing an adjustment refusal letter, then, is a delicate process, for the writer is implying that the request, which the customer views as reasonable, actually is not.

In writing an adjustment refusal, you should follow the four steps described earlier. Before starting to write, however, review the facts. Assuming that they justify a refusal, decide how best to transmit the refusal. Your two main purposes, as in any letter or memo of refusal, are (1) to state the refusal, and (2) to maintain a positive relationship with the reader. The second purpose is especially important because, by maintaining a positive relationship with customers, you can usually retain their business.

The manager of a convention hotel took this approach when responding to a request for an adjustment. The president of a student association had written to complain about the quantity of food provided by the hotel for the Keynote Night banquet.

Thank you for your letter regarding the food portions at your banquet. We appreciate your taking the time and effort to write us. — Neutral comment

From the information in your letter I suspect your group has a higher proportion of people with healthy appetites than most groups. If all our portions were large enough to satisfy them, we'd have to increase our prices substantially. Moreover, we'd likely have a lot of wastage. But you're right: the standard banquet portions considered generous to the average eater would seem inadequate to the heavy eater. — Reasons

For your next banquet, we can design a variable menu. You could offer your members a choice between normal or extra large portions. Only those who wanted an extra large meal would have to pay for it. — Implied refusal/alternative

Your group was a pleasure to host, Jim! We look forward next time to serving the exact needs of all your members. When you dine at the Park Lane, you receive the finest in freshness, quality, and attractive presentation. — Positive ending

When a rock-concert promoter was forced to make a substitution for a warmup group she had advertised, she received a complaint following the concert. She sought to reject the request for a refund without sacrificing the future business of the reader in this way:

We can certainly understand why you expected Buzzy and the Roustabouts to be the warmup act at the concern last Friday. Our clients know we begin to advertise a concert only when all of the acts on the program have agreed to perform. — Neutral comment

Occasionally something happens over which we have no control. Since two members of the Roustabouts were hospitalized only the night before the concert, — Reasons we had little time to advertise the change. Most of the spectators seemed to think that the Pinnacles did an excellent job as the warmup group. Our surveys show that most spectators attend concerts to see the headliners. Since the headline act appeared as advertised, everyone seemed pleased with the concert.

Implied refusal

We take our responsibilities to the public very seriously. If ever an advertised headliner is unable to appear, you can be sure that you will receive a full refund.

Alternative/positive ending

Loyal fans like you may soon be able to see Buzzy and the Roustabouts headlining a concert here. Our schedule for the next three months is enclosed. You're sure to find some of these concerts to your liking.

Notice that tact is always necessary. Although a small number of requests for adjustments may border on fraudulence, most do not. Sometimes correspondents who regularly handle adjustments grow cynical, an attitude that becomes reflected in their letters. Such letters often include such phrases as:

You claim that the hair dryer did not work as advertised.

We cannot understand how this quality-checked appliance could possibly malfunction.

According to you, the dryer never worked as it was supposed to.

A tactless adjustment refusal can alienate the reader

The letters written by such correspondents are tinged with distrust and suspicion. While such letters may clearly convey the message that the requested adjustment is refused, they may lose a customer.

Adjustment Refusal Guide

- Make your opening comment neutral and relate it to the subject of the letter or memo.
- Imply neither a yes nor a no in the opening.
- Keep the opening brief.
- Convey a positive rather than an apologetic tone in presenting the reasons for your decision.
- If possible, show how the reader may actually benefit from the decision because of the reasons you state.
- Present the reasons so that the reader anticipates a refusal.
- Make your refusal clear, but don't overemphasize it.
- Avoid mentioning the refusal in the ending. End the letter on a positive note.

Credit Refusals

Many businesspeople maintain that every single business letter is a sales letter. No matter what the stated purpose of a letter, you must also try to sell the reader on your organization.

When you write a refusal of credit, you face a real challenge. Although you are denying a request, you should still take a positive approach and try to retain the reader's good feelings. Many people today regard credit as a right that cannot be denied them. This attitude complicates the task facing the writer.

Denying a person credit while keeping that person's business is a challenge

Many writers seem to ignore the challenge of refusing credit. This attitude is evident in their letters. Writers who believe that you cannot deny credit and simultaneously keep a customer write uninspired letters such as:

Thank you for applying for a charge account at Wilson's Fashions Store. We regret to state that we are unable to extend credit to you at this time.

We appreciate your patronage.

A credit refusal like this suggests that the company has little hope of retaining the applicant's business. The letter is cold and impersonal. The writer presents the obvious message but pays no heed to the feelings of the applicant and makes no attempt to encourage continued patronage. The person who receives such a letter is likely to become frustrated and angry.

Rather than view this type of letter as a denial of credit, the writer might use it to convince the applicant to become a cash customer. For example, a department store de-emphasized its refusal of credit by stressing the advantages of shopping there:

We appreciate your recent application for a charge account at Astor Fashions for Men.

Much information is considered before opening a new charge account, and your application was carefully considered. Once you are employed on a full-time basis you may be able to receive an Astor's credit card.

Until that time, please allow us to serve you on a cash basis. With our fall fashions about to arrive, you may also enjoy our convenient layaway plan.

Among the many reasons for refusing a request for credit, a poor credit record is number one. Other common reasons are the applicant's having too small or unsteady an income or, perhaps, no credit experience upon which to base a decision.

Letters directed to an organization follow the same steps

Whether the applicant is an individual consumer or a business organization seeking to establish credit, the letter of refusal is organized in the same way. In either case, you will probably refer to the advantages of paying cash or making C.O.D. purchases. And you should follow the four steps for transmitting unpleasant news.

The letter to the organizational applicant may be somewhat more forthright, but it still follows the usual pattern of neutral comment, explanation, refusal, and positive ending. Here the writer incorporates a bid for cash business within the ending:

Neutral comment

Thank you for your order for 48 Evenflo seed and fertilizer spreaders. Your large order suggests that you are expecting a profitable spring. We are glad to hear that.

Explanation

Your credit references unanimously agree that you are a person of integrity and sound business principles. At this time the information about your hardware operation, however, is somewhat less positive. The competition for the hardware customer is indeed intense, and this always has an adverse impact on one's financial position.

Refusal

The expected spring upturn in the economy will most likely improve your position considerably. For the present, however, we'll be pleased to continue serving you on a cash basis, and you in turn will continue to receive a 2-percent discount for cash purchases. Another advantage of cash payment is that orders may be of any size. No minimum order is required.

Positive ending

You can reduce your present order by one half, and order replacement stock as you need it, because we can offer delivery the week you place your order. Please send us your instructions on the enclosed order form. Your shipment will be sent as soon as we hear from you.

Those who seek credit cannot be expected to be pleased when their applications are rejected. In the minds of many, a rejection of credit is a rejection of one's personal worth. Refusing credit, then, is a delicate matter meriting thoughtful consideration. Writers often err by emphasizing the refusal rather than developing a cash customer. By de-emphasizing the refusal and stressing the advantages of cash payment, writers can often retain customers they might otherwise lose.

Know your jurisdiction's legal requirements when writing credit refusals

Beyond this, the type and amount of information that a person who is refused credit has the right to know is legislated in each province. In most provinces, an individual denied credit because of information from a third party is entitled to the name and address of the reporting agency that provided the information or to the name and substance of information received from an individual or another source. In some provinces, this information must be disclosed in the refusal letter. In others, the onus is on the consumer to ask for disclosure.

Even when disclosure is not required in the refusal letter, many firms identify the source of their information. Such disclosure allows them to shift the blame for the credit refusal. Moreover, it eliminates the need for a second letter should the consumer request disclosure. However, disclosure also benefits the consumer in that it permits him or her to correct the information if an error has occurred because of identical names or other kinds of mistakes.

Credit Refusal Guide

- Begin with a neutral idea with which the reader will not disagree.
- Explain the reason(s) for the decision.
- State the refusal briefly and without using negative language.
- If possible, offer an alternative such as paying cash or using C.O.D. purchasing.
- Close with a look towards the future and without an apologetic tone.

Prewritten Messages

Many situations do not need a reply that is tailored to a specific individual. The expense of an individualized letter simply cannot be justified. When situations are so routine that individual letters are impractical, form letters are often suitable.

Form letters are composed in one of two ways. Either individual paragraphs or complete letters are prepared for use in certain routine situations. These prewritten messages allow an organization to respond quickly to much of the correspondence it receives.

You can prewrite form paragraphs or whole letters

Form Paragraphs

Prewritten paragraphs are suitable for responding to much routine correspondence.

Coach Henri Bouchard found that interest was growing in his summer hockey camps as he became better known through his successful hockey teams. Bouchard and his secretary were unable to keep up with their work because of the number of inquiries about these camps. After carefully recording the kinds of inquiries he was receiving, Bouchard prepared a series of paragraphs that answered the most commonly asked questions. He numbered the paragraphs and, after reading a letter, would tell the secretary the paragraphs to be sent in response.

For example, when asked by a potential participant about the size of the camp and the possibility of tuition grants, he told his secretary to send paragraphs 2 and 5. This is the letter that resulted.

Yes, there are openings in the July hockey camp. Enrolment is limited to 25 participants per session. As a participant you will receive intensive coaching that will help you sharpen your skills.

Partial grants are available for a limited number of participants. Please complete the enclosed application and return it to me to be considered for a grant. The enclosed brochure describes our camp in greater detail.

Respondent and typist can quickly combine prewritten paragraphs

After determining the kinds of information usually sought in incoming routine correspondence, writers can save time by preparing appropriate paragraphs in advance. Some organizations have a manual of such form paragraphs, with each paragraph assigned a reference number. The correspondent need only indicate to the typist the numbers of the paragraphs to be used and the sequence in which they are to appear.

Form Letters

Form letters are very efficient

If the same situation occurs frequently, form letters are even more efficient than form paragraphs. The entire letter is prepared in advance so that it can be dispatched more quickly than one that must be composed from prewritten paragraphs.

Because form letters are circulated widely, an organization's best writers should be assigned to develop them. Moreover, because organizational policies and procedures are constantly changing, form letters must be reviewed and updated regularly to reflect those changes.

Two kinds of form letters are commonly used: complete form letters and those with brief fill-ins. The former requires only the date and the name and address of the recipient. For example, the letter responding to an inquiry about Auto Repairs for the Layperson could be used to respond to most inquiries about the course.

The CanOil letter in Figure 9.9 is an example of a form letter that allows the writer to add information in predetermined places. It responds to a complaint concerning a specific service station. By completing the first sentence with a description of the complaint, the writer may tailor the letter to the specific complaint.

A major criticism of form letters is that they are too impersonal. However, word processing equipment now allows such letters to be "individualized." Special wording can be inserted for a more personal touch. Fill-ins can appear typed, instead of written by hand.

Word processing can add a personal touch to form letters

(Current Date)

(Customer Name and Address)

Re: (Station and Location)

Dear :

We've received your (letter/call) about (customer's complaint).
As you may know, CanOil stations are leased to independent dealers who are responsible for their own operations. However, we are always concerned when a customer is less than satisfied in his or her patronage of a CanOil station and make every attempt to assist whenever a problem occurs.

For this reason, your communication is being forwarded to our local District Management with the request that its contents be reviewed in detail with the dealer. Upon completion of their investigation, they will send you a final report.

Thank you for taking the time to write us.

Very truly yours,

GPS:

bcc: (BLIND FOOTNOTE FOR DISTRICT MANAGER)
Please conclude with customer. If applicable, forward your instructions for proper handling of customer's account to travel card centre, with copy to our office.

Figure 9.9 A Form Letter

As with any technique, individualized form letters can become offensive. One particularly irritating technique is to insert the reader's name into the text in several places. Since everyone is aware that word processors are used for this purpose, the result can often be a letter that sounds insincere.

Word processing software has given rise to another phenomenon. Many third-party software and documentation developers are providing files of "form letters to suit every business occasion." Unfortunately, these authors are generally better software specialists than they are business letter writers. All too often, the resulting form letters are simply a series of clichés strung together in an outdated format. Before you use any packaged form letters, review them carefully to ensure that they meet the ten characteristics of effective writing outlined in Chapter 5.

Appropriateness of Prewritten Messages

Prewritten messages must be used only in appropriate cases

To be effective, form paragraphs and form letters must be used appropriately. Department stores, for example, often use form letters to extend credit privileges to those who have sought them. Colleges may use form letters to acknowledge applications for admission. These uses are generally appropriate. The applicants probably prefer a prompt and clear reply and thus will overlook its impersonal qualities.

Used inappropriately, however, prewritten messages may be more irritating to the receiver than no response at all. For example, a form letter certainly would be inappropriate to acknowledge the initial order from a major new customer whose business has long been sought.

Consider a second example. Two students received identical form letters denying them permission to substitute one course for another. Bill Thompson, an excellent student, had asked permission to take another accounting course in place of a required cost accounting course. He had two years of cost accounting experience, and the required course was scheduled for a time when he had to work. He was the sole supporter of his wife and two small children.

Debra Churney, an average student, had requested permission to make a similar substitution. The required course was being offered at a time that would conflict with her duties as a volunteer photographer for the school yearbook. Although photography was only a hobby at present, she hoped to make it her profession eventually.

When the two students found they had received identical letters, they felt they had been treated with cold indifference. Personal matters certainly deserve more personal treatment and consideration.

As the volume of business communication increases, still greater reliance will be placed on form messages. If managements exercise good judgement, form letters are an effective communication tool.

Summary

Letters and memos reflect either positively or negatively on their sender (individual and company).

- Using the five-step planning process to analyze your purpose, audience, and context will result in letters that meet your readers' needs.
- When writing messages that transmit good news or neutral messages, you can ensure that they reflect positively on you and your firm by
  - getting directly to the main point in the opening paragraph
  - following up with necessary details
  - pointing to the next step in the closing paragraph
- The direct approach is used to
  - request and provide information
  - place and acknowledge orders
  - request and extend credit
  - make routine claims and grant adjustments
  - respond to problem orders
- Letters that use the indirect approach
  - begin with a neutral statement that makes the reader aware of the subject but implies neither acceptance nor refusal
  - provide reasons for your decision
  - state or imply the refusal, which should flow logically from your reasons
  - end on a positive note
- The indirect approach is sometimes desirable, particularly when refusing adjustments or credit applications.
- Prewritten messages that expedite routine correspondence can consist of
  - standard paragraphs that appear in various combinations
  - completely written form letters
  - form letters with individual fill-ins
- Prewritten messages can be effective if used with discretion.

Review Questions

1. What is meant by the direct and the indirect approach?
2. When is a direct message more appropriate than one that is indirect?
3. State the arguments for and against an organization's acknowledging every single order received.
4. In what way is a completely preprinted postcard as effective as an individual letter for acknowledging orders?
5. Describe the outline for a letter in which credit is extended to a new customer.
6. In extending credit to a new customer, should the writer state the penalties for late payment? Why or why not?

7. If the seller is clearly at fault and is giving the adjustment sought by the buyer, why is it desirable to explain the problem that necessitated the adjustment?
8. Under what circumstances might you want to use the indirect approach?
9. Explain the reasons for each of the four parts of a letter that uses the indirect approach.
10. What is meant by the expression "Every business letter is a sales letter"?
11. What criteria determine the appropriateness of a form letter for a particular situation?

Activities

Making Routine Requests

1. You are going to take a week's vacation starting on Saturday, August 1, two months from now, and you are considering taking a windjammer cruise. You have learned the schedule and rate information from advertisements, but you have the following questions: How many tourists will be on the ship? How many of them are likely to be unattached singles like yourself? You are aware that each tourist must perform some work on the ship each day and you do not object to that. You are wondering, however, how many hours per day and what kinds of duties you would have to perform. Write a letter seeking the information to Windjammer Cruises, P.O. Box 1111, Station A, Victoria, British Columbia, V8R 2W2.
2. You are a management trainee at Silvertree Farms, a large mail-order food supply firm. Using information about daytime courses offered by your college or university, write a memo to your boss, James Cohen, asking for permission to attend a course during working hours. Make sure your request is specific and answers all the questions your boss is likely to have.
3. Select a country you are interested in visiting and write a letter to its embassy in Ottawa (obtain the address from the library). Request information on points of interest for a first-time visitor. Indicate the time of year you hope to visit and inquire about the weather for that season.
4. You have been assigned to write a research paper on water pollution in the Great Lakes. You are especially interested in the industrial causes of the problem as well as the legislative changes that are currently being considered. Write a letter to your local member of parliament requesting the information.
5. While scanning a small, little-known trade publication, you find an article on a new diet plan that has become very popular in Japan

with business executives. Called the Kyoto Plan, it is a regimen of diet plus exercise. At present, you are self-employed as a sales representative for a number of different brands of exercise equipment, most of which you sell to health clubs. You are curious as to whether the Kyoto Plan diet would be acceptable to Canadians and whether they would view the exercises positively. While you are writing for answers to your questions as well as for a more thorough picture of the plan, remember that you are writing to a Japanese reader. You may want to research specific communication conventions in the library before you begin this assignment. If you decide, on the basis of your research, to modify the general guidelines for routine requests, be sure to attach a copy of the data to support your decision. Since you are unable to learn the names of any of the operatives of the plan, you should send your letter to Kyoto Plan, Inc., 14-5-201, Nihombashi Kodenma-cho, Chuo-Ku, Tokyo 103, Japan.

Placing Orders

6. Using a trade journal, magazine, or catalogue, find a company that advertises products related to your favourite hobby. Order a minimum of three products from the company. Be sure to include all the necessary information.

Credit Requests

7. You are a twenty-year-old student working part-time at the campus bookstore. You have no credit experience, but you would like an Esso credit card. Write a credit application letter to Imperial Oil Limited, 111 St. Clair Avenue West, Toronto, Ont. M5W 1K3.

Requesting Adjustments

8. In response to a newspaper advertisement, you ordered a bone-coloured Cosmopolitan Shoulder Bag. The price had been reduced from $25 to $10. You especially liked the personalized single initial on a solid brass signet plate that adorned the purse. When the purse arrived, you were disappointed to see its faded appearance, but you were even more upset when the signet plate fell off after one week. Write a letter to the company, outlining the problem and requesting a new purse. Address the letter to Cosmopolitan Specialties Ltd., P.O. Box 146-B, Richmond Hill, Ont. L4C 4Y5.
9. You have subscribed to *Contemporary Living* magazine for the past five years and have enjoyed it very much. During the past two

months you have received four notices saying that your subscription is about to expire and urging you to renew it immediately. According to your records (and you have the cancelled cheque to prove it), your present subscription still has two years to run. One year ago you renewed your subscription for three years. Write to the circulation manager of *Contemporary Living* to request that this problem be corrected. (The address is Box 9112, Station Y, Toronto, Ont. M9W 4E7.)

10. You bought a package of 100 paper plates to use at a church social. You discover that the package contained only 91 plates; 97 people attended the event. You are embarrassed by the shortage. Although the plates were inexpensive, you feel that an important principle is involved. Write a letter to Quality Paper Products, Red Deer, Alta. T4P 1C8.

Answering Requests

11. You are public relations director of Windjammer Cruises. Respond to the request for information in Activity 1. Use your imagination in responding but remind the writer that the fare for a single room is $851, which is $56 higher than for double occupancy. Write this letter to Richard Singh, 1220 Shore Dr., Apt. 1119, Toronto, Ont. M4C 3Z1.

12. You're the office manager in an import/export company, Malagar Imports. Your staff have asked for flextime, so they can avoid rush-hour traffic. You've received all the necessary approvals; write a memo advising your staff about the change. Invent the specific details about the new schedule. Just be sure all staff members know exactly what this means to their workday.

Acknowledging Orders

13. You are a salesperson for a medium-sized printing plant. After several months of seeking business from Foster's Hardware, you have finally received an order for five reams of letterhead stationery. Compose a letter to the office manager (Sharon Davis, Foster's Hardware, P.O. Box 1010, Station A, Halifax, N.S. B3H 4J5).

Granting Credit

14. As credit manager for Walsh Specialties, P.O. Box 143, Station D, Hull, Que. J8X 2T1, you are going to approve Gina Tanner's request for credit. She has just opened a lamp store called Let There Be Light (P.O. Box 840, Oakville, Ont. L6J 1C1) in a shopping centre. You are sending her the following items on terms of 3/10, n/30:

3 solid brass shell floor lamps @ $65	$195
6 solid brass 6-way lamps @ $75	450
1 Cathay table lamp @ $40	40
1 clear glass hexagon table lamp @ $35	35
	$720

All of these lamps are fashionable as well as functional and have been popular in all parts of the country. Tanner recently came to Ontario from St. John's, where she had operated a similar business. A credit report described Tanner as "generally prompt in meeting financial obligations." As with all new accounts, you will limit her credit to $1000 until she proves herself to be responsible. Write to Tanner confirming the order and extending credit up to $1000. Point out the 3-percent discount available for payment within ten days. Mention the desirability of maintaining a good credit record. Also, tell her to watch for the new Walsh catalogue, which she will receive in approximately 30 days.

Making Routine Adjustments

15. As vice president of Cosmopolitan Specialties, you devote much of your time to responding to customers' complaints. Sales of the Cosmopolitan Shoulder Bag have been better than expected, and the supply is exhausted. Because your uncle, the company's president, purchased the purses while vacationing in Sri Lanka, you cannot get any more of them. You do, however, have some spare brass signet plates. In response to complaints such as that in Exercise 8, you plan to send an initialled plate with the necessary glue for attaching it to the purse. You intend to include an instruction sheet with the letter. Write a letter responding to the letter described in Exercise 8. (You need not present the instructions.) Address your letter to Lois Holland, 1412 E. Blvd., Apt. 201, Vancouver, B.C. V7K 2E1.
16. As circulation manager of *Contemporary Living*, you have received several complaints about improper billing in the past month. A new computer system had been malfunctioning, but the situation has been corrected. Write a response to the letter described in Activity 9, addressing it to Mr. Robert Stein, 1210 4th Ave., Thompson, Man. R8N 0Z2.
17. You are industrial relations director of Quality Paper Products. You receive the letter described in Exercise 10 and must respond to it. You have been unable to learn how such a miscount could have

occurred. Write to Betty Melchuk, 404 Spruce St., Cold Lake, Alta. T0A 0V0.

18. Mrs. Ruth Guffy (1638 Pine St., Smiths Falls, Ont. K7A 3T7) purchased a Redi-quik microwave oven from your store (Ace Appliances) six weeks ago. At the time she requested that it not be delivered until she returned from a month-long vacation. Through a mixup in your shipping department, it was delivered the day after Mrs. Guffy left on vacation. A neighbour accepted it and stored it in her garage until Mrs. Guffy returned from vacation. She was distressed to learn that her new microwave had been delivered prematurely. The box the oven was in suffered slight water damage, but the oven itself was not damaged and it works well. You have learned of the mixup through a friend of Mrs. Guffy's neighbour. Write a letter to Mrs. Guffy in which you acknowledge the mistake and apologize for it. Point out that you are going to have a sale next month on all your small kitchen appliances and that many of them are colour-co-ordinated with her new microwave.

Problem Orders

19. Your company is Luggage Unlimited, a wholesaler in Winnipeg. You receive an order from Joe Ramano, owner of Luxury Imports (111 High St., Prince Albert, Sask. S6V 6E3), for one dozen #16A392 black, three-hanger Goff garment bags at $32.50 each. Luxury Imports is an occasional customer and has a good credit record.

Six months ago you stopped carrying model #16A392, since there was little demand for it. While you could get a dozen of that model, it would take six to eight weeks to do so. You have replaced #16A392 with #28C400 five-hanger Goff garment bags at $49 each.

The two models differ in several ways. The #16A392 holds three suits, has four zippered pockets on the outside, is available only in black, and is made of double-seamed vinyl. The #28C400 holds five suits, has six zippered pockets on the outside, and is made of double-seamed canvas. It comes in red, blue, and tan. You also carry complete sets of matching luggage in these three colours.

Write to Joe Ramano expressing your willingness to order the bags requested as long as the delay is tolerable. Try to show that the #28C400 is a more-than-acceptable substitute and even superior in several ways.

Refusing Requests

20. You are reservations manager for the Banff Park Lodge, a 200-room hotel in Banff. The Lodge has an occupancy rate of 88 percent and is strongly oriented towards families. In fact, 90 percent of its rentals include at least one child.

    In recent years a growing number of students have been spending their spring break at the Lodge. Unfortunately, their boisterous behaviour has sometimes upset some of the more sedate guests. You have decided to discourage the student trade in the future, but you realize that today's student will be tomorrow's desirable customer. For that reason you do not want to alienate students when you refuse to allow them to stay at the Lodge.

    Today you received the season's first request for a reservation from a student. Send your response to Joel Freitag, 120 Finnegan Hall, Carleton University, Ottawa, Ont. K1G 1A1.

21. As a service representative for Worldwide Publishing, you correspond frequently with professors who are considering adopting your textbooks for classroom use. Many professors and instructors request examination copies so that they can determine whether a book is appropriate for a particular course.

    Examination copies are free and sending them out is standard practice for many publishers. As part of your job, you must screen out the inappropriate requests and honour the legitimate ones. The criteria for making your decisions are the name of the course for which the book is being considered, the approximate size of the class, and when the class if offered. Company policy prohibits you from sending examination copies to any professor who does not currently teach courses in the relevant subject area.

    You receive a request for *Business Communication Practices* from a professor of geography who claims to be considering the book for a course in physical geography. Write a letter to Professor Shirley Zale, Geography Department, Northwest College, Thunder Bay, Ont. P7B 5E3. In the letter you should deny the request for an examination copy, but promote the enclosed list of your company's geography textbooks. Also, inform the professor that Worldwide Publishing offers a 20-percent educational discount on any book she orders, regardless of its subject. You do not want to lose the goodwill of the professor for she may become interested in some of your geography books.

Adjustment Refusals

22. You have just received a request from the seniors at Martin High School to allow them to conduct a sales campaign among the employees and on the premises of Standard Life Insurance Company. The proceeds from the sale would be donated to the children's unit of a nearby hospital. Company policy prohibits soliciting, and the firm's liability insurance policy would not cover student solicitors. Write a letter of refusal to Don Hocking, Student Council President, Martin High School, Charlottetown, P.E.I. C1A 2N3.
23. You are the promotion manager for Maple Leaf Gardens. Following a concert by the most popular group in Canada, the Gazelles, you receive this letter:

    My friends and I camped in front of your box office the night before tickets for the Gazelles' show went on sale. There were about twenty people ahead of us, but we were sure that we would still get seats in the first or second row.

    Imagine our surprise when we went to the concert and found ourselves in the sixteenth row. Not only that, but most of the people in front of us bought their tickets on the day of the concert.

    We were so mad that we went home after the concert and broke all of our Gazelles records. Besides that, we'll never attend another concert at the Gardens. We may reconsider, however, if you refund the price of our tickets. After all, fair is fair, and we should have been in the front row. I am enclosing our ticket stubs.

    There had been a malfunction in the computerized ticket operation that hadn't been discovered until the day of the concert. As a result, the last purchasers got the best seats.

    Write a letter to Stephanie Zigler, 1219 Southview Rd., Newmarket, Ont. L3Y 5X3. Deny her request for a refund, but sell her on the idea of returning to the Gardens for future concerts. Even though she was not in the first row, her seat was in the $22 section, as she had requested.

Form Letters

24. Save all the form letters you or the members of your family receive in the mail over a two-week period. When you have at least three letters, analyze them to see how effective they are in conveying their message. You can begin by applying the ten characteristics of

effective writing outlined in Chapter 5; however, you should also consider your personal reaction to them as you are the intended audience.

25. For many years Classic Mail Order House has had a policy of sending a personal note to any customer whose order will be delayed more than a week. This chore has become too time-consuming. Draft a form letter that can be sent to customers in the case of a delayed order.
26. You have just opened a sporting goods store (The Right Stuff), and you want to sent a note of appreciation to each customer who makes a purchase of $100 or more. Besides thanking the customer, you will want to mention that you intend to offer frequent unadvertised specials. Also, entry forms will be available at your store for all the road races and various softball, soccer, and tennis tournaments held in the community. Prepare an appropriate letter.
27. You are employed by Quikheat, an electrical appliance company. Approximately 10 000 toasters processed by one of your competitors, Solarist, have been declared unsafe by a government agency. Solarist has been ordered to recondition them at no expense to the owners. This widely publicized order has been misunderstood by many Quikheat owners, who have been writing to learn what they must do to get their toasters reconditioned. Prepare a form letter explaining the situation to these Quikheat owners.

Discussion Cases

Easy to Judge, Hard to Correct[1]

Professor Karen Taraki teaches a course in business letter writing at Coastal Community College. Instead of writing a final examination, the students collect letters from businesses and organizations throughout the area served by their college. These letters are then organized into a report consisting of a title page, letter of transmittal, table of contents, the letters, and critiques of each of the letters based on the criteria developed throughout the course. Finally, each letter is assigned a grade by the student.

Every term many of the students' reports contain letters that were sent by employees of the college. Inevitably these letters received grades of C, D, or even lower.

Professor Taraki concurs with these grades. The letters are often typed with many unnecessary indentations, thereby adding to the cost of the letter. They are full of *I* and *We* with little emphasis on

continued

the reader. Some of the letters are so disorganized they leave the reader wondering why they were ever written. Tired phrases abound; an insincere *thank you* is tacked on at the end of many letters even when there really is nothing for which to thank the reader. Fill-ins on form letters are not aligned and often are done in different sizes of type.

It would be a simple matter to recommend an in-house seminar on improving letter-writing skills for the staff. However, the college already employs an administrative assistant to the president who screens and approves all of the form letters that go out from the college. This assistant doesn't screen other communications. The assistant's background and experience are unrelated to business communication.

Case Questions

1. Would you recommend that the professor change the content of her course to be more in line with the letters sent out by various staff members in the college?
2. Should the professor ask the students not to include college letters in their term projects?
3. Should the professor agree with the students' critiques of college letters and do nothing to suggest improvements?
4. What alternatives besides the seminar idea could the professor propose?

Why Not Talk About It First?[2]

Jeff Webster is the Commissioner of Basketball Officials for Northwestern Ontario. Apart from scheduling the officials for all the games in his region, he is also responsible for informing the various leagues of any increases in the officials' fees for the coming season.

The 1989 to 1991 fee agreement between the Officials' Association and the community colleges ended on May 1, 1991. At their annual year-end meeting, the Association decided to increase their fees for the next year's season by $15 per game per official. This increase would add $1500 to the colleges' athletic budgets.

On May 15, 1991, Webster submitted a letter to Tom Orser, Athletic Director for the colleges. Orser, in turn, passed copies of

continued

the letter to all of the region's basketball coaches who would have to cover the requested increase. Over the years, the officials have always had their fee increase requests approved because the requests were always reasonable and never exceeded the rate of inflation.

However, the coaches took exception to this year's request for an increase. First, the budget had been set on April 1, 1991; it did not account for any fee increase. Second, they felt that the officials were already overpaid. Third, they believe in negotiation. Fourth, none can afford the increase, as financial constraints have already forced them to cut parts of their program.

During an off-the-record conversation with Jeff Webster about his concerns, Phil Ziegler, spokesperson for the coaches, concluded that the Officials' Association wouldn't budge easily from its fee increase request.

Ziegler, however, has decided to write a letter, on behalf of the coaches, to the Executive Committee of the Officials' Association, refusing to pay the increase fee.

Case Questions

1. In your opinion, how was the situation handled?
2. At what point did the communication situation begin to deteriorate?
3. What suggestions do you have for improving this situation?
4. Assuming the role of Coach Ziegler, write the letter.

Chapter 10

Persuasive Messages

Learning Objectives

In this chapter, you'll learn about the persuasion process as well as how and when to use it. More specifically, you will be able to:

1. explain the goals of the persuasion process
2. get and hold a receiver's attention by writing persuasive messages
3. explain what motivates people to respond favourably to persuasive messages
4. describe the unique characteristics of the persuasive message and the situations in which such a message may be appropriate
5. organize persuasive messages so they have the greatest impact on the reader
6. write sales letters using a four-step approach
7. describe the assumptions under which various collection letters are developed
8. develop a collection campaign in which the twin goals of payment and goodwill are achievable
9. write persuasive requests
10. write news releases

Preview Case

Jennifer O'Grady hummed softly to herself as she wandered with her husband, James, through the little shops around the town square in Cozumel, Mexico. Her parents' graduation present to her and her husband had been a complete surprise: a week at the Plaza Las Glorias Hotel in Cozumel. They'd spent the day scuba diving and had decided to wander into town to do some shopping.

"Buenas tardes," said a pleasant young man in an information booth. "Are you new to Cozumel? Let me tell you about some of the sights in our beautiful city."

Jennifer and James paused to listen and the young man showed them several points of interest on a tourist map he offered them. As they were getting ready to move on, the young man asked, "Would you like to join us for brunch tomorrow morning at the Hotel del Mar? Here are two complimentary tickets."

"What's the catch?" replied Jennifer.

"Catch? I don't understand," replied the young man. "I work for the hotel and we simply want you to consider booking with us the next time you visit Cozumel."

Jennifer and James were unprepared for what they encountered the next morning at the Hotel del Mar. "Brunch" was preceded by a one-hour sales pitch for time-share condominiums adjoining the hotel. During the brunch they were seated at a table with a representative who continued to talk about the benefits of owning a time-share condominium in Cozumel.

After twenty minutes, Jennifer and James excused themselves. James sighed deeply, "If I'd known what we were in for, I would never have agreed to go to brunch. We'll know better the next time."

Overview

We face an ongoing barrage of persuasive messages in our environment. Television commercials encourage us to buy products or services, prevent forest fires or tooth decay, and watch still other television programs. Police officers remind us to watch our speed. And our friends seek favours from us.

Persuasive messages have various effects

Our responses to these messages vary. We barely pay attention to some, so advertisers continue their search for better ways to get and hold our attention — bright colours, attractive people, catchy music, pleasing situations. Other messages do get our attention but have very little effect. We simply don't want or can't afford to buy some products, but the commercials for them are nevertheless entertaining. Still other messages do effect some change in our behaviour. We purchase the product or service. We slow down as we drive, especially when we near the place where we earned our last speeding ticket. And we help our friends, often at great inconvenience to ourselves.

To write persuasive letters, you need to understand the process of persuasion. This chapter will first describe the goals of persuasion, and then show you how to use the concepts of sender, receiver, message, and channel to accomplish those goals.

Goals of Persuasion

Although some people find the word *persuasion* so mysterious that it is threatening, persuasion is nothing new. Aristotle, Plato, and Cicero wrote about persuasion almost two thousand years ago. And popular treatments of persuasion abound today in such books as Jurd Deville's *Nice Guys Finish First: How to Get People to Do What You Want and Thank You for It*, Matthew J. Calligan's *How to Be a Million-Dollar Persuader*, and Michael Gilbert's *How to Win an Argument*. While each of these writers took a different approach to persuasion, they were all concerned about one central idea — shaping the behaviour of others.

The primary goal of persuasion is to shape someone's behaviour

In Chapter 2, you learned that the behaviour of people enables an organization to meet its goals. The essence of persuasion is to shape the behaviour of others so that some goal can be more easily reached. Simply defined, persuasion is the art of getting people to do something that they wouldn't ordinarily do if you didn't ask. By asking in a persuasive manner, you shape behaviour.

Sometimes we want to control when the behaviour takes place

When shaping others' behaviour, you often want to influence not only what they do, but also when and how they do it. The next time a mail order advertiser invites you to enter a sweepstakes, notice the extra rewards for a winner who enters the contest by an early deadline. Television commercials offering such consumer goods as records, books, and kitchen gadgets provide a toll-free number for you to call in your order. They also remind you to call immediately: "The supply is limited, so act now!" And many salespeople in department stores are instructed never to let a customer get out the door without having signed on the dotted line. In each of these cases, the persuader is aware that delay in shaping behaviour could mean no shaping at all.

We also want to control how the behaviour is performed

Some persuaders also want to influence how (or where) you perform the behaviour. The chief electoral officer simply encourages you to make sure your name is on the voters' list, but a politician is obviously interested in shaping the way you cast your ballot: "Remember to vote in the upcoming provincial election. And when you do, vote for George Jenkins." When owners of fast-food restaurants tell you, "You deserve a break today," they clearly want to influence where you take that "break."

In shaping the behaviour of others, then, you'll choose at least one of the more specific goals of:

- what the behaviour should be
- when the behaviour should occur
- how (or where) the behaviour should be performed

The Persuasion Process

After selecting your specific goals, you are ready to develop your persuasive message. Yet, as in any form of communication, certain factors will influence the success of your persuasive attempt:

1. the *sender* of the persuasive message
2. the *receiver* of the persuasive message
3. the persuasive *message* itself
4. the *channel* through which the persuasive message is sent

Sender

The more credible the source, the more persuasive the message

"Consider the source," we often say if we doubt the truthfulness of some persuasive message. Indeed, the source of a persuasive message has an enormous impact on how well it shapes behaviour. This impact is one reason the makers of an aftershave lotion use hockey players to sell their products on television and why the picture of an Olympic champion is on the front of thousands of breakfast cereal boxes. In simple terms, you are more apt to respond favourably to persuasive messages when their sender is someone you respect or admire. Your response is based upon the key sender concept, *source credibility*.

To get a better feeling of how credibility works, try this exercise. Think of the best supervisor you've ever worked for or the best teacher you've ever had. Now answer yes or no to the following statements about that person:

Some components of credibility

1. This person really knew the work. (*Expertise*)
2. This person always told the truth and kept his/her word. (*Trust*)
3. This person was active and energetic. (*Dynamism*)
4. This person would always "level" with me. (*Objectivity*)
5. This person was always interested in my personal welfare. (*Goodwill*)

How many yes responses did you give? The more you gave, the more credible the person you were thinking of is to you.

Credibility is the image of the source

Credibility refers to the overall image of the message sender. The exercise you just completed pointed to five important components of credibility. A receiver's image of the sender involves how competent, trustworthy, dynamic, objective, and well-intentioned the receiver perceives the sender to be. And the more favourable this perception is, the more likely that the sender will shape the receiver's behaviour.

As a sender of persuasive messages, you should first evaluate your own credibility. When you communicate in business, the credibility of your organization is just as important as your personal credibility.

In summary, the first step in shaping the behaviour of others is to consider your credibility. Both within and outside business, your receivers will usually "consider the source" before they act.

Receiver

As pointed out in Chapter 4, your success as a communicator frequently depends on your ability to analyze your receiver. In persuasive situations, this ability is critical. Two sets of factors to consider in analyzing the receiver of your persuasive message are those involving attention and motivation. First you get the receiver's attention; then you motivate the receiver.

The ability to analyze your receiver is vital to successful persuasion

Attention

In any persuasive situation — be it a letter, speech, or advertisement — your first function is to get and hold your receiver's attention. Knowing several things about receivers will help you do this.

People pay attention to the unexpected. Several years ago a man toured the country, giving driver-safety speeches to high school assemblies. He began every speech this way:

You can get the receiver's attention by doing something unexpected

Look around you. Look at the person on each side of you. Ten years from now one of the three of you will be dead.

The accuracy of his statistics was irrelevant. What caught his receivers' attention was the original, startling, and personal way he used those statistics. Other examples of using the unexpected abound. People attend to the unexpected, and once they attend, they're easier to persuade.

People pay attention to what is pleasing. Many persuaders use reinforcing stimuli simply to get the receiver's attention. Leaf through your favourite magazine or watch a few television commercials. You will notice immediately that many products are advertised in pleasing surroundings — physically attractive men and women, cheerful settings, attractive colours. Reinforcing words and phrases are also often used as attention-getters:

You can get attention by using reinforcing stimuli

How to Solve Communication Problems

Increasing Personal and Professional Power

Getting Noticed, Getting Ahead!

Once attention is obtained, then the real persuasive message begins.

You can get attention by emphasizing the relevant

People pay attention to messages related to their own goals and objectives. Put simply, receivers will attend to your persuasive message if that message is about something important to them. People who have dentures are more likely to watch denture-cleaner commercials on television than are people who have their own teeth. The latter pay more attention to toothpaste commercials. Pet owners attend to pet food commercials more carefully than do those who have no pets.

In summary, three attention factors are the *unexpected*, the *reinforcing*, and the *relevant*. Which factor or combination of factors you use in developing a persuasive message depends on your analysis of the receiver. Will he or she respond more favourably to an attention-getter that is not expected, one that is reinforcing, or one that emphasizes his or her important goals?

You might also consider your own credibility when choosing an attention factor. Low credibility can weaken any attempts at getting attention to persuade.

Motivation

Also involved in analysis of your receiver are motivational factors. Once you have gained the receiver's attention, what will make that person respond favourably to your persuasive attempt?

Many theories have been developed to explain what motivates people both at work and in their personal lives. One of these theories, developed by Abraham Maslow, says that people do things to satisfy certain needs:[1]

Maslow's Five Needs

1. **Physiological needs** — lower-order survival needs such as food, sleep, and air
2. **Safety and security needs** — lower-order needs for personal security (for example, a safe home) and financial security (for example, a steady income or a savings account)
3. **Belonging needs** — higher-order needs such as being included by other people in their activities and receiving affection from those people
4. **Esteem and status needs** — higher-order needs, for example, self-respect and respect from others
5. **Self-actualization needs** — higher-order needs for self-realization or fulfilment in vocation or avocation

Notice that the first two needs are called "lower order," and the last three needs "higher order." Maslow maintained that you progress from the first need to the fifth. That is, you first try to satisfy your physiological needs. Once they are satisfied, you are motivated to satisfy safety and security needs, and so on until you reach the self-actualization needs. This progression from lower- to higher-order needs is why this theory is sometimes called Maslow's Hierarchy of Needs; it is illustrated in Figure 10.1.

Maslow identified two needs as "lower order" and three as "higher order"

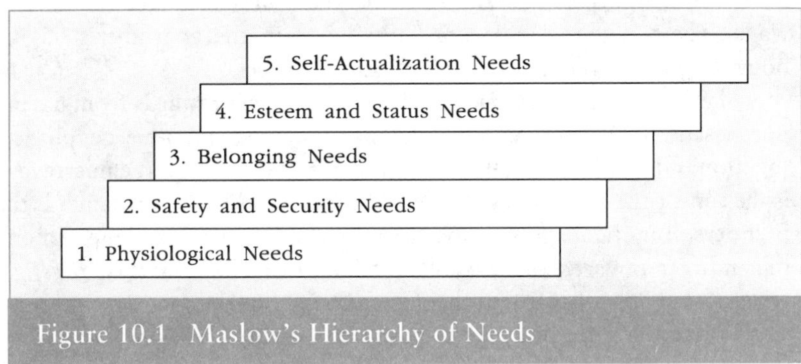

Figure 10.1 Maslow's Hierarchy of Needs

If you use Maslow's Hierarchy of Needs, your analysis of the receiver requires (1) predicting at which of the five levels your receiver is at the time of your persuasive attempt, (2) creating a message relevant to those needs, and (3) telling the receiver that the shaped behaviour you desire will satisfy the needs. The following three persuasive messages involve the same product. Yet notice how they are adapted to different needs.

Your new Phantom will be the safest car on the highway. Heavy-duty bumpers, specially moulded fenders, and our exclusive "invisible roll-bar frame" will protect you better than any other car on the market.

Safety and security needs

The Number 1 car in North America – that's the Phantom. More than thirty million people drive Phantoms. Maybe you should think about owning one, too.

Belonging needs

For the discriminating driver, Phantom's Marquis de Luxe is a step above luxury – it's a sign you've arrived.

Esteem and status needs

Direct and Indirect Rewards

Maslow's Hierarchy is only one way to analyze what motivates your receiver. Another way rests on the simple assumption that people do things for reasons, and the reasons you give in a persuasive message are built around two sets of rewards — direct and indirect.

Direct rewards come from the actual shaped behaviour

Direct rewards are those someone gets from actually buying the product or using the service; that is, these rewards come directly from the behaviour the persuasive message prompts. Think for a few moments about the rewards a consumer gets from purchasing a microwave. There's the *convenience* of being able to thaw food quickly. It's more *economical* than an electric stove because it takes less time to prepare food. Vegetables *retain more of their nutrients and colour* when they are prepared in a microwave. Utensils are *easier to clean* when food is cooked in a microwave. These rewards will come directly from the consumer's having bought a microwave. In that sense, they are direct.

Indirect rewards come from other people as a result of shaped behaviour

The consumer might also receive some indirect rewards from having purchased the microwave. Indirect rewards come from other people as a function of having performed the behaviour. Assume that the microwave is the top-of-the-line model of a name brand and that the consumer is the first person in the neighbourhood to own this superior machine. Among the indirect rewards the consumer might receive are *status*, *prestige*, *respect*, and *approval* from others in the neighbourhood.

Notice that you don't give these rewards to yourself. Doctors and lawyers have status only because others in the community assign that status to them. You may have heard the phrase "conspicuous consumption" used as an explanation for why many people purchase expensive consumer goods — flashy cars, colour-co-ordinated skis and powder suits, sophisticated stereo systems, and so on. Conspicuous means "easy to see or obvious." Thus, conspicuous consumption means that these people buy the expensive items so that others will take notice of their possessions and assign them various kinds of indirect rewards.

Direct and indirect rewards can shape behaviour on the job

In the same way that the public responds to direct and indirect rewards from business, managers and workers respond to direct and indirect rewards on the job. For example, a manager who runs a cost-efficient, productive department probably has fewer day-to-day problems and gets more job satisfaction (direct rewards) than does a manager who constantly has to respond to crises. Moreover, the effective manager usually receives regular promotions and salary increases as well as the recognition and respect of his or her peers (indirect rewards).

For workers, many companies offer cash bonuses (indirect rewards) for suggestions that will save the company money, increase productivity, or solve an ongoing problem. If the suggestion simplifies that worker's job, then the worker also gets direct rewards. If the worker is then recognized in the company newsletter, he or she receives additional indirect rewards such as increased status with fellow workers. Companies offering incentives such as these to their employees understand how to motivate their employees to better performance on the job.

You can choose from a multitude of both direct and indirect rewards when analyzing your receiver. Here are some examples:

Direct Rewards	**Indirect Rewards**
Comfort	Affection
Convenience	Appreciation
Enjoyment	Approval
Entertainment	Belonging
Health	Friendship
Less work	Pay increase
Money saved	Popularity
Personal improvement	Prestige
Problem solved	Promotion
Safety	Recognition
Satisfaction	Reputation
Sense of achievement	Respect
Variety	Status

In summary, before you build your persuasive message, you should analyze your intended receivers in terms of factors that will get their attention and factors that will motivate them to shape their behaviour in the way you plan.

Analyze receivers to determine factors likely to get their attention and to motivate them

Message

A third variable in the persuasion process is the message itself. The type of persuasive message you create depends, in part, upon the channel you intend to use (for example, sales letter, speech, advertisement). In constructing a persuasive message, you need to pay careful attention to both the organization of that message and the kinds of persuasive appeals you will use within it.

Organizing the persuasive message

No matter what channel you use, your message should contain at least three essential ingredients: an attention step (as discussed earlier); a need step (where you emphasize the needs you are appealing to or the direct and indirect rewards you are suggesting); and an action step (where you specify the behaviour the receiver should perform).

The appeals used give substance to a message

While the organizational pattern provides the skeleton for your persuasive message, persuasive appeals flesh out the skeleton and give the message substance. These appeals are like tools in a toolbox. You pick the one or ones most appropriate for your specific persuasive task. Two kinds of appeals deserve your attention here — the emotional and the logical.

Emotional Appeal

Most widely used in shaping consumer behaviour are emotional appeals, which apply to the feelings, rather than the intellect, of the receiver. Such appeals, of course, promise those direct and indirect rewards we described earlier. To give you a better idea of how emotional appeals work, here are some examples:

Shaped Behaviour	Rewards	Message
Enter a government award competition	Personal improvement, prestige	"Believing in yourself is one thing. Having others recognize your achievements is quite another. That's the kind of stimulus the Canada awards provide for your team, from the moment you enter."[2]
Join a computer dating service	Belonging, friendships, problem solved	Why spend time waiting for the perfect someone? You'll find that someone at Date-A-Match. Love is just around the corner at 100 Niagara Drive.
Sign up for a cruise	Entertainment, friendships, enjoyment	There's dining, dancing, swimming ... or, if you'd like, lounging on our spacious sundeck with the most interesting people you'll ever meet.

The bandwagon technique is an example of an emotional appeal

Some emotional appeals rely on the bandwagon technique, which speaks to a need to belong. "Everybody is doing it" is the essence of this emotional appeal. For years a certain automobile was advertised as the number-one car in Canada (meaning, of course, that "everyone" was buying this car). A well-known car rental agency advertises itself, "We're number one."

Logical Appeals

Logical appeals are used more for persuading business representatives

Logical appeals are directed towards the receiver's rational abilities. These appeals are used most often to persuade other businesspeople. One reason is that people in business — for example, purchasing agents — must be able to justify the behaviour the persuasive message produces. The result is appeals such as the following:

Shaped Behaviour	Rewards	Message
Buy a computer networking system	Problem solved	"It doesn't seem like that long ago that the company had only one microcomputer, and then there were the portables for sales staff, and the branch office. Now the challenge before you is to integrate all of these independent computers with your corporate business network."[3]
Lease cars	Convenience	"The attitude of most auto leasing companies is fairly rigid when it comes to writing customer contracts. As new kid on the block, we intend to go the other way. That's why we write our contract in pencil – it's our symbol of flexibility."[4]
Purchase a prefabricated building	Money saved, durability	The aluminum siding on Brock Buildings means that you'll get years of economical and long-lasting service.

Many persuasive messages contain a mixture of emotional and logical appeals. However, if you carefully analyze the television commercials you see and the magazine advertisements you read, you will notice that emotional appeals are more frequent, especially for consumers. You will also begin to recognize the various ways in which persuasive messages are organized.

Emotional appeals are used more for persuading consumers

In summary, the third major factor in the persuasion process is the message. In constructing the persuasive message, you use the kinds of logical and emotional appeals you think will best shape the behaviour of the receiver.

Channel

As a business communicator, you'll probably use the persuasion process in many different ways. But they'll all be divided into two basic channels of communication — oral and written.

There are two primary channels: oral and written

As part of your analysis of your receiver, decide which channel will get the best results. For example, if you want to persuade a credit customer to send an overdue payment, should you call on the telephone or write a brief collection message? If you want immediate feedback and better acceptance, oral communication is preferable. But if you need documentation or if your message is fairly detailed, a written message is better.

The appropriateness of a channel depends on many factors

Several of the other factors discussed in this chapter should also enter into your decision. You may be more able to show goodwill through an informal telephone conversation. Or you might be able to be more objective in a letter. An unexpected telephone call may certainly get attention. However, it might be better to communicate the rewards in a letter, where you can more easily control both the organization and the types of appeals you use in your message. As a persuasive source, you should weigh these channel benefits carefully when beginning your efforts to shape behaviour.

Persuasive Communication

Persuasion may be blatant and unpleasant, like that used to sell time-share condominiums in Cozumel as described at the beginning of this chapter, or it may be subtle. Regardless, persuasion plays an important role in our lives. Your happiness and your success in life are affected by your persuasiveness as well as by your receptiveness to persuasion. As a business correspondent, you will be expected to be able to persuade others through your letters. The persuasive letter is one in which you seek to "modify thought and action" of others in a certain direction.

Thus far we have considered persuasion in general. Now we will focus on those types of persuasive communication most frequently encountered in the business setting: sales letters, collection letters, letters of special requests, and press releases.

Many persuasive letters are form letters

Large organizations often send out sales letters by the thousands. Since it is not practical to compose an individual letter for each reader, a form letter may be developed. Figure 10.2 is an example of a form sales letter developed for mass distribution. A credit account application blank ordinarily accompanies such a letter.

Whether you are writing an individualized persuasive letter or a letter that will be widely distributed, the same basic principles apply. Whenever you seek to persuade someone, you should follow these four steps:

1. get the reader's attention
2. stimulate the reader's interest
3. awaken a desire in the reader
4. show that the reader's desire will be satisfied by taking whatever action you are persuading him or her to take

Giant

George R. Hanes
National Credit Marketing Manager
Giant Corporation

Dear Mrs. Smith:

I am writing to invite you to apply for the Giant Credit Card – the credit card that offers you and your family many unique benefits, conveniences, and services.

For example, the Giant Credit Card is the only credit card accepted at Giant – and the only card that lets you say "Charge it!" at 2500 Giant stores from coast to coast.

This means that no matter where you live or travel you have credit at any Giant store. And, even if you move, your Giant Credit Account will be transferred to your new location.

In addition, your Giant Credit Card opens the door to an incredible range of over 200 000 products and services you can charge, based on your particular credit level.

- You can charge family, home, and auto needs whenever it's not convenient to pay cash.
- You may budget your payments over many months, if you wish.
- There are no hidden credit charges. Finance charges are always fully disclosed on your Giant Credit Card statement.
- For more than 50 years Giant has stood behind its promise of a money-back guarantee if you are not completely satisfied.
- Shopping at Giant stores and from our catalogues is always a pleasure because of our nationwide reputation for prompt, efficient, and courteous service.

continued

Figure 10.2 A Form Sales Letter for Mass Distribution

I'm sure you're familiar with Giant's famous general catalogue. But Giant also publishes many specialized catalogues – featuring almost everything from uniforms to foreign car parts. And you can use the Giant Credit Card to order from all our catalogues by mail or by phone. (In many areas we accept phone orders 24 hours a day.) Ordering by phone from Giant catalogues lets you choose from a tremendous range of merchandise in the comfort of your own home. To get your Giant catalogues, simply inquire at your nearby Giant store.

To apply for your Giant Credit Card, just fill in and bring the enclosed application to the Giant store nearest you. (Or mail it – postage is paid.)

I know you will enjoy shopping at Giant – especially with the new convenience and budgeting flexibility the Card provides.

Very truly yours,

George R. Hanes

GRH/bsb

George R. Hanes

P.S. If you're already a Giant Credit Customer, our apologies for this duplication. And, many thanks for shopping at Giant.

These steps, sometimes called the AIDA formula (Attention, Interest, Desire, Action), are the basis for all the persuasive messages in this book. Each step will be discussed and developed as the chapter progresses.

Sales Letters

Each year millions of unsolicited sales letters are mailed to consumers, many of whom routinely discard them and disparagingly refer to them as "junk mail." That which is "junk mail" to many consumers is called direct mail advertising by advertisers, and it is big business. Almost as much is spent annually on direct mail advertising as is spent on television advertising.[5]

The results of specific sales letters are recorded

Experts consider direct mail a more precise advertising medium than television or newspapers, each of which is ordinarily directed at the general population. Direct mail advertising can be tailored for and sent to a narrow segment of the population. And since sales results can be easily related to a specific letter, direct mail advertising can be scientifically tested, with various versions of a letter compared for effectiveness.

Writing good sales letters is an art. For some people it is a full-time occupation — and a well-paying one at that. Some of the best-known practitioners of direct mail advertising are paid as much as $25 000 to develop a single packaged sales letter that will get the desired results. Since such letters are mailed out in tremendous quantities, a response rate of 1 to 2 percent is considered good.[6]

Regardless of your occupation, much of your writing will be aimed at trying to persuade the reader

While you may never become part of the direct mail advertising business, much of the writing you will do in business will be aimed at trying to persuade your reader. The obstacles you face will be similar to those encountered by the direct mail writer. In trying to persuade someone, you are trying to sell that person on an idea or a course of action. By becoming familiar with the strategy of the sales letter, you can become a more effective persuader.

The principles governing sales letters pertain to all persuasive writing

The reception a sales letter gets is considerably different from the reception given the types of letters already discussed. Letters granting requests are easy to write because they tell readers what they want to hear. Although letters refusing requests are not welcome, they will still be read, especially if they are well written, because they contain information which interests the reader.

When you write a sales letter, you often must stimulate an uninterested reader

Sales letters, on the other hand, generally fall into two categories, solicited and unsolicited. The *unsolicited* sales letter does not have the advantages enjoyed by the other types of letters. It doesn't present information likely to be considered interesting by the reader. The challenge facing the sales letter writer in this case is to create a message that, although unsolicited, will stimulate a relatively uninterested reader.

The *solicited* letter is easier to write, since the reader has expressed interest, sought information, or made a specific inquiry.

Preparation

Become completely familiar with a product before trying to write a sales letter about it

Before beginning to write persuasively, you should learn as much as possible about the idea, service, or product to be offered to the reader. You should certainly know the following about the product:

- exactly what it can do
- the materials from which it is made
- the expertise through which it was developed
- its outstanding features
- ways in which it differs from its competitors
- price extent of the maintenance required, and the expertise required to perform it
- accompanying warranty, if any

Before writing a sales letter, become familiar with the intended customers

Besides becoming very familiar with what is to be offered, you should analyze those likely to receive the letter. If you are able to appeal to the interests of the reader, the resulting letter will be more effective. Such factors as income level, occupation, and marital status may determine the appeals to be used in the letter.

At times you may have to write a sales letter with little specific knowledge about the readers. Then you must look to the product or service you will offer in the letter as an indication of the kind of person most likely to read it. For example, if you are trying to attract customers for a lawn-care service, the letter will be geared to suburban homeowners.

Once you are fully aware of the product or idea and of the potential customers, you can plan the sales message. You must determine how best to link the intended customer with what is being offered. In other words, exactly how will the reader benefit from the physical characteristics and capabilities of the product?

The physical characteristics of a certain brand of running shoes are a combination of lightweight rubber, canvas, and colour. The benefits to the owner of such shoes, however, might be that they:

- save money because they will last longer than other running shoes
- enable faster running because they are very lightweight
- improve the runner's appearance because they are so stylish and available in many different colours
- provide more comfort because they are available in many sizes
- provide more safety through their unique double-deep tread design

Readers are interested in a product's psychological benefits

Potential buyers are interested in the physical features of a product, but it may be the product's psychological benefits or features that convince the reader to buy.

Steps for Effective Sales Letters

The steps for effective sales letters pertain to all persuasive attempts

Whenever the purpose of a letter is to elicit the co-operation of others, you should follow a certain sequence of steps. Although the terminology has varied somewhat, persuasive writers have used these same steps for many years. Whether you are trying to sell something or trying to convince the reader to pursue a certain course of action, the steps we have already called the AIDA formula (other names exist) have proven effective:

1. Attract the reader's ATTENTION.
2. Stimulate the reader's INTEREST.
3. Develop a DESIRE within the reader.
4. Encourage the reader to take a specific ACTION.

1. Attention

Remember the three attention factors: the *unexpected*, the *reinforcing*, and the *relevant*. The first sentence of an unsolicited sales letter must grab the reader while leading to the remainder of the letter. In order to accomplish this, you should identify one of the most significant features of the product you are trying to sell. If possible, suggest how the reader stands to benefit from using the product. (Throughout the remainder of our consideration of sales letters, we will refer only to "product" even though the principles presented pertain to any persuasive writing.)

Unless the first sentence of a sales letter attracts attention, the reader will probably discard the letter

Many successful writers attempt to include in the first sentence that aspect of the product in which most readers are interested: its relevance. The manufacturer of an energy-efficient water heater, for example, considered economy to be the most important characteristic of the product. For that reason economy was emphasized in this opening:

How would you like to cut your water heating expense by 30 percent?

An auto dealer who felt that the new styling of the product was its most interesting aspect stressed this newness:

Come and see the all-new C-7 now and you'll be the first in your neighbourhood to own one.

No one "right" method of getting the attention of the reader exists. Only after you get to know both the product and the intended reader thoroughly are you really ready to select an appropriate method. Some of the more common methods used are as follows:

There are proven methods for attracting the attention of the reader

- Make a thought-provoking statement: "The best thing about our new line of purses is something you can't see."
- Present a startling fact: "Ninety-five out of 100 families would be bankrupt if they missed just three pay cheques."
- Offer a bargain: "Imagine, two pairs of shoes for the price of one!"
- Describe something that currently is happening: "Today more than 500 families enjoyed the *Press Journal* with breakfast."
- Present a direct challenge. "Try to tear the enclosed piece of rubberized plastic and you'll understand why our seat covers won't wear out."
- Tell an interesting anecdote: "Until I was 25 years old I thought that you had to be rich to afford a new car. The day I visited Bill Smith's Auto Market was the day I learned otherwise. That was also the day I bought my first new car."

Attention-Getting Guide

- Present what the reader will view as the major benefit of the product that you seek to sell.
- Relate the product to the reader rather than to the writer ("you-centred"). Write an original opening statement.
- Make the first paragraph interesting enough to appeal to the reader and so short that the reader will have to read subsequent paragraphs to get the important details.

Originality is an important characteristic in a sales letter

An opening is more likely to attract attention if it is written in an original manner. When the writer uses clichés, the reader is likely to think, "Here we go again," and may discard the letter. The reader is more likely to continue reading, however, if the opening paragraph is short. Conciseness is vital for an effective opening when a letter is unsolicited. If the reader has already expressed interest in the product being offered, no attention-getter is necessary.

When you are unable to attract attention, a sale is unlikely. Because attention-getting is so crucial, you must try to make your approach unique. In striving to be unique, however, you risk making an error that may cause the reader to lose interest. These are some of the most common errors made in seeking attention:

Common errors in trying to attract attention

1. Asking a foolish question. A question that has an obvious answer will not attract attention. "How would you like to double your income and shorten your work week?" is such a question.
2. Emphasizing the writer instead of the reader. Readers want to know how they will benefit. "It looks like CKUR will be number one in the ratings soon" virtually ignores the reader.
3. Presenting an irrelevant statement. A sales letter that begins: "There's at least one thing in life that you needn't be a millionaire to enjoy" sounds intriguing until the reader discovers that the product is a new deodorant soap. You must make a direct link between the opening statement and the product being sold.
4. Phrasing an idea in an unoriginal way. Avoid the use of such clichés as "A stitch in time saves nine," and refrain from using anecdotes that are already widely known.

This is how one writer began a sales letter to promote a correspondence course in electronics:

You don't need a college degree to get a good job.

The statement is not clever, but it is oriented towards the reader ("You") and it does suggest a benefit ("a good job"). This sales letter will be developed in the remaining three steps in the persuasive process.

2. Interest

Having attracted the reader's attention, you must now strive for an "I think I'd like to have that" reaction. In this section, you usually introduce the product and provide the reader with good reasons for buying it. Some authorities recommend emphasizing the reward to be derived from the product rather than the actual product at this point. Instead of selling the reader on the lawnmower, stress the good feelings associated with having an attractive lawn. In this way, the reader goes beyond the product to the pleasure experienced from its use. In the interest step, therefore, you are both describing the product and suggesting its value to the reader.

The main purpose of the interest section is to make the reader want the product

Notice that you must link this step to the attention-getting step. Unless the interest step flows naturally from the attention step, the reader will probably stop reading the letter. The writer of the following sales letter failed to link the steps:

You need a natural link between the attention step and the interest step

Want the world at your fingertips? Then, the new DMS personal compact disk text storage is for you.

It allows you to store a multivolume encyclopedia on a single compact disk. It features more data than conventional print encyclopedias. You can search for references by subject area, key words, or proper names.

The writer failed to link the attention and interest steps in this example

The writer should emphasize a central selling point throughout the letter

The key idea of the attention-getting step is that the compact disk text storage unit gives instant access to a "world" of information. The writer does not link that idea to the example of the set of encyclopedias. Hence, his letter is completely unsuccessful.

In attempting to stimulate the reader's interest the writer should emphasize some central selling point of the product. The writer of the correspondence-course sales letter did it this way:

You've probably read newspaper articles about how job opportunities are declining today. At the same time, however, there are occupations in which opportunities are expanding. The automotive service field is one in which there is a shortage of technicians. Not only is there a shortage now, but government studies show that during the next ten years the demand for automotive service technicians will increase by 21 percent. That means that for every ten electronics technicians now working, two more will be needed.

You're probably wondering who will fill all of these new jobs. The answer is people just like you who recognize an opportunity when they see one.

The writer used the availability of jobs as a central selling point. Depending on the nature of the audience, a different central selling point might have been selected. Selling knowledge for the sake of knowledge could be an appropriate approach with certain readers. Selling the challenge of electronics technician work or the potential for earning high wages are other possible approaches.

If you have successfully stimulated the reader's interest, that interest may now be changing to a desire for the product.

3. Desire

In the desire section, the writer moves the reader from the "like to have that" category to the "really need that" position. Since the reader may still be balking at the letter's basic idea, this section must justify the desire for the product by stressing its practical aspect(s).

The desire section should make the reader feel a need for the product

As described earlier in this chapter, persuasive appeals are of two types: emotional and logical. Emotional appeals apply to the feelings of the receiver; logical appeals apply to the receiver's thinking abilities. By making an appropriate appeal or appeals, the writer helps readers justify the desire for the product.

One automobile dealer, for example, may try to sell a car on the basis of the complete warranty that accompanies it. This appeal is logical. Another dealer may try to sell the same product through the idea that the reader will be the first on the block to own this distinctive new model. This appeal is strongly emotional.

The qualities of the product being sold will usually suggest whether a logical or an emotional appeal is best. Sometimes a combination of the two types of appeals is preferable.

The writer trying to sell the correspondence course sought to develop the reader's desire in this way:

As an electronics technician you can expect your choice of many attractive jobs. The pay is good and so are the working conditions. And you can learn the skills you need without leaving home. People just like you have earned an electronics certificate in their leisure time at home.

The Trotter Institute of Electronics offers a one-year correspondence course that leads to the coveted Certificate of Electronics. In only two weeks, you could be on your way to a career in electronics.

You probably think that any course offered by the Trotter Institute would have to be expensive. You're in for a surprise! You get all of your textbooks, assignments,

and consultation with our excellent instructors for only $2000, and this includes employment counselling after you graduate. There may not be many bargains available these days, but this is definitely one. You can see now that getting a better job is easier than you thought.

In the desire section the writer pointed out additional desirable features of the correspondence course and also referred to the central selling point. The price was introduced but also de-emphasized by including it in a sentence that described the product's virtues.

Emphasize price only if it is very attractive

4. Action

Now the moment of truth has arrived. The writer has pointed out the product's most significant features as well as how the reader will benefit from its use. All that remains is for the reader to take the desired action. The writer must now tell the reader what that action is. If you want the reader to complete the enclosed form and mail it in, say so as specifically as possible. Some otherwise good sales letters are rendered ineffective by the lack of the clear action close.

The action close should indicate the specific action the reader should take

The last paragraph should be brief yet purposeful. It tells the reader what to do and includes a reminder of how the reader will benefit. The correspondence-course writer did it this way:

To prepare for a better job with a great future, complete the enclosed registration form. Within ten days you'll be progressing towards an interesting and rewarding new career.

Here is an example of a sales letter in which the four steps are clearly used:

Model sales letter with four distinct steps

ASTRO LIFELONG SIDING LIMITED
2490 Scott Road
Winnipeg, Manitoba R3H 0H3

September 20, 1992

HOW WOULD YOU LIKE TO ...

Attention

continued

Figure 10.3 The Complete Sales Letter

1. make your house more attractive and valuable?
2. reduce your heating and cooling expenses by 35 percent?
3. never again have to paint your house?

Interest

Home ownership is an expensive proposition. It takes plenty of time and money to maintain a house properly. As a home owner, you're most certainly aware of your many responsibilities. If you are like most of us, you're always looking for ways to make home ownership easier. If you can do this and save money at the same time, so much the better.

Desire

Just imagine your house looking better than ever and your having more time to enjoy it. How would you like to spend weekends doing what you want to do rather than painting and fixing the house? Astro Lifelong Siding will help you take a lot of the work out of home maintenance.

You can always recognize people who own homes sided with Astro Lifelong Siding because they smile a lot. Who wouldn't smile when their heating and cooling bills are cut by 35 percent? Besides, you can retire your paint brush because your home will never need painting again.

You will save energy and money at the same time for only $4999. You will save more than that in maintenance expenses in three to five years, and your house will look better than ever.

Fill out the enclosed postage-paid card and mail it today. I'll send you a brochure that will open your eyes. When you realize how Astro Lifelong Siding will increase the value of your home, you'll say, "Why didn't I do this sooner?"

Sincerely

Edward Robinson

Edward Robinson
President

Although a step-by-step approach to writing sales letters has been emphasized, the steps are not always separate and distinct. In some sales letters the Interest and Desire steps may be indistinguishable. You may not recognize the point at which one step ceases and another begins, but the sequence of steps is obvious. Following this sequence of steps is more important than keeping the steps separate.

Brevity is desirable in business letters, but sales letters must usually be longer than most other types of business letters. Greater length usually gives you time to develop a successful persuasive appeal. However, sales letters sent to dealers are usually shorter than those sent to consumers. Appeals to dealers can be quite direct, generally emphasizing the profit to be made.

Sales letters are usually longer than most other types of business letters

Sales Letter Guide

- Begin with a brief statement or a question likely to attract attention.
- Be sure that the opening statement is clearly related to the product being offered.
- Gain the reader's interest by emphasizing a central selling point likely to appeal to the reader.
- Develop a need within the reader by providing additional evidence of the value of the product. Also remind the reader of the central selling point.
- Minimize resistance to the price by de-emphasizing it. Mention some of the strong points of the product while referring to price.
- Indicate briefly and specifically what the reader should do, and restate the reasons the reader should take the desired action.

Collection Letters

Most retail organizations invest much time and effort in training those employees who deal regularly with the public and otherwise cultivating effective relationships between salespeople and customers. Yet, these same relationships are often threatened by the organization's efforts to collect unpaid bills.

An effective collection letter will collect the bill *and* maintain the customer's goodwill

Collecting money owed should not be the only goal of the collection process. Another important goal is retaining the good feeling and the business of the delinquent customer. Many collection letter writers completely alienate the very customers in whose loyalty the company has invested heavily. Thus, much of what can be accomplished through advertising, public relations, and skilled sales personnel can be undone through inept collection procedures.

As an account becomes more past due, collection letters become more direct in tone

Virtually every type of business relies at least occasionally on collection letters to prod past-due accounts. These letters make up the collection campaign, and they are written and mailed in a predetermined sequence. The early letters, sent when an account is slightly late, are mild in tone. As the account becomes more delinquent, the letters become more directive. Collection letters should never, though, be too direct:

Your bill is overdue. Pay us immediately or I'll see that you never get credit in this town again.

Reasons for Collection Problems

Putting strict limits on credit would reduce problems — and profits

A blacksmith shop in northern Wisconsin displayed this sign prominently: "Interested in credit? See our credit manager. Please take elevator." The building was single-story. With a credit policy like this, a company would have no collection problems. But it would also have low profits and sales. People expect credit. It has become a part of life both for the creditor — the organization extending credit — and for the debtor — the person purchasing on credit.

The collection of delinquent accounts is big business

In the quest for greater profits, business organizations often extend credit to customers who, in an earlier time, would probably have been refused it. As the number of these questionable accounts increases, so also do collection problems. These problems can lead to bankruptcy for companies that let them continue unchecked. Every year, collection agencies collect millions of dollars of past-due accounts declared uncollectible by the original creditors. In return, the agencies take a percentage of the amounts collected.

People become delinquent in paying their bills for many reasons. Contrary to popular belief, many of these reasons are completely valid. Some credit managers refer to nonpayers as "deadbeats," and in doing so they impugn their motives and characters. However, the number of customers who use credit in bad faith is small.

Some collection problems are caused by misunderstanding the terms of the credit agreement

Many collection problems can be explained by such factors as illness, loss of job, or other unexpected occurrences. In some cases, collection difficulties can be traced to the debtor's misunderstanding of the terms of the credit agreement. By taking greater care in explaining the operation of a charge account, companies can prevent some future collection problems. Some debtors fail to make payments on time because their obligation has not been clearly explained to them. No matter how much care is taken in extending credit, however, some collection problems will occur.

The Collection Campaign

Company efforts to collect past-due accounts can best be described as a campaign. Like any campaign it uses a series of stages:

The four-stage collection campaign is representative of many business campaigns

1. reminder
2. strong reminder
3. inquiry
4. urgency

As a writer of collection letters, you must approach each stage somewhat differently. The assumptions you make about a debtor change as the account becomes more overdue, and you write differently on the basis of the new assumptions.

Although we divide the campaign into four stages, this division does not mean that only four letters will be sent to a delinquent debtor. More than one letter is usually sent for each stage.

A series of collection letters used by a department store follows. Note that each letter represents one of the four stages of a collection campaign.

1. Reminder – A Gentle Prod

When a customer is first recognized as delinquent, collection efforts are restrained and mild. The assumption guiding the collection correspondent at this point is that the customer has merely overlooked the bill and needs only a reminder. In fact, when the account is about two weeks late, many companies merely send a duplicate of the original bill with some reminder of its overdue status.

The first collection letter is a reminder; the writer assumes the customer has overlooked the bill

This is a friendly reminder that a portion of the unpaid balance on your account is overdue. More than likely this is an oversight that you will correct by making a payment within the next few days.

Perhaps you have mailed your remittance already. If so, we would like to thank you for your patronage.

This reminder suggests that no actual persuasion is necessary. The writer assumes that payment was not made simply because the customer forgot about it.

The number of reminders to be sent to a delinquent customer varies from one company to another. A creditor will likely send several reminders to a customer with a good credit history. To a customer viewed as a poor risk, the creditor might send only one reminder and then move into the strong-reminder stage. The process moves to the next stage quickly when it appears that the customer is not likely to respond.

Most organizations send more reminders to a good credit risk than to a poor one

2. Strong Reminder – A Direct Prod

A strong reminder may call attention to the value of the company's services

The second stage consists of a strong reminder. The assumption remains, however, that the customer has simply forgotten to pay the bill. Some companies use this occasion to remind the customer of the values available and to point out that the customer is held in high regard despite the oversight.

Most of our customers appreciate a reminder when their accounts are overdue. Therefore, we would like to remind you of your overdue account. Listed below is your present balance as well as the minimum amount due if you prefer monthly payments.

You may have already mailed a payment within the last few days. If not, won't you please do so?

As its title suggests, this letter is stronger in tone than the first one. The writer still gives the reader the benefit of the doubt, however, by assuming that the reader has merely overlooked the bill.

3. Inquiry – To Re-establish Communication

In the inquiry stage, the writer asks the customer why the bill is past due

If the reminders do not have the desired effect, you must take a stronger position. Rather than continuing to assume that it is a matter of oversight, you now assume that some other reason has kept the customer from paying. This stage is called *inquiry* because you ask why the past-due account is not being paid. If this letter doesn't elicit payment, you seek at least an explanation. If the customer responds with an explanation, there is a good chance that a payment plan will eventually result. In short, you seek to get the customer to act, preferably by paying the bill, but at least by giving an explanation.

We recently wrote to you regarding the past-due balance on your charge account. With your revolving charge account you have the option of a 30-day account or monthly payments of as little as 5 percent of the balance. At any time, of course, you may pay more or all of your balance.

Please contact us immediately if you are unable to pay the $225 now due. Together we will be able to resolve your problem. Use the enclosed envelope for your prompt reply.

At this point the writer wants either payment or an explanation of the delay. Re-establishing a link with the customer, preferably by receipt of payment, is the goal of the letter. By reminding the reader of the convenience of a charge account, the writer hopes to get a response.

While several letters may be sent to a delinquent customer in the reminder stage, usually only one letter is sent in the inquiry stage. By this time the account is approximately 90 days overdue. By suggesting that an unusual situation has caused the delinquency, the writer makes it easy for the customer to save face. At no point, however, does the writer suggest that there was any problem with the merchandise.

4. Urgency – A Genuine Crisis

If the inquiry does not lead to positive action by the customer, the collection process moves into the urgency stage. At this point the account has been delinquent for at least 120 days. A very small percentage of accounts remain delinquent for this long; however, the collection writer must be prepared to deal with the problem.

At this stage you must impress upon the customer the seriousness of the situation. To signify the gravity of the situation, a higher-level executive, rather than a collection correspondent, often signs the letter. The writer should convey the idea that this is the end of the line, though hope for a reasonable solution still exists. Do not threaten — threats may have adverse effects on goodwill. At this point you might refer to the possibility of legal action, although this would rarely be stated in very specific terms. If several letters are used at the urgency stage, sometimes only the final one mentions a specific date for action.

In the urgency stage, the writer indicates that payments must be made now

Twelve years ago this October you opened a charge account with us. Since that time we have worked hard to meet your needs. Apparently we have succeeded, for you have been a regular customer since then.

Because you have been such a loyal customer, we're surprised that we have not heard a word from you. It's a mystery to us why you have allowed your account to become overdue after such a good credit history.

We are waiting for your cheque for $260 and we must have it. If your credit record is to be protected, you must act now.

Please send us a cheque today, or at least contact us so that a payment plan can be arranged. By acting immediately, your valuable credit record may be saved.

In this letter the writer offers the debtor one last chance. The tone of the letter is serious because this problem must be corrected.

Collection strategies differ somewhat from one organization to another. In general, however, the approach of the collection correspondent follows the progression outlined above — from reminder to stronger reminder, to inquiry, to urgent appeal. Collection campaigns require thorough planning so that past-due bills are collected without sacrificing the goodwill of the customer.

Collection Letter Guide

- Be aware of the assumption under which each letter should be written.
- Get what is owed without sacrificing the goodwill of the customer.
- As a collection campaign progresses, make letters more demanding and stress collection rather than any additional sales.
- Keep the reminder letter low-key and matter-of-fact.
- In the strong reminder letter, make the customer aware of the benefits of having credit.
- Appeal to some interest of the reader in the inquiry stage when seeking a payment or an explanation.
- In the urgency stage, convey the seriousness of the situation and the fact that time is running out.

Special Requests

Special requests are a common type of persuasive communication

Large organizations may send out sales letters by the hundreds of thousands. When research shows that a given sales letter is effective, it may be used for an extended period of time. The same is true of collection letters. Another kind of persuasive letter, however, is not normally used in mass mailings. It is a letter in which you ask a favour of someone. You will write many such letters during your career.

Since there is often little reward to offer for complying with such a request, writers often dispense with the proven sales approach and get to the heart of the matter immediately. In the following example, the writer uses the persuasive sequence to try to talk the recipient into becoming a library volunteer.

This example follows the persuasive sequence

You have demonstrated, through your civic-mindedness in the past, the effect one dedicated person can have on a project. Now you again have the opportunity to improve significantly the services provided by one of our most important institutions.

Thomas Carlyle described the founding of a library as "one of the greater things we can do." Our entire community enjoys the benefits of the Woodward Library, yet one obstacle prevents its continued development. A reduced budget has resulted in staff reductions, and our professional librarians must now spend most of their time on clerical tasks.

Misusing professional librarians is a waste of tax money. Equally important, librarians are less accessible to those who come to learn and grow. You can help the library serve the public by performing some of those clerical duties so necessary for an efficient operation. There will be an orientation for new volunteers on Wednesday, September 8, at 7:00 p.m. in the conference room of the Woodward Library. As a Woodward volunteer you will enjoy being a part of a team so clearly devoted to the public good.

In this letter, the writer recognizes the reader's past contributions before describing a present problem about which the reader could do something. By following the AIDA steps, the writer presents the reader with good reasons for helping before actually requesting assistance.

Establish common ground

In the following example, the writer presents a statement with which most public relations practitioners would agree and follows with an acknowledgement of the reader's abilities. Since no request has yet been made, the reader has nothing to refuse. And since the writer has established a common ground with the reader, the reader will continue reading.

Effective public relations practitioners are able to influence the attitudes of the public on virtually any issue. You demonstrated this ability by persuading more than 40 percent of the voters to support Sunday shopping in the recent referendum.

Most students preparing for a career in public relations are unaware of all that such a career entails. Their knowledge of the field is limited to the advice of professors, many of whom are far removed from the public arena. Only through greater contact with successful practitioners will students become more attuned to the realities of public relations.

Seek agreement on the problem, which the reader can alleviate

Here the writer lays out the problem that is of concern to the reader. As a practitioner, the reader is uniquely qualified to alleviate the problem; she can, perhaps, sense an approaching request to give a speech.

Your widespread experience in both the private and public sectors puts you in a position to contribute greatly to the development of public relations students. Because you have been so successful, however, numerous demands are made on your time. Nevertheless you could lend your expertise without relinquishing any of your precious time. By sending us a packet of all of the materials you and your associates developed for promoting Sunday shopping, you would be contributing to the educational process.

State the desired action

In this paragraph the writer provides the reader with an opportunity to make a valuable contribution without expending any time. The reader will find this request hard to refuse. The writer restates the desired action and responds to a possible concern in the following close:

Respond to possible problems

Please send us a packet of your exceptional materials today and allow our students to benefit from your expertise. If you have any requests or suggestions regarding our use of the packet, we will gladly honour your wishes.

Letters of special request have countless purposes. Some of the more common are:

- seeking financial contributions
- recruiting a chairperson or a member for a committee
- requesting a letter of recommendation
- seeking co-operation for a survey
- seeking special consideration for an adjustment request

Because we write so many letters of request, competition is keen for the attention and co-operation of the reader. The letters that follow the persuasive strategy are most likely to elicit the desired response.

News Releases

News releases are the final type of persuasive communication commonly used by organizations when they wish to communicate with the general public via the news media. As with other types of written communication, and persuasive communication in particular, the purpose, audience, and context of the news release determine its content (and to some degree) its organization. Your success in your industry is generally measured by the number of minutes or column inches of print devoted to your story.

The purpose of this section is to introduce you to some general purposes for news releases and to give you practical tips for creating a news release that will get the media attention you want.

Purpose

The purposes of news releases fall into three broad categories that largely determine how you will deal with your subject matter. With each of the types discussed below, media coverage becomes progressively more difficult to obtain.

1. Public Service Announcements. PSAs generally imply that the media will print or broadcast the information as a service to the general public, usually in a time-slot or column devoted to that purpose, even when they contain no inherent news value. PSAs are generally limited to radio and print media; however, some cable-TV stations also read PSAs. Because PSAs are offered as a public service, media personnel expect them to be direct and concise even when they have a persuasive element, such as encouraging people to attend a fundraising or educational event. Before you settle on a PSA, review your situation to see whether you have exploited it to its full media potential. Often, a new angle or interesting development in an otherwise routine story will merit at least a five-minute slot on a talk show.

2. Informational News Releases. Many organizations use news releases to communicate information about developments in the organization or to effect crisis control after an event that has had adverse publicity. For example, an organization that has been responsible for an oil spill might send out a news release that deplores the situation and emphasizes how upset the company is by the event and what corrective action is being or has been taken. Informational news releases may or may not have inherent news value. Often their use depends on what else is happening on the day of the release. However, if you emphasize the availability of a good speaker on the subject, you'll more likely get better coverage.

3. Media Events. That an event is being publicized by a news release implies that it is inherently newsworthy. The primary purpose of events is to persuade the media to cover a given event as a human interest story or a news item. In such cases, the more people who may be interested in the story or the more unusual the event, the more likely the event will get news coverage. For example, if the supply of cookies for the local Girl Guides troops' annual cookie sale arrives at a local park by hot air balloon, it will more likely receive coverage than if the supply of cookies is delivered by truck. Similarly, if a major industry is having an open house, interesting and innovative displays make news coverage more likely.

Audience

Your news release has two levels of audience: the media and the general public. However, unless you get by the media, you won't have access to the public. Therefore, knowing to whom to direct your news release will increase its chances of receiving coverage. First, you need to decide which media you will contact: print (newspapers, magazines, trade journals, or organization newsletters), television, or radio. The print media rely heavily on pictures and "good quotes." Having someone who is articulate and can speak extemporaneously is less important in print than on television and radio.

Television also likes stories with high visual appeal, particularly those that have some activity or action associated with them. In addition, because much of the coverage takes place without rehearsal, articulate speakers are a must. Finally, radio requires informed and articulate speakers who are willing to be interviewed on air if the story is to receive coverage. Although your story may not be covered as a news item, it may do well as a current affairs item on a talk show.

Once you have decided what types of media you plan to include for your news release, you need to define your mailing list more specifically. For example, if you have a story that you believe is highly newsworthy, you may contact only the major television stations, radio stations, and newspapers in your area.

Alternatively, you may decide to blanket all the local media, hoping that one or two will pick up your story. In these instances, you might broaden your distribution to all television, radio, and print media in your area, including community newspapers and other periodicals. This approach has the advantage of achieving maximum coverage; however, it is time-consuming and costly.

Finally, you may decide to construct a narrow, focused list of relatively easy-to-access media sources: community newspapers, trade journals, and organization newsletters. These media will often run a well-written news release as a story. Also, they are often more willing to run a feature story based on your news release.

Your final task in defining your audience is to identify the appropriate person or department to whom to direct your news release. For example, news releases related to business would normally be directed to the business editor; those related to arts would go to the entertainment editor. In some cases, the distinction may not be so clearcut, and you will have to use your judgement. A quick phone call, even to the switchboard, can provide you with the information you need to decide who should receive the release.

Format

News releases have a standard format that people in the media will expect you to follow:

1. *Title.* At the top of the page, you should type "News Release" or "Press Release" so that the type of document is immediately evident.
2. *Date.* The date of the press release (when it's sent out) generally appears near the top right margin.
3. *Release Date.* The release date is placed immediately under the date. You may choose to say "for immediate release" or to insert a specific date. By sending your news releases out well in advance, you provide the media with the flexibility to plan to cover your events. News releases are often filed by date. When an opening becomes available on a particular date, the producer checks the date file to see whether one of the releases warrants a story.

4. *Subject Line.* Your subject line is often a clever "hook," designed to get the attention of the reader and entice him or her to read farther. It should, however, always reflect the main topic of the news release. For example, a press release for a production of *The Wizard of Oz* in New Westminster, British Columbia, had the following subject line: "Tornado Puts New Westminster in a Spin."
5. *Body.* Even if you decide to expand on the "hook" introduced in the subject line, your main idea should come near the beginning of the press release. Since most newspapers, radio stations, and television stations get dozens of press releases every day, you have very little time to get the reader's attention. Once you have introduced your main idea, you need to fill in the details (who? what? why? when? where?). Remember to use headings and lists to make the information accessible to your readers.
6. *Contact(s).* At the bottom of the release, be sure to include the name and phone number of one or more persons who are willing and readily available to speak on the subject of the news release. Ideally the phone number is one that is answered outside of normal business hours (a message service, if necessary). The people you list as contacts should be well informed and articulate. Your story will not receive the coverage it deserves if your contact gives monosyllabic responses to questions.
7. *Close.* The standard convention for closing a news release is "–30–" placed at the bottom of the document. Adhering to this convention will show your readers that you have "done your homework."

The length of the news release will vary with its purpose and context. Generally, you should attempt to have your entire release no longer than a single, double-spaced page of type. Careful, skilful editing is the best means of achieving this length. If you are sending out advance notice of a series of events (such as the entertainment lineup for the Pacific National Exhibition), your news release might extend to three of four pages. However, news releases of this length are exceptional.

Summary

- Effective persuasive messages depend on four factors:
  - sender
  - receiver
  - message
  - channel
- Four types of unsolicited sales letters were emphasized in this chapter:
  - sales letters
  - collection letters
  - letters of request (for special favours)

- news releases

- A definite strategy underlies most effective sales letters:
  - find out everything you can about the product
  - learn what the reader is likely to respond to
  - make your central selling point the feature the reader will consider most attractive
- The four-part plan helps ensure reader response to your sales letter:
  - A — attract the reader's attention
  - I — stimulate the reader's interest
  - D — develop a desire within the reader
  - A — encourage the reader to take specific action
- Although you will always try to maintain the goodwill of the customer, your collection process usually has four stages:
  - a friendly reminder that assumes the customer has forgotten the payment
  - a strong reminder that also suggests an oversight
  - an inquiry about the reasons for the overdue account
  - a final, urgent request for payment with a suggestion of legal action
- Special letters of request for which no clear reward exists should use the AIDA sequence.
- News releases must be brief and newsworthy enough to compete effectively for media time.

Review Questions

1. What is the primary goal of persuasion? What more specific goals does this goal encompass?
2. What is meant by "source credibility"? How can we use it in constructing persuasive messages?
3. What factors can you use to get and hold the attention of a receiver of your persuasive messages?
4. Compare and contrast Maslow's theory of motivation with the direct-and-indirect-reward approach to motivating receivers.
5. What four steps should be followed in writing a sales letter?
6. Explain the difference between the interest step and the desire step.
7. Four common errors in seeking attention are presented in this chapter. Describe another error and provide an example of it.
8. Describe the four stages of a collection campaign.
9. In which ways is the reminder stage in the collection campaign similar to the strong-reminder stage? How are they different?
10. What is meant by "central selling point"?
11. Describe two ways to make special requests more persuasive. Use specific examples.
12. What are three purposes of news releases?

Activities

1. Much of the "junk mail" we receive consists of sales letters of various sorts. Analyze one of these sales letters. Does it follow the four-step sequence? How does the writer try to attract the reader's attention? What specific action is the writer seeking from the reader? What is the central selling point of the letter? What changes would you suggest for this letter?
2. You are a correspondent for the Ultimate Watch Company, which is about to introduce its first chronograph, a wristwatch designed especially for runners. Its main features are: it displays hours, minutes, and seconds on a digital face; it is also a stopwatch and displays elapsed time in minutes, seconds, and hundredths of seconds; it has fewer moving parts than any other chronograph; it is shock- and water-resistant; and it carries a two-year warranty. Write a sales letter that will be sent to all those on the subscription list of several running magazines.
3. As part of your job as sales manager of Pacific Cable Television Corporation you must persuade the public to subscribe to Living Room Theatre, a channel featuring movies 24 hours a day. Many of the movies are recent films; none is more than three years old. The cost of Living Room Theatre is $15 per month. There are no commercials on this channel, and free maintenance is provided to any subscriber who experiences any difficulties with the channel. Living Room Theatre has just become available in Prince George, and you are to write a sales letter in a form that could be sent to all of the residents in that area. (If you wish to name some of the movies scheduled to be shown in the near future, let your imagination be your guide.)
4. Select a product and assume that you are employed by its manufacturer. Prepare a collection campaign including one letter representing each stage of the collection process. Prepare the four collection letters as form letters that could be sent to any consumer of the product.
5. Make the same assumptions as you did for Activity 4. This time, however, prepare four letters to be sent to dealers rather than consumers.
6. Identify the strengths and shortcomings of the following letter and rewrite it to your satisfaction:

The Program Planning Committee of the Young Business Leadership Association (YBLA) met yesterday to select a keynote speaker for its annual convention. The names of some very prominent business leaders were proposed for this honour, but each name, for one reason or another, was dropped from consideration.

Since the YBLA includes a diversity of interests, you could speak on almost any subject as long as it is somewhat related to business. Twenty to thirty minutes would be appropriate. The YBLA was founded right here in Kingston in 1970 for the purpose of keeping businesspeople abreast of current thinking in business. We have 143 members, but they won't all attend the banquet. Last year 80 members and spouses attended the banquet and 28 outsiders attended. Just as last year the banquet will again be open to the public.

The banquet will be held at the fashionable Queen's Park Hotel at 7:00 p.m. on May 28, 29, or 30, depending on your availability. We are extending this invitation four months in advance in the hopes of getting a commitment from you. Select whichever date you prefer and notify us immediately so that we can proceed with our plans.

The YBLA will pay your travel and lodging expenses. If you accept our invitation, we will reserve a room for you the night of the banquet at the Econo-Rooms Inn, which is down the street from the Queen's Park.

Thank you for considering our invitation, and we hope that you will accept. We await your prompt reply.

7. You recently purchased a spacious brick ranch-style house and hired a painter to paint the wood trim. Your intent was to cover the beige with a light green. You returned home from a business trip to discover that the trim had been painted chartreuse. The painter acknowledges that the trim is "a little bright" but assures you that the colour will fade to a light green "in a year or so." You do not intend to wait for it to fade. Write a letter to the painter's employer, requesting that the trim be repainted at no expense to you.
8. Recently you left your car at a local car wash for a deluxe wash and wax. Shortly after retrieving the car you discovered that a small camera was missing from the glove compartment. The employees of the car wash claim not to have seen the camera, and the manager disclaims any responsibility. A large sign posted prominently at the car wash denies responsibility for missing items. Write a letter to the corporate headquarters of the car wash organization, requesting payment for the camera, which you believe was taken by one of the car wash employees.
9. You have invented a new electronic game and established a small shop for its manufacture. It is called Hack-Man, and its most distinguishable feature is the humanlike hacking sound the machine makes as points are scored. As the point total mounts, the volume of the hacking increases. Your research of your community shows

that teenagers prefer Hack-Man to any other electronic game. The machine is 150 cm tall, 60 cm wide, and 75 cm deep. A feature that teenage players seem to enjoy is the attention they attract when they score well. Write a letter to be sent to the operators of game parlours. The purpose is to persuade them to return to you an enclosed postcard requesting that a sales representative visit. (Use your imagination to create for the game whatever other features you care to.)

10. You purchased a wireless burglar alarm from a mail-order discount company and are dissatisfied with it. It was easily installed, just as advertised; the problem is that the alarm goes off each time your neighbour uses her CB radio. The company has a policy of paying customer refunds only on merchandise returned within ten days of purchase. It took you more than ten days to determine that the problem could not be solved. Write a letter requesting a complete refund. Assume that you will not mail the alarm until the company has approved your request. Write the letter to General Alarms Ltd., P.O. Box 146, Calgary, Alta. T2M 2Z6.

11. You own a sporting goods store in Winnipeg and have completed a mailing list of all of the members of the various bicycle clubs in your area. Prepare a sales letter to be sent to the club members in late October saying that the Prairie winter is about to begin. Try to sell the readers on continuing to enjoy the benefits of cycling exercise by purchasing a new Exercycle. The Exercycle is manufactured in Canada, weighs only 10 kg, and sells for $110. It is a stationary bike, 120 cm long and 75 cm high. The handlebar, which is 55 cm long, is easily adjusted, without tools, for persons of any height.

12. Assume that you volunteered to take pictures at your cousin's wedding and thereby save the newlyweds the expense of hiring a photographer. You took approximately 150 pictures and gave them to a local camera store for processing. More than half the resulting photographs were badly blurred. Since you are an accomplished photographer, you know that you were not at fault. The owner of the camera store disclaims responsibility since he merely sent the film to another city for processing. He has, however, offered to give you free film equal to the amount that was blurred. Write a letter to the photo laboratory that processed the film. Since you have suffered considerable embarrassment, you feel that the photo laboratory should pay you at least $100 in damages. You intend to give whatever payment you get to your cousin. Write your letter to Master Photo Inc., P.O. Box 1212, North Vancouver, B.C. V7H 1L3.

13. In an effort to conserve energy two years ago, you replaced the caulking compound in all the windows in your eight-room house.

Now the caulking compound is badly mildewed and looks unsightly. You have complained to the owner of the store at which you bought the compound, but he was not sympathetic. "It's not advertised as mildew-resistant," he said. Write a letter to the manufacturer, requesting that a representative be sent to inspect your house and to remedy the situation. Write your letter to Home Products, Inc., P.O. Box 290, London, Ont. N5Y 3R8.

14. You have developed a new electronic bug killer known as Black Light. It electrocutes bugs instantaneously and, unlike other such devices, makes no noise. The lantern-shaped bug killer is available in black, brown, or beige. It can easily be attached to the limb of a tree, or it can stand upright on the ground or patio. It comes with a fluorescent bulb and sells for $22.50 wholesale. It is 40 cm tall, 10 cm wide, and 10 cm deep. It weighs 1.5 kg. Write a sales letter to be sent to hardware stores and lawn supply stores throughout your region.

Discussion Cases

The Nirvana Alarm Clock

You recently began your new job with a local advertising agency, and you have been given the assignment of writing a persuasive letter to be used in marketing the Nirvana Alarm Clock. You have been given the following description of the clock. The Nirvana Alarm Clock:

1. Automatically resets the alarm for the next day
2. Has a sturdy, nontip base
3. Has a five-decibel buzzer
4. Has a snooze alarm
5. Is available in the following seven colours: red, pink, blue, black, purple, green, and orange
6. Is constructed of durable polystyrene
7. Has a luminous face, and projects the correct day and time on the ceiling
8. Measures 15 cm by 15 cm by 5 cm
9. Costs $21.95, plus $3.00 for shipping and handling
10. Comes with an unconditional two-year guarantee

Thousands of these clocks have been sold nationally, but your target market will be college-level students. Write a sales letter to be sent to these students. Remember that your letter should be built around a central theme, and that you might not want to include all the characteristics listed above.

Case Questions

1. What would be your central theme for this letter?
2. Which characteristics of the clock would be of most interest to a college student? Which characteristics would be least interesting?
3. Write two "attention-getters" that you could use to begin your letter.

A Study in Credibility[8]

Imagine that you are the third-generation heir to a multibillion-dollar industry and that you are campaigning to get people to stop using the very products that provide more than half of the company's earnings. That's exactly what Patrick Reynolds, grandson of R. J. Reynolds, is doing in allying himself with the American Lung Association, which is calling for higher excise taxes on tobacco and planning a television campaign to show viewers the dangers of smoking.

On a visit to Winston-Salem, North Carolina, where RJR Nabisco Inc. is headquartered, Patrick felt the heat of his decision. "I am concerned for his lungs," remarked his half-brother, John D. Reynolds. "Some Reynolds employee might want to rip them out." Even at a local restaurant, Patrick could not escape the local outcry: a fellow diner asked, "What are you, a Communist?"

Despite the less than enthusiastic reception he has received from family and local townspeople, Patrick states: "This is one good thing that I can do, and no one can take that away from me." His credibility, enhanced because he is biting the hand that has enriched his family for three generations and because he is a reformed smoker himself, has landed him spots on "CBS Morning News" and "CBS Nightwatch." He also had a chance to testify before a Congressional subcommittee to request a ban on cigarette advertising directed at women and children. Although he long ago sold his tobacco stock, Patrick emphatically states that he will not consider giving up his $2.5 million tobacco inheritance. "Hell no," he said. "If I had to give it all up, I would find other good causes to devote myself to. You've got to take care of yourself first." Whether the sources of his personal wealth will damage his "tobacco is a killer" message remains to be seen.

Case Questions

1. Why is it important that Patrick (as opposed to you) campaign against tobacco consumption? Would anyone else be as effective?
2. What components of credibility does Patrick possess that make him believable?

3. How would you attack Patrick's credibility?
4. How does a person acquire the components of credibility so as to be believable?
5. Name and discuss individuals whom you consider credible. Why are these people believable when others you know are not?

Chapter 11

Informal Reports

Learning Objectives

In this chapter, you'll learn how to write effective informal reports. More specifically, you will be able to:

1. recognize the important role played by informal reports in facilitating organizational operations
2. select an appropriate format for your informal reports
3. recognize the underlying purpose of information reports
4. write effective incident, progress, trip, and periodic reports
5. recognize the underlying purpose of analytical reports
6. write effective problem-solving reports and proposals

Preview Case

As Joe Lopez neared retirement he became increasingly nostalgic. Thinking back on his 30 years with the company, he pondered how one's perspective changes as a person progresses along his or her career path.

The day after Joe graduated, he began working as a sales representative. He usually travelled four days a week and devoted most of the fifth to paperwork. His paperwork consisted mainly of short, informal reports pertaining to customer orders, complaints, or future prospects. Throughout his years as a sales representative, he always suspected that most of his reports were never read, that they were all a waste of his time.

After twelve years with the company, Joe was promoted to assistant regional sales manager, and his perspective began to change. He was surprised to discover that, in making decisions, he relied most on information from the sales representatives' reports. Thinking back to the many reports he himself had written as a sales representative, he realized how wrong he had been in believing they went unread. Now a major part of his job consisted of abstracting the reports of ten sales representatives and reporting the results to the regional sales manager.

During the past eight years, Joe Lopez has been the regional sales manager. Any misgivings he has ever had about the importance of reports have disappeared during this period. He now recognizes that a variety of reports enables upper management to get the "big picture" and thereby make intelligent decisions. Those informal reports, which individually may seem insignificant, collectively provide information without which organizations cannot function effectively. Because reports are so important, the ability or inability to write them has made or destroyed careers.

Overview

This chapter will discuss the kinds of informal reports commonly used in organizations. You will learn the purposes of these reports as well as how to write them. You will also learn to select appropriate formats for your reports.

Definition of a Report

Reports present findings

Reports are organized accounts of situations or problems that the writer has investigated or observed. They present the writer's findings, to help the reader make a decision. Depending on their purpose, reports may also include analyses of the findings and conclusions drawn from these investigations.

Types of Reports

Informal reports generally fall into three categories: information, analytical, or persuasive reports.

Information reports, analytical reports, and persuasive reports are the main types of informal reports

Information reports inform or instruct. Their primary purpose is to present information clearly and concisely. Your reader is looking for details of events, activities, or conditions, not analysis of the situation, conclusions, or recommendations. However, you may comment on the implications of the information. Four types of information reports are discussed in this chapter: incident reports, progress reports, trip reports, and periodic reports.

Analytical reports are written to solve problems. You not only present information, but also analyze that information, draw conclusions, and recommend changes or a course of action you want the reader to take. Problem-solving reports are discussed later in this chapter.

Persuasive reports are an extension of analytical reports: their main focus is to sell ideas, services, or products. While any problem-solving report may have persuasive elements, proposals are the most common type of persuasive report.

Differences Between Reports and Correspondence

No clear dividing line exists between informal reports and correspondence. In fact, as you'll see in the next section, reports may use letter and memo formats and, therefore, physically resemble the correspondence you've studied in earlier chapters.

Reports have a more diverse audience, more than one purpose, and more detailed information

Reports do have three characteristics, however, that distinguish them from other types of correspondence. First, they are generally written for a more diverse audience. You may, for example, find that your readers represent several levels within the organization and have different levels of understanding of the report's content.

Second, because you have a variety of readers, your reports may serve a slightly different purpose for each of them. For example, your boss might use a progress report to decide whether or not to assign additional staff to the project. She may then forward the report to her boss to support a request for extra funding.

Finally, reports generally contain more detailed and complex information. Therefore, organization and organizational aids such as headings and white space become particularly important. For a more complete discussion of the use of headings in reports, see Chapter 12.

Informal Report Formats

The distinction between informal and formal reports is generally based on format and length. Formal reports, as you will see in Chapter 12, are longer and have several distinct parts. Informal reports, on the other hand, tend to be shorter. They have fewer distinct parts, and their content and organization depend on their purpose. Their format may be that of a preprinted form, a memo, or a letter.

Preprinted Form Reports

Informal reports, which often appear on preprinted forms, play an important role in the smooth operation of any business. Without them the routine transmission of information would be greatly complicated.

Preprinted forms are used to transmit routine information on a regular basis

Most organizations use preprinted forms for reports that are required on a regular basis and are informational in nature. At the end of each week, for example, each sales representative for Falcon Products must send a Customer Contact Report to the sales manager. The report includes such information as number of customers visited, sales made, and service problems identified. Since this report is submitted so frequently and by a large number of representatives, Falcon Products provides a preprinted form for it (see Figure 11.1). The form specifies the information needed and clearly indicates where the completed form is to be sent.

From the company's perspective, the use of a form ensures that the information provided will be uniform and hence easy to compile. From the individual respondent's perspective, it simplifies the process by indicating clearly what information is to be provided. Although many workers complain about the number of preprinted forms they must complete, the use of such forms saves a great deal of time. If the workers had to develop and prepare individual reports instead of using preprinted forms, there would be much more complaining.

Memo Reports

Informal memo reports are often used within an organization

A memo is usually a brief message. However, you may also write reports using memo format. Like a memo, a memo report is used mainly for communication within the organization.

A memo report shares the advantages of a memo. It provides a written record that can reach many people simultaneously. Moreover, its standardized format helps readers find the information they need quickly and efficiently.

Customer Contact Report

Enter all visits with customers and potential customers each week. Indicate your time of arrival and departure as well as product(s) discussed. Describe any sale you made or service problem of which you learned. Describe any follow-up you intended to perform.

Date	Time	Name of contact and company	Product discussed	Sales made	Service problems	Follow-up
Mon.	Arr. Dpt.					
	Arr. Dpt.					
	Arr. Dpt.					
Tues.	Arr. Dpt.					
	Arr. Dpt.					
	Arr. Dpt.					
Wed.	Arr. Dpt.					
	Arr. Dpt.					
	Arr. Dpt.					
Thur.	Arr. Dpt.					
	Arr. Dpt.					
	Arr. Dpt.					
Fri.	Arr. Dpt.					
	Arr. Dpt.					
	Arr. Dpt.					

Note: Complete this form at the end of each work week and mail it immediately to the Sales Manager.

Signature of Sales Representative

Figure 11.1 A Preprinted Report Form

Letter Reports

Many informal reports are presented in the format of a letter. Although a letter report is — unlike a memo report — usually for external communication, it is less formal than the long reports described in Chapter 12.

A letter report looks like a letter and includes many of the same features

A letter report is similar to a letter in appearance. Since letter reports are usually sent outside the organization, they are prepared on stationery with the company letterhead. Letter reports usually include the standard parts of a letter, including sender's address, date, inside address, salutation, body, and signature. Some writers also insert a subject line between the greeting and the body of the letter report. Reports longer than one page frequently use headings to make the information more accessible to the reader.

Informal Information Reports

In an informal report, as in any business communication, the nature of the message and the response expected from the reader should determine the plan to be followed. If the reader is likely to approve of the message, take the direct approach described in Chapter 9. Begin the report with the main point, since the reader will agree with it.

If the reader is likely to disapprove of the message, you should lead him or her step by step through the information, emphasizing wherever possible the reader benefits. In writing this type of report, you should use positive language, stress reader benefits, and anticipate and respond to possible objections.

Informal reports have three main parts: the opening, the body, and the close

An informal report has three basic parts: the opening, the body, and the close.

The Opening

The opening always includes a statement of the report's purpose, background information the reader needs to understand the report, and a synopsis of the report's key ideas. In short reports, the opening may be one or two brief paragraphs under one of several headings: Introduction, Synopsis, or Summary.

Longer reports, on the other hand, generally have separate sections:

Introduction. The introduction includes the purpose of the report and the background information. It may also include a description of the way the report is organized; however, this description is not necessary in more informal reports.

Summary. The summary gives the reader a concise overview of the full report even if that report is only one or two pages long. Busy readers appreciate not having to read the entire report.

The Body

The body is the "meat" of any report. Here the reader's attention is directed to your findings. Its purpose is to show how you arrived at your conclusions. The body is always divided into sections that have descriptive headings to help the reader follow the flow of your information.

The Close

Like the opening, the close in a short report differs significantly from that in a long report. Many short reports close with a simple offer of additional assistance if the reader desires it. The closing paragraph, therefore, often deals with the relationship between the writer and the reader rather than with the contents of the report. Sometimes, in internal reports, the closing comments are omitted.

Incident Reports

Incident reports describe an unusual event, often an accident, equipment failure, or personnel problem. When simple forms exist for this purpose, a minimum of actual writing is required. Examples include accident reports, Workers' Compensation reports, and safety hazard reports. However, if you have no form, you need to know how to organize and write an incident report.

Incident reports describe an unusual event

In general, your opening should summarize the who, what, when, where, why, and how of the event. In most incident reports, you'll need only two or three sentences to accomplish this. Then, in the body, you can give all of the event's details. Here are the headings you might expect to find in an incident report that uses the memo format:

Subject. Your memo will have a subject line that clearly tells the reader what unusual event the report describes.

Synopsis. Your synopsis will tell your reader what happened, who was involved, when and where the incident took place, and what the significant outcomes were.

Description of the Incident. Next, tell your reader exactly what happened, usually in chronological order. Your description should be clear, concise, and objective. You should include only the relevant facts, not judgements, assumptions, or opinions. If you're describing a complicated incident, you may need to subdivide it into segments (events leading to the incident, description of the incident, people involved, outcomes, and so on). Some of the information might be tabulated under headings, such as who was involved and the location.

Possible Causes. This section answers the question "Why did it happen?" Normally your readers will want to know how they can prevent similar incidents in the future. Therefore, you can offer your own opinions about causes and preventive measures; however, you should be careful to let the reader know that the information is your opinion.

Action Taken. This section tells your reader what you've done to follow up or correct the incident.

Action Required. This section lists things that still need to be done. It often acts as a checklist to make sure that follow-up of the incident is completed.

The sample incident report in Figure 11.2 shows how to organize an incident report according to the guidelines given in this chapter. Notice that the description of the incident is not a description of the theft, but rather a description of the discovery of the theft.

Progress Reports

Use the same format for each progress report in a series

Progress reports, which are a kind of information report, are widely used in business, industry, and government. Depending on the nature of the organization and the project being reported, a progress report may be made only once, or as one of a series. For the convenience of the reader, each of a series of progress reports should follow the same format. Also, each report in the series should be numbered.

Progress reports usually go up the organization ladder

Progress reports are ordinarily sent upward in the organization to inform management of: (1) rate of progress compared to the schedule, (2) goals for subsequent time periods, and (3) forecast for completion of the project.

The opening of a progress report gives readers the background they need to understand the report and summarizes the main ideas. The rest of the report tells them what's been completed, what's in progress, and what's left to be done. Problems encountered and their solutions may also be highlighted for the reader.

INTEROFFICE MEMO INTEGRATED SOFTWARE LIMITED

To: Arthur Blackwell
Director of Training

From: Marion Smythe-Jones
Senior Trainer

Date: 92 November 7

Subject: Theft of Microcomputers and Printers

Synopsis

Some time between 5 p.m. Friday, November 4, and 9 a.m. November 7, three microcomputers and two printers were stolen from our training room. The cost of the stolen equipment is approximately $15 800.

Notice that the reader knows immediately when and what

The thieves entered through a basement window. Although the police have been here to investigate, we have no idea who is responsible.

Details of the Incident

When I went to the training room at 9 this morning to prepare for my 9:30 class, I noticed that three of our computers and two printers were missing. I had a class on Friday afternoon, and the equipment was there when I left at 5 p.m.

Details are presented chronologically

I called Ed Bronsky of security and together we inspected the building. We found a broken basement window with wet marks leading up the stairs. Although the window was large enough for a small person to enter, it was too small to use as an exit because of the size of the printers.

What's Missing

Here are the details of the missing equipment based on our inventory list for the training room:

continued

Figure 11.2 Sample Incident Report

Since the inventory of what was taken is important, it is detailed here

Equipment	Serial Number	Inventory Number	Estimated Cost
HAL-OD (640k)	2323234	86-2345	$1800
HAL-OD XT	1546378	88-3255	$2500
Wescot 8088	8968574	88-3256	$3000
Meson 9095	LQ-3200	88-3257	$2500
CAP-LASER 1000	CA-2424	88-3498	$6000

This section answers the question: "why did it happen?"

Possible Causes

The basement window is 50 cm by 50 cm, large enough for a small person to get through. The thieves were able to break the glass and enter through it because it had no special protection such as a metal grille to prevent entry. However, they would have had to leave by one of the exits because the printers are too large to fit through the window.

Action Taken

Listed for clarity

1. Ed Bronsky called the police. Constable Choquette arrived at 10 a.m. and took statements from Ed and me.
2. I had maintenance clean up the glass and board up the window.

Action Required

1. We need to notify the insurance company of the theft and file a claim with them. I can handle this if you like.
2. We should install a metal grille on the basement window to ensure we are not vulnerable to thefts in the future.

Progress reports are organized chronologically

The following are the headings you might expect to find in a progress report that uses letter or memo format.

Subject. You need to tell your reader you are writing a *progress* report, and name the project and dates covered by the report. If the report is one of a series, indicate the number of the report.

Synopsis. Your synopsis should briefly answer your reader's key questions: What is the purpose of this report? What have you completed? Are you on schedule and on budget? If not, why not? Any additional details are optional and will change with each report.

Work Completed. This section tells the reader what you've accomplished. It often includes a schedule so that the report can be used to plan similar projects. If you're behind schedule, this section may include reasons for the delay.

Work Underway or Problems Encountered. If you want to highlight a major, identifiable, or important part of the project, you can include this section. It is particularly useful if you are *currently* working on a problem that is delaying your progress significantly. If you are focusing directly on problems, you may want an alternative heading such as *Problems Encountered.* In describing problems, you should try to be positive — describe what you've done or what needs to be done to solve them.

Work to Be Completed. This section describes what needs to be done and how long it's going to take. If you're behind schedule, you should include a catch-up schedule and explain how you will meet the deadlines. If you're over budget, you should request additional funding and justify the costs carefully. This section may also be labelled *Action Required* or *Forecast*, depending on the nature of the project.

Figure 11.3 shows how a branch account supervisor used a memo report to describe to the bank's upper management the progress being made in a campaign to encourage the use of bank cards. Notice that the headings used in this example are a little more specific than the ones suggested in the guidelines; however, the information is still presented chronologically.

Trip Reports

Trip reports detail your findings on a trip taken at the organization's request

From time to time, your organization may send you on trips to conferences, other company operations, equipment suppliers, and demonstrations to investigate possible solutions to a problem or to learn new information and skills that may benefit the organization. When you return, you'll frequently be asked to write a trip report that details your findings. However, trip reports are more than chronological travelogues. While you may want to include your itinerary to show the scope of your investigation, it should not dictate the overall organization of the trip report.

INTEROFFICE MEMO

To: Robin Davis
Director of Marketing

From: Henry Choi
Account Supervisor
Oakdale Branch

Date: 92 April 7

Title specifies period the report covers, the subject and the number of the report

Subject: Monthly Progress Report on CardBank Usage at the Oakdale Branch (Report #6)

Reporting Period: March 1 to March 31

Includes all important details as an overview

Summary

In this reporting period, our customers used CardBank for 20 percent of all deposits and withdrawals. This is a 25-percent rise from last month's 15-percent total. New customers, that is, customers who have dealt with us for less than six months, are the most frequent users. However, with increased usage, we've also had more complaints about the machines being out of order or out of cash. We hope we've solved this problem by implementing a regular maintenance check and increasing the amount of cash left in the machine overnight and on weekends.

Present status

Present Usage

This month, CardBank transactions account for 20 percent of all deposits and withdrawals made at this bank. This represents a 25-percent increase over last month's 15 percent. We had forecast only a 10-percent increase so we are ahead of schedule.

continued

Figure 11.3 Sample Progress Report

Although the introduction of CardBank has generally been successful, we're not reaching all of our customers. In fact, the heaviest users of CardBank have dealt with us for less than six months. Our success with this group may be due in part to our policy of giving new customers personal instructions on using CardBank.

Problems Encountered

With increased usage of CardBank, the machine has been out of service six times this month, and has run out of cash every weekend. This downtime has resulted in 40 complaints from customers who were forced to drive three kilometres to our Kerrisdale Branch, or wait until the bank opened the next morning.

Problems are significant enough to justify a separate heading

The technical problems resulted from cash and deposit envelopes becoming jammed, and from problems with the computer interface. To solve the jamming problems, we've instructed the tellers who stock the machine in the correct procedures for putting cash and deposit envelopes into the machine. We've also recommended they use new bills whenever possible. To prevent computer problems, we've asked our computer operator to check the machine each night before he leaves. Since we implemented these new procedures on March 20, the machine has not been out of service.

The problem of too little cash on the weekend is more difficult to solve. Perhaps we could consider asking two employees who live near the branch to restock the machines on Saturday evening. We'd have to pay them an honorarium of, say, $25 each, but the improved public relations would be worth the extra expense.

Usage Forecast

Our customer-usage goal for April is 30 percent. A local media blitz is scheduled to begin this week. Circulars and posters in the branch will emphasize the 24-hour availability of CardBank, since our surveys show this is the least-known feature. We hope this additional publicity will reach existing customers who have not been using the machines.

Goals for the next period

The following are the headings you might expect to find in a progress report that uses a letter or memo format.

Subject. Your subject line can announce your destination and general purpose so that the reader can connect the trip with a specific company context. You may also want to include the dates during which the trip took place.

Synopsis. Your synopsis should include answers to your reader's key questions: Where did you go and why? What did you find out? How useful will this information be to the organization?

Opening. While the synopsis and opening are sometimes combined in very short trip reports, you may occasionally find that a separate opening is necessary. Your opening would include:

- a detailed discussion of the destination and the purpose of the trip
- sufficient background information to establish the context within which the trip took place
- a preview of the overall organization of information in the body of the report.

Results. Your readers will likely have two key questions when they read your report: What did you find out? How can we use this information to our advantage? This section of the report should answer those questions. If necessary, detailed information can be included as an attachment to the end of the report. If the "Results" section is longer than half a page, it may require headings to highlight your key findings.

Itinerary. The itinerary is an optional part of the report. However, a list of the places you visited, along with the names, addresses, and phone numbers of the people you met with, could be useful for future reference. You might also highlight the people who were particularly helpful. For conferences, you might include a list of the sessions you attended, along with the names and positions of the presenters.

Attachments. If you have a mass of detailed information, you should attach it to the report rather than trying to include it in the body of the report. Otherwise, you run the risk of overwhelming your reader with detail that doesn't give a clear answer to his or her questions.

INTEROFFICE MEMO PACIFIC RIM GENERAL HOSPITAL

To:	Norell Greenspan, R.N., B.Sc. Head Nurse, 3 West
From:	Gordon Chu, R.N. Staff Nurse, 3 West
Date:	92 June 15
Subject:	Report on "Advanced Modular Materials Development" Workshop

Subject line names the course

On Thursday, May 14, I attended a one-day advanced workshop on preparing modular training materials, offered by the British Columbia Institute of Technology. Overall it was a very interesting and useful course that will help me improve our teaching materials for patients in remote locations.

Workshop Details

Details of the course

Workshop Title:	Advanced Modular Materials Development
Date:	Thursday, May 14, 1992
Place:	BCIT, Burnaby Campus
Instructor:	Brian Ashlee, Instructional Designer
Workshop Content:	Motivational strategies for print learning materials, including page design, use of graphics, advance organizers, and anecdotes.

This report describes the course as it relates to patient learning materials, along with my overall assessment of the course. The course outline and handouts are attached for your information.

Workshop Description

The workshop was divided into four major sections: page design, use of graphics, advance organizers, and anecdotes.

continued

Figure 11.4 Sample Trip Report

Subheadings are used to show four sections of the workshop

Page Design

This two-hour segment covered the basics of page design: using a 10 cm column for text to make the information more readable, using white space to show relationships among "chunks of information," using descriptive headings to tell the reader what each "chunk" contains, and using the features of most advanced word processing packages to create a pleasing page layout. Since our typing pool has recently converted to word processing, I believe that we could implement many of these suggestions almost immediately.

Graphics

The two-hour graphics segment featured a demonstration of the types of graphics available with relatively inexpensive computer graphics packages. While the results were impressive, the person doing the demonstration had several years' experience as a graphic artist and computer operator. Since we do not have a graphic artist on staff, we'll need to continue using "clip art" to add graphics to our learning materials.

Advance Organizers

Advance organizers provide readers with a framework for new knowledge. They may be analogies and metaphors or something as simple as a flow chart to show how all the information fits together. While advance organizers can require considerable time to develop, I'm convinced that they could improve patient comprehension of our materials if they were well designed.

Anecdotes

The two-hour segment on the use of anecdotes in learning materials was probably the most useful portion of the course for me. I was amazed at how interesting materials became when they included typical examples written as "mini cases." Rather than simply telling the reader how important a piece of information is, you illustrate it with a story that appears real because of its details.

Evaluation

Overall this workshop was very effective. It gave me several practical ideas for improving the overall appearance and content of our patient learning packages. It was a practical, hands-on workshop that allowed us to practise some of the new skills.

I had only two suggestions for improvement of this course:

- length – had the workshop been offered over a two-day period, we would have had more time to practise our new skills
- focus – a workshop that focused specifically on patient learning materials would have been more useful to me

However, neither of these problems significantly affected my overall satisfaction with the course. I'm looking forward to applying my new skills to the module on diabetes next week.

If you would like more information about the workshop, I'd be happy to discuss it with you over coffee. Thank you for giving me the opportunity to attend.

Close invites further discussion

Periodic Reports

All organizations have some reports that must be prepared regularly. Whether prepared daily, weekly, or monthly, these reports are intended to keep others informed about some aspect of operations.

Because a periodic report is directed to the same reader on a regular basis, you can assume that your reader is generally knowledgeable about the subject. As a result, only some introductory information is needed. The sections in the body of a periodic report will depend entirely on the content of the report. However, since you'll use it several times, you should take the time to develop a standard format for your situation and use it each time you report on that situation.

Figure 11.5 is an example of a periodic report on absenteeism at a manufacturing plant.

Analytical (Problem-solving) Reports

Analytical reports require you to identify a problem, investigate its causes and possible solutions, analyze your data, draw conclusions, and recommend a course of action to your reader. While you may be asked to present the results of a complex investigation in a formal report (like the one in Chapter 12), you'll most likely use the less formal letter or memo format.

Like informal information reports, informal analytical (problem-solving) reports have an opening, a body, and a close. The following outline (page 291) shows how they're used in a problem-solving report:

INTEROFFICE MEMO

To: R.T. Bowen
Plant Manager

From: Sandra McLean
Assistant Personnel Director

Date: 92 February 5

Subject: Monthly Plant Absenteeism Record

Synopsis

During January, the average rate of absenteeism was 6 percent and the average length of each absence was 1.8 days. Both figures are down 20 percent from last January, probably due to follow-up by supervisors during the absence.

Breakdown of Absences

In January, a total of 44 workers were absent at least one day. This figure represents 6 percent of our workforce. Here is a breakdown of absences according to shift and department:

Shift	Production	Shipping	Yard Crew
first	8 of 202	1 of 28	1 of 20
second	10 of 202	2 of 28	2 of 20
third	19 of 200	n/a	1 of 10
TOTALS	37 of 604	3 of 56	4 of 50

The length of the absences varied considerably:

- 22 workers were absent 1 day
- 17 workers were absent 2 days
- 5 workers were absent 3 days or more

continued

Figure 11.5 Sample Periodic Report

<u>Notification of Supervisors</u>

On the second day of the absence, supervisors now phone workers and ask them to get a doctor's certificate explaining their absence. Although the note is not mandatory until after three days' absence, 18 of the 22 workers who were absent two or more days brought a doctor's note when they returned to work.

<u>Reduction in Absenteeism</u>

Our absenteeism rate has been decreasing steadily over the past year. Last January, 7.5 percent of our workers missed an average of 2.3 days of work. This year, 6 percent missed an average of 1.8 days of work. Thus both the number of workers off sick and the length of their absences have declined approximately 20 percent.

Summary. Because problem-solving reports are often longer than the other types of reports discussed in this chapter, the summary is often separated from the introduction and may, in fact, be on a separate page. The summary generally includes a brief statement of the problem and its implications, conclusions, and recommendations with a brief rationale.

Introduction. The introduction answers three main questions for the reader: What's this report about (the problem)? Why should I read it (why the problem concerns me)? What does the report cover (plan)? For shorter reports, the introduction may be combined with the summary. Figure 11.6 is a problem-solving report with a combined summary and introduction. Notice that the implications of the problem are discussed more fully in a separate section of the report.

Body. The body of a problem-solving report does not have any standard headings. The first section, a detailed statement of the problem, may be omitted if the problem is fully discussed in the introduction. The subsequent sections discuss all aspects of the proposed solution(s). For a more detailed discussion of problem analysis and data collection, please read *Planning Formal Reports* in Chapter 12. The process is the same for both formal and informal reports.

Conclusions. The decisions based on the information in or inferences from a report may be presented in a separate section labelled *Conclusions.* These conclusions, which should be focused and specific, should be drawn directly from details presented in the body of the report. They may be written in paragraphs or as a numbered list going from most important to least important.

Recommendations. The recommended actions or solutions may also be presented in a separate section labelled *Recommendations*. These recommendations should be presented in a numbered list going from most important to least important, or in chronological order. Each recommendation should be a specific action.

If you have only one or two conclusions and recommendations, you may combine these sections under a single heading: *Conclusions and Recommendations*. Notice in Figures 11.6 and 11.7 that the conclusions and recommendations can be directly matched with headings in the discussion.

In Figure 11.6, Albert Cunningham had hired Redcliffe Insurance Analysts to evaluate the health insurance plan provided by Falwick Industries for its employees and recommend ways to reduce costs; Redcliffe has responded with an analytical (letter) report.

Notice that the opening is a single section labelled *Synopsis*. It has a statement of purpose and a complete overview of the entire report. Approximately fifteen seconds after opening the letter, Albert Cunningham would know what Redcliffe was recommending. At that point, he might choose to send it to one of his staff for further study and action rather than getting involved in the details himself. Or he might scan the entire report, and note which solution he prefers before sending it on to his boss.

Notice that the conclusions and recommendations are combined and that they follow directly from the discussion and do not add any new information. The friendly close invites further contact with the consulting firm.

Figure 11.7 is another typical problem-solving report. Notice that all the parts in this example are separate sections of the report.

Persuasive Reports (Proposals)

Proposals are usually highly specialized problem-solving reports that sell ideas, services, or products. They require that your reader make a "yes/no" decision. Proposals recommend a course of action to solve a problem or improve a situation, evaluate the action against criteria, and point out the benefits of the action.

Typically, you would write a proposal if you wanted to change a policy, purchase equipment, improve the way something is done, bid on

REDCLIFFE INSURANCE ANALYSTS
780 Burrard Street
Vancouver BC V4C 1T2

May 1, 1992

Mr. Albert Cunningham
Director of Employee Benefits
Falwick Industries
2050 Bereford Avenue
Burnaby BC V3T 1Z2

Dear Mr. Cunningham

Evaluation of Employee Health Benefits at Falwick Industries

Synopsis

Having analyzed the employee health benefits package provided by Falwick Industries as you requested, I'm now reporting my findings and recommendations.

The cost of employee benefits will likely increase about 14 percent a year. To protect itself from these rising costs, Falwick Industries should consider a self-funded plan, which would be less costly. Although you can choose a pay-as-go insurance plan or a tax-exempt trust, I recommend the former because legislation for pay-as-go plans is changing. At present, both options are legal in British Columbia and both can be administered either by the company or by an outside administrator.

Rising Costs of Employee Health Benefits

Your concern over the spiralling costs of employee benefits is justified. During the last decade, the cost of providing employee benefits has increased at an average rate of 14 percent a year. Your employee benefit

continued

Figure 11.6 Sample Letter Report (Analytical)

plan is intended to cover medical insurance and extended benefits premiums, and to replace lost income. Because overall health costs are increasing annually while government's ability to pay is decreasing, you can expect premiums to rise dramatically. I expect that the annual increase in costs will stay at 14 percent or rise even higher.

Self-funded Benefits Plans

A self-funded plan would be less costly, since Falwick's claim rate is approximately 50 percent lower than the industry average. You would still pay basic government medical premiums; however, you would fund your own extended benefits, dental, and income-replacement plans.

At present, you can choose from two options for self-funded benefits plans: tax-exempt trust or pay-as-go insurance.

Tax-exempt Trust. A tax-exempt trust meets the unique needs of a company. First, the company forecasts its insurance requirements for the next 30 years and draws up a plan based on that forecast. Then, a tax-exempt trust is established and regular contributions are deposited to the trust. Claims and expenses are paid from the trust, and excess funds are invested to build up reserves against future claims.

Tax-exempt trusts have several tax advantages. They can be administered to qualify for exemption from federal income tax, and the employers' contributions are generally deductible as a business expense. If the employees contribute to the plan, the benefits they receive are not taxable.

Pay-as-go Insurance. Using the pay-as-go approach, the company pays claims directly from its cash flow. The firm actually becomes its own insurer and does not set aside any reserves for future claims. Most companies using this plan purchase stop-loss insurance from companies such as CU&C Health Services to protect against unexpectedly severe claims. Since Falwick Industries does not require employee contributions to its plan, you can initiate such a plan. You should note, however, that pay-as-go insurance is illegal in Quebec, and other provinces are considering similar legislation.

Administration of Self-funding Benefits Plans

Either of these self-funded plans can be administered within the organization. Some companies prefer to have a professional outside company such as CU&C handle the administration. Those companies that hire outside administrators often feel that employees more readily accept the claims decisions made by outside professionals. Whether the benefit plan is administered by an employee or by an outsider, a company such as Falwick Industries will enjoy considerable savings.

Conclusions and Recommendations

A self-funded employee health benefits plan would save Falwick Industries money. Because of the uncertainty of legislation concerning pay-as-go insurance, tax-exempt trusts are the best alternative. Secondly, outside administrators ensure fair, impartial claims decisions.

Therefore, I recommend that you

1. establish a tax-exempt trust
2. contract with an impartial outside administrator.

I shall be pleased to answer any questions that you may have.

Sincerely

Robert Simmons
Employee Benefit Analyst

INTEROFFICE MEMO Integrated Toy Design Limited

To: George Burns
Production Manager

From: Jennifer Jones
Production Supervisor

Date: 92 January 15

Subject: RECOMMENDATION TO HIRE PERMANENT ASSEMBLERS

continued

Figure 11.7 Sample Problem-solving Report

SUMMARY

To cope with monthly sales fluctuations, we have traditionally hired extra assemblers during busy months and laid them off when orders fall off. In the past year alone, this cycle has resulted in $47 000 of direct training, performance penalty, and severance costs. A temporary workforce has also reduced morale and increased accidents.

We can reduce our costs as much as $45 000 by hiring 28 permanent assemblers and training them to fill in for other workers. Therefore, I recommend that we maintain a workforce of 28 assemblers and start them on a training program immediately.

INTRODUCTION

Because our monthly sales fluctuate, we've hired extra assemblers for the busy months and laid them off during the three summer months. In addition, our production levels have been low and we've recently had to pay a $25 000 performance penalty because we couldn't meet a deadline. Severance pay and training costs have added to our expenses.

The purpose of this report is to show how hiring more permanent workers would actually save the company money and increase our production.

The report includes an analysis of the costs associated with our hire/rehire cycle and shows how these costs could be reduced by hiring more permanent workers.

COSTS OF HIRING/REHIRING CYCLE

A. Monetary Costs

Because we hire new employees when we increase production and lay them off when we decrease production, we are faced with the following expenses that directly affect the production costs of the company:

1. Training. Because our best assemblers are in demand at other companies, they generally get permanent jobs when they are laid off. Therefore, almost 80 percent of the assemblers we hire have little or no experience and require at least one week's training

before they can perform effectively on the production line. For an employee earning $12 an hour, this training costs a minimum of $400, excluding benefits. Since we hire approximately five new assemblers each fall, our annual training costs are about $2000.

2. Lost Production. Even after the training is over, the new employees still take about a month to achieve a fast and accurate pace. During this time production quotas are not met. As a result, on one contract alone, we paid a $25 000 performance penalty.
3. Severance Pay. When employees are laid off, the company has to pay severance pay. Last year, our severance costs were $20 000.

B. Nonmonetary Costs

The following costs do not directly affect the company, but do have a part in the overall profitability of the company:

1. Low Morale. Because the employees are not part of the permanent staff, they lack enthusiasm for their jobs. In addition, an indifferent employee may not be as productive.

2. Increased Accidents. Since the employees are not familiar with the equipment and surroundings, we generally experience more accidents with new employees. This leads to cost increases in compensation and insurance estimated at $5000 for 1989.

ESTABLISHING A PERMANENT WORKFORCE

A. Reduced Costs

Hiring a permanent workforce of 28, year round, would save money by:

- reducing our overall payroll costs. Having 28 full-time, permanent assemblers would mean annual salaries and benefits of approximately $621 000. This figure represents a savings of $17 000 in salaries and benefits alone over the present arrangement of having 30 assemblers during peak periods and 25 during slack periods.

continued

- eliminating severance costs for a savings of $20 000
- maintaining a well-trained workforce who can meet production deadlines and eliminate performance penalties for a potential saving of $25 000

B. Additional Savings

Additional savings could be realized by:

- improving morale by providing a stable, secure work environment
- reducing compensation and insurance costs
- increasing employee skills and versatility so that our per-unit production costs will decrease. We should be able to reduce the overall number of work stations, thereby lowering maintenance costs.

CONCLUSIONS

We can reduce our costs if we hire 28 permanent staff, instead of hiring 30 staff during peak periods and laying off 5 during slack periods. In addition, we can potentially save $45 000 by eliminating severance pay and increasing production with highly skilled assemblers.

RECOMMENDATIONS

I recommend that we:

1. hire 28 permanent assemblers
2. train employees to do more than one job.

a contract, or apply for a research grant. Proposals can be short request letters or memos similar to those you've studied previously, or they can be longer, more formal documents. However, they always arise from a need to persuade your reader to say, "Yes, we'll do it."

Table 11.1 lists the typical headings found in a proposal and matches those headings with the basic questions that each section generally answers.

Table 11.1 Comparison of Proposed Headings and Reader Questions

Typical Heading	Reader Questions
Proposal	What do you want to do?
Problem Statement	What's the problem and its background? Why do we need to act at all?
Benefits	How will your proposal solve the problem? What's in it for me? for the company?
Project Details (Implementation)	What are the details of your proposal? What are the main tasks for implementing your proposal? What specifically has to be done? How will it all work (the nitty gritty details)?
Schedule/Deadlines	What's your schedule? What are the details of that schedule?
Evaluation	How will you know if your proposal is successful? How do you plan to evaluate your results?
Other Considerations	What are the potential problems with your proposal? But what if ... ? How do you plan to overcome these difficulties?
Personnel Qualifications	Who's going to be involved in this project? What are their qualifications? Why should I believe you can do the job?
Cost/Budget	How much will all this cost? Where exactly will the money be spent?
Alternatives Considered	What else did you consider to arrive at your solution? Why did you rule those solutions out? Using what criteria?

Although the basic parts of all proposals are the same, the parts emphasized will change from one situation to another. Many of the persuasive strategies you learned in Chapter 10 are useful when you write proposals. Especially important is the need to turn features into reader benefits. Notice that in Figure 11.8 Ethan Coe not only presents the benefits, but anticipates a possible objection (the accuracy of the cost projections) by telling the reader what the data are based on.

INTEROFFICE MEMO Integrated Office Supply Limited

To: Micheline Harvey
Vice-President
Production

From: Ethan Coe
Production Planning Manager

Date: 18 November 92

Subject: PROPOSAL TO PURCHASE IBM PC 386 AND PRINTER

PROPOSAL

I propose that we purchase an IBM PC 386 or compatible with a 52 mb hard drive and laser printer for Production Planning to analyze the monthly sales and usage history data.

BACKGROUND

Because the IBM mainframe computer does not have a generalized inquiry function, access to the detailed data in the sales and usage histories is cumbersome and time-consuming. As a result, production planners use hard copies of the Monthly Sales Reports and Monthly Usage Reports to

continued

Figure 11.8 Sample Proposal

determine production requirements (each typically a 150-page report). Moreover, costly programming changes are required for all nonroutine requests for information.

BENEFITS

The PC 386 approach would give Production Planning the ability to:

- analyze the detailed sales and usage history data quickly and flexibly using a computer without costly DPSRs (Data Processing Service Requests)
- make better Production Planning decisions by using the detailed data more fully
- present the results of the analysis in a directly usable format, eliminating the need for tedious graphing and transcription of data.

This approach would also:

- reduce the use of expensive Data Processing resources for detailed data analysis
- eliminate the need for most monthly sales and usage reports (approximately 300 pages a month) for Production Planning.

PROJECT DESCRIPTION

Technical Details

To be useful, this approach requires the transfer of 2–3 million characters of data from the mainframe data base each month-end to the 52 mb hard disk on a PC 386. Data Processing staff estimate that two person-weeks of programming would be necessary to develop the most cost-efficient method for transferring these data.

continued

Once on a PC-readable medium, the data would be processed using a fourth-generation data base management system such as R:base 5000, which could generate reports and graphs that could be printed on a laser printer.

The final specification of the system, including peripherals and software, must await a more precise determination of the volume of data transfer and storage required and the method of transfer.

Cost

Even though the precise system specifications have not yet been developed, we have estimated the total cost at about $10 500. Here is a cost breakdown for the software and hardware:

1 IBM PC 386 (or compatible) with terminal simulation hardware, a 52 mb hard disk, and a monitor	$5000
1 laser printer	$2500
1 data base management system plus utilities	$1000
2 weeks of programming on the mainframe	$2000

Our figures for hardware and software are based on quotations that the Research and Development Group obtained when they purchased similar equipment three months ago. Therefore, we do not anticipate any overrun on these costs.

Schedule

If I receive your approval to proceed with this purchase, I anticipate that the system can be used for production planning in February 1993.

November 30	Complete hardware and software specifications
December 1	Solicit quotations from suppliers (deadline December 15)
December 15	Review quotations from suppliers
December 31	Complete installation of equipment and software
January 15	Complete programming of mainframe computer to facilitate data transfer

In summary, for approximately $10 500, we can reduce our data processing costs and, at the same time, make better Production Planning decisions. Please let me know your decision by Friday, November 20. If you'd like more information on the proposal, call me at local 5882.

Ethan Coe

Summary

An organization requires a great deal of communication to function smoothly. Much of this information is transmitted in the form of informal reports, of which there are:

- three types:
  - information
  - analytical
  - persuasive
- three formats:
  - preprinted forms
  - memos
  - letters

All reports have the same basic parts:

- opening
  - summary
  - introduction
- body
- closing; in analytical reports the closing includes:
  - conclusions
  - recommendations

In general, the purpose of the report will determine what information will be included and how it will be organized. However, the longer the report the more likely each part will be distinct.

Review Questions

1. How do memo reports differ from letter reports?
2. What kinds of information might be included in a progress report?
3. What is a periodic report?
4. What are some possible purposes of problem-solving reports?
5. What are the advantages to an organization of providing preprinted forms for short reports? What are the disadvantages?
6. How is a proposal different from other analytical reports?

Activities

1. As administrative assistant to the president of National Industries, you have the job of getting contributions from the workers for the president's favourite charity, the Humane Society. It is the midpoint of the month-long campaign, and you must prepare a progress report for your boss. Thus far, 41 percent of the employees have contributed, for an interim total of $1180. Of the total workforce of 325 employees, 60 percent (195) have now been contacted, and 62 have indicated that they do not plan to make any contribution. In planning this in-plant campaign, your boss forecast a 100-percent rate of participation and contributions totalling $3250. Write a progress report to your boss, Richard Cornelius, in the format of a memo report.

2. Prepare a progress report in letter form detailing your progress so far in this business communication course. Indicate the goals you hope to attain in this course and the rate at which you are approaching them. Discuss your development in such areas as written communication, oral communication, and interpersonal relations. If you can cite grades as indicators of development, do so. Address this report to your instructor.

3. Prepare a periodic information report at the end of each of the next three weeks indicating the time that you spent on school work during the week. Write each report in letter form to send to your business communication instructor. The reports should detail your work for all your classes, not simply the business communication course. Indicate the number of classroom hours and the outside-of-class time you spent studying or doing assignments for each course. Also indicate any special circumstances, such as examinations, that may have led you to devote a disproportionate amount of time to a particular course. Include weekends as well as weekdays in these reports.

4. As regional personnel research director of Metro Bank, you were assigned six months ago to investigate why there is such high turnover among the tellers and clerks employed at branches in a large metropolitan area. You instituted an exit interview program; of the 60 tellers and clerks who quit during the last half year, 32 gave the heavy rush-hour traffic as the main reason for leaving; 20 said they wanted to get a part-time job instead; and the 8 others cited personal reasons.

   You think a good solution would be to introduce a more flexible schedule. Altered work schedules, you believe, would free some workers from rush-hour driving. Another possibility would be to hire more part-time employees and to allow present full-time employees to become part-time if they wish. The cost of training new employees is very high. Anything that can be done to reduce turnover, and thereby training costs, would be worthwhile, you feel. Prepare for William Petrol, vice president of personnel, a report in which you present your findings and make recommendations. Petrol has a reputation for being against change; he feels that most modern personnel practices are actually harmful to the organization.
5. Students and faculty alike usually believe that their school could improve registration procedures. List whatever changes you consider desirable, then prepare a memo report in which you detail the steps a student would follow in registering for classes under your improved system. This report will be sent to all students who have been accepted by your school. If you are pleased with present registration procedures, your memo report should describe those.
6. As director of your school's library, you are receiving a growing number of complaints about the management of the periodical room. Twelve patrons have complained that magazines are allowed to pile up on tables before being shelved; eight complained that magazines are often put back on the wrong shelves. Also, many magazines are reported torn and no apparent attempt is made to repair them. Some students have been observed cutting articles out of magazines in violation of library policy. Write a memo to Charlene Freitag, the periodical room manager, in which you describe the complaints and make recommendations.
7. You are a management trainee in a large (1000 employees) manufacturing plant. The plant manager, Tom Dimanno, has asked you to write a report on the use of quality circles in business and industry. He wants to learn such things as what quality circles are, their uses, the extent of their usage, and their benefits. Use the *Canadian Business Index* and the *Business Periodical Index* to

locate several articles on quality circles in order to gain the knowledge necessary to write the report. Dimanno has little patience with long reports and will not read one that is more than three pages long.

8. Prepare a report describing the progress you are making in your education. Describe your goals and give details of your plan for accomplishing them. Also describe the major obstacles to accomplishing your goals and what you are doing to overcome the obstacles. Address this report to your adviser.

9. As a member of a professional association in your area of interest, you have been asked to suggest an appropriate topic for a 90-minute session at the national convention. (You are not responsible for giving the presentation, merely for suggesting an appropriate topic.) Prepare a problem-solving report in which you suggest a topic and present a rationale for its being a part of the convention. Indicate clearly why you feel that this topic would appeal to the association's members.

10. Continuing with Activity 9, in order to have as many members as possible actively participate in the convention, the association has decided that each 90-minute session will feature four presentations. Prepare a persuasive report in which you suggest a topic and a title for one set of presentations. Describe how the topic could be divided into four parts and what each presenter would cover. Explain the ways in which the topic would interest the membership and defend your suggested division of the topic into four parts.

11. You have been an instructor of business communication for several years, and you are increasingly disturbed by the attire of your students. You feel that dress has become much too informal and that this casualness has a negative effect on classes. You believe that the classroom atmosphere should be more businesslike and that more suitable clothing is the first step to a more businesslike atmosphere. Prepare a memo for all the business communication instructors in which you urge that they set and enforce certain standards of dress. Also, describe what you consider appropriate attire.

12. Log your use of time for one week. At half-hour intervals every day, write down what you did during the preceding 30-minute period. At the end of the week, prepare a letter report in which you describe your use of time. Divide your report into sections based on your major uses of time and conclude the report with a list of recommendations for improvement. Address the letter report to yourself.

13. Prepare a preprinted form for the time log described in Activity 12. Prepare this form for the use of your classmates.

Discussion Cases

Analysis of the Membership of a City Chamber of Commerce[1]

You are the vice president for membership of the chamber of commerce in a city with a population of more than 85 000. Chamber members total 153.

Within the city limits are located a comprehensive university with an enrolment of more than 16 000, a provincial mental health hospital with more than 1000 patients, a 230-bed municipal hospital, and two manufacturing plants employing more than 900 workers combined.

The chamber of commerce secretary has given you the following data about the composition of the membership of your organization:

TABLE 11.2 Characteristics of Membership, Chamber of Commerce

		Sex		Employment									
				Gov./ Ed.		Retail		Mfg.		Service		Other	
Age Group	Total	Male	Female	M	F	M	F	M	F	M	F	M	F
35 and under	3	3	0	1	0	2	0	0	0	0	0	0	0
36–44	37	22	15	4	1	11	9	3	1	4	4	0	0
45–54	68	41	27	4	2	26	13	8	1	3	11	0	0
55–64	36	21	15	4	0	9	10	7	2	1	3	0	0
65 and over	9	9	0	0	0	4	0	1	0	1	0	3	0

Case Questions

1. Prepare an appropriate table giving the percentages for the various characteristics according to the sex and the employment categories.
2. What conclusions can be drawn on the basis of the above data as to the nature of the current membership?
3. What recommendations could you as the vice president for membership offer to the chamber board of directors concerning any appropriate and desirable changes in the membership?
4. In your opinion, how should any changes be implemented?
5. Should the members of the chamber of commerce be told about this study and any changes that you will be proposing? Why?
6. Prepare a two-page memorandum to the board of directors with an appropriate table and your recommendations for changing the composition of the chamber membership.

Clear and Concise Communication[2]

The following is a letter concerning credit arrangements being negotiated by a hospital and a bank.

CITY BANK OF VANCOUVER — VANCOUVER, BC

August 3, 1993

Mr. John Smith
Vice President–Finance
Gotham Hospital
201–East 15th Avenue
Vancouver BC V5G 3X5

Dear Mr. Smith:

In line with our conversation earlier this week, we have set forth below a framework for our proposed revolving credit facility for Gotham Hospital:

Amount: $25 000 000.

Availability: $5 million available from January 1, 1990; increasing to $10 million on July 1, 1990; increasing to $18 million on January 1, 1991; increasing to $25 million on July 1, 1991; $25 million available through December 31, 1992. Commencing January 1, 1993, availability will decline in 14 equal semi-annual amounts.

Revolving Nature of Commitment: Until 12/31/92, Gotham Hospital may borrow, repay, and reborrow under the line of credit so long as amounts outstanding do not exceed the aggregate of the amount of the bank's line of credit in effect at the time.

continued

Purpose:	Loan proceeds to be utilized for the acquisition and improvement of land, the construction of new facilities, and the purchase of equipment.
Final Maturity:	12/31/99
Loan Charges:	1. Interest Rate

Closing through 12/31/90:	Prime Rate
1/1/91 – 12/31/92:	Prime Rate + 1/4 percent
1/1/93 – 12/31/94:	Prime Rate + 3/4 percent

2. Availability Fee

3/8 of 1 percent per annum of $25 million payable quarterly from date of closing to date of initial drawdown; thereafter, 1/4 of 1 percent per annum of the following amounts, fee payable quarterly in arrears:

From 1/1/90 – 6/30/90:	$20 million
From 7/1/90 – 12/31/90:	$15 million
From 1/1/91 – 6/30/91:	$7 million

3. Commitment Fee

1/2 of 1 percent per annum payable quarterly in arrears on the unused portion of the available commitment commencing on the date the committed amounts become available; fee expires on the final maturity date.

Balances: Average balances in an amount equivalent to 5 percent of the available commitment plus 5 percent of average borrowings are to be maintained in the form of non-interest-bearing time certificate of deposit.

Sincerely,

Valerie Kreskin

Valery Kreskin
City Bank of Vancouver

Case Questions

1. Explain why the format of this letter is effective.
2. Does the writer use appropriate vocabulary for this letter? If so, give several examples.
3. How does the format lend itself to a clear presentation of a complex business problem?

Chapter 12

Formal Reports

Learning Objectives

In this chapter, you'll learn how to prepare a formal report. More specifically, you will be able to:

1. explain the purpose of writing formal reports in business
2. research your topic thoroughly
3. plan your report
4. write your report
5. use visual aids in writing reports
6. prepare the various parts of a long report in business
7. package your report effectively

Preview Case

Stephanie wondered whether to get another cup of coffee. She'd had three already and felt tense. She sat at her desk watching for Scott, her boss at MicroChip Electronics.

Some weeks ago Stephanie had turned in her report on employee relations problems. She was confident that she had researched her topic well. The solutions she had proposed were, she felt, logical and desirable. But now Scott was meeting with his supervisor, Louise (the personnel manager), and Sid, the vice president. The topic of the meeting was her first semiannual review. She had known this meeting was going to take place today and who would be participating. What had caught her off guard was the sight of Sid, the ranking executive, carrying her report into the meeting. Her report was going to be used in her evaluation!

Stephanie was worried that some parts of the report — other than the research and recommendations sections — might not be correct. And, although she felt she had the "right" information, perhaps it could have been better organized.

During the six months Stephanie had been with MicroChip she had written about a dozen reports, of various lengths, for Scott. He had been gracious in guiding her in her preparation of the kinds of reports he wanted. Although her business studies had included some report-writing instruction, she had quickly discovered that she still had a lot to learn.

Now she was wondering about her report's organization, about the clarity of her conclusions, and about whether she should have included some visual support, such as charts, to illustrate her findings.

"Well," she thought to herself, "I'll know soon. Here comes Scott."

Overview

You may have felt that same uneasy feeling about one of your term papers. Of course, term papers differ from business reports, but both are used in performance evaluation, so writers may well have afterthoughts about them.

The main purpose of this chapter is to prepare you to write effective formal business reports — reports that you will *want* to be used in evaluating your performance! Like other writing tasks, preparing a formal report has two main phases: planning and writing. This chapter offers suggestions about how to plan the report. Then it discusses writing the report, as well as revising and packaging it. The chapter will also describe what Stephanie might have done to be more sure of herself in her report preparation. In fact, in the appendix to this chapter, you'll find a sample report on Stephanie's topic.

As you read this chapter, you'll find that much of the material can be applied to term papers. However, business reports are frequently different from term papers in three major ways. First, term papers are often assigned with a specific purpose, such as an assignment to describe the influence of technology on clerical workers. In business, you may initiate reports yourself and be totally responsible for defining the purpose. Second, most term papers are written for a single audience (your instructor), while business reports typically have many readers at all levels of the organization. Finally, some parts of the business report, such as the letter of transmittal, are seldom used when writing term papers.

Business report–writing skills are useful for writing term papers

Types of Formal Reports

Formal business reports, like informal reports, can be categorized by the extent of their contribution to the decision-making process. They can be informational, interpretive, or analytical in nature. Purely *informational reports*, although valuable, add relatively little to the decision-making process. A weekly absenteeism report may be an informational report that indicates only who was absent and when, the employee's department, and the number of absences to date.

Informational reports give data but no analysis

A step above the informational report is the *interpretive report*. Rather than merely presenting data, this report adds meaning to the data. The facts presented in the informational report are examined and implications are drawn. In an interpretive absenteeism report, the author would explain the meaning of the report: which employees are absentee problems, whether some departments experience higher rates than others, and what cost in time, dollars, or materials is attributable to absenteeism.

Interpretive reports assign meaning to data

As you learned in Chapter 11, the *analytical report* — the one that makes the most contribution to the decision-making process — is essentially a problem-solving report. It not only informs, but also interprets data; it analyzes the situation, reviews alternatives, examines implications, draws conclusions, and makes recommendations. If our absenteeism report moved through these steps and included, for example, a recommendation that two employees be interviewed by their supervisors to determine the cause of their extreme absenteeism, the report would become an analytical report.

Analytical reports propose solutions

Although formal reports can be informational, interpretive, or analytical, we spotlight analytical reports because they are the most involved and difficult to write. Further, the analytical report encompasses informational reports in its framework. Generally speaking, if you can write an effective analytical business report, you can probably prepare other types of reports as well.

Analytical reports are the most difficult to write

Phase One: Planning Formal Reports

As already mentioned, this chapter focuses on planning the formal report. Planning involves seven steps:

1. Determine your purpose(s)
2. Consider your audience
3. Consider the context of the report
4. Analyze the problem
5. Conduct your research
6. Evaluate your results
7. Prepare your outline

These steps parallel the writing process described in Chapter 4. However, they add three important elements: analyzing the problem, and conducting and evaluating research to solve that problem.

Step 1: Determine Your Purpose

What need will your finished report satisfy?

When your report is finished, what need will it satisfy? Will it supply information to be used by others in decision making? Are you to interpret the information? Are you to analyze the situation and supply specific recommendations along with as much information and interpretation as possible? If you can't answer each of these questions quickly and accurately, you need to clarify the purpose with your supervisor or (for self-initiated reports) spend some time reflecting on what you want to accomplish with the report.

Clearly, writing an informational report when an analytical report is desired is as inappropriate as supplying a thorough and lengthy problem-solving report when a focused and brief informational report is expected. Thus, your first step in planning a formal business report is deciding on the extent of contribution to the decision-making process that this report is to make.

In the preview case at the beginning of this chapter, Stephanie had prepared a report that recommended solutions to employee relations problems. Because of those recommendations, it can be assumed that the report was a problem-solving one.

Step 2: Consider Your Audience

Report writing requires careful analysis of the intended audience, of both the number of readers and their characteristics. One reason for Stephanie's concern on seeing her report carried into the evaluation meeting was that she had not anticipated that Louise and Sid might see her report.

Stephanie had erroneously assumed that Scott, her immediate boss, was the only person who would read the report. Had she considered her audience more carefully, she would have recognized her recommendations would eventually be considered by senior management.

Because the person to whom the report is directed is not necessarily the only reader, you should consider the information needs of both your primary and your secondary readers. For each reader, then, you need to examine several reader characteristics:

Receiver characteristics

Expertise	How much do the various readers know about the topic? Can they understand the technical jargon you might use?
Interests	How much detail will your readers want? Do they like tables, charts, and graphs for clarifying information?
Opinions	Will the readers be for or against any recommendations you make? Do they think the topic of your report is important? What do your readers think of you?

When you write term papers, you probably spend a lot of time trying to figure out what your instructor wants. When you write a formal report, your perception of your readers should also influence the way you put it together.

Step 3: Consider the Context

Knowing the context for the report can often help you to clarify and refine your audience and purpose data. The following questions should help you to define the context:

What level of formality is required? Some reports, such as those written for government or high-level management, have an extremely formal tone and appearance. Others, particularly those written in organizations where the management style is more relaxed, might be so informal that they are handwritten and relatively short. At this stage, you should have a clear idea where your report fits on this continuum.

How long should this report be? While your report should always be as long as necessary to achieve its purpose, you should know at the outset whether your audience is expecting a concise, two- or three-page document, or a fifty-page, intensive analysis of the problem.

What is the time frame for the report? Time frame involves two subissues. First, many reports are periodic: daily production reports, weekly progress reports, or annual financial reports. Other reports may be prepared only once. Second, you need to have a clear idea of the deadline for submitting the report. If you assume you have two or three weeks to complete a report, you'll be shocked to say the least if your boss asks for it after only a week.

What is the destination of the report? This question relates closely to audience; however, it goes one step farther in considering whether the report is likely to move up or down in the organizational hierarchy, whether it is an internal or external document, or whether it is directed to an audience completely removed from the organization, such as local government or the general public.

How many people will be involved in writing the report? In business, team-written reports are the norm rather than the exception. They may incorporate individually written sections into one package, or the team may work together on planning, writing, and editing the entire report. Both methods require close co-operation among team members and careful attention to the overall impression the report makes.

How will the report be received? Office politics often have a major impact on the contents and structure of a report. If, for example, you are proposing a solution to a problem that may be unpopular with one or more of your readers, you may want to discuss your recommendations with them prior to releasing the final report. Sometimes, political considerations will even affect the recommendations you ultimately include in the report. For example, if a recommendation will create such antagonism that it will receive little support, it's probably a good idea to modify it so that it's less offensive. This doesn't mean recommending a solution you know won't work, but it does mean taking a long, hard look at what will work in your organization.

Step 4: Analyze the Problem

Collecting the information for your report means answering two questions:

- What do I need?
- Where can I get it?

In planning her problem-solving report, Stephanie used a procedure most good report writers employ in answering the first question. She divided the topic into three basic categories and prepared the following chart.

A sample needs chart

Need 1 **What's the problem?**	Turnover information Absenteeism information Grievance information Morale information Unionization information
Need 2 **What's causing the problem?**	Why high turnover? Why high absenteeism? Why so many grievances? Why such low morale? Why talk of unionization?
Need 3 **What are solutions?**	More money? More fringe benefits? Better working conditions? What else?

A needs chart helps break your topic down and gives continuous feedback about your research

Not only did Stephanie's chart break down her problem into three areas of needs, it also served as her checklist. Charts can help you clearly define your information needs and can also serve as feedback devices — you can check items off as you get the information.

Step 5: Conduct Your Research

With a chart like the one Stephanie prepared, you are ready to answer the second question: Where can I get the information? Answering this question involves choosing between two kinds of information sources — primary and secondary.

Types of research

Primary sources are generally unpublished. You get them first-hand. Secondary sources are publications. Here are some examples:

Primary Sources	**Secondary Sources**
Questionnaires	Newspapers
Experiments	Government documents
Interviews	Books
Personal observations	Magazines
Organization files	Pamphlets

Your choice of sources depends greatly upon how much time you have to complete your report, your budget, and the extent of your ability in using the sources.

Secondary research is not always easier and quicker than primary research

Some people assume that secondary research is easier and quicker than primary research. Although this may often be the case, it is not always true. Don't select a secondary research technique just because it appears to be the quickest. A better rule of thumb — one that comes from scientific inquiry — is to try to do secondary research first. If someone else has already researched your topic, you may be able to rely on those findings.

You must, however, be careful of assuming automatically that because something is in print, it is correct or complete. In examining secondary research, you should ask: Is the information complete? Does it appear to be reasonable and logical? Is it biased? Is it recent? A weakness in any one of these four areas may suggest the need to conduct your own (primary) research.

As a student, you've probably had extensive experience in using secondary sources and thus feel comfortable relying on them. However, you'll find that primary sources are rich, especially for solving problems in organizations.

Specific suggestions about how to use both types of sources to help you conduct your research are offered here.

Secondary Research Sources

Secondary research is also called "library research"

Although secondary research is sometimes called "library research," it is not all done in libraries. Some items, such as newspapers, magazines, or pamphlets, you may have at home or at your office. However, a thorough secondary research project will likely take you to the library at some point.

Chances are that you are familiar with using the library to locate information sources. Therefore, a few reminders and hints on effective library use are all that's needed for this discussion.

Guidelines for secondary research

- Don't focus your search exclusively on books and neglect periodicals, or vice versa.
- Use the *Canadian Periodical Index* or other periodical indexes (which may be in magazine, hardbound, or compact disk form) to find citations by title, author, or subject. The *Canadian Business Index* serves the same function but lists only articles related to business. Here is a sample listing: "To manage well, involve people. *Plant Mgt 42* (1) F'87 p38." The compact disk format for periodical indexes is relatively new; however, if your library offers this service, you'll find that researching this source takes a fraction of the time it takes with print indexes, partially because you can print all the information directly from the computer screen.
- When you find a book on your topic, use both the table of contents and the index to locate your information. Skim both completely since

you may not know the exact term the author uses to refer to your topic.

- Let the footnotes in the books and articles you find guide you to other related sources.
- Look for sources that survey your topic. Books of this type are sometimes entitled *The Handbook of ...*, *The ... Manual,* or *An Analysis of ...* These sources often break the topic into outline form, may give its history, and frequently have many valuable footnotes.
- If you become frustrated or confused, seek help from the librarians; they're experts in locating information.
- As you locate information that you think may be of some value to you, put it on note cards.

Save time by putting notes and citations on cards

Valuable time can be saved if you take several steps now. Write down, on the top or back of the card, the complete citation for the source. Put it in bibliographic form. (The differences between footnote and bibliographic form, with examples of each, are discussed later in this chapter.) By using cards instead of paper, you'll have notes that can be easily sorted by topic, which can be helpful in developing your working outline. Furthermore, information you find late in your search can be placed between two existing cards.

Putting the bibliographic citation at the top or on the back of the card will simplify preparation of the bibliography that appears at the end of your report: you will just alphabetize your cards by the authors' last names. If someone else is typing your report, you can hand over the cards that form your bibliography instead of having to write out the citations. (Make sure your handwriting is readable, or this time-saving step will fail.)

Besides the bibliographic citation, jot down on the card the information that is of value. You may want a direct quote, your own summary, or the way the information relates to other sources. You may wish to write the publication's catalogue number on the other side of the card so you can quickly locate the source again. A sample card may look like the one in Figure 12.1.

Know when to stop your research

Be sure to limit your secondary research. The more clearly you can define your purpose and the research questions, the more successfully you can limit your secondary research. For example, if you are seeking a specific person's opinion on a topic, finding a single source that gives that opinion may conclude your research. On the other hand, if you are bringing together a variety of opinions, you clearly must examine a number of sources. Nevertheless, you can avoid exhaustion by:

- Reviewing only materials published within a given time period. Many experts suggest limiting yourself to the last five years unless you have

Smith, Carlos A. "The Usefulness of Employee Benefits in Reducing Turnover." *Journal of Applied Personnel Research*, December, 1980, pp. 365-372.

p. 371 - "The results of most studies indicate clearly that there is no relationship between liberal doses of employee benefits and turnover rates."

p. 370 -

Company	% Increase in Benefits	Change in Turnover
A.	12%	+4%
B.	25%	+1%
C.	18%	-2%

Figure 12.1 Information from a Secondary Source

a specific need for earlier information.

- Working only until you have thorough answers to specific questions. This criterion assumes your questions are such that you can tell when you have answered them. "How many four or more passenger cars were imported from Japan in 1984?" is such a question.
- Working until you are finding no new information. Once you find that your data are starting to cluster, you may be at the end of your research.

Primary Research Sources

Of the many primary research techniques, the most frequently used are probably questionnaires, experiments, interviews, personal observation, and organization files.

Questionnaires provide useful data

Questionnaires. Properly developed questionnaires can provide an enormous amount of useful data for your report. Improperly developed, however, questionnaires can give you misleading and often uninterpretable information. Proper use of questionnaires includes:

1. Selecting an appropriate sample of respondents
2. Writing the questionnaire

3. Administering the questionnaire
4. Tabulating the results

Correctly chosen, samples can accurately reflect the opinions of an entire group

Selecting an Appropriate Sample. When you hear the results of political opinion polls, you may wonder how information obtained from as few as 1000 persons can accurately reflect the opinions of millions of individuals. Yet because many opinion pollsters carefully select their samples, their predictions of election results are frequently accurate within several percentage points. Such accuracy occurs because these pollsters have clearly defined their population and then, using scientific sampling guidelines, have chosen their sample from it.

A *population* (also called a "universe") is some definable group — every item, person, or thing is either in or out of a particular population. For national opinion pollsters in Canada, the population consists of more than 26 million people. On your campus, it might be all the students or perhaps just all the female students who live in dormitories. In an organization such as Stephanie's, the population might be all full-time employees or perhaps all hourly rated employees. Your first step, then, is to define your population. What group of people should the data you gather represent?

Selecting a sample involves choosing a group to represent the whole population. Ideally, you would administer your questionnaire to the entire population. This, however, might be time-consuming and expensive. You should be able to obtain similar results by contacting only a well-chosen subgroup. The important assumption is, of course, that the sample represents the population.

The size of your sample depends on the size of the whole population, as well as the amount of time and resources you have available. For example, Stephanie was able to survey 30 of MicroChip Electronic's 300 employees, or 10 percent of the population. Tabulating results from 30 questionnaires is relatively easy. However, if MicroChip Electronics employed 5000, surveying 10 percent of that population would require considerably more time and resources. A smaller percentage of the total might suffice if the sample were well chosen.

Convenience sampling

Several types of sampling techniques exist. Stephanie might use a *convenience sample* — any available employees from the 300 in the company. For example, she might distribute questionnaires to the first 30 employees she encounters during the lunch hour. Such a sample would indeed be convenient, but Stephanie's findings would probably not represent all the MicroChip Electronics employees. She might miss employees who go out for lunch or executives who do not keep regular lunch hours. Thus, convenience is generally not an appropriate way of selecting a sample.

Random sampling

Random sampling is a more defensible approach to sampling. Using it, Stephanie would place the names of all 300 employees in a box and draw 30 as those employees to be asked to complete questionnaires. Random sampling is appropriate because each member of the employee population has an equal chance of being included in the sample.

Systematic random sampling

A third sampling technique is *systematic random sampling.* This technique is similar to random sampling, except the sample is selected by taking every *n*th member of the population. For example, Stephanie could take a list of all 300 MicroChip employees, then randomly pick a number between one and ten, such as four. By picking every fourth person from the list, she would select a systematic random sample. As with random sampling, each population member has an equal chance of being part of the sample.

Stratified random sampling

Stratified random sampling is the fourth and most sophisticated technique. Sample members are selected at random but also on the basis of some important demographic characteristics (for example, sex, race, or age). The sample is "stratified" according to these characteristics and usually reflects their proportions in the population. For example, if 47 percent of the population is female, 47 percent of the sample would be female. Of course, not all characteristics are important. For instance, in a campus political election, home town may not be important. Stephanie might decide to use the following stratifications: hourly or salary, management or nonmanagement, male or female, and more or less than five years with MicroChip.

The goal of a questionnaire's introduction is to get respondents to answer

Writing the Questionnaire. A well-developed questionnaire has three basic parts: introduction, instructions, and questions. The *introduction,* whose overall goal is to gain respondents' compliance (get them to complete the questionnaire), often includes six thoughts:

1. It identifies the purpose of the questionnaire. Unless you are concerned that stating the questionnaire's actual purpose will bias respondents' answers, state specifically why you are administering it.
2. It discusses privacy. A statement guaranteeing respondents' anonymity will help to prevent biased responses from individuals who are worried that you might try to identify them. If their names are needed, explain why. If you need to be able to identify them but will not use that identification in the report or share it with others, emphasize this point. This emphasis may be almost as beneficial as complete anonymity in gaining their response.
3. It tells respondents what to do with the questionnaire once they have completed it. For example, this section of the introduction might contain instructions for returning the questionnaire by mail.
4. It may explain why a response is important. If you are using a sample

of 100 from a population of 1000, you might explain that each respondent's opinions reflect the feelings of 10 people.

5. It indicates the amount of time necessary for completion. This indication is especially common in questionnaires that appear to be time-consuming but require only quick responses. "Only about two and a half minutes of your time are required" is the type of statement that may be helpful in gaining co-operation.
6. It identifies the researcher. Respondents prefer to know for whom and to whom they are responding. Your name and title humanize the message and improve the response rate.

The second major portion of a questionnaire is the *instructions.* The omission of thorough, clear instructions often leads to misunderstanding by the respondents. At least up to some logical stopping point, the clarity of instructions cannot be overdone. Assume that your reader is going to misinterpret your questionnaire — where will the error occur?

The goal of a questionnaire's instructions is to prevent errors in answering

The final part of the questionnaire is the *questions* themselves. The questions are the heart of the questionnaire. Their success depends on the quality of the introductory comments and instructions.

Questions can be divided into six major types or categories; each has its own purpose, strengths, and weaknesses:

1. *Demographic questions,* which frequently but not always appear first, seek information on characteristics of respondents such as age, sex, income, race, faculty department, and home town. Demographic questions have two major uses: to break down answers to other questions (for example, to see if male and female respondents differ in their feelings) and to test the appropriateness of a random sample. (For example, you know that 35 percent of your population is university educated but your question on education reveals that only 10 percent of your respondents are university educated; your demographic question has cautioned you that your sample appears non-random.)

Demographic questions gather information on the respondents

2. *Dichotomous questions* elicit one of only two possible answers. "Yes/no," "male/female," and "true/false" are examples of responses to dichotomous questions. Notice that dichotomous questions may also be demographic questions: "What is your sex?" fits both categories. Some other categories of questions may also overlap.

   "Branching" your respondents is one beneficial use of dichotomous questions. Here is an example of a branching question and instruction:

   Have you earned a bachelor's degree as of today? _____ Yes _____ No (If yes, answer questions 2 through 9; if no, proceed to question 10.)

Dichotomous questions have only two possible answers

Respondents choose one item in a list question

3. *List questions* present a list of items and ask the respondent to select one — the greatest or the least, the largest or the smallest, the most or least important, the best or worst, and so on. Here is an example of a list question:

Which of the following do you feel is most important in determining your job satisfaction?

_____Money
_____Praise from superiors
_____Doing my job well
_____Respect from peers
_____Fringe benefits

Rank-order questions ask about hierarchies

4. *Rank-order questions* are similar to list questions in that they present a list. They differ in that a response is requested for each item in the list rather than just one. Furthermore, the items are to be ranked in some way, such as best to worst or largest to smallest. Here is an example of a rank-order question:

Rank the following five items, from 1 for most important to 5 for least important, in terms of their importance to your job satisfaction:

_____Money
_____Praise from superiors
_____Doing my job well
_____Respect from peers
_____Fringe benefits

Although rank-order questions can gather substantial information, be careful in your analysis of the rankings. They determine a hierarchy among the items but not the distances between them. That is, selection 1 and 2 may be close to each other but there may be a large gap between 2 and 3.

Direct and indirect attitude questions use scales

5. *Direct and indirect attitude questions* are frequently used in questionnaires. The direct attitude question, as the name suggests, seeks a clear or obvious attitude. Since attitudes usually are not dichotomous, a Likert-type scale is often prepared. The respondent places his or her reaction on a scale that likely offers five possible positions. Here is an example:

Stimulus	**I enjoy my marketing classes**				
Scale	**Strongly agree**	**Agree**	**Neutral**	**Disagree**	**Strongly disagree**
Response	______	______	______	______	______

Indirect attitude questions seek deeper reactions. For each stimulus they offer a number of responses, usually about ten. A scale of five or seven positions is used. Here is a semantic differential question:

Stimulus My marketing classes are

Scales and responses			
	rewarding	___ : ___ : ___ : ___ : ___	unrewarding
	difficult	___ : ___ : ___ : ___ : ___	easy
	relevant	___ : ___ : ___ : ___ : ___	irrelevant
	messy	___ : ___ : ___ : ___ : ___	tidy
	active	___ : ___ : ___ : ___ : ___	passive
	weak	___ : ___ : ___ : ___ : ___	strong
	good	___ : ___ : ___ : ___ : ___	bad
	unnecessary	___ : ___ : ___ : ___ : ___	necessary
	required	___ : ___ : ___ : ___ : ___	elective
	illogical	___ : ___ : ___ : ___ : ___	logical
	fun	___ : ___ : ___ : ___ : ___	work

You can see that this kind of question elicits responses that respondents might not have thought of on their own.

Open-ended questions do not restrict answers

6. *Open-ended questions* allow respondents to express their ideas on a topic freely. When you are unsure about how your respondents might answer a question, when you don't want to limit them to your wording, or when you seek answers with richness and depth, consider an open-ended question — for example, "How do you feel about your company?" The strength of such a question lies in the richness of the answers; the weakness is the difficulty of analyzing the answers statistically. For example, you will probably have unique responses and therefore cannot say, "23.4 percent said ... "

Don't expect a high return rate from a mail-in survey

Administering the Questionnaire. Once you have selected your sample and written your questionnaire, you are ready to contact your respondents. In general, when you survey a sample of the general population by mail, you can expect a return rate as low as 10 percent. A mail survey with a return rate of more than 70 percent is considered extraordinary and can be expected only if respondents have a particular interest in making their views known.[1]

For example, when Stephanie conducted her survey at MicroChip Electronics, she knew that the employees she contacted would be very interested in making their views known about employee relations known to management. Nevertheless, she ensured co-operation by:

- keeping the questionnaire short
- mailing the questionnaire to the employees at home to guarantee anonymity
- enclosing a stamped, addressed envelope in which to return the questionnaire

Because of employee interest and Stephanie's attention to detail in administering the questionnaire, her return rate was 83 percent. In most situations, however, expecting this return rate would be unrealistic.

In some situations, questionnaires need not be distributed by mail. For example, instructors frequently distribute course (and instructor) evaluation questionnaires at the end of term. Students are asked to complete them in the class. The instructor then has one of the students collect the questionnaires to guarantee the respondents' anonymity.

Closed questions can be computer-tabulated

Tabulating the Results. Tabulating the results of closed questions is a relatively simple task, particularly if your sample is small. Because the number of potential responses is limited, the process is essentially mechanical and mathematical. For this reason, computers are often used to tabulate the results of closed questions.

Open-ended questions, on the other hand, are more difficult to tabulate. The responses are highly individual and analysis can be subjective. If you summarize the responses, you may inadvertently present biased information by assigning undue importance to some responses and ignoring others. If you do not summarize the responses, you are left to cope with an overwhelming amount of information.

Tabulating the results of a questionnaire, then, requires attention to detail and an awareness of the potential for error.

The use of an experiment implies the use of standard assumptions and guidelines

Experiments. Another method of gathering primary data is through experiments. The use of an experiment has implicit assumptions:

1. You manipulate something and then pay attention to the result.
2. You start with a specific research question or hypothesis that you test.
3. You are objective — unbiased — in your technique.
4. Most likely, you test your findings with well-defined statistical procedures.

These major assumptions, plus many other guidelines and conditions, mean that experiments can be rigorous. If the experiment is to have meaning, you must meet standard assumptions and guidelines.

Since describing even some of the important methodology in any depth is beyond the scope of this text, we will instead list a few hints and guidelines and encourage you to seek additional direction elsewhere.

Your college librarian will be able to recommend several sources.

Guidelines for primary research

- Often you will need a sample of the population for your experiment. Follow the rules of sampling.
- Always try to be unobtrusive; your presence alone can affect the data you are collecting.
- Be careful not to overgeneralize your findings — the results you observe for a sample of 50 reflects only those 50 and not necessarily the balance of the population. Conditions may change, for example, between the start of your experiment and the time you draw conclusions.
- Examine the secondary literature first to see if someone else has already conducted your research. The mistakes of others may help you.
- Keep your experiment as simple as you can. Try to control as many variables as possible. For example, if you wish to know the effect of a ten-cent rise in the price of hamburgers in the company cafeteria, don't raise the price of other items at the same time.

Interviews. Interviews have several uses in gathering data for a business report. You might conduct persuasive interviews to encourage subjects to take part in an experiment. Information giving might be used to instruct selected subjects in how to function during an experiment. For data gathering, however, you are most likely to use the information-gathering type of interview. Here are some important things to consider about data-gathering interviewing:

Guidelines for Interviews

- Sometimes only one or a few individuals need to be interviewed, particularly if they can offer expert opinions. For example, seeking the opinion of one dietitian about the nutrition of the cafeteria food may be far more valuable than seeking the opinions of many employees.
- If many people need to be interviewed, do you need a random sample? Must you meet the criteria of random sampling?
- If you are sampling and interviewing many people, are you actually conducting an experiment and therefore required to meet the criteria of an experiment?

continued

- Since interviews are such obtrusive data-gathering techniques, should you consider an alternative method?
- Does the individualized and flexible approach of interviewing justify the time and effort it will require?
- Would telephone interviewing, which has its own strengths and weaknesses, serve better than face-to-face interviewing? Telephone interviewing can gather more honest answers since the interviewees do not have to "look you in the face." But, for the same reason, it can introduce dishonesty! Telephone interviewing usually takes longer to conduct than one plans. Wrong numbers, busy signals, no answers, and number changes all take time.

Personal Observations. A data-gathering source that is frequently overlooked is personal observation. You may observe as you conduct an interview or run an experiment. But here we're speaking of a formalized approach to answering your research question.

Formal observation demands an unobtrusive observer

In addition to the usual concerns about sampling and experimentation, observation demands the rigours of unobtrusiveness. Is your presence modifying what you're observing? Can you overcome this problem by becoming a participant in the group? Perhaps you can observe, in an objective way, the effect of raising hamburger prices by joining the regular group of employees who use the cafeteria. The effect may be different from that of a stranger's walking about the cafeteria during lunch hour with a clipboard and pencil.

Much data already exists in files — but you may need ingenuity to know what to look for

Organization Files. Sometimes you can find the answer to your research question by merely looking in readily available organization files. This technique is the least obtrusive of the primary source techniques since you do not affect the existing data. If you raise the price of hamburgers in the cafeteria on a certain date, are you selling more or fewer hamburgers? Records may indicate the kilograms of hamburger purchased before and after the change. Did the 10 percent salary increase affect output? For possible changes, look to the production reports, absentee reports, tardiness reports, or number of gripes sent to the company newsletter.

Frequently you need some ingenuity to decide which records will meet your needs and to locate them. But since the information is now gathered and your presence does not affect it, you can gain in time, effort, and quality of data by using organizational records.

Step 6: Evaluate Your Results

After you have conducted your research, you are ready to evaluate your results. First, you should refer to your needs chart (like Stephanie's on page 317) and ask yourself:

- Have I collected all the information I need to answer my reader's questions about each topic on my needs chart?
- What is the answer to my initial research question?
- What gaps in information exist, and why?
- Was my sample adequate?
- Should I have applied statistical tests to make the data more meaningful?

Next, you should analyze your data and ask yourself:

- What conclusions can I draw from these data?
- Are they reasonable and logical? If not, why not?
- What action(s) should be taken?

Step 7: Outline the Report

Once you have gathered all your information, you are prepared to outline the report. As we mentioned earlier, a formal report can have many parts. For outlining, you need to be concerned with only three of them — introduction, body, and conclusion — which together make up the bulk of the report.

As you outline your report, you have two decisions to make:

Decisions in outlining a report

Decision A: In what order do I present the introduction, body, conclusions, and recommendations?

Decision B: How will I organize the body itself?

In making Decision A you have three choices:

Decisions about basic order

Choice 1 (Indirect order)	Choice 2 (Direct order)	Choice 3 (Direct order)
Introduction	Introduction	Conclusion(s)
Body	Conclusion(s)	Recommendation(s)
Conclusion(s)	Recommendation(s)	Introduction
Recommendation(s)	Body	Body

These choices may surprise you. Choice 1 seems so logical; however, you'll find that choices 2 and 3 have their own advantages. Which choice you make depends upon your analysis of the reader(s).

In choice 1, called the *indirect-order arrangement*, you save your conclusion(s) and recommendation(s) until last. Why choose the indirect-order arrangement? Here are some reasons:

Reasons for using the indirect-order arrangement

- The reader might tend to resist your conclusions and recommendations because they either contain bad news or are contrary to his or her opinion.
- The reader won't understand your conclusions and recommendations unless he or she reads the rest of the report, or the reader will need to be persuaded because a change is recommended. The problem in understanding could lie in the scientific or technical nature of your report or in the reader's lack of familiarity with its subject.

Bear in mind that the indirect-order arrangement forces your readers to spend considerable time reading detailed information before they get to the most important part. Because of this delay, many executives will find the conclusion, no matter where it is in the report, and read it first.

Choices 2 and 3 are *direct-order arrangements*. With them, you present your conclusions and recommendations either second or first. Whether you choose number 2 or 3 isn't tremendously important. However, you need to know the reasons for using the direct-order arrangement:

Reasons for using the direct-order arrangement

- The report contains good news for the reader.
- Your reader has enough background to understand the conclusions and recommendations without having to read the rest of the report first.
- The report may be easier to read, since your conclusions and recommendations provide a framework around which to interpret the detailed information in the body.

In making Decision B, you must decide in what order to present the bulk of your information. You must, therefore, organize the body so that it is concise, flows smoothly, and has the kind of impact you want.

Methods of Development

Chronological-order outline

You have several choices in deciding how to organize the body of the report. You might use a *chronological order* — that is, arrange the body according to time. We're using the chronological order in this chapter — that is, we describe a step-by-step procedure for writing a formal report. Chronological order is especially useful for writing an informational report with a topic that can be sequenced according to time.

A second way to organize the report body is *topical order*. Using this method, you organize the body around important topics. For example, if you were writing a report to help your employer choose a location for a new plant, you might organize around selection criteria.

Topical-order outline

I. **Labour market**
A. **Arnprior, Ontario**
B. **Burnaby, British Columbia**
C. **Halifax, Nova Scotia**

II. **Community support**
A. **Arnprior, Ontario**
B. **Burnaby, British Columbia**
C. **Halifax, Nova Scotia**

III. **Marketing and distribution benefits**
A. **Arnprior, Ontario**
B. **Burnaby, British Columbia**
C. **Halifax, Nova Scotia**

You can organize the report around the topics of potential sites; this *spatial organization* would allow you to discuss each location completely before moving on to the next. Here are some first-degree headings for such an outline:

Spatial-order outline

I. **Arnprior, Ontario**
A. **Labour market**
B. **Community support**
C. **Marketing and distribution benefits**

II. **Burnaby, British Columbia**
A. **etc.**

III. **Halifax, Nova Scotia**
A. **etc.**

Yet another method is the *problem-solving* order. Typically, this arrangement consists of several subparts: background, nature of problem, causes of problem (optional), proposed solution(s), evaluation of proposed solution(s), conclusions, and recommendations. The problem-solving order is perfectly suited to Stephanie's needs, since her purpose is to solve the employee problem. Her outline for the first two major headings might have looked like this:

Problem-solving order

I. Background: Employee relations in the electronics industry
A. Effects of good employee relations
B. Consequences of poor employee relations

II Nature of MicroChip Electronics' employee relations problem
A. Grievances
B. Turnover
C. Absenteeism
D. Morale
1. Methodology
2. Return rate
E. Unionization

The report body can also be organized in other ways. For example, you can use gradations of size, rank, or importance to create a pattern. In general, the most important information is presented first.

Headings Versus Headlines

Having decided how to organize your report, you're ready to decide the labels for each section. You can choose either headings or headlines to highlight each section of your report. *Headings* are key words or short phrases, whereas *headlines* are longer phrases or short sentences. Here are some examples:

Topic Headings	Sentence Headings
I. Background	I. Employee relations influence company success
A. Effects of Good Relations	A. Good employee relations produce benefits
B. Effects of Poor Relations	B. Poor employee relations produce negative consequences
II. Nature of the Problem	II. MicroChip has experienced negative consequences
A. Increased Grievances	A. Grievances have increased
B. Excessive Turnover	B. Turnover rate is excessive
1. MicroChip's Rates	1. Turnover is 25 percent
2. Reasons for Turnover	2. Employees leave for three main reasons

Headings are prepared more quickly than headlines. However, headlines will make the actual writing go faster, because they are in fact the short versions of your topic sentence for each section and subsection.

Incidentally, notice that each heading in the sample outlines has at least two subheadings below it. In the example, "Grievances" and "Turnover" are two components discussed under "Nature of the Problem" (major heading). If the report discussed only turnover, the writer would choose one heading ("Turnover" or "Problem") and use no subheading in that section. In other words, if you break an idea down, it must have at least two parts.

Notice also the important concept of parallelism. Equivalent parts of the outline use the same part of speech, have the same suffix, and have the same structure. For example, "Increased Grievances" and "Excessive Turnover" use parallel structure.

In this section we have presented the report planning process. Next, we will move to the next phase: writing the report. First, however, check your planning against this list:

Checklist for Planning the Formal Report

- Have I determined my purpose?
  - ❑ To inform?
  - ❑ To solve a problem?

- Have I analyzed my readers'
  - ❑ Expertise?
  - ❑ Interests?
  - ❑ Opinions?
  - ❑ Hierarchical position?

- Have I gathered all the necessary information?
  - ❑ Needs chart finished?
  - ❑ All secondary sources used?
  - ❑ All primary sources used?
  - ❑ Information on note cards?

- Have I analyzed my information?
  - ❑ Logical conclusions?
  - ❑ "Solid" information?

- Have I outlined my report so it will flow clearly?
  - ❑ Overall order for introduction, body, and conclusion chosen?
  - ❑ Order for body of report chosen?

Phase Two: Writing the Report

Once your planning process is completed you are prepared for actual writing. A form report can contain many parts. Some are optional; others are not. Here is a list of those parts, in the order they would appear in your final report. Those marked with an asterisk are optional.

A. Preliminary Parts

***1. Cover**	Usually a hard cover, containing only the title of your report; helpful in binding the report.
***2. Title Fly**	Sheet of paper containing only the report title that separates the cover from the title page.
3. Title Page	The report title, your name, name of receiver(s), and the date.
***4. Authorization Document**	Copy of the letter or memo authorizing you to write the report.
5. Transmittal Document	Letter or memo officially sending your report to the receiver.
6. Table of Contents	A list of the subdivisions of your report, with their respective page numbers.
***7. List of Tables**	The names of the tables in your report, showing their page numbers.
***8. List of Figures**	The names of the figures in your report, showing their page numbers.
***9. Informative Summary**	Brief overview

B. Text Parts

10. Introduction	
11. Body	In some chosen order, according to your outline.
12. Conclusion(s)	
13. Recommend-ation(s)	

C. Supplementary Parts

***14. Appendices**	Material that, while useful to your report,

might clutter the report text and slow the reader down (for example, copies of letters, questionnaires).

*15. **Endnotes/ Footnotes**	Footnotes appear on the relevant page; endnotes appear together on one page.
*16. **Bibliography**	A list of all the sources you used in researching your report.
*17. **Index**	A list, in alphabetical order, of the important key topics you used in the report, showing their page numbers.

You might think that combining all these parts effectively into one report is a formidable task. However, the task isn't too difficult if you follow two steps:

Steps in writing a formal report

1. Write the report parts
2. Package the final product

In following these two steps, you will first use your outline as a guide to writing the actual text of the report. Once this is completed, you move to the packaging step, where you add the other report parts to the front and back of the text material.

Step 1: Writing the Report Parts

Write the parts in the order that works for you

If your outline is thorough, the writing of the text parts, although time-consuming, should flow rather smoothly. Most writers find it easier to write the introduction or the body of the report before writing the conclusions and recommendations. However, since you've already analyzed the problem and decided what conclusions and recommendations you'll make, it's sometimes easier to write them first. That way you can develop a section in the body of the report for each one, showing exactly how you reached your decision.

Your introduction prepares your reader for the discussion. Therefore, your introduction should include:

- authorization (if you have no letter or memo of authorization).
- purpose of the report. Your purpose statement should clearly identify the problem you are investigating. Sometimes writers get so close to the problem they forget that their readers will be seeing this informa-

tion for the first time when they read the report. Therefore, they'll need fairly detailed information.

- history or background of the problem. If you describe the circumstances that led to the report, your reader will know why the report is significant.
- limitations of the data (circumstances or conditions that restrict the reliability or general usefulness of your information).
- scope (to let your reader know what the boundaries of your discussion are).
- method of investigation. The credibility of your data will be improved if readers can see clearly that your research methods are sound.
- sources of information (to help validate the contents of the report as your reader prepares to read the findings).
- organization of data (to give your reader easy access to specific information).

Your conclusions may change as you write

The body of your report presents your data and your analysis of those data. It is the most detailed section of your report. The act of writing the body may represent the first time you'll think about your report material in real detail. If this is the case, the body should be written before you write your conclusions or recommendations. While you will probably have some general ideas about your conclusions and recommendations when you begin to write the body, you may well discover that they will change as you write. Even if you write your conclusions and recommendations first, you should be prepared to modify them when you find that you have insufficient data to support them.

Your conclusions evaluate or draw inferences from your data. They must be based on information that is already in the body of your report. You should not introduce new material in the concluding section. Present your conclusions in order of importance: most important to least important.

Your recommendations should suggest a specific course of action for your reader. They should be specific and, where possible, should specify not only what should be done, but also who should do it.

Characteristics of Effective Reports

Apply the characteristics of effective written communication

As you write, recall the characteristics of effective written communication discussed in Chapter 5. They apply as much to long, formal reports as they do to other forms of written communication.

1. **Readability:** Consider the education level of your receiver.
2. **Tact:** Be careful to avoid sexist language.
3. **Personal:** Traditionally, the "you" attitude was not used in formal

reports; however, today, it is more common, even in very formal reports.

4. **Positive:** Use a positive tone wherever possible. (But remember that some ideas aren't adaptable to a positive approach.)
5. **Active:** Use the active voice as much as possible and the passive voice only to de-emphasize an idea.
6. **Unity:** Be sure that each sentence and each paragraph contains only one central idea.
7. **Coherence:** Use signposts, linking words, and enumerators to help the text flow clearly. Proper headings will also help.
8. **Clarity:** Avoid unfamiliar words, and use technical jargon only if you're sure the reader will understand you.
9. **Conciseness:** Avoid trite expressions, wordy phrases, unnecessary repetition, and abstract words.
10. **Mechanically sound:** Check and recheck for grammar errors (even on the typed copy).

Two of these characteristics, coherence and clarity, can be dramatically improved by using three devices: headings, tables, and figures.

Using Headings Effectively

Headings can be taken directly from your outline. They have two main purposes: they serve as signposts and improve the speed and ease with which the reader can comprehend your ideas. The many authorities who discuss the relationship between the various levels of headings do not all agree. Nevertheless, a few principles emerge:

1. Format

The appearance and spacing of headings show how ideas are related. In general, you should use upper- and lower-case letters, position, and white space to show how closely ideas are related.

Appearance. First-level headings are written in capital letters throughout and are usually centred on the page. You will normally have only one first-level heading: the title of your report.

Second-level headings are capitalized throughout, too, but they begin at the left-hand margin of the page. Third-level headings have only the first letter of each word capitalized. Fourth- and fifth-level headings are indented five spaces.

Underlining headings helps to make them stand out from the text on the page. Therefore, underlining is particularly important for headings that use upper- and lower-case letters. However, because first- and second-level headings are ALL CAPS, you may choose not to underline them. Whatever you decide, however, be consistent.

Many word processing packages (and printers) allow writers to emphasize headings by using boldface type. If you have access to this facility, you may find that you don't need to underline headings at all.

Spacing. White space between segments of a document visually reinforces the organizational pattern for the reader. In general, the more white space, the less closely related the ideas are.

Other Formats. On the job, you may be asked to use a numeric or alpha-numeric system to distinguish levels of headings. However, these systems are optional.

2. Levels

Headings and subheadings of the same level should cover information that is equal in scope and importance. For example, the first-level heading names the memo, letter, or report. Second-level headings are subordinate to the first-level headings, third-level headings are subordinate to second-level headings, and so on.

Because you are dividing something, you must have at least two parts. Therefore, you need two or more second-level headings under a first-level heading, two or more third-level headings under a second-level heading, and so on. However, each level of heading does not need to have the same number of subheading levels under it. For example, you may have third-level headings under one second-level heading but not under another.

3. Content

To be effective, headings must:

- be specific and informative. Headings such as "Discussion," "Problem," and "Solution" are too general and vague to be of much use to the reader. On the other hand, headings such as "Increased Grievances" and "Excessive Turnover" tell your readers exactly what to expect.
- stand alone. Headings are not considered part of the text; they're just signposts. Therefore, the text should make sense without the headings.
- be parallel (if reasonably possible). Headings of equal importance should have the same grammatical structure. For example, if you use a single noun for one second-level heading, all second-level headings should be single nouns (Introduction, Format, Content).

Using Visual Information in a Report

Table and figures have content and visual uses

Visuals are useful for summarizing a large amount of detailed information in a small space. They also break up the text material and thus create a more interesting appearance.

Here are some general guidelines for the use of visuals in the text of a business report:

Guidelines for tables and figures

1. Place a visual that is half a page or larger on a page by itself. A visual that is smaller can have text above or below.
2. Refer to visuals in the text. If the visual is short enough to go on the same page, place it after the paragraph that refers to it. If it is to be on a page by itself, continue your text after the paragraph with the reference and insert the visual on the next page.
3. Make sure each visual "stands alone" even though it is explained in the text. Any viewer should be able to understand the table or figure without reading the text. Therefore, each visual should have a descriptive title.
4. Put visuals in the text if the reader needs them to understand the report. If the information is helpful but not required, place it in an appendix. Lengthy visuals — several pages or more — are usually placed in an appendix.
5. When you use a visual previously presented elsewhere in published form, indicate the source — just as you would insert a footnote for quoted material in the text. The source indication, however, is part of the visual.
6. If a visual must be placed horizontally along the length of the page (instead of across its width), place it so the bottom is at the right-hand side of the report.
7. Be consistent in your presentation of information on graphs. Present the time period (years, months, and so on) on the horizontal axis. Start the vertical axis at zero and increase upward.

Using Tables

Use tables to summarize quantitative information

Tables are much more specific than figures in that they show only numbers in a column-and-row format. Figures, which are also called illustrations, include a variety of graphs, charts, and visual matter, such as maps, drawings, and photographs.

Figure 12.2 is an example of a table that Stephanie might have considered using in her report if she had compared turnover rates at several companies.

Notice that the sample table is arranged with its title first. Lines separate major divisions. A footnote explains part of the information. A writer usually arranges the accompanying text material to: first, introduce the table; second, present the table itself; and third, interpret its contents. (Notice, too, that some of the same data are shown in graph form in Figures 12.4 through 12.6.) Here are some guidelines to help you prepare tables:

TABLE 4
1980-1990 Turnover Rates for MicroChip and Some of Its Competitors

Company	Turnover Rate					
	1980	1982	1984	1986	1988	1990
MicroChip	13%	17%	18%	21%	21%	23%
Burns	18	21	16	12	11	7
Dominion	15	14	17	13	12	15
Maritime	17	24	18	16	9	10

These percentages are the percentages per 1000 employees for each company.

Figure 12.2 A Sample Table

- Limit the amount of information in any one table. If you are presenting a lot of data, use several smaller tables.
- Put figures in columns, not rows, because columns are easier to read.
- Use whole numbers wherever possible and limit decimals to three places of accuracy.
- Label each column horizontally so your reader can easily see how the information is categorized.
- Show the unit of measurement (for example, years, days, percentages).
- Use lines to enclose the table and separate major divisions.
- Put a table number and descriptive title above the table.
- Make tables easy to read by using lots of white space.

Using Figures

Among the most popular types of figures for a formal report are graphs, charts, and maps. Consider using them not only to summarize information, but also to add vividness to your presentation.

Graphs

Graphs can sometimes show information more effectively than tables

Like tables, graphs are used to present quantitative data. You'll often discover that information you intended to put into table form can be shown more effectively in a graph. Graphs show trends, comparisons, or sometimes both trends and comparisons. Four basic kinds of graphs are pie graphs, line graphs, bar graphs, and pictographs.

Pie graphs (also called circle graphs or pie charts) compare parts to a whole. As part of her research Stephanie might have gathered information about why former MicroChip employees had quit their jobs. The pie graph in Figure 12.3 summarizes those data.

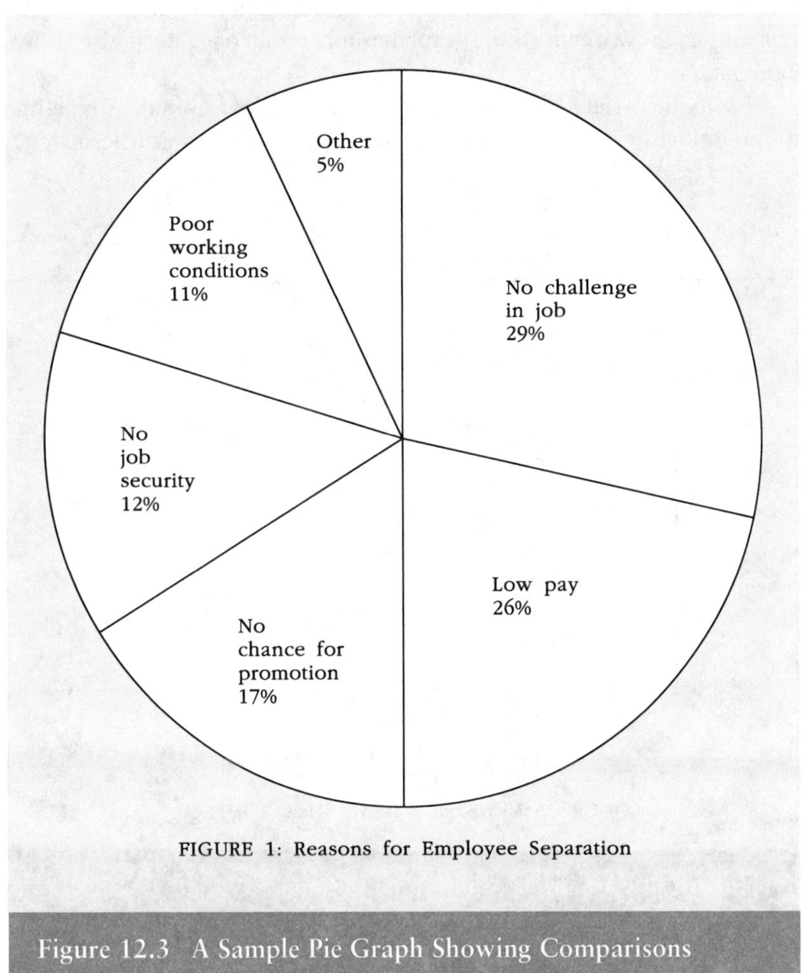

FIGURE 1: Reasons for Employee Separation

Figure 12.3 A Sample Pie Graph Showing Comparisons

These simple rules should help you construct a good pie graph:

1. Always begin your pie graph at the twelve o'clock position.
2. Enter the largest percentage first; work your way clockwise around the graph by entering the remaining percentages in descending order. However, a miscellaneous category comes last regardless of size.

3. To compute the exact space needed for each percentage, multiply 360 (the number of degrees in a circle) by the percentage. Your product is the number of degrees the percentage should make up. (For example, 360 × 29% = 104 degrees.)
4. Use a protractor and ruler to draw the graph.

Single-line graphs show trends; double-line graphs also show comparisons

Line graphs are used to show both trends and comparisons. Single-line graphs show trends. If the graph has more than one line, it also shows comparisons.

From the variety of graphs, Stephanie might have used the single-line graph in Figure 12.4 to show the trend in turnover rates at MicroChip.

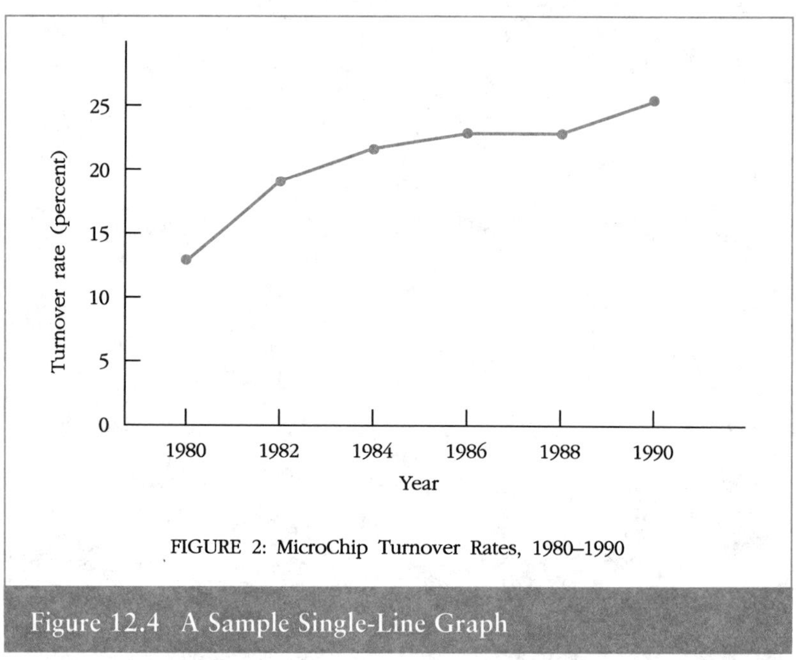

Figure 12.4 A Sample Single-Line Graph

Drawing lines for all the companies shown in her Table 4 would have been confusing, but Stephanie could have compared MicroChip to its most important competitor by using a double-line graph, as in Figure 12.5. Notice that one line is solid, while the other is dotted. Line graphs usually contain no more than three or four lines — too many will confuse your reader.

Here are some guidelines to help you prepare line graphs:

- Place the fixed (independent) variable on the horizontal or X-axis (usually time).
- Place the fluctuating (dependent) variable on the vertical or Y-axis (usually quantity or amount).
- Label the graph completely (axes, units, figure number, title, and so on).
- Remove all unnecessary detail such as grid lines and unnecessary data points.
- If you are graphing more than one set of data:
  - use a different colour or type of line for each set
  - include a legend so the reader knows which is which.

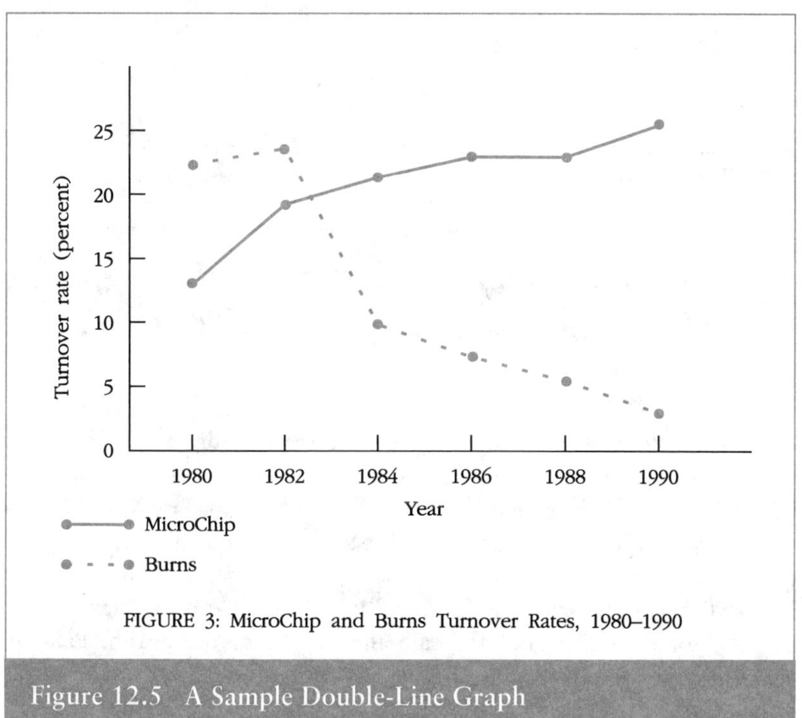

Figure 12.5 A Sample Double-Line Graph

Bar graphs best show comparisons. For example, had Stephanie wanted simply to compare the MicroChip and Burns turnover rates, she might have used the vertical bar graph in Figure 12.6. If she had drawn the graph so that the bars extended from left to right, it would have been a *horizontal bar graph*. There's a third type of bar graph, the *subdivided*

The bar graph best shows comparison

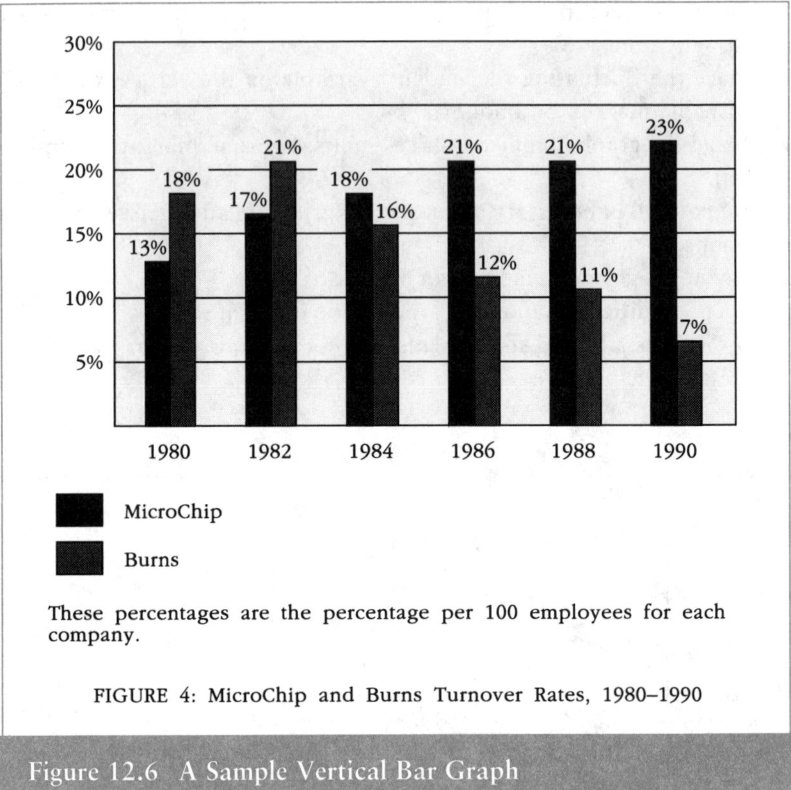

Figure 12.6 A Sample Vertical Bar Graph

bar graph, which can be used if you have more information about the contents of each bar. For example, in Figure 12.7 the information about turnover rates is subdivided by sex.

A *bilateral bar graph* can be used to show both positive and negative qualities. For example, Figure 12.8 shows the 23 percent turnover rate for 1990 broken down by plant location. Notice that on a bilateral bar graph the zero point goes through the middle of the graph. Positive quantities are entered first, beginning with the largest. Negative quantities go towards the right side of the graph, with the smallest shown first.

Here are some guidelines to help you prepare bar graphs (notice that many of the guidelines are the same as those for line graphs):

- Place the fixed (independent) variable on the horizontal or X-axis (usually time).
- Place the fluctuating (dependent) variable on the vertical or Y-axis (usually quantity or amount).

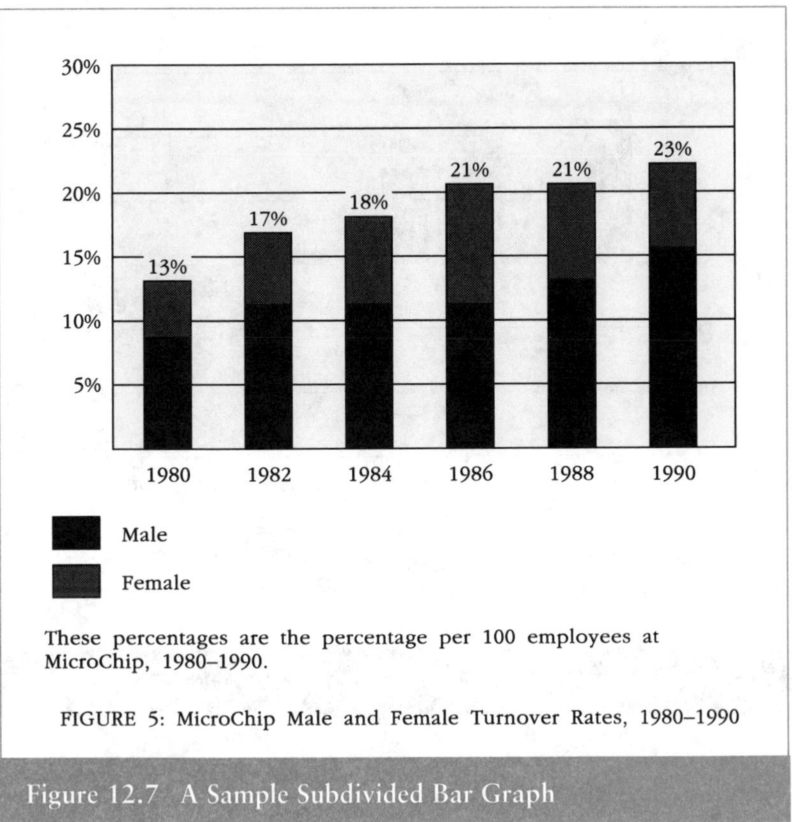

Figure 12.7 A Sample Subdivided Bar Graph

- Label the graph completely (axes, units, figure number, title, and so on).
- Use bars of equal width, and leave spaces between bars or groups of bars to balance the graph.
- If you are graphing more than one set of data:
  - use a different colour or hatching for each bar set of data
  - include a legend so the reader knows which is which.

Pictographs are the final type of graph. They are similar to bar graphs, except that symbols, rather than bars, represent the quantities being shown. The symbols can vary widely, from coins representing money to tractors representing farmers.

Charts and Diagrams

Unlike graphs, which contain quantitative data, charts and diagrams show nonquantitative information. The differences between charts and diagrams are not always clearcut. However, most diagrams show some

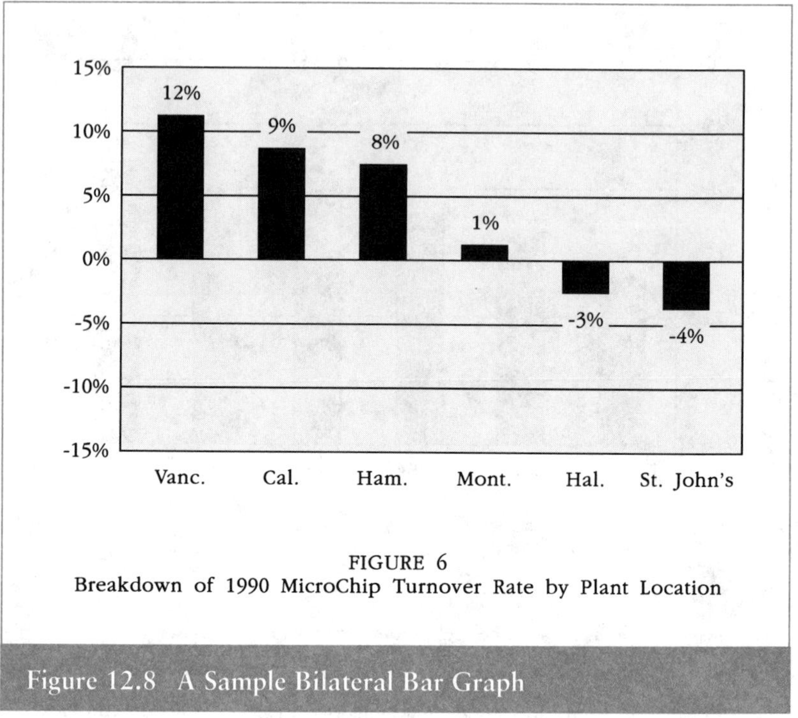

Figure 12.8 A Sample Bilateral Bar Graph

kind of process, while charts contain static information. The model of communication presented in Chapter 2 is an example of a diagram. It shows the process of communication:

encoding → decoding → feedback

An example of a chart is the organizational chart many businesses have. It is a "picture" of the organization that shows: the various positions in the hierarchy, and the lines of authority between and among these positions. For example, an organizational chart for a small shoe store with a full-time manager and three salespeople would be very simple. Figure 12.9 shows that the salespeople report to the store manager, who in turn reports to the owner.

The list of charts and diagrams you might use in a report is unlimited. Stephanie could have chosen among a variety for hers:

- an organizational chart of MicroChip Electronics
- a chart of the causes of MicroChip's employee problems
- a step-by-step diagram of how to implement her solutions to the problems

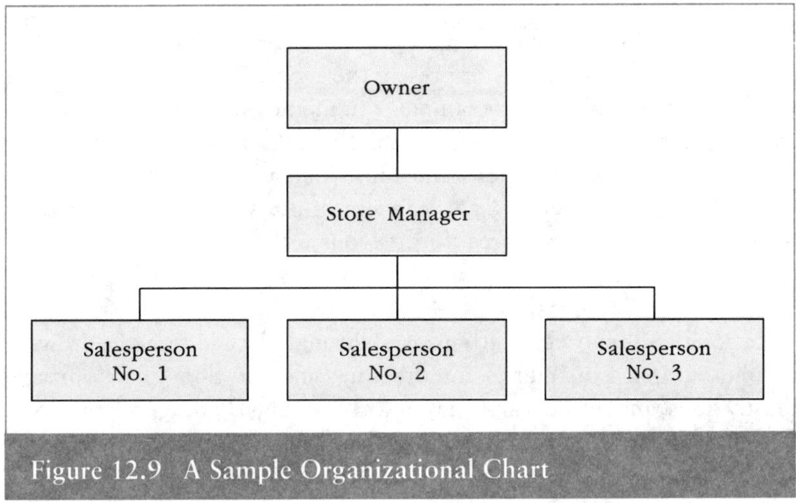

Figure 12.9 A Sample Organizational Chart

- a diagram of how low morale affects absenteeism and turnover
- a diagram of the steps in MicroChip's current grievance procedure
- a chart of the most common reasons for employees quitting their jobs at MicroChip.

Here are some additional general guidelines for preparing charts and diagrams that can enhance your written presentation by summarizing potentially unclear information:

Guidelines for preparing a chart or diagram

1. Keep the chart or diagram as simple as possible. Don't slow your readers down by forcing them to spend unnecessary time trying to understand your drawing.
2. Label each important part of a chart or diagram in capital letters.
3. If you are diagramming a process, show arrows between steps or stages in the process. Arrows will help readers follow the process itself.
4. Give the chart or diagram a number and a title. Place this information with the drawing (for example: Figure 1. Steps in Computing Compound Interest).
5. Place the chart or diagram on the page as you would a table. Introduce it, present it, and then interpret it.
6. Don't rule out the use of colour. If you only have one copy of the report to prepare, it is easy to add colour, which itself adds clarity, understanding, and interest.

Maps

Maps are used less frequently than graphs, charts, and diagrams. However, maps are a logical way to present the geographical distribution of a variety of information. For example, you might use a map of Canada to show a company's dollar sales in each province. You might also break the map into territories or regions and show increases or decreases in sales for each region. Generally, you can use any map of a city, province, region, country, or larger area if it fits your report material.

Drawings and Photographs

Drawings and photographs are sometimes useful

Occasionally, a report can be improved through the addition of a drawing or photograph. Possibilities for drawings include floor plans, artistic illustrations, and medical and anatomical drawings. Photographs are used for much the same purpose but add realism and precision. Both drawings and photographs can, of course, be presented in colour.

Computer-generated Graphics

As business increasingly relies on computers for text editing and data analysis, it will also integrate special graphics tools. Besides saving time and money, computer-generated graphics are also available in colours.

The report writer can now process, examine, and manipulate the data; prepare and edit the text; and design the maps, graphics, and drawings — all at the same computer terminal. Of course, some reports may contain illustrations prepared by someone other than the writer.

As more and more writers turn to microcomputers to generate their reports, they are likely to incorporate computer-generated graphics, which are created in four ways: from statistical packages, from spreadsheets, from graphics packages, and from packages that are combinations of other packages.

Statistical and spreadsheet software packages designed primarily to analyze data usually include some elementary graphics capability such as line and bar graphs. These figures, although almost primitive by today's graphics standards, still can quickly show numerical relationships. Although some packages will support colour output, most are limited to a single colour. Differences in data on a bar chart, for example, have to be shown with black-and-white patterns (see Figures 12.6 and 12.7).

The major value of graphics prepared by statistical and spreadsheet programs is their analytical contribution. They are usually not destined for finished reports. The outputs from graphics and combination programs, however, have presentation as their focus.

Acknowledging Sources of Information

You must acknowledge all material that is not your own

In a business report, as with any writing, you must acknowledge any information obtained from someone else, rather than claiming it for yourself by omitting the name of your source or leaving it to the reader to guess its origin. In formal reports, this acknowledgement can appear in one of these ways:

- as footnotes at the bottom of the page
- as endnotes at the end of the text
- as author-date references right in the text

Although endnotes properly belong with the supplementary part of the report, all ways of referencing sources will be discussed here.

Uses of Footnotes and Endnotes. Footnotes and endnotes are used to:

- document the source of direct quotations
- document the source of paraphrased data
- define terms
- refer to other sources or other sections of the report
- explain or elaborate a point
- explain specific tools, methods, or testing procedures
- provide supporting statistics or back-up data (brief)
- explain variables or conflicts in the data
- acknowledge assistance or support

Footnotes are the traditional method of attribution

Footnotes. The traditional footnoting approach is becoming less popular; however, you should be familiar with it. With this approach, you place a number at the end of the information you are citing; the footnote itself goes at the bottom of the same page. The number in the text is raised half a line and therefore is called a superscript. The first citation is number one, the next number two, and so on sequentially throughout the report.

Any information taken from someone else — both direct quotes and the paraphrasing of ideas — receives a number. Thus, one entire paragraph may be attributed to one author. On the other hand, one paragraph may include the ideas from a variety of sources, each of which must be cited. It's even possible for a single sentence to have several footnotes:

Many experts in finance agree with the point we have been discussing. Included in this group are Lewis,[1] Jones,[2] Harris,[3] and McWilliams.[4]

Each time you use someone else's information you need a footnote, even if you have cited that author earlier in the report. The second reference to a source can be abbreviated to include only the author's surname and pertinent page numbers.

As you have probably learned by now, footnoting is precise and

Footnoting can follow several accepted styles

sometimes tedious. You must use an accepted style that accommodates such variables as the number of authors and the type of publication (a book, an article in a periodical, a brochure, a newspaper article, and so on). Because footnoting styles vary, because it takes an entire manual to cover all possible formats, and because your organization may tell you which style to apply, the following examples present only nine footnotes that show the most-used variables. These samples follow the style suggested in *The Chicago Manual of Style*, 13th ed. The first six samples are for books and show various numbers of authors. (The works listed are worth noting since they all focus on footnoting style.) The last three footnotes illustrate citations of a magazine, a brochure, and a newspaper, respectively.

1 Charles T. Brusaw, Gerald J. Alred, and Walter E. Oliu, *The Business Writer's Handbook,* 2nd ed. (New York: St. Martin's Press, 1982), 215–20.

2 Arno F. Knapper and Loda I. Newcomb, *Style Manual for Written Communication,* 2nd ed. (Columbus, Ohio: Grid Publishing, Inc., 1983), 32–38.

3 Ruth Moyer, Eleanour Stevens, and Ralph Switzer, *The Research and Report Handbook* (New York: John Wiley & Sons, 1981), 123–68.

4 Kate L. Turabian, *Student's Guide for Writing College Papers,* 3rd ed. (Chicago: University of Chicago Press, 1976), 33.

5 *The Chicago Manual of Style,* 13th ed. (Chicago: University of Chicago Press, 1982), 485*ff.*

6 *The MLA Handbook for Writers of Research Papers, Theses, and Dissertations* (New York: Modern Language Association, 1977), 50.

7 David Gabel, "Word Processing for Personal Computers," *Personal Computing,* August 1982, 82–106.

8 *The Revolution in Software* (Berkeley, Calif.: Perfect Software, 1982), 3.

9 James A. White, "Design, Sales Strategy Help Make IBM's Personal Computer a Big Hit," *The Wall Street Journal,* southwestern edition, 15 December 1982, 33.

The footnoting approach to citation is one of the most efficient methods for the reader. Since the references are in the text itself, the reader has only to look to the bottom of the page for the information. With the advent of word processing, placing footnotes in the correct location has become automatic. *Endnotes* take the same format as footnotes; however, they are grouped at the end of the text.

Author-date citations eliminate citation numbers in the text

In-Text Citations. The second style of formal attribution is quite different. It tends to be used in academic writing, has many variations, and is rapidly gaining popularity, even in business. Its main advantage is that it eliminates the footnoting process entirely, yet delivers the information required for appropriate acknowledgement.

With this technique, wherever acknowledgement is necessary in the text, you present not a number but the author's last name, the year of the publication, and, if appropriate, specific page numbers. The citation style is the same whether the source is an article, a book, or an interview; the only exception is a work whose author is not known — then you substitute the publication name.

Here is some sample text that uses the author-date citation style. Note that the author's name may be part of the sentence.

As we continue to examine the effect of increased production on job satisfaction, we must consider classical management theory. Smith (1967, p. 307), for example, feels that production is all-important. Several other authorities agree with Smith (see, for example, McWilliams, 1956; Lewis, 1961; McAllister, 1967; Harris and Woffort, 1971; or Graber *et al.*, 1981). Probably the most sweeping comment from the opposing view is: "Smith and her cronies are absolutely wrong! Job satisfaction is so much more important than production that it can't even be mentioned in the same breath!" (Horvath, 1983, p. 227).

When readers come across an author-date citation, they have only to refer to the bibliography to locate complete information about the source. Thus, to find the Smith, 1967, citation, you move down the bibliography alphabetically until you locate Smith. If the bibliography contains several works by Smith, you can tell which one is referred to here by matching the dates of publication.

A bibliography for use with author-date citations is prepared like a standard bibliography but it is often called References or Works Cited, instead of Bibliography. The sample report at the end of this chapter uses this style of formal attribution.

Four reference styles are widely used: the University of Chicago style, the American Psychological Association style, the Modern Language Association style, and that of Turabian. Figure 12.10 illustrates these four for both footnotes and bibliography entries.

Step 2: Preparing the Supplementary Parts

Now that the writing and appearance of the text of the formal business report have been discussed, it is time to move to the supplementary parts. (Theoretically you could do the preliminary parts next, but you need to know the page numbers of the concluding elements in order to list them in the table of contents.) A formal business report may include many kinds

	Notes	Bibliography
University of Chicago Style	1. Richard C. Huseman, James M. Lahiff, and John M. Penrose, *Business Communication: Strategies and Skills*, 3d ed. (Hinsdale, III.: Dryden Press, 1988), 250.	Huseman, Richard C., James M. Lahiff, and John M. Penrose. *Business Communication: Strategies and Skills.* 3d ed. Hinsdale, III.: Dryden Press, 1988.
American Psychological Association Style	Huseman, R. C., Lahiff, J. M., & Penrose, J. M. 1988. *Business Communication: Strategies and Skills* (3rd ed.). Hinsdale, Illinois: Dryden Press.	Huseman, R. C., Lahiff, J. M., & Penrose, J. M. (1988). *Business Communication: Strategies and Skills* (3rd ed.). Hinsdale, Illinois: Dryden Press.
Modern Language Association Style	[1]Richard C. Huseman, James M. Lahiff, & John M. Penrose, *Business Communication: Strategies and Skills*, 3rd ed. (Hinsdale, Illinois: Dryden Press, 1988) 250.	Huseman, Richard C., James M. Lahiff, and John M. Penrose. *Business Communication: Strategies and Skills.* 3rd ed. Hinsdale, Illinois: Dryden Press, 1988.
Turabian Style	[1]Richard C. Huseman, James M. Lahiff, and John M. Penrose, *Business Communication: Strategies and Skills* (3d ed.; Hinsdale, Illinois: Dryden Press, 1988), p. 250.	Huseman, Richard C., James M. Lahiff, and John M. Penrose. *Business Communication: Strategies and Skills.* 3d ed. Hinsdale, Illinois: Dryden Press, 1988.

Figure 12.10 Note and Bibliography Entry Styles[2]

of supplementary parts; the most common are endnotes, bibliography, appendices, and index.

Use an endnote section if your citations require it

Endnotes. As previously discussed, endnotes are footnotes placed separately following the text. If you use this section, it is titled Endnotes or Notes and contains each of your notes in order of appearance in the report.

Your bibliography may show sources you do not cite

Bibliography. The bibliography is a list of the sources you consulted in preparing your report, including any you may not actually cite. Since the bibliography is designed to assist your reader should additional information be needed, going beyond the sources cited can be valuable. If, however, you do cite all the sources in it, the bibliography becomes a list of references.

Whether you use a bibliography or list of references, you can list your sources alphabetically either under one heading or under several subheadings. Using subheadings, you can classify your sources by types (such as books, periodicals, and government publications) or divide them into a few — say, two or three — major topics. The title of this part of your report may be Bibliography, References, or List of References.

Put useful but tangential material in appendices

Appendices. An appendix contains material that is useful to the report but not essential and might slow the reader if it appears in the text. Among the items you would include in an appendix are long quotations; details of an experiment; statistical or other measurements; complex formulas; copies of regulations, policies, laws, or bylaws; interview questions and responses; sample questionnaires and tabulated responses; sample tests and tabulated results; photographs, maps, or other visuals longer than one full page; and related correspondence.

In a formal report, each appendix is preceded by a title page that contains the label and title of the appendix. Appendices are labelled by letters starting with A, and placed in the order of their discussion in the text. Their location is identified in a table of contents; cross-references in the text read "see Appendix A," for example.

Index. Used only in lengthy reports, the index is an alphabetical list of key topics in the report with page number(s) for each entry. The index to this book is an example of a format you can follow.

Step 3: Preparing the Preliminary Parts

The preliminary parts always include a title page and a table of contents

The preliminary parts of a report may include a variety of items; generally, the more formal the report, the more items are included. The inclusion of some items, however, depends on the content of the report — obviously, a list of tables is used only when there are tables. The following list, although not exhaustive, includes most of the formal preliminary parts: title fly, title page, authorization document, transmittal document, table of contents, list of tables, list of figures (or illustrations), and informative summary.

Title Fly. An optional part used in especially formal reports, the title fly contains only the title of the report. That title should be brief yet descriptive and should indicate either the depth or the objective of the report.

Title Page. Most business reports contain a title page. It should include at least the following information: the report title, the person(s) for whom the report was prepared (perhaps with their titles), the author of the report (perhaps with his or her title), and the date (including the year).

Authorization Document. If your report was authorized in writing, a copy of that letter or memo should accompany the report. Showing this authorization can add credibility to your work. This document is likely to be found in more formal reports.

Authorization and transmittal documents usually balance each other

Transmittal Document. Also likely to be seen in more formal reports is the transmittal document. This document — a letter or memo — transfers the report to the reader. The recipient of the report is likely to be the author of the authorization document; the author of the transmittal document (and the report) is probably the person authorized to do the report. Thus, these two items are closely related.

Your transmittal document should include

1. the transmittal itself (first paragraph)
2. an overview of the report (second paragraph)
3. optional acknowledgements to other people who assisted you in preparing the report (third paragraph)
4. a courteous closing, in which you might tell what needs to be done next, express your pleasure at being able to provide the information in the report, or indicate your willingness to discuss the report in more detail (fourth paragraph)

Table of Contents. A required part of a formal report, the table of contents lists the divisions of the report, including preliminaries such as a list of tables and supplementary parts, such as your bibliography, as well as the first- and second-level headings in the text.

The table of contents page(s) is titled Contents and usually employs dots that lead the readers' eyes across to the page numbers. All items, except the title fly, the title page, and the table of contents itself, are listed. It does not, however, include tables or figures; these are identified on separate pages.

If your report has any tables or figures, you need lists of them in your preliminaries

List of Tables. If your report includes tables, a list of tables is required as a separate page, following the table of contents. This is the case even if you have only one table. The list shows the number and title of each table and the page where it is located. Title this page List of Tables.

List of Figures. A list of figures is required if you have figures in your report. Arrange the list of figures in order of appearance in the report;

you need not divide them by types (graphs, charts, maps). The format of the list should be identical to that used for the list of tables. Remember, however, that each of these lists should appear on a separate page.

When appropriate, the title may be List of Illustrations, rather than List of Figures, but the same rules apply.

Informative Summary. The informative summary, which may also be called Synopsis, or Executive Summary, provides your reader with a summary of the entire text. More and more managers are demanding such summaries on all the reports they receive. These summaries should summarize the entire report for the busy executive who wants an overview that can be read in less than five minutes.

Informative summaries are generally about one tenth the length of the report, and no longer than two or three pages, even for very long documents. However, the length varies with the complexity of the research and the report as well as with the reader's knowledge of the material and the research being conducted. Summaries may include the main headings of the report so that the reader can find and read a single section if necessary. The sample report at the end of the chapter contains an informative summary with captions (headings on the left margin) for easy reference.

In writing your summary, include some depth. Do not say, "Next we gathered some data and then analyzed them." Instead give the reader a description with details, such as, " Data were gathered by distributing an anonymous questionnaire by mail to 400 randomly selected employees. Of the 273 questionnaires returned, 60 percent were from office employees and 40 percent from the warehouse staff."

Packaging the Final Product

Now you are ready to put the report together in the order shown earlier in this chapter.

A few additional instructions may help your writing and typing of the report.

Pagination. Knowing when, where, and which type of number to place on a page is often a problem. Here are some guidelines:

Guidelines for paging

- The preliminary parts are numbered with lower-case Roman numerals. Count every page, but start showing page numbers only with the table of contents. Thus, if the table of contents is the fifth page (after the title fly, the title page, the authorization document, and the transmittal document, each of which was counted but not numbered), it is given the number *v*. Centre the number at the bottom of the page. The rest of the preliminary pages are numbered in a similar fashion.

- The first page of the body is numbered with an Arabic number, centred, at the bottom.
- All pages after page 1 are numbered at the top of the page, either at the centre or in the right corner. Be consistent: if you centre one page number, for example, centre them all.
- Many people think it is tidier not to add any punctuation or words to the page number. For example, they use just the number 2, not Page 2, -2-, 2., two, or "2".

Spacing. Many business reports are a combination of single and double spacing. Footnotes, for example, are single-spaced with a space between each citation. The text of the report may be either single- or double-spaced, but must be consistently one or the other. Double-spacing the text leaves space for comments between the lines. It also uses more paper, a factor that may be important if many copies of your report will be duplicated. Single-spacing the text is space-efficient and adds an air of formality and precision. Moreover, some people find single-spaced documents easier to read.

Many organizations have standard formats for their reports. You may be told which spacing is desired.

Cover. Often you will want to package your completed report in a binder or with a special cover. Your organization may have printed covers for all reports. Covers can add uniformity, protection, and attractiveness.

Alternative styles exist

"Correct" procedures. This chapter has frequently stated that two or more approaches are acceptable or correct. Authorities do not always agree and organizations may seek different goals with their reports. Knowledge of these different views may be of value:

- The bibliography is sometimes the first item of the supplementary parts.
- The informative summary or abstract is sometimes placed before the table of contents.
- Other formats for headings exist. For example, you can use numbers — with or without a following phrase — such as 1.3.4, and 7.5.1 — for headings. This numerical approach is most common in very formal, and in governmental, reports but may, of course, be used in other situations. Whichever format you choose, use it consistently throughout the report.
- The informative summary is sometimes double-spaced, even if the text is single-spaced.

- The table of contents does not always have leader lines. It occasionally shows third- or even fourth-level headings; the page numbers for these additional levels may or may not be presented.
- There are several approaches to pagination other than the one described above, although they are less often used.

In summary, phase 2 of preparing a formal report involves writing the text parts and packaging the final product. Here's a checklist for phase 2 (writing):

Checklist for Writing the Formal Report

____1. Characteristics
  ____a. Readable?
  ____b Tactful?
  ____c. Personal?
  ____d. Mechanically sound?
  ____e. Active?
  ____f. Unified?
  ____g. Coherent?
  ____h. Clear?
  ____i. Concise?
  ____j. Positive?
____2. Headings throughout?
____3. Tables prepared and properly placed?
____4. Figures prepared and properly placed?
____5. Packaged?
  ____a. All necessary parts included?
  ____b. Parts in proper order?
  ____c. All pages numbered properly?

Summary

- Formal business reports contribute to decision making by
  - ❑ informing
  - ❑ interpreting
  - ❑ analyzing
- Writing formal reports requires six distinct activities:
  - ❑ determine your purpose
  - ❑ consider your audience
  - ❑ analyze the problem
  - ❑ conduct your research
  - ❑ evaluate your results
  - ❑ prepare your outline

- Primary research sources include
  - questionnaires
  - experiments
  - interviews
  - personal observations
  - organization files
- Secondary research sources include
  - newspapers
  - government documents
  - books
  - magazines
  - pamphlets
- You can organize your information in several ways
  - chronological order
  - topical order
  - problem-solving order
- Once you've collected your data, you can write the main parts of the report:
  - introduction
  - body
  - conclusions
  - recommendations
  - summary
- The supplementary parts are prepared last.

Review Questions

1. What are the purposes of a formal report in business?
2. Describe the various primary and secondary sources you might use in preparing a formal report.
3. When should you use the indirect-order arrangement in presenting the introduction, body, and conclusion of your report? The direct-order arrangement?
4. Describe three ways of outlining the body of a formal report.
5. Describe the importance of comparisons and of trends in using graphs.
6. How do you number pages in a formal report?
7. Differentiate between:
   a. a bibliography and a list of references
   b. a cover page and a title page
   c. an authorization document and a transmittal document.

Activities

1. Develop your outlining skills by practising with that old standard topic, "What I Did on My Summer Vacation." Outline the body of a report on it in three ways: (a) chronologically, (b) topically, (c) problem-solving order. Use at least three levels of headings in each outline.

2. In its application for provincial funds for the 1981/82 academic year, York University reported "full-time equivalent" numbers of undergraduate and professional students as follows: Faculty of Arts, 6724; Atkinson College (part-time, mature students), 3724; Faculty of Fine Arts, 932; Osgoode Law School, 939; Faculty of Science, 1219. In 82/83 the figures were Arts, 6462; Atkinson, 3685; Fine Arts, 939; Osgoode, 951; Science, 1102. For 1983/84, the breakdown was Arts, 6341; Atkinson 3651; Fine Arts, 955; Osgoode, 963; Science, 1053. The report for 1984/85 showed Arts, 6756; Atkinson, 3757; Fine Arts, 955; Osgoode, 981; Science, 1776. Finally, the 1985/86 numbers were Arts, 7652; Atkinson, 3996; Fine Arts, 1049; Osgoode, 994; Science, 1299.

   Use the information to create a table for a formal report. Introduce the table, present it, and interpret it.

3. Using the information from your table for Activity 2:
   a. Draw a line graph (or graphs) containing all the information.
   b. Draw a bar graph showing breakdowns by faculty.
   c. Draw a pie graph showing the breakdown by faculty for 1980/81.

4. Write a formal report.[3] Select a problem or situation that needs improving. Choose one that is related to your work or, if you do not have a part-time or full-time job, one from your home, church, club, or municipal government. Prepare a report to be sent to the appropriate person because he or she has asked you to analyze and research the problem and prepare a report with recommendations for improvements or solutions.

   Use as many sources as you can to get information for your report. Try to use some primary sources, at least in the form of interviews and discussions with others involved in the situation. Reading some of the appropriate history, records, or minutes may also be useful.

   Package your report using as many of the parts of the report as possible. While your report may have all the parts, it need not be long. Write only what's needed to report the problem, your findings, and your recommendations. Remember the characteristics of effective written communication and reporting.

Discussion Cases

Breaking the Lockstep[4]

Curriculum development is a controversial topic in many schools. Administration and faculty members devote much time and energy to developing the curriculum, but the results rarely satisfy everyone.

You attend Prairie University, where students must take many required courses. The program, known as the lockstep sequence, has been the subject of many student complaints. Most students believe that the program should be more flexible and that students should be allowed to select more of their courses.

Prairie University has decided to seek ideas from the students regarding possible changes in the program. The idea of allowing students to structure more of their program is under consideration. You have been appointed to the program evaluation committee, a group assembled to provide student input on this matter.

As a member of the program evaluation committee, you must select eight courses you believe would make up a good program for you. Prepare a report to be sent to the chairperson of the program evaluation committee. In this report describe eight specific courses and your rationale for including each one. Indicate what you consider to be the goal of your program and how each course contributes to that goal.

Use as many sources as possible to get the information necessary for this report. Interview professors, administrators, and other students. Perhaps someone in a field in which you hope to work would have some insights on the subject. Also, review the catalogues of other colleges and universities, which may be available in your library. Use your imagination in developing your program. The courses that you suggest need not be presently available at your school.

Case Questions

1. Why did you organize your report the way you did?
2. Describe one other way in which you might have organized it.

Planning the Report[5]

Sally Dixon is in her final year at business college. During the past two years she has worked part-time at the local gymnasium and community centre, making appointments and scheduling classes conducted at the centre. She enjoys working there but believes the management group is not very dynamic and does not take enough opportunities to promote the centre's programs.

Recently Sally heard that the activities co-ordinator would be leaving at the end of the year. Sally would like to land the position and believes that, with the combination of her practical work experience and her business knowledge, she would make an excellent activities co-ordinator. She realizes that, although the management group is pleased with her work, they would need more proof of her business ability if they were to consider her for the position of activities co-ordinator.

One evening, when she arrived home, she found a letter from her dentist reminding her of a dental checkup. This started her thinking about a promotional campaign for the community centre where each participant could be contacted a short time after completing a class and advised of future activities at the centre. This campaign would mean setting up a new recordkeeping system, but she believed that the extra business the centre would obtain would far outweigh any cost.

Sally decided this was her chance to show the management group that she could apply her study of business systems and marketing in a very practical way. She thought the best approach would be to present the proposal to the management group in a report.

Case Questions

1. What will be the purpose of the report?
2. What aspects of the receivers will Sally have to consider?
3. What information must Sally collect for her report? Where will she get it?
4. In outlining the report, which order do you think Sally should choose? Give the reasons for your choice.

Appendix — A Sample Formal Report

The following pages contain a complete business report that illustrates the principles discussed in this chapter. It includes most of the parts of a formal report; of the preliminary and supplementary parts, only the index — exemplified at the end of this book — is omitted.

Careful examination of the writing tone as well as the appearance of the items will guide you in the preparation of your own formal reports.

EMPLOYEE RELATIONS PROBLEMS AT MICROCHIP ELECTRONICS:

NATURE, CAUSES, AND SOLUTIONS

The title fly contains only the title of the report

Aside from the title, the title page includes the name(s) of the person(s) who prepared the report and those who will receive it, along with the submission date

EMPLOYEE RELATIONS PROBLEMS
AT MICROCHIP ELECTRONICS:

NATURE, CAUSES, AND SOLUTIONS

Prepared for
Scott Millan, Personnel Director
MicroChip Electronics

by

Stephanie McQuiston, Personnel Assistant

January 30, 1992

MicroChip Electronics, Ltd.
900 West Georgia St.
Vancouver, B.C. V6C 1T9

TO: Stephanie McQuiston, Personnel Assistant
FROM: Scott Millan, Personnel Director
DATE: November 18, 1991
SUBJECT: Employee Relations Study and Report

As explained in our conversation this morning, I am directing you to research, analyze, and report on the current level of employee relations at MicroChip Electronics. As members of the Personnel Office, we know that an increasing number of grievances have been reported to us, and that the company grapevine is carrying more negative information than usual.

Brief statement of the problem

You are to conduct research, both formal and informal, to appraise the employee relations situation. If the situation warrants, analyze solutions to our problem and propose them to me.

Terms of reference

This matter is of major and immediate concern. Therefore, I need your report by the end of January. You have a budget of $10 000 for supplies and can use the steno pool for duplication needs. Bill Parsons, the new management trainee, is assigned to you for this project.

Budget for the project

Do let me know if you encounter problems or have questions.

MicroChip Electronics, Ltd.
900 West Georgia St.
Vancouver, B.C. V6C 1T9

January 30, 1992

Mr. Scott Millan
Personnel Director
MicroChip Electronics
P.O. Box 138
Vancouver, B.C.
V5G 1E9

Dear Mr. Millan:

Reference to the authorization

Brief statement of the report's purpose

Here is the report prepared as you directed me by memo on November 18, 1991. The report researches employee relations problems at MicroChip Electronics, examines those problems, looks at solutions, and proposes specific actions.

Overview of key findings

You will find that our employee relations problem is more serious than you apparently thought when we discussed this project last November. You'll want to pay particular attention to the implementation sections of the report for ways to overcome these problems.

Friendly close

This has been a most interesting project. I'll be pleased to discuss it with you, at your request.

Sincerely,

Stephanie McQuiston

Stephanie McQuiston
Personnel Assistant

iv

CONTENTS

The table of contents should have at least two levels of headings

LIST OF TABLES

The list of tables has its own page

The list of figures also has its own page

LIST OF FIGURES

INFORMATIVE SUMMARY

INTRODUCTION MicroChip Electronics is experiencing deteriorating employee relations as shown by increased grievances and turnover rates. Therefore, Scott Millan has directed me to report on the employee relations problems and recommend a plan of action to correct them.

Using the headings from the report helps to orient the reader to the structure of the complete report

CONCLUSIONS My investigation revealed that deteriorating employee relations are producing more grievances, absenteeism, and turnover, along with low morale and talk of unionization. These problems are caused by major concerns about intangible and tangible rewards.

Give specific data in your summary

RECOMMENDATIONS

1. Improve the work environment by improving jobs, feedback, and pay and benefits for employees.

2. Implement these solutions immediately by hiring Felix Graham and Associates, introducing job rotation, and beginning supervisory training.

3. Follow up with employee and industry surveys.

HISTORY The success of the electronics industry has been due, in part, to the positive employee relations that have existed. The literature supports this view: companies benefit when relations with their employees are good. On the other hand, labour unrest can have negative consequences such as reduced production and unionization.

– 2 –

NATURE OF PROBLEM	Employee relations at MicroChip Electronics are deteriorating: 1. the number of grievances has nearly doubled in the past three years 2. the annual turnover rate has risen from 2 percent in 1979 to 25 percent in 1990 3. the absenteeism rate has increased more than 600 percent since 1983 4. a survey of employees has revealed that morale is poor 5. employees are beginning to talk about forming a union.
CAUSE OF PROBLEM	Employees surveyed reported that they are dissatisfied with their pay and benefit package, the work they do, and the feedback they receive. They also feel the quality of supervision they receive is unacceptable.
SOLUTIONS TO PROBLEM	We can improve intangible rewards for employees by: • making jobs more challenging by providing job enrichment and job rotation • improving feedback through performance reviews, team meetings, and informal feedback Supervisors would be responsible for rotating jobs within their own departments. To help them develop the skills they'll need, we can • hire Felix Graham and Associates to help us design and implement a job enrichment scheme

- 3 -

- have Carrie Lewis, our industrial psychologist, design and give a supervisors' training program

We can improve tangible rewards for employees by:

- increasing the average rate of pay for hourly workers from $10.45 to $11.05 (industry wage)
- adding a dental plan to our benefits package for both salaried and hourly workers

To ensure that employee relations continue to improve, we'll need to monitor the results of these programs regularly.

INTRODUCTION

MicroChip Electronics is a young company, yet a successful one. In the thirteen years MicroChip has existed, it has grown from 20 to 300 employees. Although employee relations for the first five years were excellent, rapid expansion of the company has taken its toll. We are experiencing increased grievances and turnover rates, which seem to indicate that employee relations are deteriorating.

The introduction should include background information, a purpose statement, and a statement outlining the scope of the report

The purpose of this report is to study employee relations problems at MicroChip Electronics and recommend a plan of action that will produce a positive and satisfying work environment for our employees.

The report argues the case for positive employee relations, examines the extent of the problem at MicroChip, and recommends immediate action to solve the employee relations problem.

CONCLUSIONS

MicroChip Electronics has a history of good employee relations. However, the rapid growth that MicroChip Electronics has experienced in the past few years has adversely affected employee relations as evidenced by

Conclusions should follow logically from the discussion

Recommendations should be listed and numbered for easy reference

– 4 –

problems with grievances, absenteeism, morale, and discussion of unionization. These symptoms, our employee survey determined, are related to major concerns about intangible and tangible rewards. To regain our former closeness and team spirit, we need to improve the employees' jobs, provide more feedback, and increase their pay and benefits. To guide us in this implementation, we need expertise not available within the organization.

The cost of achieving positive employee relations will be high in dollars, time, and effort. However, we can recover some of these costs if we reduce grievances, turnover, and absenteeism.

RECOMMENDATIONS

I recommend that MicroChip Electronics

1. improve the employees' work environment by:
   - improving jobs through job enrichment and rotation
   - improving feedback to employees
   - increasing our pay and benefits package to the industry average

2. take action to implement these solutions immediately by:
   - hiring Felix Graham and Associates to design and implement a job enrichment program
   - beginning a job rotation system
   - having Carrie Lewis begin a supervisory training program

3. monitor changes in employee relations by:
   - surveying employees regularly
   - reviewing industry pay and benefits packages annually.

HISTORY OF EMPLOYEE RELATIONS IN THE ELECTRONICS INDUSTRY

Almost since its inception, the electronics industry has been characterized by positive employee relations. One authority has gone so far as to say that the electronics industry in the past fifteen years has led the country in positive employee relations (Harris, 1985). An examination of employee relations in the industry breaks down into the effects of good employee relations and the consequences of poor employee relations.

Effects of Good Relations

A company that has good relationships with its employees benefits both directly and indirectly. Direct results include higher-quality products (Harris, 1985), harder work by employees (Rosenblum, 1985), fewer injuries and days lost (Quillan and Quillan, 1987), and less absenteeism and tardiness (Rosenblum, 1985). Positive employee relationships also lead to indirect benefits: cleaner work areas (Rosenblum, 1985), happier, friendlier, more energetic employees (Smith, 1983), and lower turnover rates (Harris, 1985).

The APA Style for documenting sources uses author name and year to designate the source

Although the area between direct and indirect rewards is a grey one, and although other benefits were not mentioned, the point is clear: companies benefit when relations with their employees are good.

Consequences of Poor Relations

When a company does not have good relations with its employees, it not only loses the positive benefits discussed above, but also suffers negative consequences. Included among these are employee-family problems, poor public image (Gonzalez, 1983), sabotage of facilities (Lewis et al., 1987), leakage of corporate secrets (Armstrong, 1987), and the likelihood of labour/management distrust and alienation (Rosenblum, 1985). This distrust and alienation breaks down the existing channels of communication and, if no union exists, one is likely to see movement towards unionization.

THE NATURE OF THE EMPLOYEE RELATIONS PROBLEM

MicroChip Electronics has already experienced some of the negative consequences described above: the number of grievances has increased dramatically: turnover rates are excessive; absenteeism is unacceptably high; employee morale is low; and unionization appears imminent.

Increased Grievances

The Personnel Department handles all formal employee grievances. In addition to either acting on the grievance or forwarding it to the appropriate person, the personnel staff assign the following grievance codes:

02 an important and legitimate grievance
01 a neutral or unimportant grievance
00 a pointless or illogical grievance

The staff admit that this system is extremely subjective and add that they have coded grievances for only three years. However, during that time, the total number of grievances has increased from 35 in 1988 to 47 in 1989 to 69 this year. The proportion of each classification has remained the same for the three years: 75 percent have a 02 classification; 15 percent, a 01 classification; and 10 percent, a 00 classification

Excessive Turnover

President Rasnor has always been concerned with good employee relations. Since 1979, when he founded the company, he has maintained turnover rate records. A review of his records shows that three major clusters of annual turnover rates exist:

1. from 1979 to 1983, the turnover rate was a mere 2 percent
2. from 1984 to 1987, the rate rose to 10 percent, but this level was not considered excessive
3. from 1988 to 1990, the turnover rate has risen to 25 percent.

This dramatic rise in turnover rate coincides with the rapid growth of the company. In 1984, MicroChip had 100 employees. Today, the company has nearly 300 employees.

Knowing the turnover rate is not enough. We also need to know why people are choosing to work elsewhere. From records of separation interviews, I found that nearly three quarters of employees said they were leaving for one of three reasons: greater challenge, higher pay, or more opportunity for promotion. Figure 1 on the next page summarizes the reasons employees give for leaving MicroChip Electronics.

- 7 -

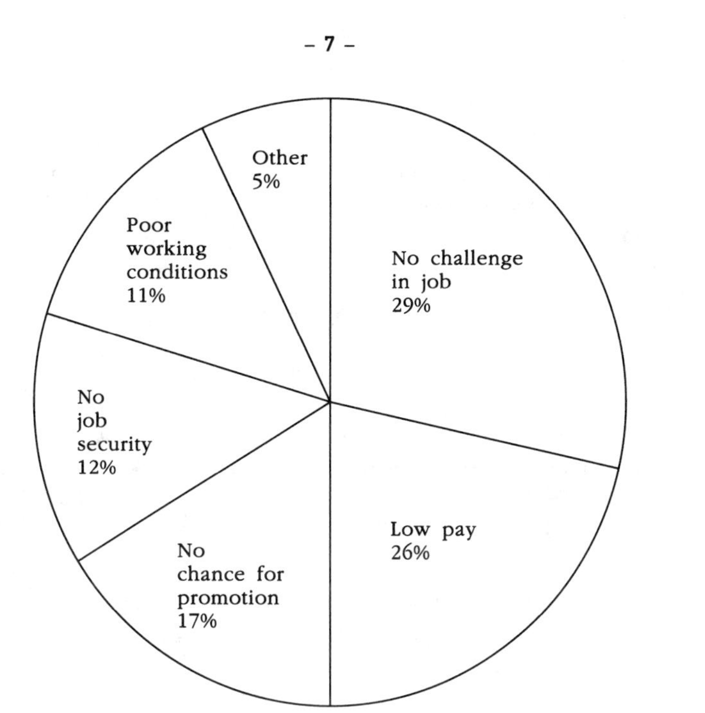

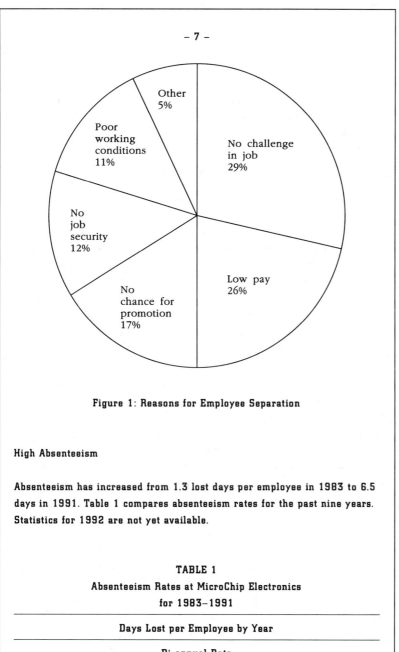

Figure 1: Reasons for Employee Separation

High Absenteeism

Absenteeism has increased from 1.3 lost days per employee in 1983 to 6.5 days in 1991. Table 1 compares absenteeism rates for the past nine years. Statistics for 1992 are not yet available.

TABLE 1
Absenteeism Rates at MicroChip Electronics
for 1983–1991

Days Lost per Employee by Year				
		Bi-annual Rate		
1983	1985	1987	1989	1991
1.3	2.7	3.5	5.8	6.5

Low Morale

To determine the current level of employee morale as well as causes for employee unrest, I surveyed a random sample of 75 employees or 25 percent of the workforce.

Method

I had the Personnel staff run a random number generator on the computerized payroll files to obtain a list of 75 employees for the survey. This procedure ensured that I obtained a random sample. Surveys were mailed to employees' homes.

Return Rate

Of the 75 surveys distributed, 62 were returned completed, 2 were returned by the post office undelivered, and 1 was returned uncompleted. The ratio of completed surveys to delivered surveys (62/73) was 85 percent. This high rate was attributed to the stamped, addressed return envelope; the survey anonymity; and reader interest in the topic.

When respondents were asked to rate the overall level of their morale on a scale of 1 to 5, with 1 being the lowest possible rating, the mean for all respondents was 1.8. Since a rating lower than 3.5, the midpoint on the scale, indicates low morale, this figure merits serious consideration.

Talk of Unionization

Although many electronics companies are unionized, MicroChip employees have never proposed unionization. However, in response to an open-ended question on the employee morale survey, 13 respondents mentioned unionization as the best way to improve working conditions and morale. Two respondents stated that they have talked with representatives of a major international union.

CAUSES OF POOR EMPLOYEE RELATIONS

In the survey discussed earlier, employees identified two major causes of low morale: inadequate employee rewards and poor supervisory methods.

Inadequate Employee Rewards

Question 2 asked respondents who rated their morale at less than 3 on the five-point scale to check all items on a ten-item list that they felt contributed to their dissatisfaction on the job. Of the ten items, three were checked by more than 75 percent of the respondents:

1. pay and benefits unsatisfactory, 71%
2. work not satisfying, 57%
3. feedback about performance lacking, 51%

Poor Supervisory Methods

The survey also uncovered two items of major concern about supervisory methods: inconsistent application of company policies and procedures, as well as lack of communication between supervisors and workers. In fact, almost 80 percent of respondents cited these items as causes of low morale.

These survey results show that, although pay and benefits are low, nonmonetary concerns are also important. Money is not the prime motivator; job satisfaction, meaningful feedback, and effective communication are equally important.

SOLUTIONS TO THE EMPLOYEE RELATIONS PROBLEM

Employee concerns of unsatisfactory pay and benefits, unfulfilling work, lack of performance feedback, inconsistent application of company rules, and poor superior/subordinate communication are the causes of MicroChip's employee relations problems. These problems have surfaced in increased numbers of grievances, high turnover, high absenteeism, low morale, and discussion of unionization.

The solution to these employee concerns and, therefore, to the symptoms

- 10 -

of discontent, has two parts. We must improve both the intangible and the tangible rewards that we provide to our employees.

More Intangible Rewards

Intangible rewards are the most important aspect of the solution package. Most of the employees' complaints and concerns uncovered by the employee survey focused on the intangible aspects of their work. This finding is not necessarily unexpected since extensive research has concluded that, once workers' basic needs are met, they quickly turn to other forms of compensation, such as friendly working conditions, praise from supervisors, respect from peers, and so on (Smith, 1983).

To improve intangible rewards on the job, MicroChip needs to:

1. make jobs more challenging by providing job enrichment and job rotation. Rosenblum (1985) surveyed companies who had implemented such schemes and found that their production increased as much as 25 percent in the first year following implementation.

2. improve feedback to workers by having managers implement bi-annual performance reviews, schedule weekly team meetings, and provide informal day-to-day feedback. Although formal feedback sessions can cost thousands of dollars, these costs can be recovered in increased production.

Supervisors at MicroChip have been contemplating a job rotation system for some time. In fact, they have already discussed ways of implementing such a system. They concluded that the system could apply to all employees except those who are classified E-3 (engineering specialists) or higher and those who do not wish to be rotated. They propose that each employee spend at least one week every month in a new job, and at least one week a year in seminars, short courses, and training for jobs other than the one currently held. All supervisors would be responsible for rotating jobs within their own departments.

A first step in improving jobs is to seek counsel on job enrichment strategies. No one in the Personnel Department professes any expertise in job enrichment or formal performance review systems. This void may well be one reason for employee dissatisfaction. I have contacted Felix Graham and Associates, the management consulting firm that MicroChip has retained for the past three years. They are available to help us design and implement a job enrichment scheme.

A second step is to begin supervisory training sessions immediately. They would focus on techniques for giving effective formal and informal feedback. Carrie Lewis, whom we hired a month ago as our industrial psychologist, has expertise in this area and has expressed interest in developing these sessions. Permission would, of course, be required from her supervisor.

More Tangible Rewards

MicroChip Electronics should improve the pay and benefits package employees receive. The survey found that 71 percent of respondents were dissatisfied with their pay and benefits package. Although the survey presents clearcut conclusions about this concern, it does not indicate the amount of improvement needed to reach acceptable levels.

Increased Pay

The average rate of pay at MicroChip Electronics is somewhat lower than the industry average. For hourly employees, the industry average is $11.05 an hour versus our average of $10.45. The rate of pay for salaried employees, on the other hand, compares well with the industry average: the industry average is $33 035 and our average is $32 985.

The electronics industry is highly competitive and is somewhat unusual in that it has several active professional associations in the area. Our employees meet with their peers in other companies and compare their working conditions. Furthermore, they tend to measure their success by how much they're paid. As a result, there is a high level of concern over a relatively minor pay differential. Although pay increases are necessary, the increases need not be great.

– 12 –

Improved Benefits

The situation with fringe benefits parallels that of pay rates: frequent comparisons with peers and personal pride account for much of the employees' concerns. Less than a year ago, an internal report prepared by our personnel staff compared the benefits package at MicroChip to those at three other companies. This report concluded that MicroChip is competitive in all areas except dental care, which is not included in our health insurance package. All of the three companies surveyed had dental plans for their employees. Therefore, we need to consider offering this benefit.

Monitoring Changes in Employee Relations

We must not allow MicroChip Electronics to come this close to disaster again. The solutions outlined above should overcome the current crisis, but we must launch a two-part follow-up system so we will not be caught off guard again. We must:

1. survey employees regularly through formal attitude surveys and informal discussions and interviews

2. review pay and benefits packages in the industry annually to avoid falling behind – or even moving ahead of – industry averages for pay and benefits.

APPENDIX

Each appendix has a separate title page

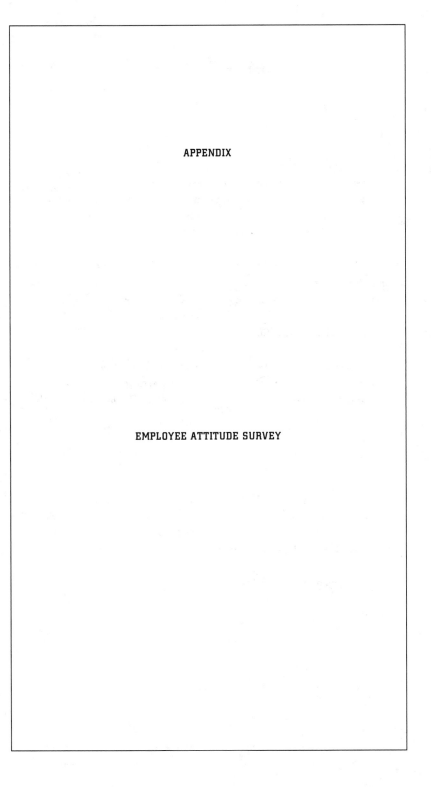

EMPLOYEE ATTITUDE SURVEY

The first paragraph emphasizes importance of completing survey

The second paragraph estimates time required and points out that it will be easy for reader to respond

MicroChip Electronics, Ltd.
900 West Georgia St.
Vancouver, B.C. V6C 1T9

EMPLOYEE ATTITUDE SURVEY

You are being asked to respond to a few questions about MicroChip Electronics. Only 75 of our employees are receiving this survey, so it is important that each is returned; your response reflects the opinions of many of your fellow employees.

Only about one minute of your time is required to complete the four questions. Your name is not needed; we are seeking only aggregate trends among our employees. You may use the stamped, addressed envelope that is enclosed to return your survey, or you may deposit it in any of the company's many suggestion boxes.

The information we receive from this survey will be used to determine employee concerns. In turn, knowing these concerns will direct our attention to improving employee needs and benefits. Thanks for your help.

Stephanie McQuiston
Personnel Assistant

1. Please rate your current morale level on the following scale, which uses a "1" in the lowest possible level and a "5" as the highest possible level. Place a single checkmark in one of the five locations:

   My current morale level is:

   High ______ ______ ______ ______ ______ Low
   5 4 3 2 1

- 2 -

2. Listed below are 10 items that relate to work conditions at MicroChip Electronics. Place a checkmark beside any of the items that represent your feelings about your job:

   ______Feedback about performance nonexistent
   ______Working conditions dirty
   ______Working conditions unsafe
   ______Not enough training sessions
   ______Pay and benefits unsatisfactory
   ______No choice in shift assignment
   ______Work unfulfilling
   ______Plant too far from home
   ______Poor parking situation
   ______Uniforms not supplied

3. Check any of the following items that you feel describe current conditions at MicroChip Electronics:

   ______No time to talk to supervisors
   ______Lack of communication between supervisors and employees
   ______Not allowed to talk to peers
   ______Inconsistent application of company rules and regulations
   ______Employees don't seem to know their jobs.

4. In the space below, write any comments you wish to share with the Personnel Office that you think might improve employee relations (use additional paper if necessary):

REFERENCES

Armstrong, William R. Vice President for Production, MicroChip Electronics. Vancouver, British Columbia: August 12, 1987. Interview.

"The Effect of Poor Employee Relations on Job Performance." *Reflections of Employee Relations.* Carlos S. Gonzalez, ed. Toronto: Prestige Press, 1983.

Harris, Mary Louise. *Employee Relations in the Electronics Industry.* Toronto: A.J. Smith and Sons, Publishers, 1985.

Lewis, Francis, et al. *The New Management.* Toronto: Unicorn Publishers, 1987.

Quillan, Sherry S., and Herman A. Quillan. "Injury in the Work Place." *Labour-Management Review* 27 (1987): 330–40.

Rosenblum, Henry. "Work and Working Relationships." *Labour Quarterly,* 1985, spring, 35–60.

Smith, Harrison. "An Examination of Happiness on the Job." Ph.D. dissertation, McMaster University, 1983.

Part Three

Oral Strategies

Chapter 13

Listening as a Communication Tool

Learning Objectives

In this chapter, you'll learn the importance of good listening skills to effective communication. More specifically, you will be able to:

1. recognize the amount of time we spend listening
2. explain the potential relationships between effective listening and various characteristics of individuals
3. describe the major perceptual barriers to effective listening
4. explain the valuable concept of "active listening"
5. explain how concentration, objectivity, questioning, and feedback can improve listening behaviour
6. explain the difference between good listening behaviour and poor listening behaviour

Preview Case

An irritating habit of mine, I've often been told by my closest friends or relatives, is to underline a passionate statement on whatever subject is under discussion with the question, "Do you HEAR me?" What I'm subconsciously asking the person, of course, is not just to listen but to "hear" my undertones, the implications.

On my desk now is a pioneering study that confirms that my question has not been as odd as it has appeared to be. For tests made as part of the study disclose that, immediately after listening to a ten-minute oral presentation, the average consumer or employee has heard, understood, properly evaluated, and retained only half of what was said. Within 48 hours, that sinks by another 50 percent.

The final level of effectiveness — comprehension and retention — is only 25 percent! Even worse, as ideas are communicated from one person to the next, they can become distorted by 80 percent.

With 100 million workers in [the U.S.], a simple $10 listening mistake by each would cost business $1 billion!

The financial toll of poor listening is enormous. Thus, more and more corporations are actively looking for solutions. Chairman and Chief Executive Officer J. Paul Lyet of Sperry Corp. (producer of Sperry Univac computers and other capital equipment products) is a leader in expanding the corporation's commitment to improve the quality of listening among its 87 000 employees.

"Poor listening is one of the most significant problems facing business today," says Lyet. "Business relies on its communication system, and when it breaks down, mistakes can be very costly. Corporations pay for their mistakes in lower profits, while consumers pay in higher prices."

If you're a poor listener, you're much more apt to make mistakes on important business matters. Letters must be retyped, appointments rescheduled, and shipments reshipped — all because the proper information wasn't heard, or understood, when first given.

If you're in the majority, though, you don't overrate your own listening abilities. For instance, 85 percent of those asked rate themselves as "average" listeners or less, while fewer than 5 percent rate themselves as "superior" or "excellent."

But your listening ability can be improved. In the few schools that have adopted listening programs, listening comprehension among students has as much as doubled in a few months.[1]

Overview

Managerial people in organizations spend up to 80 percent of their workday in face-to-face conversations, in meetings, on the phone, or writing.[2] Most people spend approximately 60 percent of the workday *listening*.[3] Yet we remember as little as 25 percent of what we hear and we can recall only half of that information after two months.[4]

Many people spend 60 percent of the workday listening

Small wonder that training employees to listen more efficiently is big business. One survey of Fortune 500 companies determined that nearly 68 percent offered listening training to employees at all levels.[5] Teachers, consultants, publishers, and counsellors interested in promoting research and listening training even have their own association, the International Listening Association.[6]

The purpose of this chapter is to increase your awareness of how much of your day is spent listening, to identify some of the major barriers to effective listening, and to learn how concentration, objectivity, questioning, and feedback can improve listening behaviour.

Effective Listening and Individual Characteristics

At one time or another everyone has had the experience of talking to another person and suddenly becoming aware that that other person is not listening. This is not a very good feeling. The fact is that most of us have no fundamental hearing deficiency, but still we do not listen very well.

How can we become better listeners? Recognizing one's characteristics and how they may affect one's listening is a good place to start. What follows are some conclusions about the relationship between listening behaviours and individual characteristics:

Eleven individual characteristics may affect listening

1. **Sex.** Although some research has shown that females comprehend slightly less from lectures than do males, the manner of testing, not inherent sex differences, probably caused the discrepancy.
2. **Personality.** As a rule, researchers have discovered no marked relationship between listening comprehension and personality characteristics.
3. **Intelligence.** Obviously, intelligence can be a determining factor in listening (aural) comprehension, but it is not the only element that affects aural proficiency.
4. **Scholastic achievement.** Moderately positive correlations exist between listening ability and cumulative grade average. Such findings indicate that students who listen well get higher grades. Furthermore, since listening and reading have similar correlations with grades, it is reasonable to conclude that scholastic excellence depends equally on aural and reading skills.
5. **Verbal ability and vocabulary.** Verbal competence is an important part of listening comprehension. An adequate vocabulary facilitates

listening and increases word retention. In fact, the effective use of words, through both listening and speaking, is a definite business and social asset.

6. **Note taking.** Since most listeners take poor notes, note taking does not have a noticeable effect on listening comprehension and retention. However, if you listen carefully and synthesize as you write, you will probably perform better on examinations.
7. **Motivation.** Motivation is one of the most significant elements of listening proficiency. Specifically, motivation, in terms of *interest*, *emotion*, and *mindset*, helps determine a person's aural competence. Listeners' comprehension improves if they are interested in the topic before the speech, if the speech creates interest, or if they know they are to be tested after the speech. The intensity of the listener's emotional reaction to what is being said also affects listening ability. Finally, various methods of producing an anticipatory mindset influence understanding. For example, if you introduce your speech by stating that it is going to be critical of, say, tax increases, your listeners are more apt to remember your criticisms. You have created, in the minds of your audience, anticipation of criticisms.
8. **Organizational ability.** Listening comprehension is directly related to the ability to organize and structure a message. The better organized the message, the higher the comprehension. This applies to speakers as well as listeners.
9. **Environment.** Research findings show that environmental factors influence comprehension. Good listeners allow for or adjust to distracting elements, such as poor lighting or extraneous noise, improper distance from the speaker, and other environmental shortcomings over which they have no control.
10. **Hearing ability.** Many think that people with some hearing loss are not good listeners; actually, the opposite is true. People with moderate hearing loss usually are better listeners than those with normal hearing.
11. **Use.** While writing skills and, to a lesser extent, speaking skills improve with use, this is not necessarily the case with listening. Just because we have been receiving the spoken word all our lives does not mean we are good listeners. Improvement requires instruction and practice in effective listening.

Everyone can become a better listener

Listening ability is a complex combination of factors. The important point to remember is that, given a stable personality and an average IQ, no particular personality trait or intelligence level excludes a person from being a good listener. Listening is a skill that can be learned: everyone can become a better listener and a better teacher of listening skills.[7]

Perceptual Barriers to Effective Listening

Before we consider suggestions for improving listening skills, let's examine some major barriers to effective listening. Note that the following are all perceptual barriers.

Major barriers to effective listening are perceptual

Have you ever heard the saying "Meanings are in people"? It means that a message is composed solely of aural (hearing) and visual (seeing) stimuli. Although the speaker (message sender) may want to convey a particular meaning, the listener's individual frame of reference — that is, his or her total life experience — determines the meaning. As a result, the speaker and listener may share similar, but not identical, meanings for a given message.

People perceive stimuli according to their individual frames of reference

Expectations are based on past experiences in similar situations. For example, suppose a supervisor is harassing a bank teller about his work performance. Each day the supervisor passes the teller's work station, examines his work, and comments sarcastically about its poor quality. In spite of these remarks, the bank teller strives to improve. Surprisingly, one day the supervisor inspects the teller's work and says, "Good job." The bank teller takes it as condescension, is offended, and promptly resigns.

People perceive stimuli according to their own expectations

The bank teller's *past experiences* completely overrode his supervisor's supportive observation. Again and again, the teller had received rude, fault-finding remarks, causing him to assume automatically that "Good job" was another hostile comment. Thus, the past climate of communication determined the teller's perception of the immediate listening situation, the speaker, and the message being sent.

Most of us are very good at distorting information so that it fits into our model of the world. This process is called *selective perception.* For example, to support the belief that their work is quite acceptable, some employees conveniently filter out criticisms from a supervisor. They refuse to hear negative comments about their work, thus avoiding an unpleasant confrontation with reality. Selective perception serves as a protective device against unwelcome aural stimuli.

People perceive stimuli according to individual attitudes and beliefs

The relationship between superior and subordinate is the most relevant case in point. Subordinates will pay close attention to a respected, credible supervisor's comments and will be more conscious of *how* they perceive communication from that supervisor. However, subordinates are likely to attach minor importance to the comments of a supervisor who has low credibility or little power.

The continuing relationship between speaker and listener plays an important role in perception

Skills for Effective Listening

What do you visualize when you think of a person listening? Listening is frequently pictured as a *passive* activity, but it is not. A good listener is *actively* involved in the listening process.

Active listening entails grasping the speaker's point of view

Several years ago Rogers and Farson introduced a concept of active listening.[8] Basically, it requires that you as a listener grasp, from the speaker's point of view, what is being communicated. More than that, you must convey to speakers that you are seeing things from their viewpoint. To listen actively, then, you must do several things.

Listen for Total Meaning

Any spoken message usually contains two important and meaningful elements: the *content*, and the *attitude* or *feeling* underlying this content. These components make up the total meaning of the message, which is what you as a listener try to understand. To illustrate, a machine operator approaches her supervisor and says, "I've finished the production run." This message has definite content and may be interpreted as a request for more work. Suppose, instead, the machine operator says, "Well, I've finally finished that production run." The basic content is the same, but the total meaning of the message is quite different.

Responding to the total meaning requires responding to the underlying attitude

This difference in meaning has important implications for both the supervisor and the machine operator. Listening sensitivity on the part of the supervisor will determine whether this conversation is a successful exchange between the two parties. Suppose the supervisor's reaction is simply to assign another production run. Would the employee feel that she had successfully communicated her total message? Would she feel free to talk to her supervisor? Would she leave feeling positive about her work and anxious to perform even better on the next job?

On the other hand, what if the supervisor responds to the machine operator with such statements as "Worked under a lot of pressure, right?" or "Glad to have it over with, huh?" or "Guess I couldn't get you to do that again!" The supervisor's reaction is in line with the employee's attitude or feeling about the completed task. In other words, the supervisor has responded from the employee's point of view. Such supportive replies don't mean that the next work assignment has to be changed or that the way is open for the employee to complain about the pressure of the job. Listening sensitivity on the part of the supervisor is simply a way to transform an average working climate into a more positive one.

Respond to Feelings

In some situations the message content is far less important than the feeling that underlies it. To interpret the full meaning of the message accurately, the listener must "hear" and be ready to respond to the feelings (attitude) component. For example, if the machine operator said,

"I'd like to disassemble the production machine and sell its parts to our competitor," responding to content would obviously be absurd. But to respond to the employee's anger or frustration over meeting tough deadlines is a sensitive and necessary reaction to the meaning of the message.

Obviously, the meaning of any message can include various degrees of feeling, so the listener must be sensitive to possible variations. What is this woman trying to tell me? What does this statement mean to this man? What is their view of the problem?

Feelings are a part of the message

Note All Cues

As we saw in Chapter 3, communication is made up of verbal and nonverbal cues. Words alone do not reveal everything that the speaker is communicating. Sensitive listening requires an awareness of several levels of nonverbal communication. Voice inflection is one factor: a speaker may stress certain points loudly and clearly and mumble others. The way in which a speaker hesitates reveals a great deal. The speaker's facial expressions, posture, hand gestures, eye movements, and breathing also help convey the total message.[9]

The concept of active listening has to do with the mental attitude you need to bring to the listening situation. In addition, several other basic concepts relate directly to listening ability. A brief review of those concepts is in order.

People are motivated to listen in varying degrees to a variety of messages. Simultaneously, they are "demotivated" from listening for many of the same kinds of reasons. Effective listeners, however, are continually and consciously motivated to listen. From the effective listener's viewpoint, whatever other individuals wish to communicate is important. Though it sometimes appears that nothing of great value may be gained through listening, effective listeners consciously strive to disprove this expectation. They become "selfish listeners," who look for potential economic benefits, personal satisfaction, or new interests and insights. In brief, each listener needs to say, "What is that speaker saying that I can use?"

Motivation and demotivation affect the listening experience

A significant differential exists between the average speaking rate (100 to 200 words per minute) and an average listener's ability to process messages (400 words per minute). Such a differential provides opportunities for mental tangents. Average listeners, therefore, tend to tune in and out of conversations. Consequently, they often fail to grasp what the speaker deems the important content of a message.

Concentration is the key to avoiding such tangents. The listener should be aware of the difference between the rates of speech and thought, and should use the time lag effectively rather than letting it destroy the listening process. See the Checklist for Listening Concentration below for some helpful tactics.

Concentration is an important determinant of listening ability

Checklist for Listening Concentration

- Anticipate what the speaker will say next. Whether or not your anticipations are confirmed, such activity serves to focus your attention upon the subject at hand. Focus on the message.
- Weigh the speaker's evidence and search for the deeper meanings. Such a tactic will help bridge the time gap created by the speech-thought differential.
- Review previous points. Recapitulate in your mind the major points the speaker has already covered. This review can help to reinforce the ideas the speaker is explaining.

Concentration, then, consists of successfully managing the time lag between speech and thought. Certain tactics can be employed both to maintain attention to the speaker's message and to facilitate retention of that message.

The use of questions is an effective listening strategy

In paired communication, such as that between a superior and subordinate, asking questions may often be an effective listening tactic. Such activity serves two purposes: it encourages the speaker by demonstrating that the listener is, indeed, actively listening, and it can clarify and develop points, thereby enhancing the listener's chances of clearly understanding the speaker's message.

Probing questions are highly useful for improving your listening capabilities. You simply ask questions that build on a speaker's utterances.

Objectivity is crucial to effective listening

Objectivity is a crucial element in effective listening. Lack of objectivity results in the assignment of distorted meanings to messages and may also jeopardize the relationship between speaker and listener. See the Checklist for Objective Listening below for some principles.

Effective listeners follow the timeworn piece of advice, "Wait your turn." They allow others sufficient opportunity to communicate their position or ideas. By adhering carefully to the rule of taking turns, the listener becomes a more effective communicator.

The Role of Feedback

Feedback is important in the listening process

Although feedback is important to listening, it is frequently overlooked in discussions of the subject. At appropriate points, listeners should provide feedback to a speaker, who may sometimes not be sure of what is (or is not) getting through. This uncertainty may cause the speaker to start repeating ideas. At this point, the listener shows even less interest and comprehension, the speaker repeats even more, and the entire communication process continues to deteriorate. This problem can be alleviated by the listener's providing appropriate and timely feedback to let the speaker know that an idea has been understood.

Checklist for Objective Listening

- Minimize the impact of emotion-laden words. Quite often a listener's perceptual process goes awry simply because the speaker utters a word or phrase that arouses an automatic, emotional response. Words and phrases such as "sexism," "reduction in force," "strike," and "grievance" can sometimes engender feelings of hostility or anxiety in a listener. When such feelings arise, the ability to think clearly and logically may be severely hampered.
- Judge content, not delivery. Listeners often discount messages largely because of some distracting characteristic in the speaker's tone of voice, rate of delivery, or pronunciation. Such subjective impressions of the value of messages seriously endanger listening efficiency. An effective listener focuses on *what* is said, not on *how* it is communicated.
- React fairly and sensibly. One of the most difficult listening functions is to avoid reacting too soon to what you hear. Consider a department head who was informed his staff must be reduced by two people. Rather than wait for an explanation or justification from his superior, he immediately responded in a defensive manner. His defensiveness led to defensive behaviour by the plant manager, and hostile feelings resulted.
- Overcome distractions. Don't let the speaker's station, appearance, or delivery affect your listening. Turn down a stereo or television that keeps you from hearing.
- Detect the central message. Don't allow isolated facts to get in the way of the total meaning.
- Ask for clarification or rewording if you are unsure what is being said.

The Role of Note Taking

A final suggestion for improving listening behaviour concerns note taking. One point needs to be made at the outset. Note taking may be useful

The usefulness of note taking depends on the situation

in some situations, but it is unnecessary in others and may even be distracting. Your purpose in listening should determine whether you need to take notes. If you think you will need to refer to the information in the future, notes are probably necessary. If the information is for immediate use, however, you are better off just listening carefully.

One other aspect of note taking is worthy of mention. Appropriate note taking may nonverbally convey to the speaker that you are paying close attention to what is being said. Such note taking shows your earnestness as well as respect for the speaker.

Ten Keys to Effective Listening

At this point it seems useful to consider the major differences between "good" and "bad" listeners. Professor Lyman Steil is a well-known authority on listening. He serves as a "listening consultant" to major corporations. In many of his talks Professor Steil summarizes the differences between "good" and "bad" listeners. These are outlined in Figure 13.1.[10]

Using the Telephone

Because of the cost and time required for face-to-face meetings, conducting business by telephone is becoming increasingly common. The telephone is used to conduct meetings (including conference calls among several people), conduct market surveys, make sales pitches, and share information. Because you cannot see the person with whom you are speaking, using the telephone for business requires particularly good listening skills. You cannot rely on gestures and other nonverbal cues to interpret the message.

The following discussion outlines ways that will help you use the telephone more effectively as a business tool.

Prepare for Outgoing Calls

How often have you hung up the phone only to realize that you had forgotten to ask the person you were calling a key question? You're not alone. Many people automatically plan for a meeting by preparing an agenda or jotting down a few key points, yet those same people think nothing of making a call without first thinking out the reasons for making it. The result? Unanswered questions and another phone call or two to get the information, and someone on the other end of the phone line who thinks you're disorganized.

To use the telephone most effectively, you need to plan your calls just

TEN KEYS TO EFFECTIVE LISTENING

These keys are a positive guideline to better listening. In fact, they're at the heart of developing better listening habits that could last a lifetime.

	The Bad Listener	The Good Listener
1. Find areas of interest	Tunes out dry subjects	Opportunizes; asks "What's in it for me?"
2. Judge content, not delivery	Tunes out if delivery is poor	Judges content; skips over delivery errors
3. Hold your fire	Tends to enter into argument	Doesn't judge until comprehension complete
4. Listen for ideas	Listens for facts	Listens for central themes
5. Be flexible	Takes intensive notes using only one system	Takes fewer notes; uses 4-5 different systems, depending on speaker
6. Work at listening	Shows no energy output. Attention is faked.	Works hard; exhibits active body state
7. Resist distractions	Distracted easily	Fights or avoids distractions; tolerates bad habits; knows how to concentrate
8. Exercise your mind	Resists difficult material; seeks light material	Uses heavier material as exercise for the mind
9. Keep your mind open	Reacts to emotional words	Interprets colour words; does not get hung up on them
10. Capitalize on the fact that thought is faster than speech	Tends to daydream with slow speakers	Challenges, anticipates, summarizes, and weighs the evidence; listens between the lines to tone of voice

Figure 13.1 A Guide to Good Listening

as you would a memo or letter. Jot down the name and phone number of the person you're calling along with the reason for the call and any key points or questions that need to be discussed during the call. That way, you'll ensure that you get or give complete information in a single call, and you'll be prepared if the person you're calling is out and returns your call several hours later.

Make the Call

When you are making a call, begin by identifying yourself, your organization, and the reason for your call. Never assume that the person you are calling will recognize your voice. If a secretary or receptionist answers the call, you may also have to state the name of the person you are calling.

If you anticipate the call will take more than a couple of minutes, check that this is a convenient time for the person you are calling. Give him or her the option of calling you back at a more convenient time.

Because the telephone relies entirely on the spoken word, you'll need to check for understanding from time to time. You can do this by paraphrasing what the other person has said, asking questions to clarify key points, or summarizing key points at the end of the call.

To ensure that you cover all your key points, you can use your preliminary list of topics as a checklist, keeping additional notes where necessary to record decisions or follow-up action.

Teleconference calls require a slightly more structured approach because only one person's speech is picked up at any one time. Therefore, if two or more people begin to speak at once, only one will be heard. Generally, assigning one person to "chair" the conference call will ensure a smooth call.

Answer Calls

Whenever you answer the phone in your office, you should identify yourself. You should also identify your department and organization, if your calls don't come through a central switchboard. At the same time, make sure you've understood the name and organization of the person calling. Having to ask for a person's name after you've been talking with him or her for ten or fifteen minutes can be very embarrassing.

When you're taking a message for someone else, be sure to get the correct spelling of the person's name and his or her organization, and the correct phone number. A record of the time and date of the call can also be useful.

Your voice tends to sound lighter and more friendly if you smile as you talk. Therefore, it's important to smile during your telephone conversations. If you doubt this is so, record yourself during a call when you are smiling and during another when you are not. You'll likely be quite surprised at the result.

Summary

In this chapter, you have learned the importance of good listening skills to effective communication.

- As much as 60 percent of the workday is spent listening
- Certain characteristics affect our ability to listen:
  - intelligence
  - scholastic achievement
  - verbal ability and vocabulary
  - motivation
  - organizational ability
  - environment
- People perceive stimuli according to
  - their individual frames of reference
  - their own expectations
  - individual attitudes and beliefs
  - their continuing relationship with the speaker
- Effective listeners
  - listen for total meaning
  - respond to feelings
  - note all cues
  - give and get feedback while listening
- Using the telephone requires good listening skills:
  - prepare for outgoing calls by making notes
  - make the call
  - answer calls courteously

Review Questions

1. On the average, how much of the workday do people spend in some type of communication? How much of that time is spent listening?
2. On the average, how much of what someone tells us do we remember immediately after we have heard it? Two months after we have heard it? What do these facts tell you about the average person's level of listening retention?
3. Select what you feel are the six or seven most important individual characteristics that affect your ability to listen. Explain your choices.
4. Give an example from a business setting of each of the major perceptual barriers to listening.
5. Explain the concept of "active listening." Why is it so important?
6. What is a "selfish listener"?

7. What tactics can a listener use to facilitate concentration? In turn, how does concentration facilitate listening?
8. The use of questions is an effective listening strategy. Explain.
9. Why is objectivity a crucial element in effective listening? In terms of objectivity what should an effective listener do?
10. What are the major differences between "good" listeners and "bad" listeners?
11. How can you increase the effectiveness of your telephone conversations?

Activities

1. You and a classmate each choose a topic of considerable personal interest. Take turns discussing your topic for three minutes. After each discussion have the listener convey the content of the message and the underlying attitude or feeling.
2. With your classmates, select a television speech that everyone can watch. (Local cable television often broadcasts city council meetings or other meetings that would be appropriate.) In the following class, discuss the concentration tactics you used to listen effectively, even when you were not particularly interested in the topic.
3. Prepare a five-minute speech on a business-related topic and present it to your classmates. Ask them to provide feedback at all unclear points in the speech. Also, give your listeners some feedback about the "messages" you received while you were giving the speech. For example, you may observe someone whose eyes are closed, someone who is talking while you are speaking, and so on.

Discussion Cases

Self-Paced, Individualized Training

Jordan Jones is the Senior Training Officer for the Lower Fraser Valley Division of Airdale Lumber, a large west-coast forest company. He's attending a three-day workshop on self-paced, individualized training given by a California consultant hired by the company.

Jordan arrives for the first session of the day fifteen minutes late: the traffic on the bridge was murder. He'd left half an hour earlier than usual and had still arrived late.

By the time Jordan reaches the workshop room, the consultant, David Lundkvist, has already started his presentation. At least,

continued

Jordan assumes it's the consultant. Hard to tell, though: he's wearing a pair of denim pants and a cord jacket.

For the next hour, Jordan listens to Mr. Lundkvist lecture on the merits of self-paced, individualized training and the evils of the lecture as a teaching tool. He uses overheads that are hard to read. Some are taken from poor-quality, dot-matrix print; others are handwritten; still others look as though they had been prepared professionally. At times, Mr. Lundkvist shuffles through the overheads and mutters "That doesn't apply here" before putting the next one up on the screen.

Jordan becomes more and more irritated during the lecture. Mr. Lundkvist uses incorrect English in his presentation — there are even spelling errors on the overheads. Throughout, he implies that anyone who thinks about it can't help but see the value of self-paced, individualized training.

Over coffee, Jordan talks to his counterpart from the Okanagan, Sylvia Ostrinski. He comments that he doesn't think he'll ever use this training method. She replies, "I've been experimenting with it for the past year. I've packaged several of the courses we offer. Now employees can study when they want to, not when I've got a class scheduled. It's saving us money too. However, if this were my first experience with the method, I'd never have tried it."

Case Questions

1. Why did Jordan react negatively to self-paced, individualized training?
2. What accounts for Sylvia Ostrinski's comment?
3. How could David Lundkvist communicate his message more effectively?

Communication Mismatch[11]

Irene DesRosiers, supervisor of the claims department of Vancouver Pacific Insurance Company, believed her department was underproducing due to outmoded computer equipment. She had thoroughly investigated sophisticated systems being used by competing insur-

continued

ance companies and concluded that Vancouver Pacific's efficiency could be significantly improved if the company replaced its aging mainframe computer with five top-end personal computers on a network.

Irene calculated that, with the new computers, claims clerks could process their own claims rather than manually completing the paperwork for input by data entry clerks. The company currently employed three claims clerks and two data entry clerks; however, Irene anticipated the need for two additional claims clerks and one data entry clerk to handle the increasing volume of business. By training her existing staff on the new computers, however, Irene felt that she could manage the increased volume of claims without hiring any new staff. These savings in salaries would help to offset the cost of the new computers.

Since Irene was aware that her boss, Cecil Cheung, was concerned about costs, she thought there would be no problem getting her request approved. She believed the advantages were obvious. When she approached Cecil for a go-ahead on the purchase, he said, "Irene, I've had a chance to look at your memo requesting five 486 personal computers. Unfortunately, I need more information."

"The advantages are clearcut. What more information could you possibly need?"

"Well, some cost figures are necessary to justify this expense to my superiors."

"My department is overworked — we never get the attention we deserve. Besides, why should you doubt my credibility? It's just not fair."

"Irene, please calm down. All I'm asking for are some cost figures. If you're so certain of the benefits of these computers, those figures should be easy to produce. I'd really appreciate them."

"I'm not an accountant. I work hard around here, you know. Why can't you take my word for it?" Irene said, and at this stalemated point the conversation ended.

Two days later, Irene received a memo from Cecil. The request had been turned down.

Case Questions

1. What went wrong in the exchange between Irene and Cecil?
2. Was Irene really listening to what Cecil said? Substantiate your opinion.
3. Could Irene have responded more appropriately to Cecil's request? How?

Chapter 14

Public Presentations

Learning Objectives

In this chapter, you'll learn how to plan, organize, and make an effective public presentation. More specifically, you will be able to:

1. explain the importance of public speaking to the individual and to the organization
2. define the general and specific purpose of your presentation
3. identify those characteristics of an audience that should influence your approach in speaking to that audience
4. organize your speech so that you accomplish your purpose
5. write a detailed outline for your presentation
6. recognize stage fright as a normal phenomenon and understand methods for controlling it
7. explain the different modes of delivering a speech and identify settings in which each would be appropriate
8. prepare visual aids that will improve the effectiveness of your presentation
9. deliver your speech more effectively

Preview Case

Bill Jones had just finished his first six months as a supervisor. Although he felt he was doing a good job, he was a little nervous as he entered the office of his boss, Hank Sims, for his formal appraisal.

The 30-minute session went better than Bill had expected. Hank was very positive about Bill's first six months as a supervisor. At the end of the session, as Bill started for the door, Hank said, "Oh, I almost forgot. We received a request from one of the local civic clubs to provide a speaker for its next meeting in two weeks. Bill, I want you to handle the speech."

Bill had such a sinking feeling in his stomach that he did not even hear the topic that Hank told him the group had requested. Bill had never given a public speech, nor did he have any desire to do so. Just the idea of standing in front of a group and talking was enough to make him break into a cold sweat. At first he looked for excuses he could use to get out of the obligation, but the fact that his boss expected him to speak made it impossible to avoid the engagement.

After worrying about the speech for five days, Bill finally started working on it. He found the research fairly easy to do, but he had a difficult time trying to organize the material. How to make this dry subject interesting to the audience also presented problems to Bill.

The nearer the day of the speech came, the more apprehensive Bill was about it. He would lie awake nights thinking about giving the speech. When he was able to sleep, he would dream about it. One night he dreamed that he completely forgot what he wanted to say; another time he saw himself fainting at the speaker's stand. His most frequent dream was one in which he gave his speech and everyone in the audience fell asleep.

"If I can get through this speech," Bill thought, "I'm never going to give another one."

To his own surprise, not only did Bill get through it, but several members of the audience were interested enough in the subject to ask him questions. He actually enjoyed handling the questions, but he vowed that there would be no more speeches for him.

Three days later, Bill received a letter from the company president, praising his speech. In the letter the president said he hoped that Bill would "continue to serve as an effective representative of the company," and advised him, "Strive to become more visible in the local community." Bill started thinking that perhaps his speech-making days were not over, after all.

Like Bill, you may be apprehensive the first time you have to speak publicly. You are not alone. A survey of 2500 North Americans indicated that more than 40 percent feared speaking before a group. By comparison, only 19 percent of those surveyed claimed to fear death.[1] This fear of public speaking can be overcome, however, by learning to approach the entire process of public speaking systematically.

The purpose of this chapter is to introduce you to a systematic approach to public speaking. You'll learn how to select and research your topic, analyze your audience in advance, organize and outline your speech, prepare effective visual aids, and, finally, deliver your speech effectively. This systematic approach will help you to speak effectively in any situation, whether you are addressing an audience of five or five hundred.

Overview

Fear of public speaking is widespread but can be overcome through a systematic approach

The Importance of Public Speaking

Public speaking ability influences personal and professional success

Being able to organize your thoughts and speak in public is a significant determinant of your personal and professional success. The way in which you speak affects the way you see yourself and the way others see you. Being able to give an effective public speech enhances your self-esteem: you feel good about yourself.

On the job, your ability as a speaker may in part determine your progress. Good ideas are usually recognized and considered only if they are presented effectively.

When June O'Hara entered the management training program, very little set her apart from the other trainees. In educational background and technical ability, the trainees were very similar. However, June soon displayed an ability to organize her thoughts and express herself in a manner distinctly superior to that of the others. By the end of the training program no one was surprised when she was awarded the choicest job assignment ever given to a trainee.

That was 24 years ago. Today June is the president of the company. She is the first to recognize the importance of technical ability, but as she sees it, "Unless a person is able to transmit information to others in a well-organized and convincing way, that person is likely to remain a technician — and a mediocre one at that."

Today, more than ever, business needs people who can effectively present the organizational viewpoint to the public. The average business organization does a poor job acquainting the public with its contributions to society.

From a communication standpoint it does not matter how pure the organization's motives are. What matters is what the public knows about a company's activities and how the public responds to this knowledge.

The public speech is a good way to present business favourably

Only through effective external communication can business present the information that will most likely result in a positive public image. One of the most effective formats in which to present that information is the public speech.

The General Purpose

As the crowd filed out of the lecture hall, Raj and Katerina began to compare the notes each had taken on the speech they had just heard. They had just listened to their Member of Parliament give a speech entitled "Canada in Crisis: The National Debt." Raj and Katerina were frustrated to learn that they disagreed as to what the speaker had actually said.

Raj and Katerina were members of a class that had been assigned to hear the speech, which was to be the subject of the following day's class discussion. It turned out that there was considerable disagreement within the class as to what the speaker had said. Approximately one third of the students felt that his main point was the need for fewer universal social programs. Another third of the class maintained that it was a need for higher taxes to pay for these programs. Disagreement was even greater among the remaining third of the class — except for the two students who said that they had no idea what the speaker's main point had been.

Some common responses to public speeches are:

- "I'm not sure exactly what he meant."
- "I couldn't find any point to the speech."
- "I don't know what she was getting at."
- "What was the purpose of that speech anyway?"

The three general purposes of speeches are to inform, persuade, and entertain

The person who made the last comment went to the heart of a significant problem. Many speakers seem unable or unwilling to determine in advance the purpose of a speech. This is a great mistake. In planning a speech you should first decide what its purpose will be. You do so in a two-step process: determine the general purpose, then determine the specific purpose. Most authorities recognize three possible general purposes: to inform, to persuade, and to entertain.

To Inform

When you try to teach listeners or explain something to them, your general purpose is to inform. The classroom lecture is an example of an informative speech. Some informative speeches are intended to acquaint the listeners with something completely new to them. That's what a personnel director is doing when she explains the company's benefit program to a group of new employees. Some informative speakers try to update listeners who are already knowledgeable about the subject. For example, when officers of credit unions attend the annual meeting of their trade association, they hear many informative speeches of this type.

To Persuade

Overt responses are easier to measure than covert responses

The second general purpose of public speaking is to persuade the listener. Persuasive speeches range from those that seek to change listeners' beliefs or attitudes to those that attempt to get them to act in a certain way. Your purpose for giving a persuasive speech can be put into two very general but distinct categories: (1) to elicit a covert response, and (2) to elicit an overt response.

A *covert response* is, as the term implies, one that is not readily apparent to the speaker or to an observer. When a union leader seeks to convince the members that the union has their interests at heart, the speaker is seeking a covert response, acceptance of an idea. It is usually difficult to evaluate a speaker's effectiveness when the response being sought is covert.

Evaluating a speaker's effectiveness is easier when the speaker is seeking an *overt response*, one that is observable and measurable. The manager who tries to get the billing clerks to reduce their errors can check future error counts for evidence of effectiveness. The production manager who urges increased output from workers can also measure results easily.

To Entertain

The third general purpose of speaking is to entertain — the response sought from the listeners is enjoyment. Many persons consider entertainment and humour to be synonyms, but they are not. Humour is certainly a common ingredient of entertainment, but it is not the only one. Perhaps you have had a teacher who thoroughly entertained the class with little or no humour. Some speakers who are enthusiastic about their subject entertain their listeners. Others are able to entertain through their flair for drama or through their picturesque language.

The Specific Purpose

The specific purpose depends on the subject and the audience

While there are only three general purposes for making a presentation, the number of specific purposes is infinite. The specific purpose of a speech is constructed with both the subject and the audience in mind.

The following examples suggest the relationship among subject, audience, general purpose, and specific purpose:

Subject	Community recycling programs
Audience	A class of undergraduate business students
General purpose	To inform
Specific purpose	To review the various recycling programs operating in the community

Subject	Community recycling programs
Audience	Residents of a neighbourhood about to start a "blue box" program
General purpose	To persuade
Specific purpose	To persuade residents to participate in the "blue box" and other community recycling programs

Subject	Use of nuclear energy for generating electrical power
Audience	Approximately 100 members of a neighbourhood home-owners' association
General purpose	To persuade
Specific purpose	To persuade listeners to write their member of the provincial legislature, expressing opposition to increased reliance on nuclear energy.

While the subject or the general purpose may remain the same, the specific purpose varies according to the audience. Although the three general purposes are usually thought of as separate and distinct, they are not. Very few speeches are entirely informative, persuasive, or entertaining. Most are, in fact, a combination of two or three of these general purposes.

Advance Audience Analysis

The more you can learn about your audience in advance of your speech, the more appropriate your speech should be.

When Lynn McLean, a member of the provincial legislature, was invited to address the monthly meeting of Wilbanks Employees Association, she immediately accepted. An election was sure to be called soon, and she was trying to get as much visibility as possible. Her party's campaign theme was to be the need for more economical government, so she planned to speak on that issue.

She arrived at the auditorium barely on time and was immediately introduced. She spoke with vigour and emotion as she lashed out at excessive government spending. Her special target was the cost of providing health care, and she emphasized the need for a "user pay" system. To say that she got a cool response would be an understatement. Although the audience numbered nearly 200, only two people asked questions, and both questions were hostile.

Had Lynn bothered to look into the Wilbanks Employees Association in advance, she would have learned that most of the active members are retired employees. After the experience, she often wondered how many votes she had lost because of that particular speech.

When you are asked to give a speech, immediately pose some basic questions whose answers will help you prepare your speech:

- How large will the audience be?
- How educated are the listeners?
- What occupations will be represented?
- What will be the age range?
- To which social, political, or religious groups will the listeners belong?

The answers to such questions will reduce some of the uncertainty surrounding your public speaking.

Audience analysis is essential

Many speakers miss their target because they make no attempt to analyze the audience in advance. A common shortcoming is to assume that what is interesting to the speaker will also interest the listener.

To be a good speaker, you must adopt a listener orientation. When preparing a speech, ask yourself how you would feel if you were in the listener's place. Before being able to answer that question, you must learn as much about the listeners as possible, and this necessitates analyzing the audience.

The best way to analyze an audience is to talk personally with all those people who will be in it. Unfortunately, this is an unrealistic approach to audience analysis because in most cases it would be impractical. A satisfactory alternative is to talk to several persons likely to be in the audience. Assuming they are similar to the rest of the members of the audience, you will then have some insight into the nature of your listeners.

When you can't talk with anyone from the audience or even with anyone familiar with the audience, you face more of a challenge. You have to infer what it will be like from the information that is available.

The more similar your listeners are in such factors as educational level, occupation, age, and group memberships, the easier it is to predict their attitudes towards you and your message. The more heterogeneous or diversified the audience, the fewer inferences you can make. The more you know in advance about an audience, the more effective a speaker you should be. Time spent in analyzing the audience is time well spent.

Researching the Topic

Much more time should be devoted to preparing a speech than to giving it

Just as an athlete spends much more time practising than actually competing, you will devote more time to preparation than to speaking. Throughout the preparation process, you should keep in mind these questions to which your listeners will seek answers:

1. How do you know?
2. Is this an accurate statement?
3. Does it agree with other sources?
4. What does it have to do with the subject?
5. What does it have to do with me?[2]

Speeches related to the speaker's own area of specialization may be based almost entirely on the observations and knowledge of the speaker. For speeches of this nature, the speaker is probably the best source of information.

When Randall Best, an assistant purchasing manager, was asked to speak to a civic club on purchasing and its effects on the local community, he spent hours in the library. He used many different sources, including textbooks, trade journals, and government documents, in preparing his speech.

He was disappointed with the audience's response — in fact, lack of response would be more accurate. At the end of his speech, he offered to answer questions, but no one asked any. There was courteous applause, but the listeners seemed mainly interested in getting out of the room.

The next day he described the situation to Joe Wiest, his boss, who was sympathetic but bluntly pointed out Randall's mistake. "Know thyself is the best advice I can give," Joe said. "As a purchasing agent you are recognized by these local groups as an expert. They want to learn about you and what you think on the subject. They don't want to be subjected to some list of figures that sounds like it's coming out of a computer. They want you."

For people like Randall Best, the insights acquired over the years in a given field are usually the best equipment for speaking knowledgeably about it. Moreover, when a speech is about a subject in which a person has been immersed and on which that person is recognized as an authority, listeners do not expect information from other sources: they want to hear what he or she has to say on the subject.

When speaking about your area of specialization, you seldom need other sources of information

Business people who do not possess all the information on a subject necessary to develop a speech can usually call on someone else in the organization for help. Through personal observations and knowledge, or with the assistance of colleagues, most business speakers are able to prepare an appropriate speech.

Printed Sources of Information

Many times speakers must go to printed sources to answer their listeners' questions. Most students, for example, lack the experience and the contacts necessary to prepare a speech without library research. That is not to say that only students rely on library research. Experienced business speakers often look to other sources to support their ideas or to improve their knowledge of a subject. Therefore, knowing how to find information in the library is an important skill.

You'll find that your college and public libraries have a wide range of books available to help you write effective speeches. Books of quotations and humorous anecdotes arranged according to subject are some of the most useful sources of information for the speech writer. However, you need to take great care in choosing material that is relevant to your subject and purpose.

If you haven't learned how to use your college or university library effectively, researching your topic can be a slow process. If you've never used the catalogue or the indexes before, ask the librarians for help. They may suggest that you use one of the self-teaching packages available in many libraries. These packages lead you systematically through the research process.

Organizing the Speech

Speakers often make the mistake of believing that they are ready to speak once they have completed their research. What results is usually a speech that is unclear in purpose and inconsistent in direction. Such speakers have overlooked the necessity of organizing their material.

When trying to organize the results of your research, you should have an overabundance of materials so that you can then select those that are most appropriate. Inexperienced speakers often question the value of

Too much material is better than too little

doing more research than necessary; however, after preparing several speeches, you will know why. It is painful to a speaker and obvious to listeners when a speech is short on ideas, for it is then that a speaker is likely to include digressions, redundancies, and irrelevant statements.

A speech is made up of three main parts: introduction, body, and conclusion. Although the body follows the introduction, most speakers develop the body first. It is in the body of a speech that its actual message is presented.

The body of a speech contains the central idea, main ideas, and supporting evidence

The body of a speech in turn has three main components: central idea, main ideas, and supporting materials. The *central idea* is the major theme. It is what the speaker wants the listeners to remember even if they forget all else. A campaigning politician may present many ideas in a campaign speech. The central idea, however, is usually "Vote for me." Although central ideas are generally longer than that, they should be limited to one sentence. A training director recently gave an informative speech in which the central idea was this: A person should not be made a supervisor until having satisfactorily completed a course in interpersonal communication. A good central idea is brief and clear. Remember that the central idea represents the minimum that you want the listeners to remember.

After determining the central idea, you seek ideas to support it; these are the *main ideas*. Since the main ideas are second in importance only to the central idea, you hope that the listeners will retain them, too. For that reason, you should not have many main ideas; four or five are sufficient for most speeches.

Several main ideas support the central idea; each should have multiple supports

Once you have selected the main ideas, look for ways to support them. Since an argument that convinces some listeners will not necessarily convince others, you should seek enough *supporting materials* to reach all of your listeners.

Among the methods of support most frequently used are quotations, examples, analogies, and statistics. In deciding on the appropriateness of a given form of support, these are the questions the speaker should consider:

Quotations (or Testimony)

1. Will the person being quoted be recognized by the listeners?
2. Will the listeners regard the quoted person as an authority?
3. Does the person being quoted have credibility with the listeners?

Examples

1. Can the example be understood by the listeners?
2. Is the example clearly related to the main point?

Analogies

(An analogy draws parallels between two different things. For example, when we use gasoline unnecessarily, it is as though we are reducing the number of future trips we will be able to take.)

1. Is the analogy appropriate for the subject being considered?
2. Will the listeners be able to grasp the relevance of the analogy?

Statistics
1. Will the statistics be understandable to the listeners?
2. Will the listeners recognize the relationship between the statistics and the main point they are intended to support?
3. Are the statistics recent and reliable enough to be acceptable to the listeners?

Sequence of Main Points

Once the central idea, the main points, and the supports have been selected, the speaker must decide in what order to present the main points. Some of the most common organizational patterns are chronological, topical, spatial, and logical. The sequence that is most appropriate depends on the topic, the speaker's purpose, and the interests of the listeners. Effective speakers are equally adept in using any of these sequential arrangements.

In selecting an appropriate sequence, consider the topic, your purpose, and the interests of the listeners

Chronological Sequence. In this sequence, the speech progresses from one point in time to another. This sequence is regularly used when explaining a process.

When the plant manager explained paper making to a class of undergraduates, he started by explaining how lumber is purchased and what is done to it in the wood room. He described the entire process for the listeners through to the packaging of the paper and the shipping from the mill.

The chronological sequence can also be used to describe the evolution of an idea or to explain how to do something.

Topical Sequence. When a topic is divided into several different parts, it is arranged according to the topical sequence. The more natural the divisions, the easier it is for the listeners to understand and retain what the speaker is presenting.

At the annual meeting of the shareholders of Tendril, Inc., the president spoke on the declining productivity of Tendril employees. He first spoke about the causes of this problem as perceived by management. Then he presented the causes as perceived by labour. He concluded by discussing those causes perceived differently by the two sides.

The topical sequence seems to be the one used most frequently. Some speakers tend always to use it, even though another sequence would be more effective.

Spatial Sequence. As the name implies, this sequence uses space to determine the arrangement of ideas. The speaker arranges the material according to physical location. For example, something might be described directionally, from east to west. Or a building might be described from its first to its top floor.

When the city planner presented the board's first recommendations for a mass transit system, she talked about the ways in which each suburb would be affected by the system. She described the location of the main stations in the inner city and the system's accessibility to downtown workers and shoppers. She also described the major northern, southern, eastern, and western routes and the terminus of each.

Speakers who use the spatial sequence describe the physical location of certain points and the relationship between these points. Use of the spatial sequence should enable the listeners to visualize what the speaker is telling them.

Logical Sequence. Several different patterns of arrangement are included in the logical sequence. Among the most common are the causal and the problem-and-solution sequences.

In using the causal approach, speakers have two options. One is to point out certain forces and the results that follow from them; the other is to describe events and then explain the forces that caused them.

When a chamber of commerce official spoke, he described the group's efforts to attract new business to the city. He then listed the organizations that have moved to the city as a result of those efforts.

When a representative of Pollution Probe discussed water pollution, she pointed out the growing health problems associated with it. She then listed discharges from manufacturing plants and lax sewage control as the causes.

The problem-and-solution approach is quite similar to the cause-and-effect approach in that the speaker presents two main points. For example, in discussing an increase in customer complaints about sales personnel (the problem), the personnel director urged that greater emphasis be placed on employee training (the solution).

Introduction and Conclusion

Until you have decided what you will present in your speech, knowing how best to get the listeners involved is difficult. For that reason you should develop the body of the speech before the introduction and the conclusion.

An introduction should establish rapport with listeners while gaining their attention

Your introduction has three purposes: to establish rapport with the listeners; to gain their attention; and to introduce your topic.

You can introduce your topic to your listeners in several ways:

1. Make a startling statement
2. Refer to the audience
3. Refer to the occasion
4. Quote a recognized authority
5. Ask a rhetorical question
6. Use humour that is relevant

Regardless of the approach you use to introduce your speech, remember to gain the acceptance of your listeners and tell them what the speech is about.

In concluding a speech you should, at a minimum, restate your central idea. A good conclusion provides closure for the listeners — that is, it indicates to them that the topic has been thoroughly covered. Some of the most common ways to conclude a speech are:

1. Summarize the main points.
2. Propose a solution.
3. Quote a recognized authority.
4. Challenge the listeners to accomplish some specific goal.
5. Describe the future if your proposal is or is not accepted.

Outlining Your Speech

In outlining a speech you arrange its parts into a sequence that allows for an orderly presentation of ideas. The outline helps you determine if the relationship between ideas is clear and helps your listeners follow your train of thought. A training director giving an informative speech to an undergraduate professional management society used this outline:

By outlining a speech, you can clarify the relationships among ideas

I. Introduction
  A. Brief history of the training function within the business organization
  B. Increased specialization and ongoing automation changes as purposes of training

II. Central idea:
The job of the training director is varied enough to be challenging and very important to the organization

III. Body (main ideas)
  A. The training director must learn the training needs of the organization
    1. Through observation of operations
    2. Through interviewing upper management
    3. Through interviewing line workers
  B. The training director must develop training programs to meet organizational needs
    1. Determine the target audience for the program
    2. Locate and schedule competent instructors for the program
  C. The training director must evaluate the effectiveness of the training program
    1. Test participants on the subject matter
    2. Interview superiors of the participants, and use other criteria to measure improvement

IV. Conclusion
  A. Summary of speech body
    1. Training director must learn training needs
    2. Training director must develop appropriate training programs
    3. Training director must evaluate the effectiveness of the programs
  B. The job of the training director is important to the organization and challenging to the individual.

Outlining the Persuasive Speech

Although the outline of the persuasive speech is similar to that of the informative speech, the two types of speeches are not developed in the same way. Since the informative speech is usually factual and not controversial, gaining the listeners' acceptance is not a problem.

Gaining the listeners' acceptance, however, *is* a challenge to the persuasive speaker. Researchers have shown that the more a persuader's ideas conform to the way people think, the more likely it is that successful persuasion will occur.

The Motivated Sequence

The Motivated Sequence is a method of speech organization based on an analysis of the thought process.[3] If you follow this sequence, you will present your ideas in the order that people naturally follow when thinking through to a solution of a problem. Listeners who are led along these steps will be motivated to accept your proposition. The Motivated Sequence consists of five steps:

1. Getting attention
2. Showing the need
3. Satisfying the need
4. Visualizing the results
5. Requesting approval or action

Just as readers grow oblivious to advertisements in magazines and newspapers, listeners also tune out when speakers try to persuade them. This is certainly not surprising: during an average day most of us are bombarded by numerous attempts to persuade. For these reasons a persuader must first get the *attention* of the listeners. In trying to do this, you have available the options presented in the discussion of introductions and conclusions earlier in this chapter. The most appropriate approach depends on many factors, including the occasion and the nature of the audience. The opening least likely to get the attention of the listeners is "My topic today is ... "

To *show the need* to the listeners, you describe a problem. In addition, you may clarify the situation through the use of examples. The examples will be more effective if they illustrate the seriousness of the problem and if you point out to the listeners how the problem affects them.

To *satisfy the need*, you present a solution to the problem raised in the previous step. You show how the solution will satisfy the need of the listeners who now know something about it. At this point you clearly state the attitude or action you are asking the listeners to adopt. Through the use of examples or other supporting materials, you show that your proposal will work. While explaining how the solution will meet the need, you should anticipate likely objections and address them during this step.

By describing future conditions, you help listeners to *visualize the results* of the proposed solution. Some speakers describe the results likely to occur if the solution is accepted. Others approach it negatively and describe future conditions if the solution is not accepted. The hoped-for result of the visualization step is to intensify the desire of the listeners.

By *requesting approval or action*, you focus the thoughts of the listeners on the theme developed in the speech. The request you make should be brief, to the point, and unmistakably clear.

This is the outline of a persuasive speech given by a production manager to a group of supervisors. Notice how it follows the steps of the Motivated Sequence.

I. Introduction

A. You have within you the power to grant yourself a pay increase because of our company's profit-sharing plan Attention

B. You also are in a position to generate more business for the company

Need

II. Body (main ideas)

A. Industry-wide research shows that we trail our competitors in two significant factors

1. We have the highest rate of lost-time accidents in the industry

2. We have a worse-than-average rate of consumer complaints about product defects

Satisfaction

B. You can take some actions that will increase your earnings and improve the company's position within the industry

1. Enforce all of the safety regulations all of the time

2. Stress ongoing quality control and make more spot checks yourself

Visualization

C. If you follow our supervisory manual to the letter, lost-time accidents will be reduced by 50 percent and consumer complaints will be reduced by at least 30 percent. You will benefit directly by

1. Increased profit sharing at year-end

2. Less nonproductive paperwork to complete concerning accidents

Action

III. Conclusion

A. Report all violations of safety regulations

B. Be a good model in every respect for your workers

Writing Your Speech

You can't write a speech

Some authors maintain you can't "write" a speech.[4] Instead they recommend that you talk about each of your key points into a tape recorder and only then write down what you have said. At the very least, you should read what you've written into a tape recorder to determine how it sounds. Whatever method you choose to "write your speech," the following guidelines will help you produce an effective oral presentation.

Writing for the Ear[5]

Writing for the ear requires different skills

Writing for the ear is different from writing for reading. When we read a letter or memo, for example, we can scan the entire document to determine the main ideas. We can read all of the document or only a portion. More importantly, we can read the document over and over again to grasp its meaning. When we listen, we rarely get a second chance. The message must be understood immediately.

Because of this immediacy, speeches should be more concise than conversation. The key points should be highlighted at the beginning and reinforced throughout the presentation. Listeners should be able to identify the overall structure of the presentation and speakers should refer to and reinforce that structure periodically.

The K.I.S.S. principle (Keep It Short and Simple) is essential when writing for the ear. Short sentences and paragraphs that contain specific, descriptive, active language will help to create vivid, memorable images for your listeners. Consider the differences in the following examples:

K.I.S.S.

Poor — Sales in the fourth quarter were less than anticipated because of economic conditions beyond our control.

Better — Our sales dropped 10 percent in the fourth quarter because of the recession.

Poor — One can conclude from the information presented so far that

- good employee relations are to be sought
- there has been a major increase in turnover rates at MicroChip Electronics in the last ten years
- our turnover rates are rising while our major competitor's rates are constant or slightly improving.

Better — This information suggests three conclusions. First, we need good employee relations. Second, our turnover rates have increased by 20 percent in the past ten years. And third, our turnover rates are increasing faster than those of our major competitor.

Notice that the second "better" example uses four short sentences instead of one long one. It also uses numerical cues to help the listener organize the information: "three,", "first," "second," and "third." In a written presentation, the "poor" example might be perfectly acceptable in that the reader could see the organization of the information on the page.

In general, your speech will be much easier to understand if you:

- Use relatively short sentences, but vary their length so your presentation doesn't sound "choppy."
- Choose the present tense and active voice whenever possible: "The Deer Lake General Hospital takes pride in providing high-quality patient care."
- Use sentence fragments occasionally for effect: "The bottom line? Our profits dropped 10 percent last year."
- Employ the "you attitude" to involve your audience emotionally in your presentation: "Look around you. One in three people won't be here when you graduate in 1995" is much more effective than "One third of all people who enter university fail to graduate."
- Use contractions to give your presentation a more conversational tone: for example, "can't" and "isn't."

- Get rid of unnecessary words: "It is said that ... "
- Use verbal organizers to help your listeners follow your presentation: numbers such as those in the example above are most common; however, you can use other transition words. Words such as "however" show a change in direction; words such as "therefore" show you are moving on to your conclusion.

Preparing to Give the Speech

Once you have a speech you are satisfied with, you need to prepare some aids to help you deliver your speech successfully. These aids include note cards and various kinds of visual aids.

Note Cards

Use note cards but do not read your speech

Even the most experienced speakers prepare notes they can refer to during their speech. The easiest method is to use note cards with key words and phrases on them rather than complete sentences from your speech. That way you will be sure to present all of your main ideas, but you will not be tempted to read to your audience. The Guide for Preparing Note Cards below gives some helpful hints.

Guide for Preparing Note Cards

- Use 7.6 by 12.7 cm (3 by 5 inch) index cards for your notes.
- Use large printing for convenient reference.
- Number the cards so that they can be sorted quickly if they get out of sequence.

Visual Aids

Visual aids improve interest and message retention

Studies have shown that visual aids have several benefits for speakers and their audiences. Speakers are perceived as being better prepared when they use visuals, the length of the presentation is reduced (perhaps because the speaker is better organized), and retention rates increase to 50 percent from as little as 10 percent.[6] Therefore, you can heighten listeners' interest in a speech and increase their retention of main ideas through the use of visual aids.

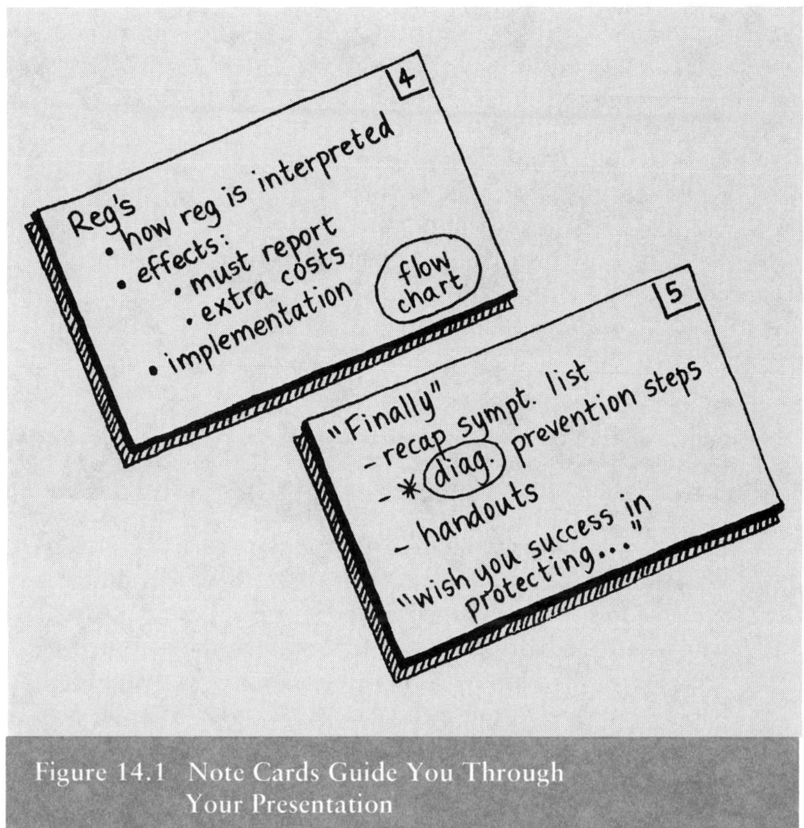

Figure 14.1 Note Cards Guide You Through Your Presentation

While some organizations have graphics specialists who prepare visual aids for company speakers, many speakers have to select and prepare their own. The guides on Uses for Visual Aids, Media Choices, and Design and Colour Basics below will help you do this successfully.

The function of a visual aid is to reinforce the message you are presenting. No matter how effective, however, a visual aid is not a substitute for the speech itself. The burden is still on you to convey the intended message.

To use a visual aid effectively, you must:

1. Be familiar enough with using the aid so that doing so adds to rather than detracts from the message
2. Learn in advance the most appropriate time to use the visual aid
3. Refer specifically to the visual aid in your speech
4. Display the visual aid only when you are referring to it (otherwise it can distract your audience)

Uses for Visual Aids

- Add humour or interest
- Outline a talk (use key words and phrases only)
- Reinforce or emphasize an important idea
- Clarify a difficult concept or idea
- Give impact to statistics (use graphs and charts)
- Show examples (see Figure 14.1)

Media Choices

- **Blackboards and whiteboards,** the traditional media for visual aids, are still very effective for developing diagrams during a presentation. If you're uncertain about your ability to draw "on command," consider drawing your image on the board, using faint pencil lines, prior to your presentation. That way, you'll be relaxed during your presentation and your audience will marvel at your ability to produce a professional illustration. When using the blackboard, remember to erase any material not related to your presentation and to limit the amount of information on the board at any one time.
- **Computer-generated illustrations** are the latest presentation visuals. Using a special attachment with a liquid crystal screen to link your computer with an overhead projector, you can project a series of visuals directly from the computer. This medium is particularly useful for demonstrating the capability of computer software or for presenting material that will change so frequently that the cost of preparing slides or overheads is prohibitive.
- **Flip charts** are most effective for small groups and they are readily available and can be prepared with a minimum of materials. You can prepare flip charts in advance or create them as you deliver your presentation. Again, faint pencil lines will help give you a more professional product. In workshops, many leaders post the completed flip chart sheets around the room so that the audience can review them.

continued

- **Handouts** should not be overlooked as a visual aid. They are particularly useful for detailed drawings that will reproduce badly on a slide or overhead projector. If you are using handouts, decide in advance when to distribute them. The audience will flip through a handout as soon as they receive it. Therefore, if the handout covers your entire presentation, distribute it at the beginning; if it covers only one portion, distribute it just before you reach that portion in your presentation. Some professional presenters provide the audience with copies of their overheads as a note-taking outline.
- **Overhead projectors** are popular because all that's needed for viewing is a well-lit room, and the transparencies are relatively easy to prepare. Moreover, the projector is situated in front of the audience so that the speaker can face the audience while presenting or completing the visuals. You should always remember to turn the overhead projector off when you are not using it. The light on the screen or even the last visual will distract your audience when you move on to your next point. (*Hint:* Frame your overhead transparencies to minimize extraneous light and define the borders of your graphic.)
- **Slide projectors** are favoured by speakers who have several visuals because the slides can be changed easily. However, slides usually have to be prepared professionally, adding to their cost.

Design Basics

While full-colour computer-generated slides create a very professional presentation, you will most likely rely on much simpler graphics. The following guidelines for colour and design should help you to make the most of the medium you choose.

Guide to Design Basics

- Use a horizontal format for slide and overhead transparencies. This will minimize the amount of material below the audience's line of vision.

continued

- Limit the amount of material on each visual; your listeners should be able to read and understand a visual in five seconds or less.
- Be sure your visuals are large enough to be seen by everyone in the room. On overhead transparencies, for example, the lettering should be 0.5 cm to 1 cm in height.
- Use a simple, easy-to-read, block lettering style.
- Use diagrams, graphs, and charts instead of words whenever possible.
- Eliminate unnecessary detail from diagrams, graphs, and charts.
- Use colour carefully and sparingly.

Colour Basics

- Use colour for emphasis, but limit the number of colours that you use on any one slide or transparency. Two or three different colours are generally sufficient.
- For slides, use white or yellow text on a blue or black background for maximum readability.[7]
- For overhead transparencies, use dark text on a light background.
- Use the rainbow colour spectrum if you want to colour code points in sequence (Roy G. Biv: red, orange, yellow, green, blue, indigo, violet).[8]
- Remember that red usually signals losses in business, and black profits ("in the red; in the black").

Delivering the Speech

Nervousness can be expected in giving a public speech, but much of it can be overcome

Some people feel that, if a speaker has attended to all of the other preliminaries, the delivery of a speech will take care of itself. The advice they are most likely to give to beginning speakers is "Be natural." They may also advise speakers, "Imagine that you are carrying on a conversation with the audience and act accordingly."

Such advice, while well intended, is not helpful. Your body may make it difficult for you to be natural in what is an unnatural situation.

Consider the bodily changes that usually occur when you are about to give a public speech: blood pressure and pulse rate increase; digestive processes slow down; perspiration increases; and breathing becomes irregular. These phenomena are among the many signs of anxiety that speakers may experience when facing an audience. Even experienced speakers report trembling hands, dryness in the mouth, and butterflies in the stomach.

Feelings of nervousness in a public speaking situation are to be expected — they are completely normal. As you become more experienced, such signs may become less pronounced, but they never completely disappear. Even extreme nervousness — of which you may be so painfully aware — is not nearly as noticeable to the listeners as you may think.

A positive aspect of nervousness is that it gives you a slight edge, which is evident in greater alertness and sensitivity to the listeners. In fact, speakers who are relatively anxious very often give better speeches than do those who are fairly calm. All in all, delivering a speech is a challenge that can provide satisfaction.

Guide for Reducing Stage Fright

- Select a topic in which you are genuinely interested.
- Learn as much as possible in advance about your audience and about the setting in which you will speak. The more knowledge you have on these matters, the less uncertainty you will feel.
- Prepare your speech thoroughly. Lack of preparation is a major cause of stage fright.
- Write your main points on a note card to avoid forgetting.
- Practise, practise, practise — but do not memorize.
- Space your practice sessions. Rather than practising for two hours the day before your speech, practise for shorter periods over six or seven consecutive days.
- Each time you practise go through the entire speech. In this way, you will get a feel for the whole message.
- Throughout your preparation, always keep your main purpose in mind.
- While awaiting your turn to speak, sit in a relaxed, even limp, position.
- While waiting your turn, breathe deeply.

continued

- Know your introduction especially well — this will ease you into your speech.
- Refer to your note card when necessary, but do not read to your listeners.
- Focus your thoughts throughout your speech on your message and the response you are seeking, rather than on yourself.
- Use gestures and movement to emphasize important points, and your tension will be reduced.

Vocal Factors

While your primary message as a public speaker is the verbal one, you also communicate through many secondary channels. Volume, rate, and pitch of speech contribute to the impression you will make.

Since noise pollution has become an issue in society, we have grown increasingly aware of the volume, or loudness, of those around us. When you speak to a group, adjust your volume according to such factors as room size and those noises over which you must be heard.

Fred Rosen is a well-organized and articulate speaker. He has one fault, however, that greatly reduces his effectiveness. He begins each sentence with enough volume to be heard easily but then gradually reduces it so much that many of the listeners are unable to hear the ends of sentences. This practice has led his subordinates to call him "Half-a-Sentence" Rosen.

A public speaker who regularly speaks more softly towards the end of each sentence is probably using improper breath control. If you have this problem, use shorter sentences or consciously pause at natural breaks to take a breath.

The speed, or rate, at which you speak will influence the way others respond to you and your message. Nervousness sometimes leads inexperienced speakers to speak too quickly. Speaking too rapidly causes other problems: breath-control difficulties and a tendency to give all ideas equal emphasis. Your main ideas should "leap out" at the listener, but they won't unless you slow down ... though not to extremes.

Professor Whittaker is a well-known geneticist. With all the public interest in heredity and cloning, he receives many invitations to give public speeches. Despite his interesting topics, however, he is unable to hold the attention of the audience for very long. After twenty years of lecturing slowly enough so his students can take notes, he seems unable to break the habit. After fifteen minutes of his slow and steady rate of speech, the most interested of civic groups is fighting sleep.

Delivery Guide

- Record your speech at least once while practising and carefully evaluate it.
- Vary your rate, pitch, and volume so that you emphasize your main points.
- Avoid vocalized pauses. Unnecessary "uh's" cause listeners to lose interest in the message.
- Silence is preferable to vocalized pauses.
- Maintain eye contact with your listeners. Watch them to see how they are responding.
- Develop an urge to communicate by selecting a topic in which you are interested.
- Unless you are obviously interested in your topic, your listeners will not be.
- Lessen the distance between you and your listeners. Distance constitutes a barrier that must be overcome.

The highness or lowness at which you speak is referred to as pitch. Although there is no one "correct" pitch, you have a certain pitch level at which your voice is most effective.

Variety is the key to the successful use of these vocal factors. By varying your volume, rate, and pitch, you will become more interesting to listen to, and your message will be more memorable. Many of the other nonverbal factors described in Chapter 3 also greatly influence the impression you make on others.

Modes of Delivery

Public speakers use four main modes of delivery:

1. Impromptu
2. Extemporaneous
3. Memorized
4. Manuscript

Each of the main modes of delivery has advantages and disadvantages

The *impromptu* speech is delivered with little opportunity to prepare. Its main virtue is that it is spontaneous; its main shortcoming is that it is usually not well planned. When you are urged to "say a few words" without any warning, what results is an impromptu speech.

Extemporaneous speaking is somewhat more formal than impromptu speaking. You have an opportunity to plan, and the resulting speech is better organized than an impromptu speech. You usually rely somewhat on notes, but you do not read to the listeners. Most public speeches are delivered extemporaneously.

A *memorized* speech allows for a well-planned expression of ideas. When presenting a speech from memory, however, many speakers tend to lose a certain amount of naturalness and sometimes sound and look quite wooden. The possibility of forgetting the speech is another negative aspect of the memorized speech.

Manuscript speaking is relied on for more formal occasions. When you speak from a manuscript, you can be very precise and carefully control the exact message you send the listeners. Of course, it generally takes longer to develop a manuscript speech. And the manuscript frequently becomes a barrier between speaker and audience.

Team Presentations

Team presentations can be effective if well planned and if individual presentations are mutually exclusive

Although individual presentations are much more common, presentations by teams of individuals are becoming increasingly popular. Continuity is especially important in team presentations.

Planning and delivering a team presentation is a lot like putting together a jigsaw puzzle. You start with the complete picture on the cover of the box and all the various pieces inside.

In team presentations, the introductory segment should preview the entire presentation for the audience, giving them a sense of the "complete picture" as well as the key pieces that will follow. When introducing each segment, each speaker should link his or her segment to the "complete picture" as well as to the segment that immediately preceded it. And, when concluding, each speaker should introduce the next speaker, and his or her topic. The speaker responsible for the concluding segment should review the "complete picture" to ensure that the audience understands how all of the pieces fit together.

When these transitions are managed effectively, the overall presentation will appear as a single, unified whole, rather than as a series of unrelated presentations. Repetition, when it occurs, will be carefully orchestrated and designed to reinforce key points and provide links among the various segments.

When the chamber of commerce sought to attract a National Hockey League team, it assembled a group to present the city's case to the owners of those clubs with an interest in moving.

The first speaker described the area from which the team would draw spectators. Through the use of flip charts, she showed the makeup of the population according to educational level and age now and projected three, five, and ten years into the future.

The second speaker presented the findings of a wage survey done in the community. He described the various income levels and estimates of the amount of discretionary income at each level. His presentation was supplemented by computer-generated slides showing the statistics in colourful graphics.

Transportation facilities were the subject of the third speaker. She presented information about the airport and flight schedules, plus an explanation of the city's public transport. The urban freeway system was also graphically described, using a series of simple, but effective overhead transparencies.

The fourth speaker described the sports complex in which the team would play. This final speaker listed the specific financial incentives and tax benefits the city would provide the team that accepted its offer.

After agreeing to move to the city, the team officials cited "the attractive package" and "persuasive presentations" as major reasons.

All of the principles of effective communication that have been discussed also pertain to the team presentation. The team presentation format also requires some other principles.

Manage your audiovisual aids carefully

The management of audiovisual aids can present challenges when various speakers choose to use different media. Ideally, all the audiovisual aids should be set up prior to the presentation and left in place. In reality, it's sometimes necessary to move the flip chart closer to the audience, move the overhead projector to the side so that it doesn't obscure the screen, and raise the screen if one speaker chooses to use the blackboard or whiteboard. As with set changes between scenes in live theatre, having someone not directly involved in the presentation assist in rearranging the equipment is a good idea. Regardless of the method chosen, you should practise these "set changes" just as frequently as you practise the presentation itself.

Decide how to handle questions in advance

Prior to the presentation, you'll need to decide whether you'll have one question period at the end of the entire presentation or a series of short question periods, one at the end of each segment. If you choose the latter, you might want to have a moderator for the presentation. Having the same person lead each of the question periods will help to control the length and scope of the discussion.

Team Presentation Guide

- Plan the team presentation as a group, and divide the topics into logical and well-balanced segments.
- Anticipate those questions likely to be directed to you and be prepared to respond to them.
- Unless you are the first speaker, begin your speech by referring to the previous speaker, thereby increasing the continuity of the team presentation.
- Direct your speech primarily at the larger audience rather than at the other speakers.
- Stay within your time limit. Do not encroach on the time of the other speakers or on the patience of the listeners.
- While giving your speech, do not lose sight of the goal of the team.
- Listen to the speeches of the other participants and refer to them where appropriate in your speech.

Summary

The fear that many people express at the prospect of giving a speech can be overcome through preparation.

- Determine your purpose
  - the general purpose (to entertain, to inform, to persuade)
  - the specific purpose (what you want to accomplish)
- Analyze your audience so you can appeal to your listeners' interests
- Jot down your central theme, main ideas, and supporting details
- Decide how you'll organize your speech
  - by topics (topical)
  - by time (chronological)
  - by place (spatial)
  - by logic (logical)
- Select techniques for illustrating main ideas
  - quotations
  - examples
  - analogies
  - statistics
- Draft your speech so that it includes
  - an introduction (written last)
  - a body (written first)
  - a conclusion

- Write for the ear
  - k.i.s.s.: keep it short and simple
  - use verbal organizers to orient your speaker
  - use sentence fragments for effect
  - use a conversational, but concise style
- Use visual aids effectively
  - blackboards and whiteboards
  - computer-generated graphics
  - flip charts
  - handouts
  - overhead and slide projectors
- Choose one of the five modes of delivery
  - impromptu (unlikely if you've got time to plan)
  - extemporaneous
  - memorized
  - manuscript
  - team
- Practise, practise, practise

Review Questions

1. In your own words, explain why public speaking is so important to the individual and to the organization.
2. Describe the two-step process used to arrive at the purpose of a speech.
3. Compare a covert response to one that is overt. Give three examples of each.
4. What is meant by audience analysis?
5. What are the five basic questions to which you should seek answers when analyzing an audience?
6. Explain the relationships between central idea, main idea, and supporting materials.
7. What are four commonly used forms of support?
8. What are four commonly used sequences of main points?

Activities

1. Develop and present to your class a five-minute informative speech. Afterwards, encourage comments and questions from the class members. Write a memo to your instructor, outlining the changes you would make in the speech if you had to give it again.
2. Do a written audience analysis of your business communication class. Detail the ways in which the class members are similar and the ways in which they are different.
3. Assuming your class is an audience, develop a five-minute persuasive speech on a subject about which you feel strongly. Describe those

factors from your audience analysis (Activity 2) that most influenced your approach.

4. Give a one-minute impromptu speech on a topic selected by another member of your class. During that minute try to present one main idea and support it as well as you can.
5. Tape-record one of your speeches and write a two-page evaluation of it.
6. In groups of four or five, prepare a team presentation to be given before the class. Select a subject, and divide it among the team members. Each team member should have a specific role. The class members who are the audience should be told the kind of group they are to represent. Following each team presentation the class will do an evaluation.
7. Name two public figures whom you have seen give speeches (either in person or on television). Describe what you think each should do to become a better public speaker.
8. Consult a professional journal in your field to find out about a new development. Report your findings to your class in a five-minute informative speech.
9. Select a product or service and develop a ten-minute persuasive presentation to sell the product or service to your class.

Discussion Cases

The City Council Meeting[9]

Jeffrey Faught is the director of the chamber of commerce in Eastman, a small town with a population of approximately 3000. Although the town is relatively small, it is growing every year.

Faught has been working to bring industry to Eastman for about two years. Presently the town has no industries at all. Most of the people in Eastman are local businesspeople or farmers. Faught believes the town needs some industry, because it would not only strengthen the economy, but also create more jobs. With jobs come people, and people need homes to live in; therefore, real estate would gain from industry as well.

Faught's problem is with the city council and the townspeople. The townspeople want a park and recreational area built where the plant would be built. The city council must decide whether to grant a zoning change for the new industry or the new park.

The second Tuesday night of every month, the city council

continued

meets. The public is also invited. This particular Tuesday, both Faught from the chamber of commerce and the townspeople who favour the park plan to attend.

Faught decides he must make his stand known to both the council and the people. He has not given many speeches, but he knows this presentation must be very persuasive.

The townspeople have wanted a park for their children for years. They believe their town is doing just fine without industry. In the past, the city council has shared this same belief.

Faught is faced with the job of convincing both the council and the people to change their views.

Case Questions

1. What should Jeffrey Faught take into consideration when analyzing his audience?
2. How might he organize his presentation to accomplish his persuasive purpose?
3. Knowing that Faught has to overcome the objections of the council and the people, what modes of proof should he attempt to employ?

The Campus Planning Meeting[10]

Jessica Schuyler is president of the Student's Association at Deer Lake Community College (DLCC). DLCC has a population of 4000 day students and 6000 night school students. The campus is spread over a large city block, 1 km by 2 km, and is located in the city of Deer Lake, which has a population of 40 000. Although there are residence halls on campus, most of the students live off campus and commute by car. A city bus route runs by the campus, but most students prefer to drive.

For three years, the SA has worked with the idea that more student parking is needed on campus. There are parking lots designated for faculty, staff, and handicapped students, but most of the students scramble for a very few parking spots that are farthest away from the main campus buildings. They come early to get a space or face the prospect of parking illegally on city streets near

continued

the campus. Because most students live off campus, the SA feels the time has come for DLCC to provide more student parking.

The Administration and Campus Planning Department meet every week to discuss development plans for the campus. Their priorities range from a new science complex to the construction of a performing arts centre. In the past three years, they have made it clear that they believe buildings and facilities must take precedence over parking lots.

This year, Jessica, as president of the SA, has been given a place on the agenda to present the students' views. She has made many speeches and presentations. With her facts and figures in mind, she must both educate the committee to the problem and persuade them to make campus parking for students one of their priorities. She must be the students' voice.

Case Questions

1. When analyzing her audience, what characteristics of the committee should Jessica keep in mind?
2. Because Jessica has to both educate and persuade the committee, how should she organize her presentation?
3. What modes of proof could Jessica use to overcome the objections of the committee?
4. What visual aids could Jessica use to add to her presentation?

Chapter 15

Communication and Decision Making in Small Groups

Learning Objectives

In this chapter, you'll learn how to be an effective leader of and participant in small groups. More specifically, you will be able to:

1. participate effectively in small-group communication situations
2. explain the purposes of small-group communication in organizations
3. discuss the advantages and disadvantages of reaching decisions in small groups
4. use a problem-solving agenda to guide small groups towards effective decision making
5. explain the role of focus groups in organizational decision making
6. use brainstorming to generate ideas and solutions to problems
7. describe how to overcome the problem of individuals who distort group decisions
8. describe the critical concept of cohesion as it affects the successful functioning of small groups
9. differentiate the various styles of group leadership
10. describe how specific behaviours of group leaders and members can help move the group towards its goal

Preview Case

"I've got a million things to do today," Alex was thinking as he entered the conference room. "The last thing I need is another meeting." The purpose of this meeting was to explain to the supervisors the new worker involvement program the company was about to implement.

Theresa Staub, the plant manager, conducted the meeting with the assistance of an outside consultant. In the first part of the meeting, the consultant described the benefits other companies experienced through worker involvement programs. After that the consultant explained the process and the critical role the supervisor played. Alex found the concept of worker involvement interesting. He was sceptical, however, about it working in this company.

In accordance with what he had been taught, but with considerable apprehension, he called a meeting of his people. He explained the worker involvement program and described how everyone stood to benefit from the program's success.

"Concentrate on quality control," he told his workers. "What are some things you think should be done to improve quality control?" After an awkward silence a few members made half-hearted suggestions. Fortunately, the time had come to end the meeting. "Same time next week," Alex reminded his people, all the while dreading the prospect of another such meeting. "Between now and then, keep thinking of ways to improve quality control," he said.

At the next meeting, Alex realized that his fears had been unfounded. The group members required no prodding to participate. The members obviously had given some thought to quality control, and they were no longer hesitant about expressing their thoughts.

Alex was pleasantly surprised by the transformation of a collection of individuals into a group. As a result of this experience, he began to recognize the many values to be derived from working with groups.

Overview

Small groups are an integral part of your business and social life. Your family is the first group to which you belonged. As you grew, so did the number and range of your groups. Neighbourhood, school, and church affiliations are all groups in which interaction takes place.

The organizations within which you work, or will work, are additional groups. Most business organizations make extensive use of groups. In fact, many managers spend as much as half of each workday working in small groups. A large percentage of the decisions made in business organizations are made by groups.

The ability to lead and to participate in groups is an important skill in any business organization. It is also a skill that can be learned. The purpose of this chapter is to help make you an effective participant in small groups by increasing your awareness of factors that significantly influence group communication.

The Role of Groups in Organizations

Business has traditionally made extensive use of groups. Until the last several decades, however, the makeup of such groups was exclusively managerial. Managers and staff participated in meetings and conferences for fact-finding and decision making. Plans were developed and policies were made by groups that rarely included anyone else because the activities were considered the role of management alone.

Until recently most decision-making groups were managerial

Today the use of groups pervades all levels of the organization. In the quest for greater productivity and employee satisfaction, many companies have moved towards *participative management*. With this method employees at every level become involved in job-related decision making. Worker involvement groups such as the one described at the beginning of this chapter are a technique of participative management.

The growth of the quality circle movement mirrors the growing emphasis on participative management. *Quality circles* are small groups of workers that meet regularly with management to discuss problems of productivity and of the workplace in general. Quality circles appear to have a significant impact on employee commitment to the organization, as well as on organizational productivity and development.

The emphasis on participative management has been accompanied by a greater emphasis on groups

Whatever job you eventually assume in an organization, you will become a part of various work groups. Your ability to work and interact effectively in them will significantly determine your occupational success. While a knowledge of the contents of this chapter will not in itself turn you into a polished team player, it will help you move in that direction.

Characteristics of a Small Group

Imagine that you participated in two groups today. Your first group gathered in the plant cafeteria 30 minutes before starting work. The group, which consists of you and five friends, meets most mornings before work and usually discusses sports, politics, and the opposite sex, not necessarily in that order.

Your second group was the plant grievance committee, a group with seven members that meets weekly to consider employee grievances. You were selected to represent the shipping department.

Small groups have certain characteristics

Technically, each of these groups is a small group; only one, however, meets the criteria necessary to be designated a small group for our purposes. The characteristics of a small group are:

1. A Common Purpose

Members must share a common nonsocial purpose

The members of the plant grievance committee gather with a common purpose to consider the grievances of employees. The individuals who get together in the cafeteria meet because they especially enjoy talking to one another about sports or current events. The six individuals meet most mornings on a social basis but do not share a common professional purpose.

2. A Small Number of Participants

Group size influences productivity and satisfaction of members

The size of a group has a significant impact on productivity as well as on the satisfaction of group members. A group that is too small will be limited in the quantity of information it can generate. Individual members would, however, have greater opportunities to participate. The increased opportunities will often result in more satisfied members.

A larger-sized group can generate more ideas. There will be fewer opportunities for individual participation, however, and members may be less satisfied with their groups. Although there is no magic number, groups of five members are often regarded as ideal for effectiveness.

3. Interdependence Among Members

There is an interdependence among group members

Groups assemble with the intent of capitalizing on the combined efforts of the members. Members not only influence one another but also rely on one another for information and support. A bond develops between the members that leads to an interdependence that facilitates communication within the group. Members remain aware of the collective nature of the group.

4. Face-to-Face Interaction

Interaction between members is face to face

Another characteristic of a small group is that the members interact face to face. The members meet and exchange information verbally and nonverbally.

5. Roles

The roles that group members assume are a function of the type of group as well as the characteristics of individual members. If group members belong to a *command* group of superior and subordinates, the roles they play will depend on their organizational positions as well as their relationships with the group's formal and informal leaders. If the group were a group of friends, the role and role expectations would be entirely different.

The role of the group member depends on the type of group as well as the individual

In any group, individuals can choose whether to play a task or a maintenance role. A *task role* focuses on accomplishment of the task set before the group. Conversely, a *maintenance role* centres on the emotional and psychological needs of the group members. Both roles are essential for effective group functioning. A closer inspection of the task and maintenance roles is included later in this chapter in the discussion of the functions of the small-group leader.

The *grievance committee* possesses all of the characteristics of a small group. The cafeteria group does not, since it lacks both a common professional purpose and interdependence among its members. A *small group* may be defined as a collection of a few individuals who interact face to face, verbally and nonverbally, for a common professional purpose, and whose members are interdependent.

Small groups are used in a wide variety of situations. However, they usually have two basic purposes: information sharing and problem solving. Frequently, these two are combined within the same group.

Advantages and Disadvantages of Small Groups

Small groups have advantages in making decisions

When faced with a decision you should consider the advantages of using small groups. For many, participation in small-group communication is motivational. Most of us prefer to participate in a group and be a part of the decision-making process rather than have someone simply hand down a decision to us. Other advantages of using small groups include:

1. Quality of Decision

As long as the group members have appropriate knowledge and expertise, a group decision is usually superior to the decision of an individual. A plant manager who expects first-line production supervisors to select the plant's new air filtration system, however, is probably assuming too much about the supervisors' expertise.

2. Acceptance

Subordinates who are included in the decision-making process will usually accept a decision more readily. For example, suppose that the clothing manager in a retail store is faced with requests from three full-time salespeople to have the same week off as vacation. One of the three must be asked to reschedule so that the business can function normally. This is not a decision about quality — any one of the three salespeople could perform adequately alone. If the department manager makes the decision, the unlucky salesperson will be upset and may become hostile. However, the three salespeople are asked to work out a decision among themselves, so that each has the opportunity to discuss his or her own viewpoint. A group decision in this instance improves the chances that all the salespeople will accept the final agreement.

3. Commitment

The elements of acceptance and commitment are closely related. Commitment, however, goes beyond acceptance. When individuals are directly involved in analyzing and solving a problem they become more committed to the effective implementation of the decision. Thus, a company considering such motivational tools as job enrichment, wage incentives, or profit sharing might benefit from involving employees in selecting the appropriate program.

4. Status

Participants gain a sense of heightened status and recognition from the responsibility and interaction in group decision making.

You should also consider the disadvantages of using small groups.

Using small groups also has definite disadvantages

1. Time

Preparing for a meeting or conference takes time, especially if you are responsible for leading the session. To be an effective participant, you must devote some time to preparing. And, the actual meetings are time-consuming. Many managers spend more than one third of their working hours in meetings.

2. Cost

Expense is another disadvantage since group meetings take employees away from their regular duties. When individuals make decisions, less time is lost and, consequently, the decision making is less expensive.

3. Unclear Individual Accountability

Accountability refers to the expectation that someone will do some specific things to accomplish a specific goal. When an individual is assigned a task, that person is accountable for its satisfactory completion. When a group pursues a task, accountability is blurred.

Someone once said, "Success has a thousand fathers; failure has none." Although the person wasn't specifically referring to groups, the quotation suggests a disadvantage of groups. When a group effort is successful, individual members will often try to take credit for the success. When a group effort is unsuccessful, individual members will often seek to disassociate themselves from the results. From the standpoint of individual members, unclear accountability may be viewed as an advantage of small groups. From the standpoint of group productivity, however, unclear accountability is a definite disadvantage.

4. Undue Conformity

Sometimes a group is dominated by one individual with whom the other members acquiesce in order to avoid conflict and speed decisions. At other times, a group may perceive a member as more knowledgeable than is the case and, therefore, go along with that person's opinions. The more a group interacts, the greater the pressures on members to conform. Peer pressure, the influence of the other members, is likely to ensure conformity. The greater the conformity, the less likely it is that a group will benefit from all members' expertise. At the extreme, such conformity is called groupthink. This phenomenon is discussed later in the chapter.

Solving Problems in Small Groups

Nearly every small group brought together to solve a problem follows a format or agenda. In this section, we'll discuss four common methods for problem solving in groups.

The Dewey Format

The most widely used format is based on John Dewey's Reflective Thinking Process:[1]

Group problem solving using Dewey's Steps of Reflective Thinking is common

1. Defining and Analyzing the Problem

First, the precise nature of the problem is specified and its underlying causes investigated. Consider, for example, a small retail firm that has low employee morale, a considerable decline in sales, and an unusually high rate of employee turnover. The leader might begin by describing these problems and delineating them with available facts. By concisely depicting the present state of affairs, the leader is defining the problem.

Once each participant understands the nature and scope of the problem, the group can investigate potential causes. In this example, group members would offer their perceptions of what might be causing the morale, sales, and turnover problems. These perceptions are discussed, modified (if necessary), and recorded by a leader or appointed group member.

Suppose the group perceives the following four possible causes: lack of communication between superiors and subordinates; poor motivational programs; conflict between the sales and delivery departments; and insufficient advertising. After analyzing information from attitude surveys or grievance and exit interviews, the group might decide that inadequate motivation is the major cause of the problem. When the problem is defined and the suspected cause is identified, the group can move to Step 2.

2. Establishing Criteria for a Solution

The criteria step in the problem-solving sequence may be postponed until solutions are actually evaluated. Suppose, however, that this group, after considerable discussion, determines that any potential solution must: include all nonmanagement employees; become effective within two months; and cost no more than 2 percent of the company's gross profits.

In some cases, the criteria may be dictated by circumstances outside the control of the group itself: legislation, company policy, budget realities, market conditions, and so on. In any event, the group has three criteria and is ready to begin Step 3 of the problem-solving process.

3. Proposing Possible Solutions

In this step, participants suggest as many solutions as possible. Each participant attempts to propose solutions that meet the specified criteria. Although members may amend the solutions offered by others, no solutions are evaluated at this time. The third step is essentially brainstorming, and it is important to keep the basic rules of brainstorming in mind. These rules are:

a. Ideas are expressed freely without regard to quality. The emphasis is on quantity. Generate as many ideas as possible.
b. Criticism of ideas is not allowed until the brainstorming session is over.
c. Elaboration and combinations of previously expressed ideas are encouraged. The theory is that creativity will build as one idea triggers another. A record of the possible solutions generated is kept by the leader or appointee.

Suppose that the group suggests the following five potential solutions: better fringe benefits, increased commissions, profit sharing, a sales contest, and wage incentives. The group can now move to Step 4.

4. Evaluating Possible Solutions

In Step 4, the group members evaluate each of the proposed solutions. Each solution is weighed against any criteria outlined in Step 2 as well as against other proposed criteria. The group's aim is to identify the advantages and disadvantages of each solution. For example, the wage incentives might be pertinent to all nonmanagement employees and easily set up within two months but, nevertheless, too costly and not relevant to the needs of the commission salespeople.

A matrix with the criteria on one axis and the proposed solutions on the other is a useful format for recording the discussion during this phase. Once the advantages and disadvantages have been assigned to each solution, the group can proceed to Step 5.

5. Selecting a Solution

A critical point to keep in mind is that the group is not obligated to select only one of the proposed solutions. The most effective decision might combine two or three proposed solutions or an altered version of only one. Whatever the outcome, during Step 5 a final decision must be made concerning the best possible solution. The precise details of the solution should also be decided. Suppose, in this example, that the group chooses to increase commissions by 1 percent across the board. In addition, the group decides on a three-month sales contest between hard- and soft-line divisions and that the winners will receive cash bonuses and gift certificates. The participants are now ready for the final step in the problem-solving sequence.

6. Plotting a Course of Action

This final step concentrates on how best to execute the solution. Before the meeting can end, the participants must agree on a specific, detailed method for enacting the solution. Group members may volunteer to be responsible for certain aspects of the program, or the leader may assign specific tasks to participants. Whatever approach is chosen, agreement must be reached before the problem-solving process can terminate.

Checklist for Dewey Reflective Thinking Format

- Define and analyze the problem
- Establish criteria for a solution
- Propose possible solutions
- Evaluate possible solutions
- Select a solution
- Plot a course of action

For the sake of illustration, suppose that two department heads have volunteered to direct the sales contest. Together they will work out the details and report to the store manager within one week. Finally, the store manager announces that the 1 percent commission increase will become effective at the beginning of the next month.

The Ideal-Solution Format

The ideal-solution format is another approach to problem solving

Although Dewey's six-step approach is the best-known and most widely used method for problem solving, other formats are used. One is the *ideal-solution* approach developed from observing the problem-solving process followed by many business groups. In the ideal-solution approach, group discussion follows this sequence of questions:

1. Are we all agreed on the nature of the problem?
2. What would be the ideal solution from the point of view of all parties involved in the problem?
3. What conditions of the problem could be changed so that the ideal solution might be achieved?
4. Of the solutions available to us, which one best approximates the ideal solution?[2]

The Single-Question Method

The single-question method is sometimes used in problem solving

The single-question method is another approach to group problem solving. Groups using this method focus on a single objective and thereby are less likely to pursue digressions. In the single-question method, this sequence of questions is followed:

1. What single question will yield the answer that is all the group needs to know to accomplish its purpose?
2. What subquestions must be answered before this single question can be answered?
3. Do we have sufficient information to answer confidently the subquestions? (If yes, answer them. If not, continue.)
4. What are the most reasonable answers to the subquestions?
5. Assuming that our answers to the subquestions are correct, what is the best solution to the problem?[3]

The ideal-solution and the single-question methods appear to be more direct than the Dewey approach. The Dewey approach, however, is more thorough and more likely to develop the group members' analytical skills. As a group matures and remains intact over long periods of time, it adopts a more abbreviated approach to problem solving. Its new approach may be the ideal-solution or the single-question method, or the group may adopt another approach specifically tailored to its environment and needs.

Focus Groups

One specialized small group popular in businesses today is the focus group. Focus groups have long been the tool of market researchers, but today they are being used in a variety of other settings.

A focus group has certain characteristics

In market research, a focus group provides informal communication to the business about the probable success of its plans for a product. For example, a soft drink firm may want to investigate how best to advertise a new soft drink soon to go on the market. The company would gather together a group of eight to twelve individuals who are more or less homogeneous. The company's focus group in this case might consist of either full-time female college students or males in their senior year of high school. These two diverse groups would not be mixed in the same focus group because of the differences in their lifestyles and objectives.

Once the focus group is assembled, the moderator opens the discussion and makes sure it continues. The moderator does not direct the discussion in any one direction. The result is freewheeling talk, often not in the anticipated direction. Focus group discussions are frequently recorded for later review, and the people in charge of making the decision may watch the group interact from behind a one-way mirror.

Spontaneity is the primary advantage of focus groups

Lack of structure is the primary advantage of the focus group: what the group members say is spontaneous. Traditional market research relies upon questionnaires that force the respondent to choose one of the answers provided. The focus group allows the communication process between the consumer and the company planners to be dynamic and free flowing. In short, the planners may uncover ideas that they have not considered.

The experience of Curlee Clothing with focus groups is indicative of the benefits of a company's uncovering problems that its planners had never considered. Curlee Clothing set out to evaluate its advertising and product strategies and organized several focus groups to uncover deficiencies in these areas. What the researchers found was that the group members centred their discussions on distrust of the sales personnel and not on styles, prices, quality, or advertising. The informal communication provided by the focus group was instrumental in the company training its retail sales personnel to be more responsive to customer needs, instead of needlessly attempting to improve its advertising.[4]

Some unlikely organizations and individuals are now using focus groups

The Wall Street Journal has reported that users as unlikely as universities and lawyers are testing their ideas with focus groups before implementation. In 1985, Syracuse University used focus groups of alumni to determine how best to appeal to the university's alumni in a $100-million-plus fund drive. The promotional film shown to the focus groups stressed science and research; the focus groups were unimpressed. Said Harry W. Peter III, vice-chancellor for university relations, "We were so proud of showing off our technology toys that we had underestimated the abiding interest [alumni] had in their undergraduate, humanistic education."[5]

Lawyers, too, are using focus groups to test their courtroom strategies before the actual trial. In one case, focus groups indicated that nonworking jurors would be more impartial towards a defendant, an office products manufacturer, because people who worked in offices regarded the defendant's products so highly they found it impossible to believe the defendant company could be guilty of any wrong.

Focus groups do have their limitations. First, finding out what eight to twelve people think about a soft drink advertisement is not the same as finding out what eight to twelve million people think. Generalizing the findings of focus groups can thus be very risky for a company, a university, or a lawyer.

Second, the moderator must be trained to lead the focus group. Even the most experienced moderators have a difficult time not imposing their opinions on what the group has said. The moderator can also contaminate the process — and its outcome — by shifting topics too rapidly or by leading the group in one direction instead of another. Last, focus groups are expensive. The cost of the facility, the moderator, and the participants (who are typically paid a small fee) can be prohibitive for small companies.

Avoiding Defective Decision Making

Individuals can distort group decisions

Sometimes defective decisions are reached in small groups because of certain characteristics of individuals. For example, powerful individuals sometimes dominate groups and keep others from actively participating in the group process; poor decisions often result. You may encounter a group member who digresses and consumes valuable time on unrelated topics. On other occasions, individuals in the group may press for a quick decision before all the important aspects of the problem have been carefully considered. In numerous other ways, individuals can dilute the decision-making potential of groups.

Maintaining Cohesion

Group cohesion is the product of the mutual attraction of members and the commitment of members to the group. While there are many theories on what makes groups effective, most people will agree that, if members feel loyal towards their group, it is destined to be more successful than one that has no such loyalty. Such factors as loyalty, unity, and attraction in groups are encompassed in the term *cohesion.*

Three factors that determine the extent of group cohesion are the degree of agreement on goals, the frequency of interaction, and the amount of intergroup competition.

Cohesion is more likely when there are frequent meetings, agreement on goals, and intergroup competition

1. Agreement on Goals

When a group agrees on goals, members are more attracted to it. Kim Cochea quit her sorority after one year out of a sense of frustration. She, along with some other members, believed the sorority should pursue a small number of campus improvement projects each year. Other members believed the group's main purpose should be to plan and hold as many parties as possible. Because this disagreement on goals was not resolved, group morale declined and several members left the sorority.

As long as group members cannot agree on what a group's goals should be, the group's effectiveness will be neutralized. Cohesion is virtually unattainable as long as such basic differences exist.

Just because there is agreement on goals, however, does not mean there will be an absence of conflict or disagreement among group members. Deciding on the means of accomplishing a goal is also the cause of many problems in groups. Nevertheless, when the group agrees on its goals, cohesion is likely to develop.

2. Frequency of Interaction

The more frequently a group meets, the more likely that group will become cohesive. As members get acquainted, they become more interested in their colleagues and in their common tie, the group. Cohesion comes from familiarity, and familiarity from the frequency of interaction.

3. Intergroup Competition

Few situations bind a group as does a perceived threat to the group. In many business organizations, managers intentionally create a threat by developing competition between groups, and increased cohesion results. When one group is pitted against another, both groups will usually benefit. In some plants, for example, competition is developed between shifts, with the most productive shift receiving an award.

While competition between groups heightens cohesion, competition within groups results in division and discord. Members become polarized, taking sides against the other, and interpersonal friction develops.

Cohesion is a significant ingredient in effective groups. Some of the by-products of cohesion are high morale, good communication, and members' willingness to work hard. As is often true, it is possible to have too much of a good thing, and cohesiveness is no exception.

Groupthink

Groupthink hampers decision making

Groups that are overly cohesive suffer from groupthink.[6] Groupthink occurs when agreement, rather than critical thinking, becomes most important. Under such conditions, a group may make decisions that the individual group members, acting alone, would probably not have made. The cliché "Don't make waves" expresses a sentiment that often prevails in groups beset by groupthink. Here are the symptoms of groupthink:

1. An illusion of invulnerability, shared by most or all the members, creates excessive optimism and encourages taking extreme risks.
2. Collective efforts to rationalize and discount warnings might lead members to reconsider their assumptions before they recommit themselves to their past policy decisions.
3. An unquestioned belief in the group's inherent morality inclines members to ignore the ethical or moral consequences of their decisions.
4. Stereotyped views see opposition leaders as too evil to warrant genuine negotiation or as too weak.
5. Direct pressure on any member who expresses strong arguments against any of the group's stereotypes, illusions, or commitments makes clear that dissent is contrary to what is expected of all loyal members.
6. Self-censorship of deviations from the apparent group consensus reflects each member's inclination to minimize the importance of any doubts and counterarguments.
7. A shared illusion of unanimity concerning judgements conforming to the majority view (partly resulting from self-censorship of deviations and augmented by the false assumption that silence means consent).
8. The emergence of self-appointed mindguards — members who protect the group from adverse information that might shatter their shared complacency about the effectiveness and morality of decisions.[7]

Groupthink can be prevented

Groupthink is both prevalent and destructive to genuine group efforts and its presence defeats the main reason for assembling groups — critical thinking. By adhering to the following suggestions, however, it is possible to prevent groupthink:

1. Have the group leader assign the role of critic to each member. Doubts and objections are thus more likely to be exposed and discussed than to be suppressed. Group leaders must set the example by accepting criticism of their ideas and thoughts on the matter at hand. Acceptance of criticism does not often come naturally, so it may have to be learned by group members.

2. When assigning a decision-making mission to a group, the leader should be impartial instead of stating preferences. When executives in an organization give guidance to decision-making groups, they often unwittingly introduce bias by being too specific in outlining what they want accomplished. If the time is short, more guidance will hasten the decision.

   However, less guidance means there is less chance that the executive's notions will unduly influence the group's decision. Certainly the leader should not be so specific as to indicate which of several alternatives is personally preferable. Admittedly there is a delicate balance between just enough guidance to get the job done and too much guidance so that group members believe they have been manipulated. That balance is what a group leader should strive for.
3. Members of the decision-making group should seek advice and counsel from trusted associates in their own departments within the organization. Fresh perspectives on a problem can be gained by introducing thoughts from those outside the decision-making group. The reactions of their associates should then be taken back and introduced to the group. Discretion must be used in implementing this suggestion when the decision involves highly confidential planning of goals or policies that should not have wide dissemination.
4. The tendency to see a consensus could be effectively thwarted by using a "devil's advocate" at each group meeting. The role of devil's advocate, to be most effective, should be rotated among the group members, and in some cases more than one may be desirable. Criticism by this person should be taken seriously and discussed to the satisfaction all present.[8]

The Role of the Group Leader

An important role in every group is that of the group leader. The group leader is responsible for planning the meeting, circulating an agenda and information related to the items on that agenda to participants in advance of the meeting, structuring and controlling the discussion during the meeting, and ensuring that the proceedings are recorded.

Planning the Meeting

All too often business meetings suffer from a lack of clear purpose, direction, or results. Such meetings can leave their participants feeling angry and frustrated. When you are responsible for leading a meeting, you need to start planning well in advance. As with other types of communication, you should first consider your purpose and your audience:

1. Decide on Your Objective

Meetings need a clear purpose

Having a clear and necessary reason for meeting is essential. Groups that meet on a weekly or monthly basis because "we've always done it that way" can unintentionally waste thousands of dollars. For example, a one-hour department meeting attended by five individuals earning an average of $15 an hour costs $75 in salary alone. Lost productivity can increase this amount.

2. Decide on Topics

Once you've decided on your objective, you can list the topics that need to be covered in order to achieve that objective. For example, if you are meeting to plan for the unveiling of a new product, you might want to introduce the participants to the features of the new product, review the strategies that have been used previously, and brainstorm ways to introduce this product.

3. Decide Who to Invite

The right people need to be there

Although some groups have a constant membership, it's a good idea to check to see that everyone needed to accomplish the meeting's objective is invited. For example, introducing participants to the features of the new product may mean inviting its designer to present the information.

4. Look at Options

Before you prepare your agenda, ask yourself if there's a less expensive way of achieving your objective. While you may well decide to go ahead with the meeting, at the very least you will have a clear rationale for the meeting when you make your opening remarks.

5. Circulate an Agenda

Agendas announce the meeting's purpose and schedule

A meeting agenda is essentially a schedule of events for the meeting. It includes details about the date, time (including overall length), and location of the meeting. Frequently it is circulated as a "Notice of Meeting" memo (see Figure 15.1). It tells participants what will be discussed and what they need to do to prepare for the meeting. Where appropriate, it includes information attached to it relating to items on the agenda.

Notice that the agenda in Figure 15.1 also includes the amount of time you anticipate spending on each item. A full two thirds of the meeting will be devoted to the main objective; however, twenty minutes are allowed to ensure that members are clear about what was accomplished in the last meeting (minutes and business arising) and have an opportunity to deal briefly with issues that concern them (other business). Such limitations help you, as the leader, to ensure that all topics are covered and that the amount of time spent on each one reflects its importance at that particular meeting.

If someone other than the group leader is responsible for specific items on the agenda, it's a good idea to include that person's name beside the item(s) he or she is responsible for. The name serves as a gentle reminder that extra preparation may be necessary on that item.

Subject: NOTICE OF MEETING: ENGLISH LANGUAGE PROFICIENCY COMMITTEE

The English Language Proficiency Committee will meet next week to consider the draft policy of English Language Standards at Columbian College. Please review the draft policy and be prepared to offer suggestions for revisions.

DATE: Wednesday, May 15, 1991
TIME: 1230 to 1330
PLACE: Boardroom 2B
Campus Administration Building

AGENDA

1. Introduction	2 minutes
2. Minutes of the last meeting (attached)	3 minutes
3. Business arising from the Minutes	10 minutes
4. Draft Policy: English Language Standards (attached)	40 minutes
5. Other business	5 minutes

Figure 15.1 Sample Meeting Agenda

Conducting the Meeting

The leader's role is critical to the meeting's success

As the group leader, you will most likely be responsible for chairing or leading the meeting. While there are rules for conducting formal meetings, known as "Robert's Rules of Order," named after their originator, most meetings are less formal. If you do need to conduct a formal meeting, you can consult *Robert's Rules* in your library. This chapter dicusses leading informal meetings.

At the outset of the meeting, you should assign someone to take "minutes" or record the key points in the discussion. At the very least, minutes should contain a record of all decisions and the names of those responsible for implementing those decisions. As group leader, you will be too busy to take comprehensive notes yourself. While some groups have the luxury of a professional secretary to take minutes, most rotate the responsibility among the group members. By focusing only on key points and decisions, members should not find the task too onerous.

Task and Maintenance Functions

The two major functions of the leader of the small group are the task function and the maintenance function.

The behaviours included under the *task function* have to do with completing the group task:

1. Define the problem to be discussed.
2. Agree on the sequence of topics.
3. Ask for information about the problem.
4. Clarify the contributions of group members.
5. Ask for evaluation of information.
6. Ask for solutions.
7. Ask for evaluation of solutions.

The behaviours included under the maintenance function keep the group working together:

1. Encourage participation by all members.
2. Develop a permissive and informal group atmosphere.
3. Make group members feel secure.
4. Ensure that contrasting views are presented.
5. Allow for the release of tension.
6. Resolve differences among group members.

If the discussion becomes heated and all present begin to talk at once, you may find a speaker's list is useful. By acknowledging a group member and adding his or her name to the speaker's list, you'll find that members are more willing to listen to what others have to say and wait their turn.

Before closing the meeting, you should ensure that everyone knows what will happen next and that those assigned specific tasks have a clear understanding of those tasks and a deadline for completing them.

Following Up on the Meeting

Following the meeting, the group leader should meet briefly with the person who recorded the proceedings to ensure that all important information has been included. These minutes can then be word-processed and circulated to group members. Ideally, group members receive the minutes within a couple of days and so have a written reminder of their tasks.

Minutes generally include the following information: the name of the group; the date, time, and location of the meeting; at least one entry recording the outcome of every item on the agenda; and a list of key decisions and the people responsible for implementing those decisions.

Although the duties of the group leader remain relatively constant, leadership styles can vary dramatically.

Leadership Styles

In carrying out their duties, group leaders can adopt a variety of leadership styles:

1. Authoritarian Leadership

Authoritarian leaders usually determine the specific task for each participant because they often believe that group participants are limited in ability and need strict guidance and control. This style of leadership, therefore, is rigid and inflexible. Authoritarian leaders often dominate discussion and are usually reluctant to acknowledge those who disagree with them. Such leaders discourage member participation, causing members to resign themselves to the fact that the leader will make all the decisions no matter what anyone else might have to contribute. Leaders who employ the authoritarian style may very quickly reach the solution they want, but in terms of group morale, the costs are very high.

The emotional consequences of authoritarian leadership are serious. One might wonder why a group leader would use this style. In many situations leaders want the group to know beyond any doubt that they are in control. Because such leaders so completely dominate their groups they are unaware of and probably unconcerned about the members' perception of them as leaders.

There are some situations for which authoritarian leadership is appropriate — when there is a crisis, when time is extremely limited, or when the matter under discussion is trivial. Authoritarian leadership, however, is overused and counter-productive.

Supervisory leadership is useful when efficiency is critical

2. Supervisory Leadership

Supervisory leadership that stops short of autocratic control is useful when efficiency is critical. Supervisory leaders almost always introduce the problem for discussion with a lengthy description. They usually decide what problem will be discussed in the meeting and frequently summarize what has so far taken place in the group. Such leaders are not as formal or rigid as the authoritarian ones, but they give little attention to the needs of the group.

Democratic leadership encourages active participation

3. Democratic or Participative Leadership

Both authoritarian and supervisory leaders depend upon methods that limit the participation and freedom of other group members. Democratic or participative leaders, on the other hand, encourage group members to participate actively in discussion. Rather than restricting group members, this style of leadership has a positive effect. A leader who employs the participative style seeks to accomplish the following:

a. All group members participate freely
b. Communication directed to all members, not just the leader
c. Group decisions perceived as group achievements
d. Group members able to satisfy some personal needs in the group environment
e. Group members able to identify with the group

Employing the participative style of leadership is a difficult assignment when the leader must co-ordinate both the task and the group maintenance functions. This type of leadership, however, is most frequently used because it promotes a high degree of group cohesion and at the same time spurs the group towards accomplishing the task.

4. Laissez-faire or Group-centred Leadership

Laissez-faire leaders expect group members to be self-directed, and refrain from structuring the group in any way. They listen but do not show approval or disapproval, and although they may clarify on occasion, they are careful not to impose their own thoughts. The atmosphere is extremely relaxed. This kind of leader always tries to view the discussion from the frame of reference of the member who is speaking.[9]

The Role of Group Members

The success of small-group decision making also depends on the participants. They can make the leader's job easier by trying to follow the agenda and by being aware of the flow of the discussion. Group members can help move the group towards its goal by:

1. Contributing Information

The problem-solving group needs information to reach decisions. Effective group members bring information they have gathered about the topic. Some participants have a tendency to divulge all their information the first time they have the opportunity to speak. This leads to disorganization. People need to develop the ability to see where their information on the topic applies. Timing is a critical element in presenting information.

2. Evaluating Information

Group participants need to bring several critical skills to the problem-solving situation. One of the most important is the ability to examine carefully all information presented to the group. Participants should offer supporting or contradictory evidence when they have it. Fallacious reasoning and unsupported assertions should be exposed. Good reasoning and accurate information are essential to the group problem-solving process. Participants should resist the tendency to accept everything that is said during the discussion.

3. Asking Questions

Group participants perform an important function by asking pertinent questions at appropriate times. Such questions help to expose inaccurate information or to clarify a point that one of the other members is attempting to make. The use of questions encourages feedback, aids the understanding of all group members, and helps keep the participants on the main subject of the discussion. The attention of the entire group can be focused on the central issue of the discussion by a well-phrased, pertinent question.

4. Listening Empathetically

As previously noted, listening is of key importance in the communication process. Effective group participants listen to the content of what other members are saying and also "listen between the lines." The empathetic listener tries to see the topic from the speaker's frame of reference. It's important to be sensitive to the attitudes and feelings of the other group members.

5. Thinking as a Group

Group members should be aware that group thinking (not groupthink) is different from individual thinking. Participants should relate their comments to the group's thinking and refer to what their fellow members have said, and what has already been agreed to. Usually the longer people participate in a group, the more skilled they become in group thinking. It's not a good idea to move ahead too quickly: for the group to function effectively, it must think together.

Group Leadership Guide

In conducting a meeting, you should:

- start the meeting on time
- keep the group aware of the goals of the meeting
- control the discussion by discouraging digressions
- encourage quiet members to participate
- provide frequent summaries to clarify what has happened thus far
- end the meeting by summarizing what has been accomplished

Group Participation Guide

As a participant in a meeting, you should:

- be on time
- be alert both in attitude and in physical bearing
- participate early in the meeting and as often as you have something relevant to say
- keep your comments brief — contribute several times, making one point at a time rather than making several points at one time
- take notes to retain specific information

Summary

Groups are playing an increasingly important role in organizations.

- Small groups have certain characteristics:
  - a common purpose
  - a small number of participants
  - interdependence among members
  - face-to-face interaction
- Small groups have several advantages:
  - higher-quality decisions
  - greater acceptance
  - greater commitment

- Small groups also have disadvantages:
  - increased time requirements
  - greater cost
  - unclear individual accountability
  - undue conformity
- Four methods can be used to solve problems in small groups:
  - the Dewey Reflective Thinking Process
    - define and analyze the problem
    - establish criteria for a solution
    - propose possible solutions
    - evaluate possible solutions using the criteria
    - select a solution
    - plot a course of action
  - the ideal-solution approach
    - agree on the nature of the problem
    - identify an ideal solution
    - identify conditions for change so the ideal solution will work
    - select the best approximation of the ideal solution
  - the single-question method
    - identify a single question
    - generate subquestions
    - collect information
    - answer subquestions
    - identify the best solution
  - focus groups
    - find out what homogeneous groups of eight to twelve people think about an issue
    - use that information to develop a solution
- Avoid defective decision making by:
  - maintaining cohesion
    - get agreement on goals
    - meet frequently
    - create intergroup competition
  - avoiding groupthink
    - assign a member to be "critic"
    - choose a leader who's impartial
    - seek advice from experts
    - appoint a devil's advocate
- The group leader is responsible for:
  - planning the meeting
    - determine your objective
    - list the topics to be discussed
    - decide who to invite to the meeting
    - look at other options

        - circulate an agenda
    - conducting the meeting
        - assign someone to take minutes
        - attend to task and maintenance functions
        - use a speaker's list to avoid multiple speakers
    - following up on the meeting
        - ensure minutes are prepared quickly
        - circulate minutes
- Four leadership styles have been identified:
    - authoritarian
    - supervisory
    - democratic or participative
    - laissez-faire or group centred
- Group members are responsible for:
    - contributing information
    - evaluating information
    - asking questions
    - listening empathetically
    - thinking as a group

Review Questions

1. What are the identifying characteristics of small-group communication?
2. Discuss the major advantages and disadvantages of reaching decisions in small groups.
3. You are a student government officer who wants to serve the needs of students. Explain how you might use focus groups to guide your decisions.
4. Explain the steps of a problem-solving agenda.
5. Why is brainstorming effective for generating ideas?
6. Define the concept of cohesion as it relates to small-group decision making. Why is it so critical in determining successful group problem solving?
7. What is groupthink? How is it different from thinking as a group?
8. What are the major styles of group leadership? Which style best fits your personality? Why?
9. Group members play a vital role in successful group decision making. In what ways can the participants help move the group towards its goal?

Activities

1. Divide the class into groups of five or six and use the brainstorming technique to generate solutions to a problem that confronts your school.

2. Attend a meeting of the local city council or watch one on community television. Observe the interaction of council members. Record your observations.
3. Critically evaluate a meeting connected with your interests at school — student government or student professional association, for example. Include both the pros and the cons of the proceedings in your evaluation.
4. Select a problem that is common to yourself and a peer group. Reach a decision on your own, then discuss it with the group. Record any new viewpoints that the group brought up that you overlooked in your original decision.
5. Have everyone in class make a list of the problems one experiences as a new member of an established group. Then, in groups of five or six and using the individual lists, construct a master list for each group. Each group should then identify ways in which group members can overcome these problems.
6. Using the problem lists generated in Activity 5, identify ways that group leaders can assist members in overcoming those problems.

Discussion Cases

The Realty Tangle[10]

Kilgore and Mitchell, Realtors, is a Calgary real estate firm with a total of ten agents and two full-time secretaries. The firm has been in business for fifteen years and has a good reputation in the community. Recent problems are having a detrimental effect on the usually harmonious atmosphere of the company office.

Virginia Bolt, 55, has been with the firm less than five years, but she has built a reasonably large clientele. Before coming to Kilgore and Mitchell, she had spent twenty years in various clerical positions in banks and with government agencies. She successfully passed the real estate examination and received her licence at the age of 50.

As a clerk Virginia had done an excellent job, but she did not remain with any of her employers for long due to her inability to get along with people. She has an aggressive personality and tends to manipulate people — traits that could be assets in the sales field.

Her recent actions in the real estate firm indicate a renewal of this people problem. In addition to antagonizing other people in the firm by back stabbing, she has allegedly violated an important

continued

company policy by advertising property in her own name with no reference to Kilgore and Mitchell as her employers.

Donald Mitchell, the junior partner in the firm, wants to fire Virginia. He feels that her unethical actions could damage the firm's good name. He also believes that her personality is disrupting an otherwise smooth operation.

Senior partner, James Kilgore, disagrees with Donald and wishes to give Virginia another chance. His reasoning is that her successful record in sales outweighs her shortcomings in other areas.

Case Questions

In groups of five, analyze the case study, keeping in mind the field of human relations and the psychology of communication:

1. Considering the feelings of all the individuals involved, decide what should be done about Virginia's tenure with the firm.
2. How should this decision be communicated to Virginia and to other personnel in the firm? Why?

The Springwood Drive Plaza[11]

Canada is facing a problem it has never faced before, related to the phenomenon called the "greying of the population." Decreasing infant mortality and increased life expectancy mean that a large portion of our population will be over the age of 65 in the next few decades.

The aging process creates two major problems for both the aging individual and society as a whole. As people age, they often become less able to care for themselves. It frequently becomes necessary for the elderly person to either obtain help within the home or move into some type of institutional setting. Society has the responsibility of ensuring that home help services and care facilities are available.

The Springwood Drive Plaza is one facility that offers a unique approach to these problems. It provides apartments for elderly individuals and couples, support services on site, and supervision by caring, skilled personnel.

continued

The Plaza is managed by Marie, Susan, and José. Marie and Susan are registered nurses, and José is a social worker. The three have worked extensively with the elderly in a variety of settings. Their combined skills and backgrounds provide the expertise required to accurately assess, plan, carry out, and evaluate strategies designed to meet the needs of the tenants. In addition, they are familiar with and know how to cope with the type of stress generated in caring for the elderly.

Marie, Susan, and José have maintained an effective and satisfying working relationship during the three years their business has been in operation. Though they are partners, Marie is considered the leader of the group and is officially recognized as the administrator of the organization.

The relationship has been characterized by open communication. The partners chat over coffee and meet informally during the week to discuss any problems that arise. Once a month, they and their families get together for a supper or barbecue. They also meet formally once a month to review major problems and to evaluate their success in helping the elderly tenants retain independence and meaning in their lives.

Eight months ago, an additional service was added to the package offered to the tenants. Tom, a massage therapist and physiotherapist, had persuaded Marie, Susan, and José that a program of massage and exercise would help the tenants feel better and maintain the physical strength needed to carry out the activities of daily living. The results of the program have been positive in both areas.

Gradually, Tom began to spend more time talking to José. He mentioned to him over coffee one day how satisfying it was to work independently and not have to deal with the restrictions of a hospital bureaucracy.

During Tom's fourth month at the Plaza, he asked José if he could participate in the monthly meetings. José discussed the request with Marie and Susan, and as a group they decided to include Tom in the meetings.

Tom has attended two meetings. At the first, he contributed little to the discussion. When he did speak, it was to boast about the success of his massage program. At the second, he spoke in an authoritarian manner when addressing Marie and was openly critical about how the status of the tenants was assessed.

Case Questions

1. What fostered cohesiveness within the small group consisting of Marie, Susan, and José?
2. Why might Tom be acting as he is?
3. What type of leadership style would you use with a group member such as Tom? Why?
4. How would you encourage Tom to become a contributing member of the group?

Part Four

Strategies in the Job Search

Chapter 16

Marketing Yourself

Learning Objectives

In this chapter, you'll learn how to plan and conduct a successful job search. More specifically, you will be able to:

1. explain the importance of a systematic job search
2. prepare a personal inventory
3. identify prospective employers
4. develop a comprehensive marketing strategy for yourself

Preview Case

It was May 30. Tom Solomon would graduate in ten days, but he didn't have a job yet. He'd been through three interviews on campus, each of which he thought had gone extremely well. Yet in the past week he'd received rejection letters from all three companies. The letters had all said much the same thing: "You have fine qualifications, but at present they don't fit the position we are filling. Please keep us in mind in the future."

"So much for a degree," Tom thought, as he packed his now huge collection of textbooks in boxes for shipment home. "Here I am with an A+ average, and I can't even get a job. Maybe I should go to graduate school."

Overview

Each year thousands of college and university students have experiences like Tom's. Desperation sets in as graduation approaches and no job offers appear. Other students find jobs, many of them because they studied in fields where jobs are abundant. Yet most students who secure attractive, entry-level positions in business do so because they carefully plan and carry out strategies for getting the best possible jobs. The purpose of this chapter is to help you plan and implement your job search.

Job Prospects for the Nineties

The days when young men and women joined a company on graduation, moved up within the organization, and stayed with the company until retirement are long gone. Today, the average worker changes jobs every three to five years. Those entering the workforce in the next few years can expect to change *careers* two or three times.

The types of jobs available are also changing. In the past forty years, "Canada has gone from having a workforce that was more than 60 percent in the goods sector (natural resources, manufacturing and construction) to over 70 percent in the 'softer' service industry."[1] Employment and Immigration Canada has projected that the greatest opportunities for jobs in the next decade will be found in health care and medical technology; engineering and engineering technology; computer programming and systems analysis; hospitality and travel; and that demand will be high for senior managers and professionals who can manage information, teachers, mechanics, highly skilled tradespeople, social and community workers, and biotechnicians and biotechnologists.[2]

To cope with these changes, employers are looking for flexible people who know how to learn new skills and knowledge, who can communicate effectively, and who are effective problem solvers. Figure 16.1 contains sound advice for meeting the challenges of the job market of the '90s.

HOW TO SUCCEED IN THE '90s

Job security is dead. That's the bad news. The good news? There will be plenty of opportunity for those who stop relying on their employer to look after them and start taking responsibility for shaping their own future. How to do it:

■ Know yourself. The better you understand your skills, interests and values, the more secure you will be. Many people go wrong by squeezing themselves into slots that don't fit them. Malcontents and misfits are more likely to antagonize the boss and undermine the company's goals — and get the axe. If you're not sure what you want, a career counsellor can help you sort it out.

■ Choose an industry with growth potential. Horizons are shrinking in the airline industry, heavy manufacturing and real estate and development. The odds look better in packaged goods, pharmaceuticals, telecommunications and high-tech. If you're willing to compromise on salary, consider the non-profit sector. As charities and hospitals struggle to stay afloat in tough times, they are looking for people with solid business skills.

■ Make sure your job helps your company stay competitive. If you don't know how you are making money for the company, or who will use the output of your work, then your job is in jeopardy.

■ Want to get ahead? Get ready to work harder. If you think it's competitive now, just wait until the mid-'90s when all those baby bulgers start trying to fight their way through that narrowing funnel to the top jobs.

■ Think seriously about consulting. Companies will do anything to avoid building up the payroll again.

■ Be prepared for frequent moves. People have expiry dates like groceries on the shelf; they now spend an average of only 3.6 years in a job. Make yourself known at industry associations, build ties with people who can help you, and publicize your achievements.

■ Take advantage of training opportunities. Some companies offer more than others. You are only as current as your skills, and they'll require frequent updating in the fast-changing workplace of the '90s. If you regard yourself as a finished product, you might as well quit now.

The Globe and Mail Report on Business Magazine, March 1991.

Figure 16.1

Strategies for Getting Started

Getting a job has been compared to marketing a product.[3] In this case, *you* are the product. As with any successful marketing campaign, you need to do three things: decide what you're looking for in a job, become thoroughly familiar with the features and benefits of the product you're marketing (yourself), and find out whether there's a market for that product.

Setting Your Goals

Know what you want in a job

People who enjoy their jobs are generally effective and productive employees. In order to find work you will enjoy, it's important to know what you're looking for. Too often, especially when jobs are difficult to find, people are so concerned with "getting a job, any job" that they don't take time to think about their future and what they really want from a job. As a result, they find themselves vaguely dissatisfied with what they're doing, and move from one job to another without any apparent direction. You can avoid this hazard if you answer the following questions honestly and thoughtfully:

- Where do I want to be in one year? in five years? in ten years? It's important that goals be realistic and achievable. Otherwise, you're programming yourself for failure and disappointment.
- What am I looking for in a job (salary, duties and responsibilities, working conditions)? Jobs that appeal to one person may be totally unacceptable to another. For example, some people will accept a lower-paying position if the company offers opportunities for advancement or has an above-average benefits package, flexible working hours, or a convenient location. "According to a Conference Board of Canada survey ... 35 percent of employed Canadians aged 25 to 44 would forgo some of their salary for more time off."[4]
- How will my job fit in with the rest of my life? For example, are you willing to travel or to relocate? Extensive travel can disrupt your participation in community activities such as sports and service groups. Moreover, with two-career families becoming increasingly the norm, you'll need to decide just how much you and your partner are prepared to sacrifice for a promotion.

Not only will these questions help you determine where to start looking for a job, they may also help you in the employment interview. Recruiters frequently want to know whether an applicant has thought seriously about his or her future. They recognize that individuals who have a "game plan" for their own lives will have the skills to set objectives and get results on the job. Of course, they also want to know whether you have concrete strategies for achieving your goals.

Compiling a Personal Inventory

Know what you have to offer

Just as companies conduct periodic inventories of their assets, you need to take an inventory of your qualifications, skills, experience, and personal qualities to determine what you have to offer an employer right now, and what additional qualifications you need to achieve your long-term goals.

This personal inventory collects, in one place, all the information you need to conduct your job search. Ideally, you have already begun to keep a file that documents your education, work experience, and accomplishments. If you haven't, now's the time to start. Your personal inventory file should include:

- copies of all certificates, diplomas, and degrees you've earned
- transcripts from all your courses
- a list of scholarships and awards you've received
- a list of all courses, workshops, and conferences you've attended, even if they were offered by an employer
- a list of employers that includes the name, address, and phone number of each company; the names of your supervisors; dates of employment; job descriptions for each position you held; dates of promotions; as well as detailed salary records
- letters of recommendation
- a list of all volunteer positions you've held that includes the names, addresses, and phone numbers of the organization; the names of the persons to whom you reported; brief descriptions of what you did; and the dates involved
- a list of organizations to which you belong
- copies of past résumés and letters of application (you can use them as a starting point for updates)
- copies of recent job advertisements in your field (even those you don't apply for)

Understand the employer's needs so that you can address them

While this factual data will help you decide what you have to offer an employer, you need to go one step farther: understand the employer's needs so you can decide how to respond to those needs. Employers are faced with problems: meeting the payroll requires hard cash; overhead and production costs are too high; profits are too low; sales are up or sales are down.[5] Your success or failure will depend on your ability to persuade potential employers that you can help solve their problems. To do that, you have to tell employers how you can help them, and provide concrete evidence that what you say is true.

Identify your attributes

The following questions will help you to identify the less tangible attributes you bring to the job:

- What personal qualities will make you a good employee? To answer this question, imagine that your best friend is describing you to someone you haven't met. How would this friend describe your best qualities? What concrete examples could they give to support their descriptions?
- How can I demonstrate that I can learn independently? that I have good communication skills? or that I am an effective problem solver? Each of these questions calls for a subjective opinion. However, if you spend a little time on them, you should be able support your opinion with specific details. For example, one of the most effective methods for demonstrating your written communication skills is to write an effective résumé and letter of application.

If you've prepared a résumé or letter of application in the past, you may have considered some of these issues already. If you haven't, now's the time to start.

Identifying Prospective Employers

Some authorities estimate that as few as 20 percent of all job openings are ever advertised outside the organization. Therefore, your task is to identify those organizations that have openings — even if they haven't advertised them. Obviously, you can't contact every existing company. You need to narrow your list of prospects to companies that fit your job objective and, if important, your geographic preference. For example, if you want to work for an insurance company in Toronto, you might search the Toronto Yellow Pages for the names of prospective employers. Trade publications are also a good source of information. If, for example, you want a job with a publishing company, you could consult the annual *Canadian Publishers Directory* put out by the trade journal *Quill & Quire*. Here are some additional ideas for identifying prospective employers:

- Keep a record of all the jobs advertised in your field — starting yesterday!
- Find out what companies employ people with your background

Sources of companies for a direct-mail campaign

Campus Placement Office. Many campuses have a branch of Employment and Immigration Canada on site. The staff in these offices are extremely helpful sources of information.

Career Planning Annual. Published by the University and College Placement Association, it provides information on employer-members who recruit at the college and university levels.

College Placement Annual. Published by the College Placement Council, it contains a list of companies in both Canada and the U.S. who are seeking college and university graduates.

Canadian Trade Index. Provides information about Canadian manufacturers.

Dun & Bradstreet Canadian Key Business Directory. Provides information about businesses in Canada.

Dun & Bradstreet Million Dollar Directory. Provides information about more than 30 000 companies whose net worth in each case exceeds one million dollars.

Dun & Bradstreet Middle Market Directory. Similar to the *Million Dollar Directory*, but information is about more than 30 000 companies whose net worth is between $500 000 and $999 999.

Moody's Manual of Investment. Contains information about a variety of companies, including banks, utilities, insurance firms, and industrial firms.

Newspapers such as *The Globe and Mail* and *The Financial Times* often contain profiles of companies and/or executives, as well as announcements about expansions, new products, or the appointment of key personnel. These articles are a wealth of information for the job hunter.

Standard & Poor's Register of Corporations, Directors, and Executives. Contains an alphabetical listing of more than 35 000 corporations in Canada and the U.S., showing products and services, officers, and telephone numbers.

Don't overlook sources about specific industries and/or regions. Two of the hundreds of examples are:

Canadian Miner's Handbook. Provides information about the Canadian mining industry.

B.C. Lumberman's Green Book. Provides information on the British Columbia forest industry.

Making Yourself Known

Get to know as many people in your field as you can

Ideally, you will have begun making contacts in your field long before you graduate. That way, by graduation, you'll have a fairly clear idea of what's available and where to apply. You'll also have a long list of contacts. These contacts are very important because people generally are more willing to hire someone they know. If you haven't already started, get to know as many people in your field as you can.

To begin with, ask friends, relatives, and acquaintances to let you know if they hear of any job prospects. If they work in your field, take advantage of their knowledge by talking with them about their jobs — most people are delighted to talk about what they do.

Become an active student member of associations in your field or related fields. Not only will you meet potential employers, but you'll also benefit from the educational component commonly a part of these associations. While it's perfectly acceptable to let people know you are looking for work, don't overdo it. You'll find members avoiding you if you habitually show up with a handful of résumés and constantly ask them if they have any openings. A far more effective approach is to get involved, particularly in those tasks that are often unpopular — phone committees, social committees, clean-up detail. You'll quickly get a reputation as a hard worker who's not afraid to do whatever's required to get the job done.

Attend trade shows. Trade shows are a great place to meet potential employers and to find out what's new in your field. Some schools organize booths at important trade shows to tell the industry about their programs and their graduates. These booths can offer an excellent opportunity to practise your communication skills.

Another method of introducing yourself is to contact potential employers for help with a student project. Just remember to be considerate of their time and follow up with a brief thank-you note such as the one shown in Figure 16.2. Notice that you can send along a résumé to indicate your interest in working for the company.

Information Interviews

Information interviews refer to appointments scheduled with potential employers for the express purpose of gathering data. They warrant close

Ms. Marion Williams
Integrated Forest Products
1231 West Broadway
Vancouver BC V5Z 1V7

92 January 19

Dear Ms. Williams

Thank you for taking time last week to help me with the research for my technical communication project. My instructor was so impressed with the quality of my information that she asked me to share it with the rest of the class. I've enclosed a copy of my report for your information.

For my part, I was delighted to learn that you hire new graduates as supervisor trainees and encourage them to develop their management capabilities. If you have any openings in the next six months, I'd like an opportunity to compete for the position. The enclosed résumé summarizes my qualifications.

I'll call you in May just before graduation to see whether you have any openings.

Sincerely

Gerald Kozinski
3232 Windy Place
North Vancouver BC V7N 3R4

encl.(2)

Figure 16.2 Sending a Résumé with a Thank-You Note

attention because many job hunters have found them to be useful in helping them to:

- learn about the job opportunities that exist in their field

- learn about companies and their criteria for hiring
- demonstrate "employee potential"

By scheduling an interview before you submit an application, you show employers that you have:

- initiative
- enthusiasm for your field and their company
- good communication skills (oral and written)

Plan carefully for your information interview

To make a good impression on the prospective employer, you need to prepare carefully for the interview:

Find out all you can about the company in advance. Annual reports are a good place to start with public companies. The Public or Media Relations Department is another option. Your research shouldn't stop there: use the library to find out more about the company specifically or to locate articles on the particular industry you are researching. The more you know in advance, the more you will learn during the interview.

Decide what your objective is. It's unrealistic to expect someone to give you more than a half-hour of their time even under the most favourable circumstances. Therefore, you need to have a clearly focused objective for the interview. For example, you may be interested in finding out about the type of work available to people with your general qualifications or you may want to know more about the market that the company serves.

Formulate your questions prior to the interview. Although you may not use every question during the interview, you should draft three to five general, open-ended questions that will encourage the person you are interviewing to talk. For each general question, having two or three supplementary questions related to specific topics or examples is a good rule of thumb. Having the questions written out, with space to enter the answers during the interview will make note taking easier.

Schedule the interview. You should schedule the interview by telephone or in person. Be prepared to accommodate the schedule of the person you wish to interview, but do suggest some times. Most people feel uncomfortable with a completely open meeting time, but faced with suggestions will agree to one of them or offer an alternative. Once you have the appointment, write a brief confirmation letter that includes your specific areas of interest.

Conduct the interview. You should begin by summarizing the reason you're there and explaining your objectives. Then you can begin asking your questions. Don't be surprised if the person anticipates and answers some of your questions before you've asked them. By summarizing responses to each general question, you'll give the interviewee an opportunity to correct any misconceptions. And, in the process, you'll demonstrate effective listening skills.

End the interview on time. Even if the interviewee seems to be enjoying the process, be sure to complete the interview on time. Be sure to thank the interviewee for his or her time. Then leave quickly.

Follow up with a thank-you letter. If you decide that you'd like to work for the company, you may send your résumé with your thank-you letter. Under no circumstances should you take a résumé to the interview.

Conducting Your Marketing Campaign

You can market yourself using three strategies

You can use three basic strategies to market yourself: a direct-mail campaign; responses to newspaper advertisements; and campus placement office appointments. Each will help you to reach a different market segment. Your objective, though, remains the same: to get an employment interview.

In seeking employment interviews, you will either be contacting companies that have not announced an opening or be responding to a known opening. The letter of application you send to the company with a known job opening is a *solicited letter*. (Your knowledge of the opening need not have come through formal channels; you may have learned of the job from a family member or an announcement on a bulletin board, rather than through a newspaper advertisement or an announcement from a company recruiter.) A letter of application sent to a company without a known opening is called an *unsolicited* or *surveying letter*. The direct-mail approach usually involves writing unsolicited letters.

Conduct a Direct-Mail Campaign

A direct-mail campaign announces your availability

The direct-mail approach is a shotgun approach. You may write to many companies, but the number of interviews you are invited to will be small. Nevertheless, if jobs are tight in your field or if you wish to maximize your chances for acquiring interviews, the approach can produce results.

Some students select as many as 200 companies for their direct-mail campaigns; more typically, they choose 75 or 100 key prospects. If you send your application to 100 firms, you can expect a rejection rate of approximately 85 percent. You won't hear at all from some of the other companies. However, should you get six or seven job interviews from such a campaign, your strategy has been successful.

Much of the reason for the low number of positive responses in a direct-mail campaign lies in the breadth of the approach. The more you narrow the focus of your campaign, the greater your success. Some ways to narrow your list of prospects are to

1. pick companies that offer the type of job in which you're interested
2. select companies with jobs for which you're qualified
3. locate companies that are known to provide advancement in your field
4. find companies that are centred or have branches in geographical locations of interest to you
5. omit companies you are sure you would not accept a job from if one were offered

Once you have selected your prospects, you will have to prepare and mail your résumé and cover letter. Résumés and letters of application are discussed in Chapters 17 and 18.

Respond to Newspaper Advertisements

As indicated earlier in this chapter, newspaper advertisements account only for about 20 percent of all job openings. However, you can be sure that when you respond to a help-wanted advertisement in a newspaper, literally scores of other applicants are also responding to it. Thus, you must make your application stand out from those of the masses. Again, researching the company to find out as much as you can about its needs is the key to success.

Use Your Placement Office

Using your campus placement office to line up interviews is quite different from using direct mail or answering newspaper advertisements. The direct-mail and newspaper-advertisement approaches are general in scope, frequently cannot be personalized, and are based on the assumption that, if you apply to enough companies, you'll receive some interviews.

Campus placement offices offer many valuable services

The placement office, on the other hand, is individualized and, in some cases, leads directly to an interview. One valuable way to use the placement office is as a library. Often it has available the latest publications on how to interview or write résumés. Many companies send placement offices their annual reports and other recruiting literature. In addition, the placement office personnel can offer guidance. They can help you with career decisions and tell you about the most recent trends in industries. Some placement offices will maintain your records, including letters of reference and résumés. The staff can even review your résumé or application letter. And, of course, they may also know of the latest job openings.

Another major activity of the placement office is the scheduling of on-campus job interviews. Frequently companies visit the campus and interview thirteen to fifteen students a day in 30-minute interviews. The placement office undertakes co-ordination of room scheduling and time-period assignments, makes company literature available, and gathers interviewees' résumés.

Signing up in a time slot for an interview through the placement office is far easier than using a letter of application to achieve an interview. For this reason, as well as to gain the other benefits mentioned, regular communication with your placement office is usually wise.

Keep Accurate Records

Recordkeeping is vital during your job search

Throughout your job search, recordkeeping is essential. Keep a file or log on each company to which you've applied, copies of your letters, the responses to them, records of interviews, names of interviewers, dates and content of phone calls, and so on.

Usually responses from your prospects arrive about two weeks after you mail your letter and résumé. If you don't hear from a company after about fourteen days, consider a follow-up by phone or letter. The phone call is quicker but may be perceived as pushy. If you decide to call, try to reach the person to whom you addressed the letter. Ask about the "progress of your application."

Summary

- Job hunters are facing new challenges, including:
  - decreased job security
  - a move from a goods-based to a service-based economy
  - an increased need for flexibility
- To get started on your job search, know:
  - what you want
  - what you have to offer
- Plan your job search by:
  - identifying prospective employers
  - making yourself known
  - conducting information interviews
- Use all three strategies for contacting potential employers:
  - conduct a direct-mail campaign

    - respond to newspaper advertisements
    - use your campus placement office
- Be sure to keep accurate records of your job search

Review Questions

1. List specific strategies you have for coping with job prospects for the '90s.
2. Why is a personal inventory important? What should it include?
3. How can you identify prospective employers? What sources do you know about from personal experience?
4. Why are information interviews helpful in conducting a job search?
5. Describe the three basic strategies for conducting a successful job search.

Activities

1. The year is 2010. You've been working for several years in your chosen field. Take a few minutes to describe the job you hold and your lifestyle in general. Share your description with a classmate.
2. Select a company in your area that you would like to work for. Research and plan for an information interview. You'll need to:
    a. find out as much as you can about the company
    b. decide what type of information you want to get from the interview
    c. identify a specific person you can interview
    d. formulate a series of questions for the interview
3. Conduct the information interview you researched and planned in Activity 2. Write a brief report summarizing your findings.
4. Working in groups of three, reflect on the successes or opportunities for improvement in your handling of information interviews. What worked well? What would you change the next time?

Discussion Cases

Why the Differences?[6]

Paul Couture worked for one of the world's largest computer companies, with more than 55 000 employees worldwide. The company had sales offices in 64 countries and operated manufacturing plants in 12 locations in North America, Europe, and Southeast Asia. The Canadian operations headquarters were based in Toronto. Growth, measured in terms of new staff, was approximately 15 percent a year.

continued

Paul joined this multinational corporation in Toronto after graduating from university with an engineering degree in the mid-1970s. He quickly developed an interest in the marketing area, and was promoted more rapidly than many of his university friends who had joined more traditional firms in building and construction that were not experiencing the same growth rate.

Paul's company encouraged frequent job mobility, and it was not long before he was transferred to the company's headquarters in the United States. While there he concentrated on marketing computer systems for the technical and scientific markets. When the company decided to concentrate on this aspect of its European operations, he was also able to spend several years working at the European headquarters in Frankfurt.

Meanwhile, Paul had married April, a colleague from his office in the U.S., and she accompanied him to Frankfurt when he moved there in 1985. April chose to work for a different organization when they arrived in West Germany. By 1990, the couple had two young children and April was offered a senior management position with her company in their Toronto office.

Since April's job offer was very attractive, and the couple was anxious to raise their children in Canada, Paul decided to ask for a transfer to the Toronto office. The company reluctantly agreed; however, the position they offered was less attractive than his current position. Paul's manager expressed surprise that he would even consider giving up his current position under the circumstances.

April and Paul moved back to Toronto, and Paul began almost immediately to look for another position.

Case Questions

1. What are the implications of Paul and April's decision for each of their careers? for the company Paul works for? for society in general?
2. Two-career families are a fact of life nowadays. How would you choose a course of action in a similar situation?
3. How do you think organizations should address the issue of two-career families?

My Next Career?

Kelly Szwec had always known she would go to university. In the late 1980s, she completed her English Literature degree at the University of Manitoba. Jobs were scarce for arts graduates, so she accepted a secretarial position in a teaching hospital while she looked for something more suitable. Gradually, she noticed that she was being given responsibility for drafting letters and reports from her meeting notes. She was even more surprised to find that she actually enjoyed the task.

After several months, Kelly realized that she was spending more than half her time drafting or editing documents — at secretarial wages! Kelly decided then and there that she would approach her boss to ask for a new job description and a raise. She listed all the jobs she had completed in the past two months and tried to anticipate her boss's possible objections to the request.

Just as she was trying to get up enough courage to schedule an interview with her boss, he called her into his office. Kelly was delighted. He probably knew what she was planning and was making it easier for her.

As she shut the door, her boss announced, "I'm afraid I'm going to have to let you go. It's not a reflection on your work, you understand. It's just that we have to reduce our deficit before the end of the fiscal year. You have the least seniority in the department, so we'll have to lay you off. You have one month's notice, of course, since it's in the contract. Feel free to schedule interviews during the day if you need to."

Kelly was devastated. She could barely get out of her chair. Unable to concentrate on her duties, she left the office for the day. "How could they?" She had gone above and beyond the call of duty. She'd performed well beyond her job description. What was she going to do now?

Kelly also had more immediate problems. She'd just moved into a new apartment where her share of the rent was $400. Because she'd been working only a short time, she had relatively little money saved.

Case Questions

1. Imagine you are Kelly. What are her options under the circumstances? Where should she go from here?
2. What resources might Kelly use to start her own job search? Be as specific as possible.
3. If you were Kelly's boss, how would you have handled the layoff notice?

Chapter 17

Writing a Résumé

Learning Objectives

In this chapter, you'll learn how to prepare an effective résumé. More specifically, you will be able to:

1. describe the components of an effective résumé
2. select information for your résumé
3. package your résumé effectively

Preview Case

Ginette Pfeiffer, personnel manager for Barrington Industries, pulled open her file drawer and quickly flipped through it. Pulling out a file marked "Applications — Manager Trainees," she returned to her desk and emptied onto it 250 résumés, all of which she'd received in the past two months.

She began sorting the résumés into piles. During her fifteen years in personnel work, she had developed a system for choosing potential employees by looking at their résumés. First Ginette sorted the résumés by appearance — creating a neat, professional-looking résumé was the least someone would do if he or she was sincerely interested in the job. Since she was often faced with reviewing literally hundreds of résumés, Ginette found herself positively influenced by résumés that she could scan in a minute or less — that meant résumés with lots of headings and lists. Only then, did Ginette look at details on the selected résumés to see how well the applicant's qualifications matched the requirements of the job.

In just over 45 minutes, Ginette had selected fifteen résumés from the stack. She placed the remaining résumés into the file, slid it to one side of her desk, and began calling fifteen fortunate applicants to schedule job interviews with them.

Overview

Ginette Pfeiffer is fairly typical of people who make hiring decisions. They have to screen literally hundreds of résumés when openings are advertised, particularly for entry-level positions. Your objective in preparing your résumé is to appeal to recruiters like Ginette Pfeiffer.

After collecting all the information you need to prepare your résumé, and after having developed the comprehensive marketing strategy outlined in Chapter 16, you are ready to write an effective résumé that will not only help you obtain an interview, but be of value in the interview itself. This purpose will be accomplished by discussing the components of a résumé and by describing how to fit these components into a format suited to your specific needs.

Remember, in reading a résumé, the recruiter seeks the answers to five basic questions:

1. Do you have the basic credentials for the job (a business degree or diploma, basic job experience, for example)?
2. Do you have any education or experience that elevates you beyond the basic qualifications?
3. Do you have the personal qualities that will make you an effective, reliable, long-term employee?

4. Are you good at what you do?
5. Do you know what you want?

Most résumés transmit information to answer the first question, and many supply answers to the second and third. Few, however, take full advantage of the fourth and fifth questions. Yet, the fourth is the most important to many recruiters. They prefer an applicant who is good at, say, ditch-digging to one who is only mediocre in a job related to the open position. The enthusiasm, leadership, and responsibility that emerge when you hold a job indicate your effectiveness. If you can show a winning track record, recruiters will anticipate your continued success, even in a new field. For new graduates, unrelated work experience is particularly important.

Many résumés omit details that are important to recruiters

The fifth question is important to recruiters who are looking for long-term employees who can progress within the organization. Too often they are faced with applications from people who are concerned with "getting a job, any job." These applicants often move from one job to another without any apparent direction. Therefore, you should let the recruiter know that you have definite short-term and long-term goals as well as a clear idea of the type of work environment you prefer. Keep these last two questions in mind as you begin to write your résumé.

With the advent of word processing, many recruiters expect applicants to tailor their résumés to the position they are applying for. As a new graduate, you will probably need both a standard résumé that you can use for comprehensive job searches and more position-specific résumés for applications resulting from advertisements for specific jobs.

Components of an Effective Résumé

Résumés are defined by three characteristics: they are factual, categorized, and tabulated. A *factual* résumé is one for which the information can be substantiated; it is not opinion. The date and location of your high school graduation, for example, can be verified. Your belief that you're enthusiastic cannot be verified.

Categorized means your information is grouped under headings, such as Education or Job Experience. The headings tend to be mutually exclusive. Information in a résumé is not presented in sentence form; it is *tabulated*, much like a balance sheet, with headings, subheadings, and responses to implied queries, such as Health: excellent.

Just as résumé formats vary widely, so do résumé components. Further, the order of the components may determine the image or tone of the message. Just as persuasive letters are organized differently from positive letters, résumés need to be organized to serve a specific situation.

You must choose the presentation that is best for you for this job

Even though you probably won't use all the possible components in your résumé, we'll discuss each one, so that you can choose those you think best represent your accomplishments. Remember, though, that our presentation is not necessarily in the order that is most efficient for you for all job applications.

Component 1: Résumé Heading

A required part of every résumé, the heading should contain your name, address, and telephone number. If you have two addresses, one at school and one at home, put both in the heading. Listing your home address will help an employer contact you when you are no longer in school. The word *résumé* itself is an optional part of the heading and is being used less often at present.

Here is an example of a résumé heading:

Robert J. Anderson

Address (until June 1, 1992)	Address (after June 1, 1992)
134 Ansley St., Apt. 4B	1897 Clearwater Road
Vancouver, B.C. V5Z 1C2	Kamloops, B.C. V2C 3S6
(604)863-2717	(604)422-5799

If you have only one address, you can place it either where you see the Ansley Street address in the example or directly beneath your name.

Leave the picture off your résumé

You may wonder why no picture is called for at the top of your résumé. Ten or fifteen years ago, pictures were standard items on résumés. However, laws now prohibit employers from discriminating on the basis of several factors, including race, sex, and, in some jurisdictions, age. So, omit the picture — if you put one on your résumé, you may put your potential employer in an embarrassing position.

Component 2: Availability Date

Availability dates help employers find you an opening

Companies budget many of their position openings to coincide with graduation dates. For example, Ginette Pfeiffer's organization might have five openings beginning June 1 (for April and May graduates), two September 1 openings (for August graduates), and two January 1 openings (for December graduates).

Openings do occur in every month of the year, of course. But as a courtesy and convenience for your potential employer, place your date of availability on the résumé. If you do so, the employer can more easily fit you into a budgeted position.

Give the month and year and, if possible, the specific day of your availability:

AVAILABLE: **June 1, 1992**

If you are available for a position at the time you complete your résumé, you might write the availability component like this:

AVAILABLE: **Immediately**

Component 3: Objective

The impression you make on your potential employer comes in large part from how clearly defined your goals are. As you'll see in the next chapter, interviewers normally ask about both short- and long-term goals. To many interviewers, applicants with clearcut goals show more maturity and readiness to pursue a profession than applicants who have no clear goals in mind.

Here's an example of a goal statement:

OBJECTIVE: **Responsible career position in accounting or finance.**

The objective shows your potential employer you have planned for the future

Choose your words carefully. The word *responsible* says that you want and are willing to assume responsibility. Don't let a potential employer wonder whether or not you are responsible.

The word *career* says to the reader that you want to stay with the company that hires you. Employees are expensive to replace. In some organizations, the cost of hiring you (or replacing you if you quit) could be as high as $5000 for such things as hiring and training your replacement. Therefore, in the front of every interviewer's mind is the question: "How long will this applicant stay with my company?"

Be sure that the position you list in the goal statement is as specific as you can make it. Accounting and finance are fairly closely related. Try to avoid general statements (for example, "general business") or statements that represent you as a jack-of-all-trades (for example, "accounting or real estate").

Are you willing to relocate or to travel? If so, then state your willingness after your objective:

OBJECTIVE: **Responsible entry-level position in personnel management with ample opportunity for advancement. Willing to relocate and travel.**

Although not actually part of your career or job objective, this information is placed in a part of your résumé that every reader will notice.

A willingness to relocate and travel may help you get the job

Information on willingness to relocate and/or travel is tremendously important to businesses. In recent years, many managers in large companies have turned down promotions and salary increases simply because relocation was involved. If you are willing to relocate, let the reader know as soon as possible. Remember, willingness to travel is a requirement for many sales positions. And no matter what position you seek, there may be some travelling involved, especially during the training and orientation period.

Component 4: Education

The education section of your résumé contains five important items:

1. when you received your degree(s) or diploma(s)
2. where you earned your degree(s) or diploma(s)
3. your major, department, faculty, or field of concentration
4. relevant course work
5. your grade average, if appropriate

Where you place this component in your résumé depends partly on which format you decide to use. Most students finishing school place their education directly beneath their objective because their education is the strongest qualification they have for the position.

If you have or are expecting to receive a university degree, you might write your education component like this:

EDUCATION:

June, 1992	**Bachelor of Commerce (Honours), University of British Columbia. Major in Industrial Relations Management. Minor in Marketing. Course work included wage and salary administration, personnel selection, personnel administration. Maintained 85% average. Graduated summa cum laude.**
June, 1988	**Graduated with honours from Richmond Senior Secondary, Richmond, B.C.**

If the location of the college or university from which you receive your degree is well known, omit the city and province. But always include the city and province for your high school information.

Be clear about relevant course work

The course work you list should be related to the objective in the previous section of your résumé. Be careful about listing courses by name.

Often the name of a course is misleading or ambiguous. For example, if a course called "Human Resource Management" focuses primarily upon such topics as leadership and interpersonal relations, then your course work statement should include "leadership and interpersonal relations."

Finally, list your grade average only if you want to call attention to it. Generally, mention only an average higher than 75 percent (B+). However, many employers are more interested in your major, work experience, and activities than in your overall average. If it is not high but you achieved high marks in your major, then state, "85 percent average in major."

You may list or omit your grade average

If you are a graduate of a community college, technical institute, or Quebec CÉGEP, you might use this format for your education component:

EDUCATION:

June, 1992	Diploma in Business Administration, Northern Alberta Institute of Technology, Edmonton. Concentration in marketing management. Course work included administrative practices, business communication, marketing principles, and accounting theory.
June, 1986	Graduated with honours from Central High School, Lethbridge, Alta.

Finally, if you have a university degree but also attended a community college, you can work both schools into your résumé like this:

EDUCATION:

June, 1992 (Expected)	Bachelor of Commerce, University of Toronto. Major in Personnel Management. Minor in Marketing. Course work included wage and salary administration, personnel selection, personnel administration. Maintained a 79% average.
September, 1984 to June, 1985	Attended Selkirk College, Castlegar, B.C. Maintained an 85% average.
June, 1983	Graduated with honours from Kitsilano Senior Secondary, Vancouver, B.C.

If you write your résumé before you receive your final degree, you can place "Expected" beneath the date when you expect to receive the degree.

If that date is only two or three months away, however, you might omit the word. Most potential employers reading your résumé will understand that the date you have listed is the expected date.

Component 5: Work Experience

For any full-time or part-time job that you have had, include the following information:

1. when you held the job
2. what your job title was
3. who your employer was
4. what your responsibilities were
5. what your accomplishments were

Here is an example:

WORK EXPERIENCE:

September, 1987 to present	Part-Time Registration Clerk, Holiday Hotel, Vancouver. Responsibilities include registering hotel guests, making reservations, processing check-outs, and handling guest problems. Have earned approximately 30% of university expenses.
Summer, 1987	Sales Representative, Legal Book Company, Toronto. Responsibilities included calling on potential customers, processing orders, and delivering merchandise. Was top salesperson in 12-person territory. Earned 70% of university expenses for 1987/88 year.

Don't dismiss the listing of menial jobs

First, notice that your jobs are listed in reverse chronological order — most recent job first. Second, if you have held a number of jobs during school, you may not want to list them all. Choose those most related to your objective. Just remember that no matter how menial the job seemed to you, to a potential employer your having worked says two things: this applicant has been out in the "real world" and therefore has actual business experience, and this applicant shows initiative and responsibility.

Dates of Employment. Notice that the dates in the example are not exact — you don't need to list the actual days you began and ended your employment. If you held the same job at different times, you can state

"Summers, 1988, 1989," or "Summers, 1990, 1991, and Christmas 1990." On the other hand, including the month in the date helps show continuity. Many potential employers suspect that you may be hiding periods of unemployment when you don't include the month.

Job Title. Some jobs don't have specific titles. If you have had such a job, simply make up a descriptive title for it. For example, if your job was serving customers at the counter of a fast-food restaurant, you could call it "Counter Clerk." Notice that each job title is underlined so that it stands out.

Name of Employer. When you list your employers, show both their names and their locations. If your potential employer wants to call for a reference or verify your employment, having the information will make that job easier.

Responsibilities. Notice that we have called them "responsibilities," not "duties." Again, your purpose is to show that you are capable of assuming responsibility. You need not list all of your responsibilities — just those that you think are the most important.

Accomplishments help set you apart from other applicants

Accomplishments. Any accomplishment that your potential employer can verify belongs in your list of accomplishments. In the example, we illustrated two kinds of accomplishments: earning money to attend school, and succeeding as a salesperson. Other types of accomplishments to list include supervising other people or training your replacement; many potential employers regard both as showing leadership skills. If you assumed your own supervisor's duties while he or she was absent, include that information. Perhaps you made some suggestion that was adopted by your employer. If so, list it. Even seemingly minor accomplishments, such as an employee-of-the-month award, can impress the person who reads your résumé.

Component 6: Honours

Honours and activities may be combined

Any school-related honour you have received belongs in the honours section of your résumé. If you have no honours, simply omit this section. If you have only one honour, consider including it in the activities section and renaming that section "Honours and Activities." Here's a sample honours section:

HONOURS:

University	**The Society of Management Accountants Award in Accounting (academic achievement), 1991**

	The Financial Executives Institute Award (academic ability and leadership), 1991
High School	Chosen class valedictorian, 1988
	Scholastic Achievement Award, 1988

Notice that a brief explanation of each honour is provided as well as the year of reception. Never list your honours in paragraph form. An interviewer is likely to forget what honours you have received. But if you list them, he or she may at least remember how many you have.

Component 7: Activities

After your field of study and your work experience, the activities in which you have been involved constitute the most important part of your résumé. To most potential employers, the activities you list show your interest in other people, practice in developing interpersonal relationships, and possession of social skills. If you have served as an officer in some organization, you may also have leadership skills.

Include in your activities organizations at school as well as volunteer and other outside activities. Your activities can show skills of interest to your potential employer.

ACTIVITIES:

University	Vice President, Society for the Advancement of Management, 1989/90-1990/91
	Business representative, student association, 1989/90
	Chairperson, campus Red Cross Blood Drive, 1988/89
High School	Spanish Club, 1984/85-1985/86 (President, 1985/86)
	Captain of basketball team (provincial champions), 1985/86

Component 8: Interests

You may have wondered, when filling out an application for a job, why you were required to list your hobbies or interests. To many potential employers, your interests are as important as your activities. What many employers seek is a person who has a balance of individual and group interests. Consider the following:

INTERESTS: **Reading, jogging, skiing, photography**

Show a mix of group and individual interests

Some interviewers perceive a person with interests like these to be too isolated because no real group pastimes are listed. Other interviewers have an equally negative perception of:

INTERESTS: **Tennis, basketball, chess, backgammon**

Interests such as these might suggest a total group orientation and draw the reaction, "Perhaps this person is too dependent on others."

In short, your interests should include a mix of group and individual pastimes. However, do not list interests that you don't actually have. An interviewer may ask you to discuss the book you've read most recently or how often you jog. If you don't actually read or jog, you've placed yourself in an embarrassing predicament.

Component 9: Personal Data

All Canadian jurisdictions prohibit employers from making selection decisions based on various personal factors, unless the factor in question is a bona fide occupational qualification. The grounds on which discrimination is specifically forbidden vary among jurisdictions. All include race, religion, ethnic origin, marital status, and sex. Several also specify mother tongue, age, nationality, and physical handicaps. The interpretation of laws changes frequently; usually the changes are a broadening of their application.

Given these prohibitions, the personal data section of your résumé is optional. However, if you do not mind revealing some kinds of personal data, doing so may help you get the position. For example, if you are an unmarried female who is willing to relocate, your marital status might help you (although legally it should not).

Don't include personal data unless you think it will help you

An entry pertaining to military service may be appropriate. Persons with Canadian military service receive bonus points when applying for federal public service positions from outside the public service. If your military service was extensive (more than two years) and ties to your objective, you might enter it as part of your work experience component. Otherwise, list it briefly with other personal data.

Personal data on a résumé usually includes the following:

PERSONAL: **Age 22; Excellent Health**

If you have only one address at the top of your résumé (see the résumé heading component), you might place your personal data at the top right-hand corner so as to create balance and save space:

Age: **22**

Marital Status: **Single**

Health: **Excellent**

Military Service: **Canadian Armed Forces, 1987-1989, discharged as lieutenant after service on destroyer escort**

Component 10: Licences and Other Accreditations

List all your licences and certificates

Possessing a licence or professional certificate may be important to your getting a position. For example, if you are applying for a real estate sales position, having your licence should help. Other examples of licences or accreditations that might be entered on your résumé are Registered Nurse, Licensed Practical Nurse, Registered Nursing Assistant, Chartered Accountant, Certified General Accountant, Radiology Technologist, and any teaching certificate relevant to your objective. An entry for this component can look like this:

PROFESSIONAL LICENCES:

Licensed Practical Nurse, Province of Saskatchewan

Registered Nurse, Province of Saskatchewan

Component 11: Special Skills

If pertinent, list your special skills, including abilities in languages

Some jobs require special skills. For example, many computer programmers are expected to know several computer languages as well as different types of computer systems. If you are one of these persons, your special-skills component can appear in this way:

COMPUTER SKILLS:

Languages: **COBOL, FORTRAN, RPG, and PASCAL**

Systems: **IBM 360, 720, and 1030; CYBER 370 and 380**

In Canada, fluency in both official languages may be an advantage, particularly if you are applying for a position in the federal civil service or an area with both Anglophone and Francophone populations. You can list knowledge of both languages as a special skill:

LANGUAGES:

Fluently bilingual. Received most of my elementary education in French and have prepared French correspondence and French-English translations for local community centre.

You may find it better to list the information earlier in your résumé as a separate item or with personal data:

PERSONAL:
Age 24; married, 1 child; good oral French

Knowledge of one or more foreign languages may be necessary for positions in international business or for working with ethnic populations. Even if it is not required, it may be an asset in many situations. So if you know a foreign language and are not sure of its pertinence to your résumé, consider including the skill:

FOREIGN LANGUAGES: **Speak and read German and Spanish fluently.**
Read and write Italian.

Any other special skill you possess should be entered on your résumé, provided that the skill is relevant to your objective.

Component 12: Professional Memberships

Many students are members of campus chapters of professional organizations. Your membership in such organizations can be listed under the activities component, unless you'd like to draw special attention to it. Here's an example:

Professional organizations can be combined with activities

PROFESSIONAL MEMBERSHIPS:
Personnel Association of Toronto, 1988 to present

Component 13: References

Some experts advise including references on your résumé; others advise bringing a list of references to the interview. You'll need to decide which strategy you prefer.

Decide whether to list your references on the résumé

Unless you are changing jobs and want to keep your decision to make a change to yourself for as long as possible, some experts suggest that you list your references on your résumé. They see phrases such as "References available on request" as an inconvenience to the personnel specialist, who must either call or write you, ask for your references, and then contact them. You'll save the specialist time if those references are on the résumé. He or she may be more inclined to consider you if your references are easy to check. However, by including your references, you may subject the people who've agreed to provide references for you to phone calls from employers who are only mildly interested in hiring you.

On the other hand, including phrases such as "References available on request" ensures that only potential employers who are seriously interested in you as a candidate will contact your references. Besides, in many cases, checking references is the final step before a person is offered a position.

References may be professional, character, or educational

You supply references for possible verification of the facts you have presented elsewhere on the résumé, or for additional information. References fall into three main categories: (1) professional references, who can speak about your professional ability for this job, such as your knowledge of accounting or computer science; (2) character references, who know your personality and can speak about factors such as your industriousness or ambition; and (3) educational references, who can respond to questions about your scholarly achievements and background, such as your performance in a management class.

Former employers are frequently used as professional references; friends, neighbours, or colleagues as character references; and teachers as educational references. Keep in mind, though, that it's *how* they know you that determines the category of reference they serve. A boss may be a friend (character reference), for example. Of course, one reference may fit more than one category.

Some types of people should generally be avoided as references. Employers assume family members, clergy, and fellow students are biased in your favour. Their opinions, therefore, are discounted.

Never list a person as a reference until you have obtained his or her permission to do so and you are confident he or she will provide a positive reference. Also, try to provide the people who've agreed to act as references with some information about the type of positions you're applying for so that they can anticipate the questions potential employers will ask. When a potential employer tells you he or she will be checking your references, a quick phone call to those references to let them know they will be contacted is often appreciated.

Here is an example of a reference section from a résumé.

REFERENCES:

Dr. Lillian Patterson
Department of Commerce
University of British Columbia
P.O. Box 3561
Vancouver BC V5Z 2C5
(604) 731-8265

Mr. William Luciano, Distribution Manager
Legal Book Company
4324 Brownsboro Rd.
Toronto ON M2W 1X0
(416) 923-4832

Ms. Betty Hakamura
Department of English
University of British Columbia
P.O. Box 3561
Vancouver BC V5Z 2CS
(604) 731-8143

List a title (for example, Dr., Mr., Mrs., or Ms.) for each of your references so the personnel specialist who telephones them will know how they are to be addressed. Give the complete business address and telephone number (never list the reference's home address unless the reference prefers it).

What your references say about you will not — unless it is negative — have a great impact on your evaluation. Some potential employers will not even contact your references, though others will. Employers expect that anyone you list as a reference will support your application. Nevertheless, you will be required normally to submit at least three names of people who are willing to recommend you.

Should you decide not to list your references on the résumé, you might use the following statement:

REFERENCES: **Excellent references available upon request.**

In summary, in writing your résumé, you can choose from thirteen components those that you think will best show your accomplishments. The rest of this chapter shows you how to package these components into a compelling résumé format.

Résumé Formats

You can select from a variety of formats the one you think presents your résumé components in the best way. This chapter will introduce you to the two most commonly used formats: chronological and functional. You will also be shown an example of a résumé that combines elements of both formats.

Chronological Résumé Format

The chronological résumé is especially useful if you are graduating from school and entering the job market with little work experience. Figure 17.1 is an example of this format that incorporates most of the thirteen components that have been described.

The appearance of your résumé is almost as important as its contents.

With the increasing availability of word processors and desk-top publishing, employers are interested in applicants who can use this technology to their advantage. Notice (in Figure 17.1) that Robert has used a two-column page layout so that each of the components is readily identifiable. He has used a larger font size for the headings in the left-hand column so that they stand out clearly on the page. Thus, readers can quickly find the information they are looking for. For example, some will want to read about your work experience first; others, your education.

In the second column, the actual information is blocked attractively, several spaces in from the section headings. Solid lines lead the eye from the heading to the first item in the section. Italics are used to emphasize key information such as degrees and positions.

Finally, the references are listed across (not down) the bottom of the page. This approach will save space and make your references easier to identify. It also ensures that the résumé does not exceed two pages — the length recommended by most experts.

Figure 17.2 is another example of the chronological résumé format, written for Laura Bailey. Notice how Laura has used her education to her best advantage. She gives specific details that focus on what she accomplished during her training rather than simply listing the courses that she took. She also mentions her portfolio so that potential employers know she has examples of her work.

If you have extensive work experience, the work experience component appears early and describes each position in detail. Notice that in Figure 17.3 the individual's work experience consumes the most space. Work experience also precedes education, since it is more important.

Functional Résumé Format

The functional format emphasizes job qualifications

The functional résumé differs from the chronological in that it is organized according to skills and qualifications. When using the functional format, choose the qualifications you think are important for the position you want, list each separately, and show how you came to possess it. The functional résumé is becoming increasingly popular because of its focus on qualifications — what you have to offer the employer — rather than on length of service.

As you read the following example (Figure 17.4), however, notice that it does list actual positions. Even if they are impressed with your qualifications, employers want to know where you have worked in the past. You may, if you wish, omit the dates of your jobs when you use this format. However, recognize that many potential employers will wonder if you have something to hide when you omit dates from your work history.

Robert J. Anderson
1897 Clearwater Rd.
Kamloops, BC • V2C 3S6
(604) 422-5799

Address until June 1, 1991
134 Ansley St., Apt 4B • Vancouver, BC
V5Z 1C2 • (604) 863-2717

Available June 1, 1991

Objective — Responsible career position in accounting or finance.
Willing to travel and relocate.

Education — June, 1991
Bachelor of Commerce (Honours),
University of British Columbia.
Major in Accounting, Minor in Finance.
Course work included:

- Accounting Principles
- Tax Accounting
- Accounting Law
- Financial Analysis
- Financial Planning

Maintained 85% average; graduated summa cum laude

June, 1987
Graduated with honours from Richmond Senior Secondary,
Richmond, BC

Work Experience — September, 1987 to present
Part-Time Registration Clerk
Holiday Hotel
Vancouver
Responsibilities include:

- registering hotel guests
- making reservations
- processing check-outs
- handling guest problems

Have earned approximately 30% of university expenses

Summer, 1987
Sales Representative
Legal Book Company
Toronto
Responsibilities included:

- calling on potential customers
- processing orders
- delivering orders
- delivering merchandise

Was top salesperson in 12-person territory
Earned 70% of university expenses for 1987/88

continued

Figure 17.1

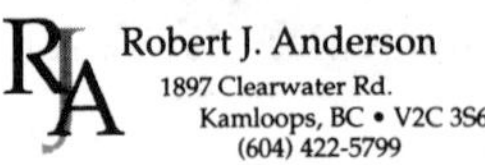

Awards

Postsecondary
- The Society of Management Accountants Award in Accounting (academic achievement), 1990
- The Financial Executives Institute Award (academic ability and leadership), 1990

Secondary
- Chosen class valedictorian, 1987
- Scholastic Achievement Award, 1987

Activities

Postsecondary
- Alpha Kappa Psi Business Fraternity (Vice President), 1989/91
- Business representative, student association, 1988/89
- Chairperson, campus Red Cross Blood Drive, 1987/88

Secondary
- Spanish Club, 1983/84, 1986/87 (President, 1986/87)
- Captain of basketball team (provincial champions), 1986/87

Interests
- reading
- tennis
- photography
- basketball

Personal
- age 22
- no children
- married
- excellent health

References

Dr. Lillian Patterson
Department of Commerce
University of British Columbia
PO Box 3561
Vancouver, BC
V5Z 2C5
(604) 731-8265

Mr. William Luciano
Distribution Manager
Legal Book Company
4324 Brownsboro Rd.
Toronto, ON
M2W 1X0
(416) 923-4832

Ms. Betty Hakamura
Department of English
University of British Columbia
PO Box 3561
Vancouver, BC
V5Z 1C3
(604) 731-8143

Laura Bailey ❧

#117 - 2714 West 10th Avenue • Vancouver, BC • V6K 2A5 •733-6308

Education

Currently working towards completion of Certificate Program in Business Communications and Media Techniques through night school classes.

Desktop Publishing/Graphic Arts
McCain Technical Institute, 1990

- 300 hours of intensive training in typography, design, and page layout using a computer
- over 200 hours of hands-on computer experience
- projects included logos, a newsletter, an ad, stationery, and a travel guide

Applied Communication (1st year completed)
Camosun College
Victoria, 1989 - 1990

- intensive full-time studies concentrating on print, radio, and video production
- experience with all aspects of the print process
  - typesetting
  - page layout and design
  - paste-up
  - mechanicals
  - process camera and offset darkroom capabilities
  - line negatives, halftone negatives, PMTs, and platemaking
  - offset lithography
- assisted in production of monthly magazine and acted as art director
- hosted weekly radio program
- produced audio projects including news and sports report, concert promotion, and four-track recording and sound mixing
- instructed in use of 35 mm SLR camera as well as processing and development of black and white film
- produced video projects such as 3-minute campus tour and 5-minute historical video

continued

Figure 17.2

Laura Bailey ❧

Work Experience

Computer Graphic Artist

Microtech Ltd.
Vancouver, BC
April 1991 - present • consultant
December 1990 - March 1991 • full-time

- designed technical drawings from instructional designer's specifications
- documented entire on-going graphics revision process of all courses and modules being worked on by group
- daily and weekly maintenance of extensive file management system of over 200 disks and 200 hard copy files

Desktop Designer - practicum

Dan Miller & Associates
Advertising Inc.
Vancouver, BC
October 1990

- intensive, on-the-job training with PageMaker and FreeHand on a Macintosh
- laid out a variety of multi-page documents such as itineraries, newsletter/magazines, and proposals
- produced advertisements, brochures, logos, business cards, forms and price lists from designer specifications, meeting set deadlines

Technical Skills

- Macintosh Plus/ SE/II/IIx/IIci
  - Aldus PageMaker
  - Aldus FreeHand
  - Adobe Illustrator
  - Microsoft Word
  - MacDraw/MacDraw II
  - MacWrite
- typing 40 wpm
- process camera
- AB Dick 360 offset press
- Comp/Set Varityper direct entry/memory entry phototypesetter
- 35 mm SLR photography
- Ilford black and while film processing and development

❧ **References and portfolio available** ❧

Joyce Lauffer

4255 Tufts Road
Brandon, Manitoba, R7A 4M8
(204) 614-8432

Age: 27
Health: Excellent

Available: Immediately

Objective: Responsible and challenging management position in health care administration.

Experience: May, 1988 to present
Assistant Administrator
Health Sciences Centre
Brandon, Manitoba

Directly responsible for:
- Hiring all hourly-wage employees to staff 100-bed hospital.
- Administering wage and salary program for all staff members.
- Writing policies and procedures for employee handbook.
- Supervising four department heads and two clerical workers.

Accomplishments:
- Implemented technical training program for all health-care employees. Received highest possible rating from Hospital Accreditation Board.
- Implemented employee suggestion system which has resulted in net savings to hospital of $75 327.

September, 1986 to April, 1988
Director of Nurses
Health Sciences Centre
Winnipeg

Responsibilities:
- Scheduled working hours for all nursing staff.
- Supervised three shift supervisors.

Accomplishments:
- Promoted use of paraprofessional to assist nursing staff.
- Awarded the Manitoba Nurses' Association "Supervisor of the Year Award," 1983.

June, 1984 to August, 1986
Nursing Supervisor
Groveland Hospital
Winnipeg
- Responsible for all first-shift nursing operations at 250-bed hospital.
- Made recommendations concerning patient care and staff grievances. All were implemented.
- Supervised 25 registered nurses and 13 nursing assistants.

continued

Figure 17.3

Joyce Lauffer

4255 Tufts Road
Brandon, Manitoba, R7A 4M8
(204) 614-8432

Age: 27
Health: Excellent

Education:

1988 to present
University of Manitoba
Working toward a Master's Degree in Hospital Administration. Completed 60 hours of course work.

June 1984
University of Manitoba
Bachelor of Science degree in Nursing. Graduated with high honours.

Professional Memberships:

- Canadian Hospital Association
- Manitoba Association of Health Care Administrators
- Registered Nurses Association of Manitoba

Community Activities:

- Canadian Cancer Society
- Canadian Red Cross
- United Way (Campaign Chairperson, 1987)

Interests:

- antique collecting
- golf
- public speaking

References: Available upon request.

ALAN THIBEAU
25 Clarkston Place
Montreal, PQ
H1K 1H6
(514) 236-5926

Available Immediately

Age: 25
Marital Status: married, no children
Health: excellent

Objective
- Responsible general management position in textile or related field. Willing to travel or relocate.

General Management
- Supervised more than 100 hourly-wage workers in two textile plants. Responsible for scheduling and employee-relations problems.

Quality Assurance
- Met or exceeded quality standards 95 percent of the time.
- Helped establish quality standards for new product.

Production
- Assisted in introduction, set-up, and operation of new machines. Am familiar with Crossland and Weaveright equipment.

Motivation
- Used MBO, goal-setting, and piece-rate systems.

Work History
- 1989 to present: Production Manager, Bostick Mills, Montreal
- 1985 to 1989: Production Supervisor, Brun & Frères, Trois-Rivières

Languages
- Fluently bilingual in English and French; some Portuguese.

continued

Figure 17.4

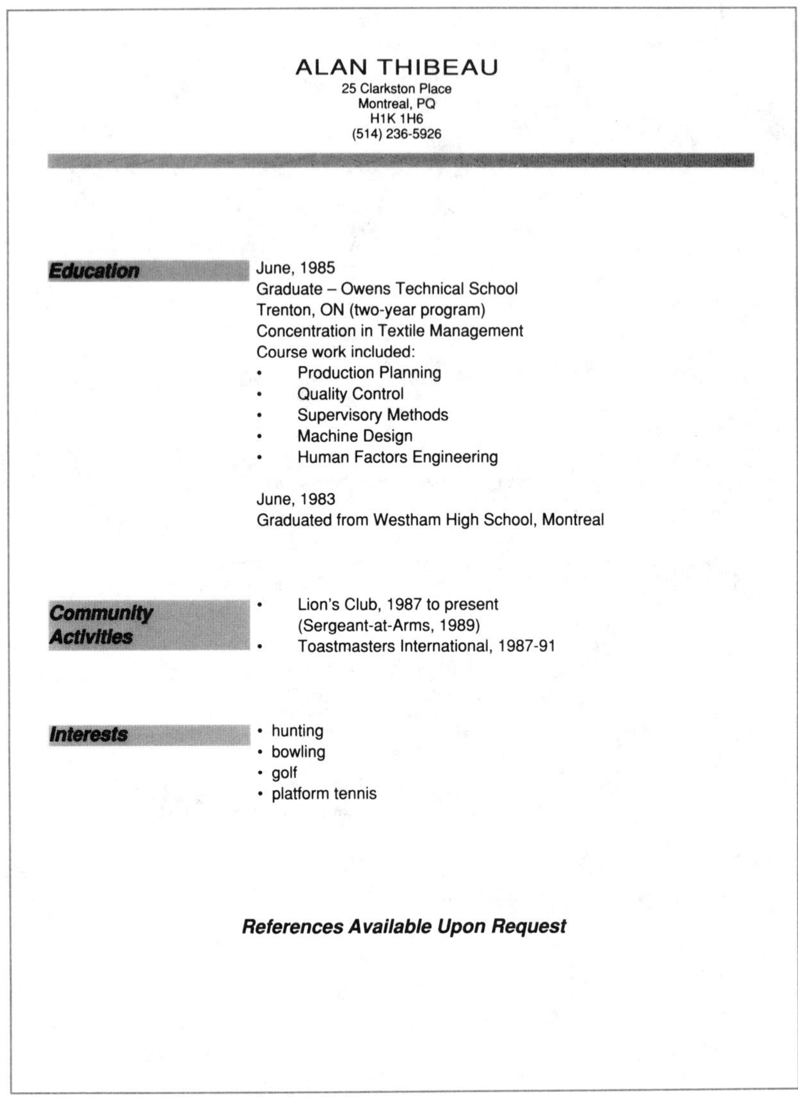

ALAN THIBEAU
25 Clarkston Place
Montreal, PQ
H1K 1H6
(514) 236-5926

Education

June, 1985
Graduate – Owens Technical School
Trenton, ON (two-year program)
Concentration in Textile Management
Course work included:

- Production Planning
- Quality Control
- Supervisory Methods
- Machine Design
- Human Factors Engineering

June, 1983
Graduated from Westham High School, Montreal

Community Activities

- Lion's Club, 1987 to present (Sergeant-at-Arms, 1989)
- Toastmasters International, 1987-91

Interests

- hunting
- bowling
- golf
- platform tennis

References Available Upon Request

Combination Formats

You can create a résumé format that combines the best elements of both the chronological and the functional résumé. This combination format is often useful when you are tailoring your résumé to a particular job. You can use the Special Skills section at the beginning to highlight your suitability for the position without having to redesign your résumé completely. Notice the use of graphic elements in Figure 17.5 — particularly effective for someone whose training includes architectural drafting and design.

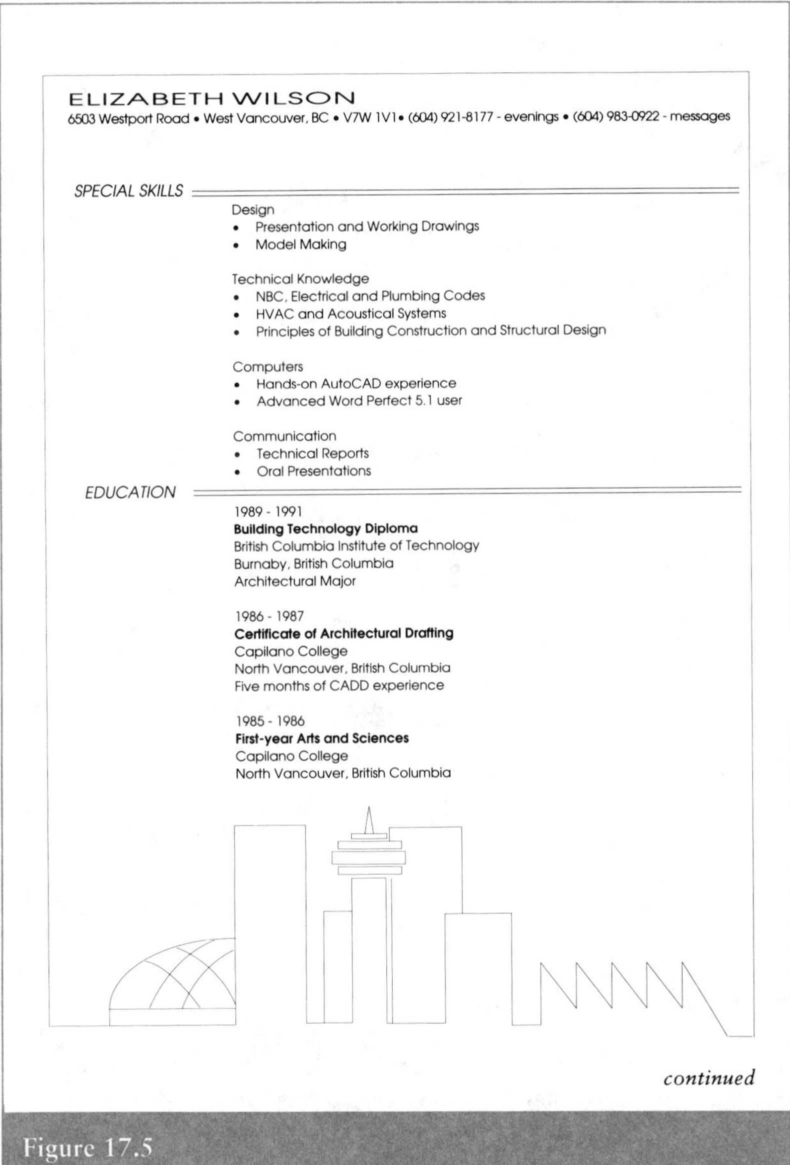

ELIZABETH WILSON
6503 Westport Road • West Vancouver, BC • V7W 1V1• (604) 921-8177 - evenings • (604) 983-0922 - messages

SPECIAL SKILLS

Design
- Presentation and Working Drawings
- Model Making

Technical Knowledge
- NBC, Electrical and Plumbing Codes
- HVAC and Acoustical Systems
- Principles of Building Construction and Structural Design

Computers
- Hands-on AutoCAD experience
- Advanced Word Perfect 5.1 user

Communication
- Technical Reports
- Oral Presentations

EDUCATION

1989 - 1991
Building Technology Diploma
British Columbia Institute of Technology
Burnaby, British Columbia
Architectural Major

1986 - 1987
Certificate of Architectural Drafting
Capilano College
North Vancouver, British Columbia
Five months of CADD experience

1985 - 1986
First-year Arts and Sciences
Capilano College
North Vancouver, British Columbia

continued

Figure 17.5

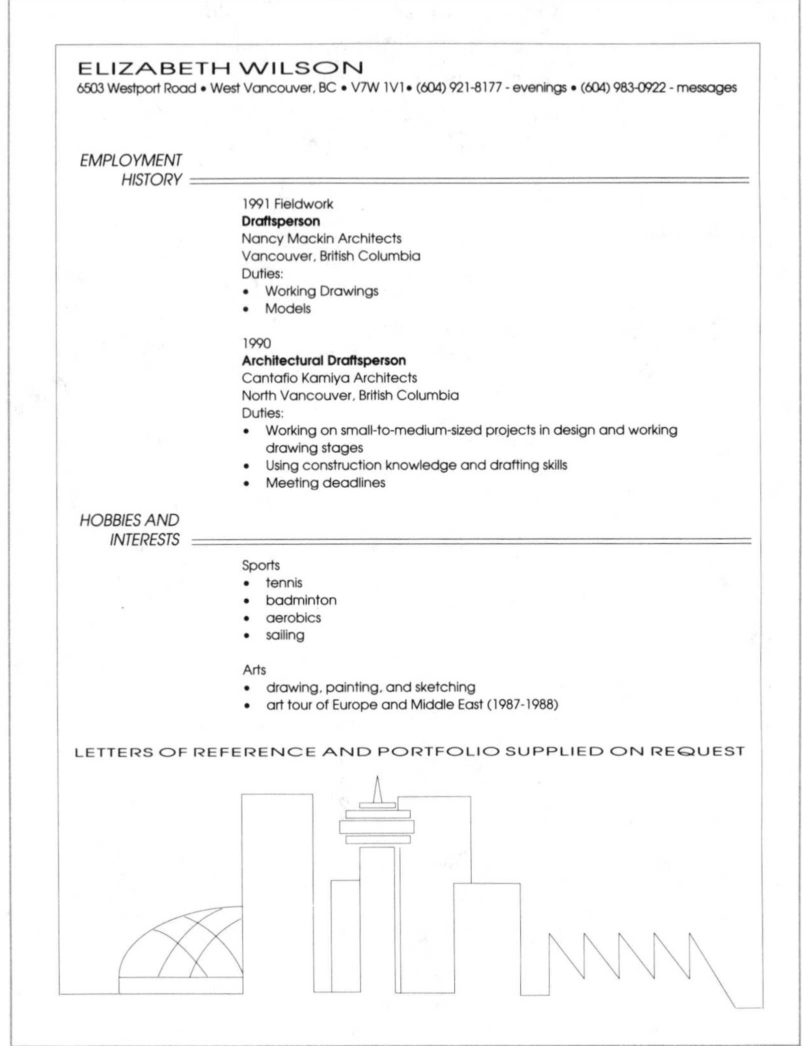

ELIZABETH WILSON

6503 Westport Road • West Vancouver, BC • V7W 1V1• (604) 921-8177 - evenings • (604) 983-0922 - messages

EMPLOYMENT HISTORY

1991 Fieldwork
Draftsperson
Nancy Mackin Architects
Vancouver, British Columbia
Duties:
- Working Drawings
- Models

1990
Architectural Draftsperson
Cantafio Kamiya Architects
North Vancouver, British Columbia
Duties:
- Working on small-to-medium-sized projects in design and working drawing stages
- Using construction knowledge and drafting skills
- Meeting deadlines

HOBBIES AND INTERESTS

Sports
- tennis
- badminton
- aerobics
- sailing

Arts
- drawing, painting, and sketching
- art tour of Europe and Middle East (1987-1988)

LETTERS OF REFERENCE AND PORTFOLIO SUPPLIED ON REQUEST

Preparing Copies of Your Résumé

Word processing and desk-top publishing have revolutionized the production of résumés. Many students have access to sophisticated computers and software packages that they can use to prepare their résumés.

Alternatively, they can have someone else prepare the final copy — many student associations provide this service for their members at a nominal cost.

Try to keep your résumé to one or two pages. Even if you have extensive work experience or other information, select only the most useful information to include on any one résumé.

Reducing the résumé to one page

One way to get a lot of material on one page is to use reduction. If your résumé takes more than one page and you are using a professional word processor, have your final draft printed on 21.6 cm by 35.6 cm (8 1/2 by 14 inches) with no margins at the top or sides. Many print shops can reduce this long sheet to standard-sized paper when the résumé is copied. If your long copy requires no more than a 20-percent reduction, the final résumé should have an attractive appearance.

The final copies of your résumé should be printed on good-quality white or off-white bond paper. Many print shops have a variety of bright colours from which to choose; however, colours are not used for résumés as often as they were a few years ago.

Summary

This chapter has given you the information you need to write an effective résumé. It shows you:

- how to answer a recruiter's key questions
  - highlights your suitability for the job
  - documents your education, both formal and informal
  - details your employment record, including references
- what the components of a résumé are
  - preliminary data: heading, availability date, and objective
  - education
  - work experience
  - additional related data: honours, activities, interests, and personal data
  - licences, accreditation, special skills, and professional memberships
  - references
- two different résumé formats
  - chronological
  - functional

Review Questions

1. What does the education component of a résumé contain? The work-experience component?
2. What is meant by a "balance of interests" on your résumé? Why is this balance important?
3. Describe the differences between two résumé formats.
4. What are "special skills" on a résumé?
5. When should you emphasize your ability in French? Why?
6. Briefly discuss the final production of a résumé.

Activities

1. Write a draft of your own résumé using the chronological format. Exchange your résumé with a classmate's. Evaluate each other's drafts, suggesting changes.
2. Rewrite your résumé using the functional format. Do you see any advantages in this format for your own résumé?
3. Make an appointment to interview a personnel officer in a company in your community. Your purpose in this interview is to find out: what he or she considers most important in a résumé; how he or she uses résumés in making selection decisions; and what he or she does not like in a résumé. Write a brief report summarizing your interview findings.

Discussion Cases

Ray's Résumé[1]

Many new graduates have less-than-outstanding scholastic averages and only meagre work experience. Yet they must compete with apparently better-qualified graduates for the available job openings. Raymond Cortez is one such graduate. Here is what he told his friend about his predicament:

"Susan, Pioneer Technologies has asked for résumés to screen candidates before it interviews for two sales-support openings. Sales-support people get data from the engineers and the production personnel and translate it into benefits and procedures for the marketing representatives to use when selling to potential customers. Sales-support staff do some customer contact, too, so they're half sales, half technical. And it's all state-of-the-art stuff! I really want that job, but so do at least 30 other grads I've talked to. Pioneer will interview only 12, and I'm not really even qualified. The company wants a minimum average of 75 percent and all I've got is 70 percent. Look, here's my résumé. What do you think?"

Résumé
RAYMOND F. CORTEZ

481 Ferris Street, London, Ont. N6K 2X2; 830-4145

OBJECTIVE:	**Responsible position in sales with opportunity for advancement.**
EDUCATION:	**University of Western Ontario, London, Ont., 9/88-6/90.** **Faculty of Business Administration, marketing major.** **Maintained a 70% average.**
	Graduated from Eaton High School, London, Ont. 6/88.
WORK EXPERIENCE:	**Helper, Al's Auto Service, summers, 1988-9.** **Helped with all areas of auto service and repair.**
	Attendant, Frank's Pizza Place, part-time, 1986-87. **Made and served pizzas.**
	Newspaper route, *London Free Press*, after school, 1985-86.
SPECIAL SKILLS:	**Chauffer's licence**
ACTIVITIES:	**Football, restoring old cars.**
REFERENCES:	**Rev. Michael Walsh** **First Unity Church** **Main and Circle Streets** **London, Ont. N5W 2Y1**	**Julia Tibor, Instructor** **University of Western Ontario** **London, Ont. N6G 1G3**

"What do I think of it? You don't stand a chance with this résumé," said Susan.

"Yeah, my grades ..." Ray sighed.

"That's not the worst of it. There are misspellings, it's incomplete, it's not well spaced. Even the objective is wrong — it's for a sales job, not ... ," said Susan.

"But this is a standard résumé!" Ray said.

"Change it. At least say that you're graduating. And don't start out with your poor grades — that's starting with a negative point.

continued

And let's see what we can do with the job titles and descriptions to show that you can work effectively with technical people, marketing people, and customers," said Susan.

After interviewing Ray for a gruelling hour and a quarter, Susan found out that Ray expects to graduate with a B.Comm. in June 1990. In addition to marketing courses, he took courses in management, organizational behaviour, interpersonal communication, psychology and group dynamics, as well as sales promotion and audio-visual presentation. His average in his major (marketing) was 74 percent.

The auto service job had no formal title, but it could legitimately be called "mechanic's helper." He wrote up customer orders, repaired transmissions, and became the resident expert on lubricants and high-performance (racing) equipment. If he does not find a job in his field, he will probably return to the shop this summer as Al has asked him back. During each of the two summers he worked for Al, he made enough money to cover almost all his tuition without using the Ontario Student Aid Program loan he was eligible for.

At Frank's Pizza, Ray ordered supplies, opened and closed when Frank wasn't there, and created a contest idea and a profitable "Kitchen Sink Pizza" (everything on it) as well as a hotline service for delivery to Western's student residences. He also fixed some of the equipment. On the newspaper route, he started with 30 customers and had 54 when he quit after finding that the job interfered with his school football schedule.

Ray has joined few campus organizations and has won no academic honours. He likes dancing and, with a girlfriend, won a dance contest last year. He also enjoys hockey and played on the school team, though his career was undistinguished. He was a fourth-string defence player with a lot of bench time. One semester, when he was injured, he served as an assistant manager; he was responsible for uniforms and some promotion work, and travelled with an assistant coach as part of an advance team to set up for away games.

continued

Ray has no formal training in French beyond required high school courses, but he has had no trouble meeting Francophones and carrying on conversations during several trips to Quebec. His Spanish-speaking grandmother taught him her language when he was a child.

During the past year, Ray bought two wrecked European cars and restored them with the help of original-language manuals (French and Italian); he sold both cars at a profit. He got a Class A driver's licence thinking he might drive a truck some time. The summer before he started at Western, he worked for his father's swimming pool business and wrote a customer quality checklist, but he quit after two weeks because he did not like the business.

Case Questions

1. How would you revise Ray's résumé? Defend your revisions.

The Résumé: Path to an Interview — and a Job[2]

Now that you are familiar with the theory of résumé writing, you should be able to pinpoint the devices that distinguish an acceptable résumé from a truly effective one.

Figures 17.6 and 17.7 show two résumés prepared by a young marketing graduate who set himself the goal of landing a job in sales with IBM.

He updated the résumé he had used in his senior year in college and mailed it directly to IBM's Toronto-area marketing manager. When he received no reply after two weeks, he phoned and learned from the secretary that the company had no sales openings.

continued

Using his marketing experience — he was, after all, selling himself — he revised his résumé and resubmitted it. This time he received a phone call from the marketing manager asking him to come in for an interview. And he did get the job he wanted.

WILSON OWEN
140 Crossroads Drive
Winnipeg, Manitoba
R3B 3T6
(204) 775-0179

EXPERIENCE: *1988 to present*	Prairie Greetings Corporation Winnipeg *Accounts Manager:* Promoted from sales representative in supermarket division to accounts manager of a top national drug chain. Maintained customer satisfaction with successful sales through the development of innovative merchandising techniques and analysis of market trends. Supervised six employees. *Accomplishments:* Over forecast in 1990 by 32 percent and 1991 by 71 percent with eleven new accounts opened. Percentage of new stores successfully prospected is up to 40 percent in 1991 over previous two years.
1981 to 1988	Magic Chef Delicatessen Winnipeg *Night Manager:* Worked up from apprentice clerk to night manager with responsibilities for preparing and closing the store. Paid all school and travelling expenses with job.
EDUCATION:	Bachelor of Commerce in International Business from the University of Manitoba in June 1988. Member of the Student World Trade Association.
AWARDS:	Earned Scholastic Achievement Award from the Faculty of Commerce in 1986 on the basis of scholastic accomplishments and debating skills.
INTERESTS:	Building fine furniture, playing golf, and racquetball.
REFERENCES:	References available upon request.

Figure 17.6

WILSON OWEN
140 Crossroads Drive
Winnipeg, Manitoba
R3B 3T6
(204) 775-0179

OCCUPATIONAL OBJECTIVE

To be an active participant in sales with a progressive company.

EXPERIENCE HIGHLIGHTS

1988 to present
Prairie Greetings Corporation
Winnipeg
Accounts Manager:
Initially employed as a sales representative in the supermarket division. Promoted to accounts manager, requiring supervision of merchandisers, sales analysis, development of innovative merchandising techniques, and customer relations.

1982 to 1988
Magic Chef Delicatessen
Winnipeg
Sales Clerk:
Worked up from apprentice clerk to night manager with the responsibilities of preparing for the next day and closing the store. Paid for all school and travelling expenses with job.

EDUCATION

B. Comm. in International Business from the University of Manitoba, 1988.
Played on college golf team. Member of the Student World Trade Association. Earned Scholastic Achievement Award from the Faculty of Commerce in 1986.

COMMUNITY SERVICE

Six years of volunteer work with Canadian Cancer Society.

PERSONAL INTERESTS

- building fine furniture
- playing golf
- handball

PERSONAL DATA

- age 26
- no children
- height 170 cm
- excellent health
- married
- weight 90 kg

REFERENCES

Personal and business references available upon request.

Figure 17.7

Case Questions

1. Place yourself in the marketing manager's position. You don't have any current openings, but you can make room for an exceptional applicant. Which version would arouse your interest enough to call the applicant for an interview?
2. Why? Defend your selection with specific examples.

Chapter 18

Job Search Letters and Interviews

Learning Objectives

In this chapter, you'll learn how to conduct a successful job search. More specifically, you will be able to:

1. write effective job search letters
2. write interview follow-up letters
3. plan for job interviews
4. anticipate the kinds of questions job interviewers often ask
5. improve your performance during a job interview

Preview Case

Carla Chavez has landed an interview with Tom Coates, regional sales manager for Nirvana Computers. During the interview, Tom asked Carla, "Why do you want to work for Nirvana?"

Carla replied: "Well, Mr. Coates, that's why I asked for the opportunity to meet with you today. I want to be sure that Nirvana is the right company for me.

"I've read a great deal about Nirvana and I've met a few of your employees. I also had the opportunity to hear a presentation by one of your campus recruiters. Everything I've heard and read has been extremely positive. I'm especially impressed by your concern for employees and service to customers.

"But I wanted to see some of this for myself. I'm not sure that I can get a real feeling for the Nirvana culture without visiting and finding out how I would fit the profile of a Nirvana sales representative. I have a few questions that I need answered before I can be sure."

"Go ahead and ask. I'll answer your questions the best I can," replied Tom.

Carla asks a few specific questions about various Nirvana policies, and she probes until she is satisfied that she has the information she needs.

Tom leans back in his chair, clasps his hands behind his head, and says, "I like your style, Carla, and I think you've got the making of a top-notch Nirvana sales representative."[1]

Overview

When you are looking for a job, your primary goal should be to schedule as many job interviews as you possibly can. You follow this strategy for two reasons: the experience and the greater likelihood of finding a job it allows for.

Most students have had little or no experience in interviewing for a career position. Such interviews can be ego-threatening and even traumatic, especially when an interviewer asks a question you are not prepared to answer (for example, "What is your major weakness?"). As you progress through a number of interviews, you become more confident and able to sell yourself because you have learned from practice and from your own mistakes.

The more interviews you have, the greater your chances of finding an attractive position

The more interviews you have, the greater the likelihood that you'll be offered a job. The assertiveness Carla Chavez showed in her interview came only when she was confident about her own interview performance. You will be offered a job only when your qualifications match the position being filled and you are better qualified than all the other individuals who have applied for that position. Nevertheless, you'll find that your communication skills are often judged on the basis of your performance in the employment interview.

Whether you are conducting a direct-mail campaign or responding to a specific job advertisement, you'll need to write letters of application and follow-up letters to obtain the all-important interview. Chapter 16 showed you how to develop an overall strategy for your job search. This chapter will show you how to write those letters and how to make the most of your opportunity when you are called for an interview.

Unsolicited Letters of Application

Cover letters sent as part of a direct-mail campaign are not in response to a specific request for applications; therefore, they are often call unsolicited letters of application. To be successful, these unsolicited letters must have three characteristics: they should be personal; they should include a reason for wanting to work for the company; and they should be persuasive.

Your cover letter is important

When you are conducting a direct-mail campaign, never use the salutations "Dear Sir or Madam" or "To Whom It May Concern." A personal touch is critical. Usually, the person you want is the personnel officer of the company. Often you can obtain this name by consulting the sources listed in Chapter 16 or by calling the firm and asking for the personnel officer's name and title (for example, personnel manager, vice president for personnel, recruiting officer).

Second, successful letters give a reason for applying to the company. You can include this reason in your cover letter as a way of showing interest in the firm.

An unsolicited job letter is a kind of sales letter

Third, successful letters are persuasive. You might use the AIDA format discussed in Chapter 10. Figure 18.1 is an example of an unsolicited application letter that uses the AIDA format. Notice first that this unsolicited letter clearly indicates the position for which the person is applying. Second, it calls attention to the résumé and briefly summarizes some of the writer's qualifications that are related to the position. Third, it provides convenience for the receiver by stating when the writer can be reached by phone. Finally, the letter follows the AIDA approach and saves the desired action (the interview request) for the final paragraph. The unsolicited job letter is much like a sales letter: you are establishing a need in the reader to talk with you.

Your application letters should never be longer than one page. If you have enough space, mention information that relates your abilities to known job requirements. But only highlight your qualifications, since your résumé, which is enclosed, expands these thoughts.

May 30, 1992

Ms. Patricia Markham
Personnel Manager
Able Computers, Inc.
P.O. Box 1511
Toronto, Ontario
M5W 3G1

Dear Ms. Markham

Subject Line

Application for Entry into Your Management Training Program

The reputation and growth of Able Computers have led me to apply for a position in your management trainee program. Information in the Career College Planning Annual indicates you hire university graduates with business degrees. The Annual states you prefer computer, management, and sales or marketing majors.

Interest

My B.Comm. degree from Queen's University incorporates a major in management and a minor in marketing. Further, my two years of part-time work for the Bank of Montreal in its data processing department used capabilities acquired in my three university-level computer classes.

The fact that Electronic Industry Magazine rated you number 1 in its poll of the most promising companies of the 1980s is impressive. The challenge of helping you maintain your position of leadership in the volatile computer industry is especially exciting.

Desire

As you will note on my attached résumé, I am willing to accept challenges and carry them through to successful completion. Mr. Grover Jefferson of the Bank of Montreal has offered to support this view. His address and the names and addresses of other references are on the résumé.

Action

May I have an interview at your convenience? I am available at (416) 922-9676 between 2:00 p.m. and 6:00 p.m., weekdays.

Sincerely

Jennifer Jones

Jennifer Jones
33 Burford Place
Oakville, Ontario
M4Z 1V9

Figure 18.1 Sample Persuasive Application Letter (Unsolicited)

Just as you were extremely careful to prepare a letter-perfect résumé, you should also be careful in the preparation of the cover letter. Some recruiters are so concerned about correct typing, grammar, and spelling that they don't even answer letters with errors!

Solicited Letters of Application

The cover letter you send in response to a newspaper advertisement is known as a solicited letter of application. It generally resembles an unsolicited letter of application. However, there should be some differences. In the first paragraph, you should refer to the advertisement, identifying where and when you read it, as well as to the position for which you are applying.

When you are highlighting the qualifications outlined in your résumé, you should concentrate on those qualifications that match the ones listed in the advertisement. One way to do this is to use key words from the advertisement itself. For example, if the ad calls for someone with "experience participating in and leading internal and external committees" and you were president of your campus student association, you would try to use the key words *experience*, *leadership*, and *committees* when you were highlighting this aspect of your qualifications.

In responding to an ad, emphasize qualifications that match those specified

Figure 18.2 is a sample advertisement to which the letter in Figure 18.3 responds.

Computer Systems Planner

We are looking for an experienced computer professional to assume both technical and consulting responsibilities. A strong background in business, and industrial applications on a variety of computer systems is required. Good communication skills and a minimum of four years experience are essential. Please submit your résumé to:

Mr. Edward Delaney
Compuware Consulting Ltd.
101-800 Bloor Street West
Toronto, Ontario M5W 1E8

Figure 18.2 Computer Systems Advertisement

92 11 02

Mr. Edward Delaney
Compuware Consulting
101 - 800 Bloor St. W.
Toronto, Ont. M5W 1E8

Dear Mr. Delaney

Application for Position as a Computer Systems Planner

Your advertisement in last Friday's *Globe and Mail* calls for an experienced computer professional with a strong background in business and industrial applications; this description matches my qualifications. As a computer systems planner, I could serve you and your clients well.

I have four years' experience in computer systems development. Holding increasingly responsible positions, I have worked on both commercial and engineering applications. I am equally at home calculating cost of sales, solving complex equations, and scheduling industrial processes.

In each of my positions, I have learned how the business functioned so that I could talk to the users in their own terms. This knowledge allowed me to understand and contribute to discussions at development meetings and to produce clear proposals with realistic examples.

When you have had an opportunity to review my résumé, I would appreciate an interview to discuss my qualifications with you. You can phone me at 922-6804, local 304, during office hours to arrange an appointment.

Sincerely

Joshua Cherny

Joshua Cherny
152 Bedford Road
Toronto, Ontario M4E 2B6

encl. (1)

Figure 18.3 Responding to an Advertisement

Follow-up Letters

As indicated in Chapter 16, following up on your applications is extremely important. Two weeks is generally accepted as a reasonable time to wait before making a follow-up contact with an organization. Often a follow-up letter or phone call will result in your making the short list rather than being left out. Figure 18.4 is an example of a follow-up letter. Strategies for the follow-up phone call are included in Chapter 16.

June 15, 1992

Ms. Patricia Markham
Personnel Manager
Able Computers, Inc.
P.O. Box 1511
Toronto, Ontario M5W 3G1

Dear Ms. Markham

Follow-up: Application for Position as Management Trainee

Several weeks ago I wrote you applying for a management traineeship with Able. In case my application letter has been lost in the mail, I do wish to ensure that you know of my enthusiasm for Able. As my June 15 letter stated, I am impressed with your position of leadership in your industry.

You are interested, I understand, in recruits with computer, management, and marketing abilities. My management major, marketing minor, and data processing job experience meet those qualifications.

The enclosed résumé presents more information about how my educational, job, and extracurricular activities prepare me well for your traineeship.

An interview with you, at your convenience, is still my goal. My schedule remains the same; I am still available at (613) 922-9676 weekdays from 2:00 p.m. until 6:00 p.m.

Sincerely

Jennifer Jones

Jennifer Jones
33 Burford Place
Oakville, Ontario M4Z 1V9

Figure 18.4 Sample Follow-up Letter

With a letter, you can organize your thoughts to achieve your follow-up goal. Notice first, in the sample letter (Figure 18.4), that the writer uses tact by implying that the original letter and résumé may have been lost in the mail. Second, another résumé is enclosed in case the original is indeed missing. Third, another summary of relevant qualifications is provided. New information can, of course, be added at this time. This is another opportunity to emphasize your qualifications. Finally, available times for receiving phone calls are repeated.

Interview-Confirmation Letters

If a firm grants you an interview as a result of your direct-mail campaign or your response to a newspaper advertisement *and* if you have sufficient time, you might write a letter confirming the date, time, and place of the interview and expressing your appreciation for being given the interview. Here's an example of the body of such a letter:

Sample interview-confirmation letter

Thank you for scheduling an interview with me about opportunities in Able Computer's manager trainee program. I am looking forward to our meeting.

As you requested during our telephone conversation, I'll be in Room 117 of the Able Building at 10:00 a.m. on Thursday August 9.

Your interest in my application is appreciated.

Job Interview Performance

Your actual, face-to-face interaction with a representative of the company is the most critical step in your job search process. The job interview is the major selection tool for most organizations.

A successful job interview involves three steps:

1. Planning
2. Performing
3. Following up

Interview Planning

Planning in every business-communication situation has been emphasized throughout this text. Planning is of paramount importance to the job interview as well. Here are some suggestions to help you prepare.

Review Your Qualifications

Match your qualifications with the job requirements

Your job search will be successful when the employer's representative realizes that your qualifications match the requirements of the position being filled. The question "Is this person qualified?" remains uppermost in every interviewer's mind, even after reading the résumé and the covering letter. Your goal is to show this match during the interview, to demonstrate that, as in Figure 18.5, the pieces of this job-selection "puzzle" do fit together.

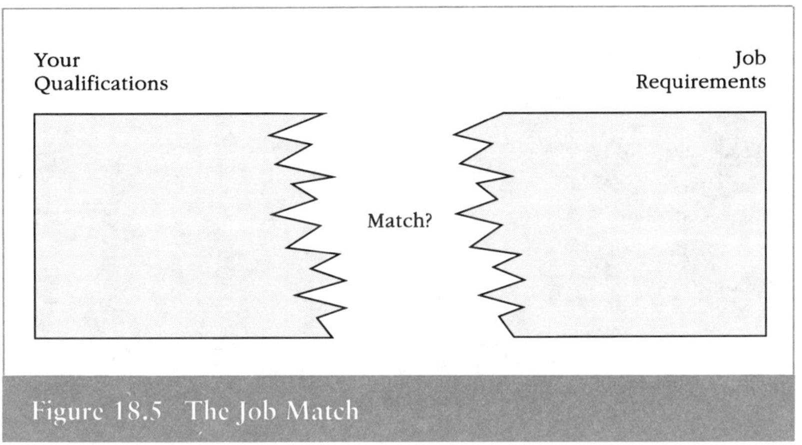

Figure 18.5 The Job Match

Be able to document your best qualities

As we pointed out earlier, your qualifications for a job include not only your previous applicable work experience, education, and extracurricular activities, but also any saleable personal characteristics you have. Figure 18.6 lists qualities that employers consider to be important. As you place a checkmark in the appropriate blank next to each quality, don't forget to consider all your work- and school-related experiences. You should be able to justify clearly any high rating you have given yourself. Trained interviewers are not interested in statements such as "I'm a self-starter" unless you can give evidence of your initiative. Be prepared to show that you are dependable, adaptable, mature, and so on.

Any activity in which you have been involved can provide evidence. For example, playing basketball or any other team sport requires the ability to work with others. Earning part or all of your college expenses shows initiative. A clear and logical explanation of why you changed fields or transferred from one school to another can indicate decision-making ability and, perhaps, adaptability. Leadership skills can be shown through various activities, including holding offices in organizations,

	Superior	Above average	Average	Below average	Poor
Ability to learn	_____	_____	_____	_____	_____
Initiative (self-starting)	_____	_____	_____	_____	_____
Decision-making abilities	_____	_____	_____	_____	_____
Written communication skills	_____	_____	_____	_____	_____
Problem-solving skills	_____	_____	_____	_____	_____
Oral communication skills	_____	_____	_____	_____	_____
Adaptability	_____	_____	_____	_____	_____
Professional appearance	_____	_____	_____	_____	_____
Ability to work with others	_____	_____	_____	_____	_____
Leadership skills	_____	_____	_____	_____	_____
Enthusiasm	_____	_____	_____	_____	_____
Dependability	_____	_____	_____	_____	_____
Self-confidence	_____	_____	_____	_____	_____
Maturity	_____	_____	_____	_____	_____

Figure 18.6 Am I Qualified?

working as a counsellor in a summer camp, or even training your replacement for a job you left.

In short, pick your major qualifications, document them, review them, and be prepared to talk about them during the interview.

Research the Company

Before the interview, find out all you can about the company

One of the most important steps in preparing for an interview is to research the company. You need to know the size of the company, its products or services, its position in the industry, some of its history, the locations from which it operates, its financial considerations, the employment situation, the types of jobs being filled, and whether it is a subsidiary of an American company. For this information, look to the company's annual report, recruiting literature, and the *Canadian Business Periodical Index*, as well as to the sources mentioned in Chapter 16.

When recruiters discuss major problems or errors in interviews, they invariably point to interviewees' lack of knowledge about the company as a serious shortcoming.

Anticipate What Will Happen in the Interview

Knowledge of interviews will help you prepare for the interview and reduce your anxiety as well. Here's what you can expect:

1. the types of interviews
2. the types of interviewers
3. the flow of the interview
4. the types of questions asked

Types of Interviews. Most interviews or interview situations are found in one or more of the following classifications.

Interviews fall into at least six types

1. *The screening interview*, as its name implies, screens prospects into groups, such as "Interview them further," "Reject them," or "Hold for future decision." Such an interview usually occurs before other categories of interviews and typically lasts about 30 minutes.

2. *An open-ended interview* (sometimes called an "unstructured" or "non-directive" interview) follows no discernible pattern. Your answer to an initial question may determine the next question. The interactions and responses direct the interview.

3. *A panel interview* involves one interviewee and more than one interviewer. Since an interviewee may feel overwhelmed by only one interviewer, imagine the pressure you are likely to feel with several people questioning and observing you! On the other hand, if the company feels your interview is important enough to justify the time of two or more recruiters, perhaps it is already impressed with you.

4. *The group interview* is the reverse of the panel interview — several interviewees are present with one interviewer. You're likely to encounter a group interview in a social setting, such as a party to which many job prospects are invited or a mass screening situation when the company has a large number of applicants for few positions. Since these interviews may not last long, each interviewee seeks to make a quick and positive impression — often at the expense of other applicants. Do try to impress your interviewer but avoid direct comparison to others in the room if possible.

In a group interview, try to make a good impression quickly but without comparison to other candidates

5. *The stress interview* — probably the most unpleasant of the six categories — places the interviewee in a stressful situation in which the interviewer carefully observes reactions. Examples of these situations are inviting you to smoke but not supplying an ashtray and putting you in a lengthy business simulation full of tricks and pitfalls. Questions the interviewer knows to cause stress may also be used. At one time deliberate stress questions and stress interviews were fairly common. Today they are

less frequent, but they are sometimes used, especially for high-level executive and high-stress positions (high-pressure sales, for example).

Office visits may mean six or seven hours of being evaluated

6. *The office visit* (or plant headquarters visit) is not a single interview but a series of them that may incorporate several of the categories already discussed. Some of the interviews may be stressful, others may be conducted by a panel, and still others may be open-ended. A six- or seven-hour day, including breakfast, lunch, and coffee breaks with company officials, is not unusual. You are constantly being evaluated, not only in the formal interviews but also in the casual, information discussions; therefore, never let down your guard. In addition to interviews, the visit may include psychological or ability testing, building tours, discussions with potential peers or subordinates, and the completion of application or travel reimbursement forms.

Types of Interviewers. Just as there are many types of interviews, there are also different types of interviewers; the major ones are the practitioner and the personnel office representative.

The practitioner interviewer is difficult to predict

1. *The practitioner* is a person who is currently doing the type of job for which you would be hired, that is, an accountant who interviews prospective accountants, and so on. The interviewing practitioner may be the person who would be the immediate superior of the new employee. The practitioner is not likely to have formal training in interview procedures; therefore, it is difficult to predict the course of the interview. Likely discussion topics are the job's required area of expertise and background about the company. Because of their lack of training in interviewing, practitioners are more likely to ask stress questions at inappropriate times or ask questions deemed illegal by the relevant human rights guidelines.

The personnel interviewer is difficult to "read"

2. *Personnel office representatives* probably have, as part of their job descriptions, the role of recruiter. Training in selection methods, appraisals, and interviewing prepares them for this role. Because of their training, representatives of personnel offices are difficult to "read." They will be pleasant and courteous but seldom will you be certain that you have "blown" the interview or that you have it "sewn up."

Typical Interview Flows. A description of a typical screening interview may help prepare you for it. The interview may last 15 to 45 minutes or so, but 30 minutes is traditional. A typical 30-minute period might break down as follows:

First 5 minutes	Introductions, small talk, questions of low priority

Next 10 minutes	Focus on interviewee's abilities and responses to interviewer's questions
Next 10 minutes	Responses by interviewer to interviewee's questions and description of company and job
Last 5 minutes	Closing comments, explanation of next steps

The schedule for a full-day office visit depends, of course, on the organization and the type of job. However, a visit to an office for a management job might proceed through these steps:

9 a.m. – 10 a.m.	Breakfast with the interviewer who conducted the screening interview
10:15 a.m. – 11 a.m.	Introductions to other personnel office employees
11 a.m. – noon	Meeting with vice president of related area
Noon – 1:30 p.m.	Lunch with two members of personnel office and prospective immediate superior
1:30 – 2:30 p.m.	Meeting with prospective immediate superior
2:30 – 4 p.m.	Half-hour meetings with three potential peers
4 p.m. – 5 p.m.	Completion of company forms and tour of facilities with personnel office representative
5 p.m.	Depart with screening interviewer for the airport for flight home.

As you can see, by the time you get home, you will have had a long, tiring, and eventful day.

Types of Questions Asked. Another way you can help yourself through anticipating what will occur in an interview is by knowing the types of questions you may be asked and when they usually occur in an interview. Questions fall into five major categories:

1. *Questions to which the answers are really inconsequential* usually start an interview. The purpose of these questions is to break the ice and get the interview moving. Trained interviewers know that you'll be anxious about the interview. After all, much rides on how you perform in a short period of time; you're in a strange and perhaps bleakly appointed interview room; you're meeting a total stranger and talking, in some cases, about personal thoughts and feelings.

For these reasons questions about the weather or last night's hockey

The manner in which you answer opening questions is important

game occur first. The recruiter doesn't care too much about what you say but rather about how you say it. Your enthusiasm for a certain hockey team makes more of an impression than which team you prefer.

2. *The important questions* start shortly after you start to relax. They focus on your interests, your knowledge of the company or the job, and why you think you can do the job. The recruiter will listen carefully to your responses and is likely to build on them with follow-up questions. You are evaluated on the speed, depth, and quality of your answers.

Many of the important questions will be open-ended so you can decide how much or how little to include in your answer. As a general rule, answer such questions in three to seven sentences, depending on the complexity of the question.

3. *Stress questions*, as mentioned earlier, are designed to place pressure on you. They may occur at any time in an interview but are most likely to appear after some important questions. It is hard to plan how to respond to stress questions — by definition, they are intended to catch you off guard. Still, just knowing they may occur should help you.

4. *Inappropriate questions* are either illegal or unrelated to the position at hand. Interviewers are not supposed to ask questions on subjects related to forbidden grounds of discrimination. For example, questions about your race, ethnic background, marital status, or religion are not allowed in any Canadian jurisdiction. Each province has a list of other forbidden topics, which may include age, physical disabilities, political beliefs or affiliations, club memberships, language, criminal record, and sexual orientation. Exceptions occur when the information is directly related to the job — for example, you may be asked about your French if the position is bilingual. (Notice that some provinces permit a prospective employer to collect information on sex, marital status, and age on the application form, although it may not be asked in the interview or used to discriminate in hiring.)

Think carefully if you're asked an illegal question

What do you do if you are asked one of these questions? You have several options. If you do not find the question offensive or the answer potentially damaging, you can answer it. If the answer to the question is personal or if you think it is not related to the job, you can tell the recruiter so politely. You may wish to ask the purpose of the question; there may be an unanticipated good reason for it.

Be prepared to ask your own probing questions

5. *Questions you ask* the recruiter are the final type of interview question. Most interviewers allow time for you to learn more about the job and the organization. Your questions can be valuable for two reasons: the better the question, the better its reflection on you, and you probably

have some questions you would really like answers to. Before the interview, prepare yourself with five or six questions. The interviewer may answer some of them in the company or job description segments of the interview. But, when given the opportunity, you should be able to raise several probing questions. Avoid trite or shallow questions. Aim for open-ended questions rather than those that yield only a yes/no answer. Consider asking questions about the extent of responsibility you would be given, the types of assignments encountered, and even about the negative aspects of the job.

Here are some examples of questions you might ask:

1. Where does your typical manager trainee wind up in five years' time?
2. How important are advanced degrees, such as an MBA, to advancement in this company?
3. Do you normally promote from within the company?
4. What kind of orientation program or training do you provide for new employees?

Be sure to avoid questions that might create negative feelings in the interviewer. For example "How do you handle grievances?" is inappropriate. "Will I have to work much overtime?" might characterize you as having little initiative. You should avoid questions about salary unless starting salaries are the same for all incoming employees (for example, some teaching positions, government jobs, and even management-trainee programs).

Prepare answers to common questions

The following list contains 50 questions that are frequently asked by campus recruiters. Examine them to get the "flavour" of the typical interview. Since some of these questions are likely to be asked of you, you may want to think out your answers to them.

As you read the questions, you will notice that some of them seek your opinions whereas others ask for facts. Most interviewees have much more difficulty with the opinion questions, since the "right" answer isn't clear.

Questions Most Frequently Asked by Campus Recruiters[2]

1. What are your future vocational plans?
2. In what school activities have you participated? Why? Which did you enjoy most?
3. How do you spend your spare time? What are your hobbies?
4. In what type of position are you most interested?
5. Why do you think you might like to work for our company?
6. What jobs have you held? How were they obtained and why did you leave?

7. What percentage of your university (college) expenses did you earn? How?
8. Why did you choose your particular field of work?
9. What courses did you like best? Least? Why?
10. How did you spend your vacations while in school?
11. What do you know about our company?
12. Do you feel that you have received a good general training?
13. What qualifications do you have that make you feel that you will be successful in your field?
14. What extracurricular offices have you held?
15. What are your ideas on salary?
16. How do you feel about your family?
17. How interested are you in sports?
18. If you were starting your postsecondary school all over again, what faculty or department would you choose?
19. Can you forget your education and start from scratch?
20. Do you prefer any specific geographic location? Why?
21. How old were you when you became self-supporting?
22. How much money do you hope to earn at age 30? 35?
23. Why did you decide to go to this particular school?
24. How did you rank in your graduation class in high school? Where will you probably rank in your university (college) class?
25. Do you think your extracurricular activities were worth the time you devoted to them?
26. What do you think determines (a person's) progress in a good company?
27. What personal characteristics are necessary for success in your chosen field?
28. Why do you think you would like this particular job?
29. What is your father's (mother's) occupation?
30. Tell me about your home life during the time you were growing up.
31. Are you looking for a permanent or temporary job?
32. Do you prefer working with others or by yourself?
33. Who are your best friends?
34. What kind of boss do you prefer?
35. Are you primarily interested in making money or do you feel that service to your fellow human beings is a satisfactory accomplishment?
36. Can you take instruction without feeling upset?
37. Tell me a story.
38. Do you live with your parents? Which of your parents has had a more profound influence on you?
39. How did previous employers treat you?
40. What have you learned from some of the jobs you have held?

41. Can you get recommendations from previous employers?
42. What interests you about our product or service?
43. Have you ever changed your major field of interest while in university (college)? Why?
44. When did you choose your department (field of concentration)?
45. Which of your years in school was the most difficult?
46. Do you feel you have done the best scholastic work you can?
47. How did you happen to go to university (college)?
48. What do you know about opportunities in the field in which you are trained?
49. How long do you expect to work?
50. What is your major weakness?

Here are some suggestions for dealing with several of the questions students have found difficult:

Question 7: What percentage of your university (college) expenses did you earn? How? It is a paradox of our society that most of us envy the wealthy, such as students who don't need to work summers, but that prior experience and indications of industriousness are paramount in employee selection. All things being equal, the recruiter is more impressed with the student who has worked to pay educational expenses, even doing menial or non-career-related activities, than with the wealthy student who has shown no indication of a willingness to work. Therefore, the stronger a case you can build for yourself in percentage of expenses earned, the better your evaluation.

On the other hand, if you have not held a job but have volunteer experience, especially in your field, you can show that you have initiative to further your career.

Question 19: Can you forget your education and start from scratch? Your goal in answering this question is to underline the importance of your education but at the same time to show a willingness to learn new things. Thus, an appropriate answer might be something like this: "I can't really forget my education, because I think I've learned some things that will be helpful to me in my work. However, I know that my education isn't completed yet. I'm willing and eager to learn new things."

Question 37: Tell me a story. Many students have heard this question in job interviews. One approach to answering is to tell a factual story containing a "moral" about yourself or someone you know. For example, you might describe a conflict situation with a roommate in which you became so frustrated that you finally sat down and leveled with him or her. Because your interaction had a healthy outcome, you realized the importance of simply communicating with someone with whom you're in conflict. Or you might tell a story about a relative who, although lacking formal education, started a business, worked long hours, and succeeded. You can draw "morals" from a story like this one about persistence, perseverance, initiative, energy, or optimism.

Question 50: What is your major weakness? Three important factors in answering this question are: that you identify a weakness, that you show that you've analyzed it, and that you show that you are overcoming it or have a clear plan for doing so. One example is a fear of getting up in front of people to make a speech. You are voluntarily taking a public speaking course (or joining the local Toastmasters Club) to overcome this weakness. Other examples of weaknesses you might consider are having too high expectations of other people, having too much desire to take control of situations involving other people, and not knowing how to accept compliments from other people. Whatever weakness you choose to discuss, try to make sure that the interviewer cannot interpret it as an uncorrectable personality trait.

Know What the Recruiter Is Seeking

What you are is more important than what you know

You can prepare for an interview better if you have some feeling about how and on what you will be evaluated. Many students are surprised to learn that often they are not evaluated on what they know. Instead, recruiters assume that your degree or diploma shows you have some basic information and the ability to learn. It also indicates an interest in specific areas. Now, if the company hires you, it will teach you in depth the specifics it wants you to know. Therefore, recruiters ask few questions about your knowledge of subjects, such as, "Can you tell me the difference between a closed-end and a limited open-end mortgage bond?" or "How would you apply Maslow's Theory to a management trainee job?" Questions are asked to determine such characteristics as tact, enthusiasm, industriousness, maturity, congeniality, or communication ability. Your directedness, initiative, competitiveness, and intelligence will be scrutinized as well.

Most companies use an interviewee evaluation form, which the recruiter completes after the interview. Since the importance of various characteristics differs by company, no standard form exists. The sample form in Figure 18.7, however, is typical in the type of attributes evaluated, and the length and depth of response requested.

Consider Your Appearance

Appearance shouldn't cost you a job, but it might

Don't let the simplicity of this suggestion mislead you. One survey found that in a twenty-minute interview the average interviewer had made a selection decision within the first four minutes.[3] Some interviewers claim

INTERVIEW APPRAISAL FORM

Name ____________________ School ____________________

Campus Address ____________________ Phone Number ____________

Post-graduation Mailing Address ____

________________________________ Phone Number ________

Availability Date ____________________ Geographical Preference ____________________

Career Interests ________________________ G.P.A. ____________

SELECTION STANDARD Relates to selection standards and to information reported by applicant	EXCEEDS	MEETS	DOES NOT MEET

PRESENTATION	Forcefulness, Organization, Conciseness — ask related questions.
ACHIEVEMENTS	Academic, Technical, Professional Contributions to previous employers. Do they relate to our needs?
AMBITIONS	Career Goals, Financial Goals — are they realistic?
CONTRIBUTIONS	Long- and short-term, what can the candidate add to the organization?
IS CANDIDATE SOLD ON COMPANY	Understands Career Opportunity.
OVERALL REACTION	

HIGHLY RECOMMENDED __________

RECOMMENDED __________

REJECT __________

____

Recruiter's Signature

Figure 18.7 A Sample Interview Appraisal Form

that they can decide whether or not an applicant is suitable for a job the very instant he or she enters the room. Obviously, these early decisions are based in large part on physical appearance.

Generally, you should dress as you would in the job for which you are applying. This guideline often means that men should wear a suit and tie, and women a dress or suit. If you aren't sure, it is probably better to dress in simple business attire, giving consideration to what is socially acceptable.

Prepare for the Unusual

Stories abound about "tricks of the trade" that interviewers use to catch an applicant off guard. Although it is unlikely that you will be confronted with any of these, you should nevertheless be aware of and be prepared for them. Examples are:

"Tricks of the trade" are not used by most interviewers

Silence	The interviewer says absolutely nothing at the beginning of the interview. Instead, he or she simply looks at you. You, therefore, must begin the interaction.
Sell Me	During an interview for any kind of sales or marketing position, the interviewer slides an ashtray or a pencil across the desk to you and says, "Here. Sell this to me."
Turnabout	The interviewer says, "I've been interviewing people all day and I'm tired. Why don't you interview me?"
Choose a Chair	When you enter the interviewer's office, you see two empty chairs. One is near the interviewer's desk, the other is several feet away from it. The interviewer says simply, "Have a seat," but doesn't tell you which chair to choose.

If these situations seem frightening to you, remember that very few interviewers use tricks. Most are highly trained, competent business-people who want to evaluate your qualifications in a straightforward manner.

In summary, your first step in successful job interviewing is to plan for the interview. The six suggestions offered should help build your confidence before an interview and improve your actual interview performance.

Interview Performance

The second step in your strategy for a successful job interview is your behaviour during the interview. Here are several suggestions:

Successful performance involves both verbal and nonverbal communication

Arrive Early or on Time. Being late for a job interview shows lack of dependability (one of the qualities discussed earlier). If you must be late, call the interviewer and explain why. Consider making a trial run before the interview to determine travel time, parking facilities, and exact location of the building and room. Arriving late will put unneeded pressure on you.

Have a Firm Handshake. Shake hands with the interviewer. A handshake is a sign of acceptance and greeting in a business situation. Also, remember that some interviewers perceive a weak, fishlike handshake as characteristic of a weak personality.

Establish and Maintain Eye Contact with the Interviewer. Like the weak handshake, an absence of eye contact denotes a weak personality to many interviewers. To a few of them it also indicates that the interviewee may be lying.

Consider Your Posture. Interviewers sometimes form negative perceptions of applicants who slouch in chairs, cross their arms and legs, and face away from them. Sit erect, facing the interviewer. Don't cross your legs and arms at the same time. Some interviewers believe the stereotype of the person who sits in such a closed position as being someone who is trying to shut the other person out.

Don't Fiddle with Objects. Playing with objects (for example, a pen or pencil) during the interview communicates unusual nervousness to many interviewers. Often they translate your nervousness during the interview to mean that you cannot perform well in stress situations on the job. Under no circumstances should you fiddle with objects on the interviewer's desk.

Don't Criticize Past Employers. An interviewer may interpret your criticism of past employers as an indication that you are a complainer who criticizes all your employers. Also, such criticism may be seen as a rationalization for the real (and damaging) reasons you left your previous employers.

Don't Evaluate Previous Jobs — Simply Describe Them. Because many students consider their work experience menial, they are often inclined to communicate that perception during the interview: "Well, really all I did was fry hamburgers," or "The job really wasn't much — I just waited on people." Yet no matter how unimportant you think a job was, an interviewer will ask questions about it in order to assess a number of your qualities, among them dependability, leadership skills, ability to work with others, and initiative.

Ask Questions about the Company. During interview planning, you prepared questions about the company. Remember to ask them before the interview ends.

Be Honest. Don't try to be someone you're not. Allow your true personality to emerge. Try to make a good impression, but avoid developing an image that is inaccurate. The company will make hiring decisions on what shows in the interview. Problems may occur if the "real you" who turns up for work is substantially different.

Express Appreciation for the Interview. As the interview closes and you are about to leave, remember to thank the interviewer for discussing employment opportunities with you. If possible, express appreciation for any constructive suggestions the interviewer has made, especially if you think you will not be considered for the job.

In summary, the second step in successful interviewing involves polished, professional behaviour during the actual interview. You can gain the needed skills by practising the above suggestions with anyone (classmates, friends, relatives) who will take the time with you.

Interview Follow-up

A job interview follow-up consists of three steps: immediate follow-up, delayed follow-up, and follow-up to letter of acceptance or rejection.

1. Immediate Follow-up

Immediate follow-up should occur one to two days after your interview

As soon as possible after the interview, write the interviewer a follow-up letter. Basically, this letter consists of three paragraphs:

Paragraph A Express appreciation for the interview and your continued interest in the position.

Paragraph B Add any important information about yourself that you failed to mention during the interview. Or emphasize one of your qualifications that the interviewer stressed as important, especially if you feel personally confident about the qualification. Or mention some information you learned about the company during the interview and that impressed you. Try to say something that will remind the reader of you and the interview; pick something that would not have been discussed with other interviewees. You may also mention, when appropriate, that you have completed and enclosed an application form.

Paragraph C Communicate your willingness to answer further questions about your qualifications and assume a positive attitude towards hearing from the interviewer.

Here's an example of such a follow-up letter:

Sample follow-up letter to an interview

Dear Ms. Markham

Thank you for the time you spent with me on Thursday discussing employment opportunities in Able Computer's manager trainee program. Your description of Able's program was very impressive and reinforced my serious interest in the position.

You mentioned during the interview that Able is interested in individuals who can assume responsibility. Both my work experience (where I trained new employees and replaced the manager when she was out of town) and my extracurricular activities (where I assumed leadership positions in three different campus groups) show the kind of responsible experiences you might be seeking in an applicant.

If you wish to discuss any questions about my qualifications for the manager trainee position, please call me. I look forward to hearing from you.

Sincerely

Your follow-up letter may also serve as a cover letter for a job application form. Most companies use application forms that ask for much the same information as is supplied on your résumé. You may be asked to complete the organization's form before a screening interview, immediately after the screening interview, or at the office visit. Frequently, at the completion of a successful screening interview, you are asked to take a form with you and return it by mail. This request can be an indication that you are proceeding through the job-getting process. As you complete the form, keep in mind that neatness, spelling, grammar, and punctuation are important.

2. Delayed Follow-up

Advantages of follow-up

Most interviewers close a job interview by telling you how soon a selection decision will be made: "We'll let you know something by the fifteenth of next month." If you don't hear from the company by the deadline specified, telephone the interviewer to check on the "progress" of your application. If a decision has not yet been made, you will have simply gained the advantages of immediate follow-up. If a decision has been made and you have not been chosen, you will at least know where you stand.

If you are turned down, you have little to lose by remaining diligent. Recruiters sometimes talk about the employee they hired who wouldn't take "no" for an answer.

A final note on follow-ups: You might have wondered why follow-ups have been emphasized so extensively in this chapter. Certainly, it creates more work for you. However, the follow-up (whether by letter or telephone) has two purposes. First, it is a public relations device designed to enhance your relationship with the interviewer. Second, it is a means of bringing your name back to the interviewer's attention. Recall that many interviewers, especially those who do campus recruiting, interview as many as fifteen applicants in one day. You want to stand out as a qualified person who is genuinely interested in the position.

3. Follow-up to Letters of Acceptance or Rejection

You'll probably get both kinds of letters — some offering you a position with a company and some turning you down. You should respond to both kinds of letters.

If you are offered a position that you accept, your follow-up letter should:

a. Formally accept the position.
b. Express appreciation for the offer.
c. Confirm the details of the offer, including:
  1. salary
  2. starting time
  3. location of position
  4. name of person to whom you'll be reporting.
d. Show anticipation of doing good work.

Here is an example of such a letter:

Dear Ms. Markham

Sample letter accepting a job offer

Your offer of a position in Able Computer's manager trainee program is enthusiastically accepted. Thank you for your confidence in my potential to perform well in the program.

Confirming your letter offering the position, I understand that the starting salary is $23 150 per year, to be paid monthly. I will report to Room 236 of the Able Building at 8:00 a.m. on Monday, January 4, and ask for Phillip Woo, who is to be my training co-ordinator.

As we discussed earlier, I am impressed with the opportunities Able Computers provides qualified applicants. I will do all I can to justify your trust in my potential.

Sincerely

If you refuse a position offered by a company, your letter of refusal should:

a. Express appreciation for the offer.
b. Compliment the interviewer or the company offering the position.
c. Clearly refuse the position and explain your refusal.
d. Express appreciation for the offer again.

Here is an example of a letter refusing a job offer:

Dear Ms. Markham

Sample letter refusing a job offer

Thank you very much for your letter of September 23 offering me a position in Able Computer's manager trainee program. I am sincerely impressed by both your confidence in my potential and the opportunities Able offers to qualified applicants.

Just this morning Stover Chemicals offered me a training position in their employee relations department. Because of Stover's proximity to my home and the immediate opportunity to work directly in the employee relations field, I have decided to accept that offer.

Your interest in me and your consideration of my application are appreciated.

Sincerely

If you receive a letter rejecting your application for a position, you should follow it up, especially if you might reapply with the company in the future. Such a letter should:

a. Express appreciation for considering your application.
b. Express appreciation for the learning experience the application process has provided you.
c. Introduce future application possibilities.

Here is an example of a response to a letter of rejection:

Sample response to a letter of rejection

Dear Ms. Markham

I received your letter of September 23 indicating that I will not be offered a position in Able Computer's manager trainee program.

I do appreciate your time and effort in considering my application. Interviewing with you has been a learning experience that has provided me with valuable insight into my qualifications and opportunities for improvement.

As we discussed earlier, I am genuinely impressed with the opportunities Able provides qualified applicants. Therefore, when I have taken the courses you suggested in your letter, I intend to reapply for a position with Able. Please keep my application on file.

Sincerely

Sometimes an applicant receives a job offer from one company but wants to wait and see if another, better offer arrives. If this happens to you, you may wish to write a letter asking to delay your decision. Recruiters assume you are interviewing elsewhere and are not disconcerted by such requests.

On the other hand, they often have deadlines to meet or other applicants to whom they would like to give your job offer. Therefore, your request needs to be tactful. Your letter should:

a. Express appreciation for the offer.
b. Indicate that your goal is to select the company at which you can be of the most benefit and your career will be most enhanced.
c. Explain that your interviewing process is not quite complete and that you wish an extension of the decision deadline (give dates).
d. Reaffirm your interest in the job and the company.

Do not say that, if forced into a decision now, you would turn the offer down; this sentiment is better left unsaid.

Here is a sample delay request letter:

Dear Ms. Markham

Last week you offered me a position at Able Computers as a Management Trainee, starting June 1, at a salary of $23 150. I am very pleased to receive this offer and am giving it much thought. With your offer, you asked that I make a decision by February 1.

Sample request for delayed decision

As I told you during my visit to Toronto, I am seeking a position in which I can make a valuable contribution while moving towards my career goal of high-level management. To be fair to myself and the company for which I will work, it is necessary to explore the job market fully. My exploration is almost over but is not yet complete.

Would it be convenient, Ms. Markham, to delay my decision about your offer from February 1 until February 20?

Your job offer continues to impress me, and I am excited by it. This delay will enhance the quality of my decision – a decision that is important to both of us.

Sincerely

Summary

- Write both solicited and unsolicited letters of application.
- Follow-up all job applications with a phone call or a letter.
- Plan for the interview by:
  - reviewing your qualifications
  - researching the company
  - anticipating what will happen in the interview
  - practising answering questions
  - considering your appearance
  - preparing for the unusual
  - arriving on time
- During the interview,
  - have a firm handshake
  - establish and maintain eye contact
  - consider your posture
  - avoid fiddling
  - avoid criticizing past employers
  - avoid evaluating past jobs
  - ask questions about the company
  - be honest
  - express appreciation for the interview
- Following the interview,
  - write a follow-up letter

- ❑ call if you haven't heard by a specific deadline
- ❑ respond to letters of acceptance and rejection

Review Questions

1. Describe the contents of both unsolicited and solicited letters of application.
2. What are the steps in planning for a job interview?
3. Describe five kinds of nonverbal behaviour you should be conscious of during the job interview.
4. Discuss the importance of follow-up as it applies to job interviews.
5. Describe three situations in which you would be likely to use a follow-up.

Activities

1. You are a campus recruiter for Goldwin's, a chain of novelty stores with locations in Halifax, Charlottetown, Saint John, and Fredericton. You are looking for an applicant who shows three major qualities: dependability, initiative, and willingness to assume responsibility. The chosen applicant will become a manager trainee at Goldwin's in Saint John.
   a. Interview one of your classmates for this position.
   b. Write a brief (no more than two-page) report that summarizes: how you assessed your classmate against the three qualities; what your classmate said that made you feel that he or she possessed each of the qualities; and how your classmate's nonverbal communication affected your perception of him or her.
2. Form a trio with two of your classmates. Person A is the interviewer; Person B is the interviewee; and Person C is the observer. A should interview B for approximately ten minutes, asking any of the 50 questions listed in this chapter. A and C should give feedback to B about his or her answers and nonverbal communication. Allow B to practise answering difficult questions. Then switch roles for the next twenty minutes, making sure that each member of your trio plays each person in the exercise.
3. Fill out the qualifications checklist presented earlier in this chapter. Then write a brief report justifying your rating on each qualification. Use your work experience, activities, honours, and interests as evidence.
4. Make an appointment to interview the personnel officer of a local company. Your purpose in this interview is to find out:
   a. what kinds of questions the person likes to ask in job interviews
   b. the role this person thinks nonverbal communication plays in the job interview
   c. the most difficult problem this person has in selecting among applicants

d. what qualities this person looks for in people with your level of education

Summarize your findings in a brief report or a short oral presentation to the class.

Discussion Cases

Lost Opportunity[4]

On the advice of a friend, Sid Flaccus called Data Preparation Associates and obtained an interview for an entry-level technical writing position DPA was seeking to fill.

Flaccus is 22 years old and has a B.A. in English. He now works part-time for Personnel Service of London, Ontario, where he writes manuals, letters, memos, and reports.

Sid arrived fifteen minutes early for his interview with Betty Boman, the chief editor of DPA. He was dressed in a suit and tie and had even shined his shoes. Two days earlier he had had his hair styled and cut short.

Ms. Boman was dressed casually and appeared relaxed. Sid could see that she was an experienced interviewer. She let Sid do most of the talking, but interrupted his digressions about his writing experiences to ask pointed questions about his knowledge of computer software.

Sid knew a little about computers from his required course in computer science, and he added that he "didn't see much difference between journalism and tech writing." He recommended that Ms. Boman read a recent article taking computer software writers to task for their jargon and quoted several humorous examples from it.

When the conversation turned to Sid's writing, he quickly pointed out that he had a scholarly paper on poetry published in a Canadian journal, as well as several short stories in the campus magazine. He also mentioned that his English professors had praised his writing and encouraged a writing career.

The interview lasted nearly an hour, and for the last half-hour Ms. Boman asked no questions. She and Sid discussed the novels of Margaret Atwood, in whose work they shared an interest. The interview ended cordially, and Ms. Boman told Sid to call in about a week.

When Sid called a week later, he was surprised to find that another applicant had received the job.

Case Questions

1. What do you suspect caused Ms. Boman to turn Sid down?
2. What would you have done differently at the interview that might have changed its outcome?
3. Would you tell Sid to do anything differently at his next interview? What?

Trouble in the Ranks[5]

By the mid-1980s, there was such demand for courses in computing at Central Business College that the governing body of the college decided to create a new position of Dean — Computing Science, responsible for the co-ordination of all existing computer courses at the college, as well as for the introduction of new programs.

When the position was advertised in the national press, there was a large number of applicants both from the Toronto area as well as from across Canada.

Two teachers already on the staff of the college also applied. One, Janet Kizt, already taught several computing courses as part of a science course, while the other, Elizabeth Holt, had considerable knowledge of computers, although her expertise was in marketing. She also had less managerial experience than Professor Kizt.

When the selection committee met to discuss the applications received they found that at least four external candidates were as qualified as Professor Kizt for the new post, whereas it appeared that an additional five should be included if Professor Holt was considered an appropriate choice for the shortlist.

The committee reluctantly decided to interview only the top five candidates, including Professor Kizt but not Professor Holt, even though it was the general policy to interview all internal applicants as a matter of courtesy. The committee asked the chairperson to make a personal explanation to Professor Holt, explaining to her the very strong qualifications that the five short-listed candidates had, compared with hers.

Several days later, the chairperson wrote a formal letter to Professor Holt explaining the situation, and indicating that he now considered this the end of the matter as far as Professor Holt's application for the position was concerned.

When Professor Holt received the letter from the chairperson,

continued

she was outraged. At the time, she made the following comment to one of her colleagues:

"I think I've been treated badly. Most people around here know how committed I am to the college. The chairperson couldn't even find time to talk to me. I didn't even get a chance to put my ideas across. I can cope with not getting the job, but I consider the way I missed out highly insulting. It's typical of the management style around this place."

Case Questions

1. Can you understand Professor Holt's strong reaction? Give reasons for your answer.
2. Why should she have felt that the difference between a letter and a personal interview was so significant?
3. Discuss this case in terms of the differences between formal and informal communication channels.

Notes

Chapter 1

1. Carolyn Leitch, "Giving All for Dear Old Firm Begins to Pall on Employees: Workplace Values in Transition," *The Globe and Mail*, February 6, 1990, B1, B5.
2. Carolyn Leitch, "Learning Begins After School's Out: Basics Best Equip Students for Business," *The Globe and Mail,* February 6, 1990, B23, B24.
3. Leland Brown, *Communicating Facts & Ideas in Business*, 3rd ed. (Englewood Cliffs, N.J.: Prentice-Hall, 1982).
4. Mary K. Kirtz and Diana C. Reep, "A Survey of the Frequency, Types, and Importance of Writing Tasks in Four Career Areas," *The Bulletin*, 53 (4) (December 1990): 3–4.
5. *Report to the President by the Presidential Commission on the Space Shuttle* Challenger *Accident* (Washington, D.C.: Government Printing Office, 1986).
6. Carl Stieren, "Nirvana or Nightmare: Views Differ on Tomorrow's Wired Workplace," *The Globe and Mail*, February 6, 1990, B23, B24.
7. Adapted from a case by Vivienne Hertz, Southern Illinois University.
8. Adapted from a case by Larry R. Smeltzer, Arizona State University.

Chapter 2

1. For a more detailed discussion of reinforcing and aversive stimuli, see David Thompson, *Managing People — Influencing Behavior* (St. Louis: Morby Company, 1978).
2. Daniel Katz and Robert Kahn, *The Social Psychology of Organizations* (New York: John Wiley, 1966), 188.
3. Lee Thayer, *Communication and Communication Systems* (Homewood, Ill.: Richard D. Irwin, 1968), 195–203.
4. Adapted from a case by Jim Stull, San Jose State University.
5. Adapted from a case by David B. Parsons, Lakehead University, Thunder Bay.

Chapter 3

1. Albert Mehrabian, "Communication Without Words," *Psychology Today*, September 1968, 53–55.
2. M. Knapp, *Nonverbal Communication in Human Interaction*, 2nd ed. (New York: Holt, Rinehart and Winston, 1978), 220–32.
3. John T. Molloy, *Dress for Success* (New York: Peter Wyden, 1975).
4. Molloy, *Dress for Success*, 27–28.

5. John T. Molloy, *The Woman's Dress for Success Book* (Chicago: Follet Publishing Company, 1977), 43–44.
6. Molloy, *The Woman's Dress for Success Book*, 35
7. Susan Bixler, *The Professional Image: The Total Program for Marketing Yourself Visually* (New York: G. P. Putnam's Sons, 1984), 26–27.
8. Adapted from a case by Mildred W. Landrum, Kennesaw College.
9. Adapted from a case by Mary Jane Nelson Riley, Central State University.

Chapter 4

1. Michael Gelb and Nancy Margulies, *The Mind Map* (Washington, D.C.: High Performance Learning, 1990). (Brochure available from High Performance Learning Center, 4613 Davenport Street, N.W., Washington, D.C. 20016.)
2. Gelb and Margulies, *The Mind Map.*

Chapter 5

1. Carolyn Crawford Dolecheck, "Are You Teaching Affirmative Action Writing?" *ABCA Bulletin* 41 (4) (December 1978): 21.
2. Herta A. Murphy and Charles E. Peck, *Effective Business Communication* (New York: McGraw-Hill, 1976), 457.
3. Koreo Kinosita, "Language Habits of the Japanese," *ABCA Bulletin* 51 (4): (September 1988): 35–36. (Reprinted with permission from *Japan Echo* 13 [4] [1986]. Submitted to *The Bulletin* by Margaret Bahnuik, Cleveland State University.)
4. Adapted from a case by David B. Parsons, Lakehead University, Thunder Bay.
5. Adapted from a case by Dr. Beryl D. Hart, West Liberty State College.

Chapter 6

1. This definition of arguments and of inductive and deductive reasoning is adapted from *About Thinking* by W. Ward Fernside (Englewood Cliffs, N.J.: Prentice-Hall, 1980).
2. W. Ward Fernside, in *About Thinking*, also includes the inductive category of hypothesis in addition to the three listed in this chapter.

Chapter 7

1. Adapted from a case by Richard Pompian, University of Texas, Austin.

Chapter 8

1. Jerry Zeidenberg, "Market for Laptops Among the Hottest: Variety of Laptops Available." *The Globe and Mail*, March 6, 1990, C1, C2.
2. Leslie Ellis, "Walkabout Computing: Pen," *The Vancouver Sun*, February 6, 1991, B10, B11.
3. "Artificial Intelligence: The Second Computer Age," *Business Week*, March 8, 1982, 66–69.

Chapter 9

1. Adapted from a case by Lynne K. Anderson, Tidewater Community College.
2. Adapted from a case by David B. Parsons, Lakehead University, Thunder Bay.

Chapter 10

1. Abraham Maslow, *Motivation and Personality* (New York: Harper & Row, 1954).
2. First paragraph in a two-page advertisement for the Canada Awards for Business Excellence, a program of Industry, Science and Technology Canada.
3. First paragraph from an advertisement for Antares Technologies Inc., a company that markets computer networking systems.
4. Introduction from an advertisement for Autoflex leasing company.
5. Jim Powell, "The Lucrative Trade of Crafting Junk Mail," *The New York Times*, June 20, 1982, F–7.
6. Powell, "Crafting Junk Mail," F-7.
7. Adapted from a case by Richard Underwood, Ball State University.
8. Adapted from a case by Wesley C. King, Jr., Miami University.

Chapter 11

1. Adapted from a case by Anthony S. Lis, University of Oklahoma.
2. Adapted from a case by Jeremiah J. Sullivan, University of Washington.

Chapter 12

1. Charles Backstrom and Gerald Hursh-Cesar, *Survey Research*, 2nd ed. (Toronto: John Wiley & Sons, 1982), 118.
2. *The Chicago Manual of Style*, 13th ed. (Chicago: The University of Chicago Press, 1982); *Publication Manual of the American Psychological Association*, 3rd ed. (Washington, D.C.: American Psychological Association, 1983); Joseph Gibaldi and Walter Achtert, *Modern Language Association Handbook for Writers of Research Papers, Theses and Dissertations* (New York: Modern Language Association, 1979); and Kate Turabian, *Student's Guide for Writing College Papers*, 3rd ed. (Chicago: University of Chicago Press, 1976).
3. I would like to acknowledge the part played by Marjorie Holmes in creating Activity 4.
4. Adapted from a case by James M. Lahiff, University of Georgia.
5. Adapted from a case by Kath Ralston, Chisholm Institute of Technology, Victoria, Australia.

Chapter 13

1. Sylvia Porter, "Now Hear This: Americans Are Poor Listeners," *Tampa Tribune*, November 15, 1979, 15–A.
2. "The Act of Listening," *Royal Bank of Canada Monthly Letters* 60 (January 1979).

3. Leland Brown, *Communicating Facts and Ideas in Business*, 3rd ed. (Englewood Cliffs, N.J.: Prentice-Hall, 1982).
4. Judy C. Nixon and Judy F. West, "Listening: Vital to Communication," *The Bulletin of the ABC* 52 (2): 15.
5. Carolyn Gwynn Coakley and Andrew D. Wolvin, "Listen to What's Being Said About Listening Training," *Performance & Instruction* 30 (4): 8–10.
6. Nixon and West, "Listening," 15–17.
7. The review provided on listening research is based on Charles R. Petrie, Jr., "Informative Speaking: A Summary and Bibliography of Related Research," *Speech Monographs* 30 (1963): 79–91. See also Sam Duker, *Listening Bibliography*, 2nd ed. (Metuchen, N.J.: Scarecrow Press, 1968), and *Listening Readings*., vols. 1 and 2 (Metuchen, N.J.: Scarecrow Press, 1966, 1971); Larry Barker, *Listening Behavior* (Englewood Cliffs, N.J.: Prentice-Hall, 1971); and Carl Weaver, *Human Listening* (Indianapolis: Bobbs-Merrill Company, 1972).
8. Carl Rogers and Richard Farson, "Active Listening," in *Readings in Interpersonal and Organizational Communication*, ed. Richard Huseman, Cal Logue, and Dwight Freshley, 2nd ed. (Boston: Holbrook Press, 1973), 486–87.
9. Rogers and Farson, "Active Listening," 486–87.
10. Adapted from *Effective Listening: Key to Your Success*, by Lyman K. Steil, Larry L. Barker, and Kitty W. Watson. Professor Steil and colleagues adapted their material from "Listening Is a 10-Part Skill," by Ralph G. Nichols, *Nation's Business* (July 1957).
11. Adapted from a case by Martha Shoemaker, Coca-Cola Company, U.S.A.

Chapter 14

1. David Wallechinsky and Irving Wallace, *The Book of Lists* (New York: William Morrow, 1977).
2. Robert T. Oliver, Harold P. Zelko, and Paul D. Holtzman, *Communicative Speaking and Listening*, 4th ed. (New York: Holt, Rinehart and Winston, 1968), 104.
3. Alan H. Monroe and Douglas Ehninger, *Principles of Speech Communication*, 6th ed. (Glenview, Ill.: Scott, Foresman, 1969), 260.
4. C. Dickson, "You Can't Write a Speech," *Training and Development Journal* 41 (4): 70–72.
5. This material has been adapted from the class handout of Jennifer Nachlas, Instructor, Communication Department, British Columbia Institute of Technology.
6. Margaret Cole and Sylvia Odenwald, *Desktop Presentations* (New York: Amacom, 1990), 3.
7. Cole and Odenwald, *Desktop Presentations*, 145
8. Cole and Odenwald, *Desktop Presentations*, 145.
9. Adapted from a case by Julie C. Burkhard, Charlottesville, Virginia.
10. Adapted from a case by Julie C. Burkhard.

Chapter 15

1. John Dewey, *How We Think* (Boston: D.C. Heath, 1922).
2. Carl Larson, "Forms of Analysis and Small Group Problem Solving," *Speech Monographs* 36 (1969): 453.
3. Larson, "Forms of Analysis," 453.
4. D.I. Hawkins, "Curlee Clothing Comany," *Harvard Intercollegiate Case Clearing House*, #9-572-681 (1972).
5. "Once a Tool of Retail Marketers, Focus Groups Gain Wider Usage," *The Wall Street Journal*, June 3, 1986, Sec. 2, 31.
6. Irving L. Janis, *Groupthink*, 2nd ed. (Boston: Houghton Mifflin Company, 1982).
7. Janis, *Groupthink,* 197–98.
8. Janis, *Groupthink,* 198–99.
9. This discussion of leadership syles is adapted from Charles R. Gruner, Cal M. Logue, Dwight L. Freshley, and Richard C. Huseman, *Speech Communication in Society*, 2nd ed. (Boston: Allyn & Bacon, Inc., 1977), 258–60.
10. Adapted from a case by Doris D. Phillips, Ph.D., School of Business Administration, University of Mississippi.
11. Adapted from a case by Judith V. A. Dietrich, R.N., M.S.N., formerly Sessional Lecturer, School of Nursing, University of British Columbia.

Chapter 16

1. Robert Sheppard, "Where Do the Jobs Come from After the Factories Close?" *The Globe and Mail*, February 19, 1990, B1.
2. Carolyn Leitch, "Health Care Careers Head Top 10 List for Growth, Income," *The Globe and Mail*, February 6, 1990, B1.
3. Herman Holtz, *Beyond the Resume: How to Land the Job You Want* (New York: McGraw Hill, 1984).
4. Carolyn Leitch, "Giving All for Dear Old Firm Begins to Pall on Employees: Workplace Values in Transition," *The Globe and Mail*, February 6, 1990, B1, B5.
5. Holtz, *Beyond the Resume.*
6. Adapted from a case that appeared in the Australian edition of *Business Communication: Strategies and Skills.*

Chapter 17

1. Adapted from a case by Richard Pompian, University of Texas, Austin.
2. Adapted from a case by R. Barnhard, San Francisco State University.

Chapter 18

1. Adapted from a case by Jim Stull, San Jose State University.
2. From a list of 93 in *Making the Most of Your Job Interview*, a booklet prepared by the New York Life Insurance Company, New York.

3. Robert L. Dipboye, Richard D. Arvey, and David E. Terpotra, "Equal Employment and the Interview," *Personnel Journal* 55 (October 1976): 521.
4. Adapted from a case by Michael T. O'Neill, Personnel Finders of Arlington, Inc.
5. Adapted from a case that appeared in the Australian edition of *Business Communication: Strategies and Skills.*

Index

To the Owner of this Book:

We are interested in your reaction to *Business Communication*, 3rd Canadian edition, by Huseman, Stockmayer, Lahiff, and Penrose. With your comments, we can improve this book in future editions. Please help us by completing this questionnaire.

1. What was your reason for using this book?
   ____ university course
   ____ college course
   ____ continuing education course
   ____ personal interest
   ____ other (specify)

2. If you used this text for a program, what was the name of that program?

3. Which school do you attend?

4. Approximately how much of the book did you use?
   ____ 1/4 ____ 1/2 ____ 3/4 ____ all

5. Which chapters or sections were omitted from your course?

6. What is the best aspect of this book?

7. Is there anything that should be added?

8. Please add any comments or suggestions.

(fold here)

Business
Reply Mail
No Postage Stamp
Necessary if Mailed
in Canada

Canada Post Postes Canada
43652

POSTAGE WILL BE PAID BY
Heather McWhinney
Editorial Director
College Division
HARCOURT BRACE JOVANOVICH CANADA INC.
55 HORNER AVENUE
TORONTO, ONTARIO
M8Z 9Z9

(tape shut)